Aging and Mental Health

Aging and Mental Health
Second Edition

Daniel L. Segal, Sara Honn Qualls, and
Michael A. Smyer

A John Wiley & Sons, Ltd., Publication

This second edition first published 2011
© 2011 Daniel L. Segal, Sara Honn Qualls, and Michael A. Smyer

Edition history: Blackwell Publishers (1e, 1999)

Blackwell Publishing was acquired by John Wiley & Sons in February 2007. Blackwell's publishing program has been merged with Wiley's global Scientific, Technical, and Medical business to form Wiley-Blackwell.

Registered Office
John Wiley & Sons Ltd, The Atrium, Southern Gate, Chichester, West Sussex, PO19 8SQ, United Kingdom

Editorial Offices
350 Main Street, Malden, MA 02148-5020, USA
9600 Garsington Road, Oxford, OX4 2DQ, UK
The Atrium, Southern Gate, Chichester, West Sussex, PO19 8SQ, UK

For details of our global editorial offices, for customer services, and for information about how to apply for permission to reuse the copyright material in this book please see our website at www.wiley.com/wiley-blackwell.

The right of Daniel L. Segal, Sara Honn Qualls, and Michael A. Smyer to be identified as the authors of this work has been asserted in accordance with the UK Copyright, Designs and Patents Act 1988.

Library of Congress Cataloging-in-Publication Data

Segal, Daniel L.
   Aging and mental health. – 2nd ed. / Daniel L. Segal, Sara Honn Qualls, and Michael A. Smyer.
      p. cm. – (Understanding aging)
   Smyer's name appears first on the earlier edition.
   Includes bibliographical references and index.
   ISBN 978-1-4051-3075-2 (pbk.: alk. paper)   1. Older people – Mental health.
2. Geriatric psychiatry.   I. Qualls, Sara Honn.   II. Smyer, Michael A.   III. Title.
   RC451.4.A5S66 2011
   618.97'689–dc22
                              2010021917

A catalogue record for this book is available from the British Library.

Printed and bound in Malaysia by Vivar Printing Sdn Bhd

[001]   [2011]

Daniel L. Segal: To Cindy and Shaynie
Sara H. Qualls: To Mark, Morgan, Lea, and Marcus
Michael A. Smyer: To Piper, Brendan, and Kyle

Contents

Preface

What is important in knowledge is not quantity, but quality. It is important to know what knowledge is significant, what is less so, and what is trivial. (Leo Tolstoy)

In this book we have tried to take Tolstoy's maxim to heart, sorting out the significant from the trivial in the domain of aging and mental health. As we did so, we had two audiences in mind: today's clinicians and the clinicians of the future. The first group includes clinicians who are already in practice settings but who want to know more about the intricacies of working with older adults. The second group encompasses students in the professions that work with older adults (e.g., psychology, social work, nursing, psychiatry).

Both groups must face the issues of aging summarized by Michel Philibert, a French philosopher: "Of aging, what can we know? With aging, what must we do?" (Philibert, 1979, p. 384). These are also issues that older adults and their family members must face. In a way, they are variations on the questions that often arise in clinical settings. Consider the following example:

Betty was worried about Alex. His memory seemed to be failing him more often. He'd get to the store and forget half of the things she'd sent him there for. He seemed more tired than usual, with less energy for his hobbies at the end of the day or on weekends. He didn't want to go out with friends to the movies or to dinner. Alex didn't notice anything different in his behavior. Betty called to ask your advice: "Should I get him tested at the local Alzheimer's Center?"

How would you answer Betty? What would you need to know? Which portion of her story is significant in forming your answer? Which less so?

In answering these questions, you are implicitly answering Philibert's queries as well. You are implicitly making a differential diagnosis of Alex's situation: Is this a part of normal aging? Is this a pathological pattern? Is it a combination of the two? (Of aging, what can we know?)

You may also be linking your answer to an implicit action plan. Betty certainly is: Diagnose the problem and then decide what kind of treatment is most appropriate. (With aging, what must we do?)

To fully answer Betty's question requires much more information about aging in general, about patterns of mental health and mental disorder in particular, about Alex's distinctive history and pattern of functioning, and about the contexts in which she and Alex live and receive services. This book is designed to provide you with frameworks for considering each element.

Part I is an overview of basic gerontology, the study of the aging process. This background information forms a context for answering the simple question often posed by clients and their relatives: Should I be worried about this pattern of behavior (e.g., Alex's apparent memory problems)? To answer this deceptively simple question requires that we sort out the influences of physical illness, basic processes of aging, and the intersection of historical and social trends as they affect older adults' functioning. In Part I we outline the basic parameters of mental health in later life, providing the foundation upon which later chapters build.

In Part II we consider basic models of mental disorders. Each model provides a set of assumptions about mental health and the development of mental health problems, their assessment, and their treatment. These assumptions direct the clinician's attention to specific aspects of older adults and their functioning. For example, assume for the moment that Alex's memory problems are not organically caused. The behavioral perspective might highlight the context of the older adult's behavior. Several important models of mental health and mental disorder are outlined in the chapters of Part II. In each chapter we focus on an important question for older adults and those who work with them: How is this approach relevant to older adults and the problems they encounter in later life?

The third and final part focuses attention on the most commonly occurring mental health problems and disorders in later life: cognitive impairment, depression, serious mental disorders (e.g., schizophrenia), anxiety, substance use, personality disorders, and other common disorders. In each chapter we outline the prevalence of the disorders, the most appropriate assessment approaches for older adults, and the most effective treatment strategies for older adults. We were fortunate to be able to call upon Stephen J. Bartels for his expertise in the diagnosis and treatment of chronic mental disorders (Chapter 9). Part III concludes with a capstone chapter on the contexts and settings of geriatric mental health practice. One physical setting is particularly important in geriatric mental health care: nursing homes. Although they were not designed for it, they are a major treatment setting for mentally ill older adults. Of course, other contexts (e.g., health care settings, social service settings, legal issues) affect how, where, and why mentally ill older adults are diagnosed and treated. We discuss these contexts in this final chapter.

Colleagues and friends in several settings have helped us write this book: colleagues in the Department of Psychology, the CU Aging Center, and the Gerontology Center of the University of Colorado at Colorado Springs, and the faculty, students, and staff in the Center on Aging & Work at Boston College and in the Provost's office at Bucknell University. Early in the development of the first edition we benefited from the guidance and advice of Jim Birren and two anonymous reviewers. The process of revision was supported by input and advice from our academic and community services colleagues as well as a new set of anonymous reviewers. We eagerly acknowledge our debt to each, while also admitting that any remaining flaws are ours. We also express our deepest appreciation to our friend and editor at Wiley-Blackwell, Constance Adler, whose patience and diligence ensured that this second edition came to fruition. Finally, we remain grateful to our family members for their ongoing love, encouragement, and support.

Our goal throughout this book is to provide information and a set of frameworks that will be useful in working with older adults and their families. In the end, we hope that you will conclude that there is much to hope for in aging, and much that we can do about mental health and mental disorders later in life.

Part I
Introduction

1

Mental Health and Aging
An Introduction

Consider the following case description:

> Grace, director of a Senior Center in your area, calls you about Mr. Tinker. Although Mr. Tinker used to come to the center three or four times a week, he hasn't come at all since the death of his friend, Ed, four months ago. Grace had called Mr. Tinker at home to say how much he'd been missed. When she asked if he wasn't coming because he was still upset over Ed's death, he denied it. Instead, Mr. Tinker said that he wanted to return to the center, but he was in terrible pain. In fact, he was in so much pain that he really couldn't talk on the phone and he hung up. Grace was worried that Mr. Tinker might not be getting the medical attention that he really needed. She asked you to make a home visit, which you agreed to do. You call Mr. Tinker and set up an appointment.

As you prepare to visit Mr. Tinker, what are the basic questions you might ask about him and his situation? Which factors do you think are important to explore with Mr. Tinker? How would you assess Mr. Tinker's functioning?

Your answer to these simple inquiries reflects your implicit model of mental health and aging. In this book, especially in Part II, we will illustrate several different conceptual models of mental disorders and aging. In doing so, we will emphasize the links between starting assumptions and subsequent strategies for assessment and intervention. You will come to see that your philosophical assumptions about mental health, mental disorder, and aging shape the interpretive process of working with older adults and their families.

Mr. Tinker's current functioning raises a basic question: Is his behavior just a part of normal aging or does it represent a problem that requires professional attention? Our answer represents implicit and explicit assumptions regarding the continuum of functioning that runs from outstanding functioning through usual aging to pathological patterns of behavior.

Aging and Mental Health, 2e. Daniel L. Segal, Sara Honn Qualls, and Michael A. Smyer
© 2011 Daniel L. Segal, Sara Honn Qualls, and Michael A. Smyer

What is Normal Aging?

The starting point for mental health and aging must be a general understanding of *gerontology*, the study of normal aging, and *geriatrics*, the study of the medical aspects of old age and the prevention and treatment of the diseases of aging. In Mr. Tinker's case, we want to know if his reaction is a part of a normal grieving process or an indication of a disease process (e.g., a mood disorder, such as major depressive disorder). To answer this requires a starting definition of normal aging.

A conceptual definition

Discussions of this issue focus attention on three different patterns of aging: normal or usual aging; optimal or successful aging; and pathological aging (e.g., Rowe & Kahn, 1998). Baltes and Baltes (1990a) provide definitions of normal and optimal aging:

> Normal aging refers to aging without biological or mental pathology. It thus concerns the aging process that is dominant within a society for persons who are not suffering from a manifest illness. Optimal aging refers to a kind of utopia, namely, aging under development-enhancing and age-friendly environmental conditions. Finally, sick or pathological aging characterizes an aging process determined by medical etiology and syndromes of illness. A classical example is dementia of the Alzheimer type. (pp. 7–8)

A statistical definition

Distinguishing between normal aging and optimal aging requires us to sort out statistical fact from theoretically desirable conditions. For example, the Baltes and Baltes definition suggests that normal aging does not include "manifest illness." However, in the United States today, chronic disease is typical of the experience of aging: More than 80 percent of those 65 years old and older have at least one chronic medical disease, and 50 percent have at least two chronic medical diseases (Centers for Disease Control and Prevention and The Merck Company Foundation, 2007).

For example, half of those over age 65 report having arthritis (Hootman, Bolen, Helmick, & Langmaid, 2006). By 2030, 54 percent of adults with arthritis are expected to be over age 65 (Hootman & Helmick, 2006). Moreover, among the oldest old groups (75+ or 85+) there are substantially higher rates. Thus, from a statistical perspective, arthritis is certainly modal, and may be considered a part of normal aging. We will return to this in Chapter 2.

A functional definition

Another approach to defining normal aging arises from defining "manifest illness." By focusing not on presence or absence of a chronic disease, such as arthritis, but on the *impact* of that disease, we may get another depiction of "normal aging." Here, again, though, the definition of terms can affect our conclusion regarding normal aging.

Consider the prevalence of disability among older adults. Functional disability could be considered one indicator of manifest illness among older adults. So far, so good. However, how shall we define functional disability? The answer may determine our conclusion about what is or is not normal for later life. Again, Mr. Tinker's situation may help us clarify the issues:

> When you get to Mr. Tinker's house, you find an apathetic, listless, very thin man of 81. He seems to be fairly isolated socially, having few friends and even fewer family members in the area. (He never married and he has no living siblings.) Although he seems physically able to cook, he says that he hasn't been eating (or sleeping) regularly for quite a while – and he doesn't care if he never does again.

Is Mr. Tinker functionally disabled? If so, is this normal for someone of his age? According to the US Census Bureau, most persons aged 75 years old and older have a disability: 56 percent of those 75–79 years old had any type of disability with 38 percent having a "severe disability" (Brault, 2008). In contrast, Manton, Gu, and Lamb (2006) reported that 78 percent of the 75–84 age group was "non-disabled." How could such differing pictures of older adults emerge?

The answer lies in the definition of disability. The Census Bureau focuses on difficulty with functional activity for its specific definition of disability. The range of functional activities is somewhat broader than traditional definitions: lifting and carrying a weight as heavy as 10 pounds; walking three city blocks; seeing the words and letters in ordinary newsprint; hearing what is said in normal conversation with another person; having one's speech understood; and climbing a flight of stairs. In contrast, Manton et al. (2006) focused on activities of daily living (ADL; e.g., eating, getting in or out of bed, getting around indoors, bathing, dressing, using a toilet) and instrumental activities of daily living (IADL, e.g., light housework; doing the laundry; meal preparation; grocery shopping).

Not surprisingly, these different definitions of disability produce different depictions of functioning and normal aging. The metric we use in assessing functional ability is important for two reasons: the specific activities may be important in and of themselves; and the ability to complete activities (such as ADL and IADL activities) acts as a proxy for underlying physical, cognitive, and social skills (Kemp & Mitchell, 1992). Thus, depending upon the range of functioning we wish to assess, we may conclude that Mr. Tinker is either disabled or not and that such a pattern of functioning is either normal or unusual aging!

What is Abnormal or Unusual Aging?

Thus far, we have considered merely one side of the dilemma: What is normal aging? We have also limited ourselves to *physical* and *functional* definitions, steering clear of similar issues focusing on *mental* health problems or disorders.

> You notice that Mr. Tinker doesn't mention being in any terrible pain – that is until you mention his friend Ed. When you do, Mr. Tinker grabs his side and says

how much it hurts to talk. You suggest that he lie down and rest for a minute, which he does.

From the couch, Mr. Tinker begins to talk about Ed. It turns out that the two men were not just "friends" as Grace had implied. They were like brothers (if not closer) and had been since they were boys. "I'm good for two things," Mr. Tinker said, "no good and good for nothing. But Ed was my buddy anyway. Don't know why he bothered with me. I never made much of my life. But I do know that it won't be hunting season without him. Just can't do it alone and nobody in their right mind would want to hunt with an old fool like me."

Again, Mr. Tinker challenges us. Is he mentally ill? The answer depends upon resolving other issues: How will we define mental health among older adults? Conversely, how will we define mental disorder among older adults? In Part III of this book, we will discuss assessment and treatment approaches for many specific mental disorders. Here, however, we start at the beginning: definitions of mental health and mental disorder.

Mental Health and Mental Disorder

The Centers for Disease Control and Prevention and the National Association of Chronic Disease Directors (2008) summarized the importance of mental health in later life:

> The World Health Organization defines health as "a state of complete physical, mental, and social well-being and not merely the absence of disease or infirmity" [WHO, 1948] … Because mental health is essential to overall health and well-being, it must be recognized and treated in all Americans, including older adults, with the same urgency as physical health … In fact, the mental health of older Americans has been identified as a priority by the Healthy People of 2010 objectives [US Dept. of HHS, 2000], the 2005 White House Conference on Aging [US Dept. of HHS, 2006], and the 1999 Surgeon General's report on mental health [US Dept. of HHS, 1999].

Mental health among older adults is a multifaceted concept that reflects a range of clinical and research activity, rather than a unified theoretical entity (Qualls & Layton, 2010; Qualls & Smyer, 1995). Definitions of mental health in later life combine several complex elements: statistical normality; the link between individual functioning and group norms; the extent to which specific disorders can be effectively treated or controlled; and ideals of positive functioning (Butler, Lewis, & Sunderland, 1998).

In contrast, there is greater agreement on definitions of *mental disorder* among older adults. For both clinical and research purposes, operational definitions of mental disorder usually follow the American Psychiatric Association's guidelines in the *Diagnostic and Statistical Manual of Mental Disorders* (DSM-IV-TR; American Psychiatric Association, 2000). Thus, mental disorder in older adults is operationally defined by patterns of disorders as outlined in the DSM-IV-TR, which is the prominent classification system for much of the developed world (Segal, 2010). Several hundred mental disorders are defined in the manual, which lists the specific diagnostic criteria for each disorder.

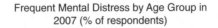

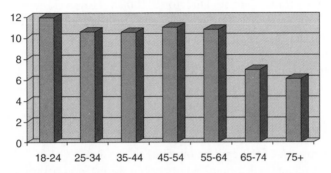

Figure 1.1 Frequent mental distress by age group in 2007 (% of respondents).
Source: Adapted from CDC (2007).

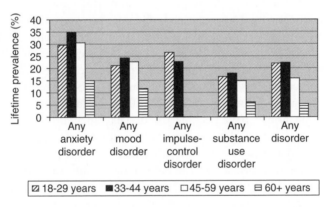

Figure 1.2 Lifetime prevalence of DSM-IV/World Mental Health Survey disorders by age group from the National Comorbidity Survey Replication sample.
Source: Adapted from Kessler et al. (2005).

Data from the Centers for Disease Control's Behavioral Risk Factors Surveillance System (BRFSS) revealed that in 2007, 6.9 percent of adults aged 65–74 reported frequent mental distress as defined by having 14 or more mentally unhealthy days. The percentage was slightly lower (6.1 percent) for the 75 or older group (CDC, 2007). Older age groups had the lowest prevalence of frequent mental distress compared to all younger age groups (see Figure 1.1).

A similar pattern emerges when the focus is on diagnosed mental disorders. Kessler, Berglund, Demler, Jin, and Walters (2005) reported data from the National Comorbidity Study, which included interviews with a nationally representative sample of over 9,000 people. Again, older adults had lower levels of diagnosable anxiety disorders, mood disorders, impulse-control disorders, and substance use disorders compared to younger adult groups (see Figure 1.2).

Depression is clearly not a part of normal aging. In 80 percent of cases, depression is a treatable condition (Centers for Disease Control and Prevention and the National Association of Chronic Disease Directors, 2008). However, geriatric depression reflects the difficulty of discerning "normal aging" from pathological aging. Depression in later life appears in several guises. When using the Beck Depression Inventory, older adults have low rates of moderate depression and anxiety (6.1 percent lower) in comparison to young adults (Goldberg, Breckenridge, & Sheikh, 2003). Only 5.0 percent of adults age 65 or older currently have depression and 10.5 percent have had a lifetime diagnosis of depression (Centers for Disease Control and Prevention and the National Association of Chronic Disease Directors, 2008). However, the prevalence of depressive *symptoms* among older adults is much higher. (See Chapter 8 for a full discussion of the epidemiology of depression.)

Again, the challenge is distinguishing between normal and pathological aging: Are Mr. Tinker's sleep and appetite disturbances a sign of depression, a part of the normal aging process, or a combination of the two?

Another challenge is that rates of mental disorders vary by setting. For example, older adults in institutional settings present a very different picture: In a sample of older medical inpatients, 46 percent had mild depressive symptoms and 27 percent had severe depressive symptoms (Linka, Bartkó, Agárdi, & Kemény, 2000). Similarly, a recent study analyzed data from Minimum Data Set assessments and found that 27 percent of newly admitted nursing home residents were diagnosed with schizophrenia, bipolar disorder, depression, or anxiety disorder (Grabowski, Aschbrenner, Feng, & Mor, 2009). Grabowski and his colleagues (2009) summarized the impact of these patterns: "Nursing homes have become the de facto mental health care institution as a result of the dramatic downsizing and closure of state psychiatric hospitals, spurred on by the deinstitutionalization movement" (p. 689).

A final relevant issue is not simply the rates of mental disorder in older adults, but rather the pattern of the *age of onset* of mental disorders (e.g., the average age at which people tend to first experience the disorder). Informative data from Kessler et al. (2005) indicated that the median age of onset was much earlier for anxiety disorders (11 years old) and impulse-control disorders (11 years old) than for substance use disorders (20 years old) and mood disorders (30 years old). For all of the mental disorders included in this large study, 50 percent of all lifetime cases start by age 14, 75 percent of all lifetime cases start by age 24, and 90 percent of all lifetime cases start by age 42. Thus, the first onset of most mental disorders is in childhood or adolescence and a much smaller percentage of disorders have an onset in later life. Among older adults with a mental disorder, it is clinically relevant to determine when the disorder began. For example, an older adult who has suffered from lifelong depression will likely have a lengthier and more complicated treatment than an older adult who experienced depression for the first time in later life. The issue of age of onset is further explored in many of the chapters on specific mental disorders in Part III of this book.

Linking the Physical and Mental in Later Life: Comorbidity

Mr. Tinker's pattern of symptoms – his lethargy, social withdrawal, and his reported physical pain – remind us of the importance of *comorbidity*: combinations of more than one mental disorder, physical illness, or combination of both. Cohen (1992) provides a context for understanding comorbidity by outlining four useful paradigms for the interaction of physical and mental well-being among older adults:

- Psychogenic (or psychologically based) stress may lead to health problems.
- Health problems may lead to psychiatric disturbances.
- Coexisting mental and physical health challenges may interact.
- Social and psychosocial resources may affect the course of physical or mental disorders.

Indeed, one's initial concern about a client or patient may be raised by either a physical or mental health problem.

First, psychogenic stress may lead to physical health problems: In Mr. Tinker's case, abdominal pain may be a reaction to his grief over Ed's death. For Mr. Tinker, this physical symptom may be a more socially acceptable way for him to express pain.

Second, the direction of causality may be reversed, however, with a physical disorder leading to psychiatric disturbance. Consider the following sentence:

The five senses tend to decline with senescence.

Remove the f's, s's, and th's. Now try to make sense of what's left:

e ive en tend to decline wi ene e.

This example mimics high frequency hearing loss among older adults (Butler et al., 1998) and gives you a sense of how easily such a hearing loss might lead to delusions and confusion among older adults.

A third possibility is that coexisting physical and mental disorders may interact. One category of mental disorders among older adults underscores this interplay: cognitive impairment, including the dementias. Cognitive impairment among older adults is a challenge for interdisciplinary diagnosis and treatment. Distinguishing among age-related cognitive change, mild cognitive impairment (MCI), and Alzheimer's disease or other dementias can be difficult (Buracchio & Kaye, 2009; Green, 2005; Peterson, 2004). In addition, differential diagnosis and prompt treatment requires ruling out a myriad of potentially reversible causes of confusional states: drug reactions; emotional disorders; metabolic disorders; impaired vision and hearing; nutritional deficiencies; dehydration; brain tumors and traumas; infections. This requires an interdisciplinary collaboration designed to assess complex patterns of comorbidity (see Chapter 7).

Currently, resources are being invested in research on the biological bases of Alzheimer's disease and related disorders (e.g., Anderson, Litvack, & Kaye, 2005; Bertram, McQueen, Mullin, Blacker, & Tanzi, 2007; Brouwers, Sleegers, & Van Broeckhoven, 2008), the social impact of these diseases (e.g., Kim, Knight, & Longmire, 2007; Montgomery & Kosloski, 2009), and the potential for preventive interventions aimed at avoiding the personal and economic devastation that accompany dementia (e.g., CDC & Alzheimer's Association, 2007; Day, McGuire, & Anderson, 2009; Teri, Logsdon, & McCurry, 2008; Willis et al., 2006).

Again, national data reflect the individual and societal importance of this work: Estimates are that as many as 5.3 million Americans currently have Alzheimer's disease and related dementias (ADRD), with 70 percent of these patients aged 71 or older suffering from Alzheimer's disease (AD) (Alzheimer's Association, 2009a). Estimates suggest that the number of ADRD patients will increase to more than 11.8 million by the year 2040 (National Academy on an Aging Society, 2000).

Similarly, recent work (Plassman et al., 2008) indicates that, for older adults age 71 years and older, two estimates of disorders are important to assess: those with already-diagnosed Alzheimer's disease (approximately 3.4 million people) and those who have cognitive impairment without dementia (approximately 5 million people). Taken together, these two categories produce a prevalence rate of 22 percent for those 71 and older (Lichtenberg, 2009).

A global estimate of the prevalence of dementia suggests that there are currently 24 million people worldwide with dementia (Ferri et al., 2005). This number is projected to double every 20 years to 42 million by 2020 and to 81 million by 2040 (Ferri et al., 2005). Perhaps surprisingly, 60 percent of those with dementia are estimated to live in developing countries, a rate projected to rise to 71 percent by 2040 (Ferri et al., 2005).

Fourth, and finally, Cohen (1992) suggests that social and psychosocial resources can affect the course of physical and mental disorders. As we discuss in the stress and coping model (see Chapter 5), social support can buffer the negative effects of life stress and help people cope better with a myriad of problems. Even among those with a dementing disorder, a positive social environment can enhance the person's dignity and quality of life.

Individual Differences and Assessment of Risk

Thus far, we have sketched general patterns of mental health and mental disorder among older adults, as a context for working with Mr. Tinker. One question has been implicit in this discussion: How is Mr. Tinker like other older adults of his age? In this section, the emphasis shifts to another question: How is Mr. Tinker different from other individuals his age?

What do we know about Mr. Tinker that would differentiate him from other 81-year-olds? What are the categories of information we would use in sorting older adults? Socioeconomic status (SES) dramatically affects the experience of aging. Consider the relationships among age, having a chronic health problem, and SES (see Figure 1.3). Data from the Behavioral Risk Factors Surveillance System (CDC, 2007) showed that individuals in the lower SES categories have the highest rates of chronic conditions throughout adulthood.

Moreover, by early mid-life (ages 35–44), those in the lower SES group already have chronic health problems at higher rates than those in the highest SES group at ages 55–64, 65–74, and 75+. Variability in risk among older adults is not limited to the physical or functional domains, however. There are similar patterns of variability in risk of mental disorders. Consider the risk for suicide. We resume our conversation with Mr. Tinker:

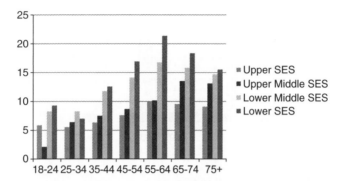

Figure 1.3 Percentage of respondents reporting that they have a chronic health problem stratified by age and SES.
Source: Adapted from CDC (2007).

"I never made much of my life. But I do know that it won't be hunting season without Ed. Just can't do it alone, and nobody in their right mind would want to hunt with an old fool like me."

These words have a haunting finality to them. As you hear them, you begin to wonder about Mr. Tinker's will to live and his plans for the future. Should you ask him about these elements, about his potential for suicide?

Psychiatric epidemiological data can be helpful in tracing overall patterns of suicide risk among older adults, as well as differential patterns of risk (see Figure 1.4). The threat of completed suicide is substantial in later life, with the highest rates appearing among those 65 years or older (14.7/100,000 vs. 11.0/100,000 for the general population; Centers for Disease Control and Prevention and the National Association of Chronic Disease Directors, 2008). Older adults are more likely to complete suicide than any other adult age group, due to more lethal methods of suicide attempt. Suicide among older adults is associated with diagnosable psychopathology (most often affective disorders, especially depression) in approximately 90 percent of cases (World Health Organization, 2005).

When gender and ethnicity are included, the group at highest risk for death by suicide is White men over the age of 85, with a rate of suicide two and a half times higher than the nation's rate for men (American Association of Suicidology, 2008). Sadly, the majority of older suicide victims had seen their primary care physician within the month prior to suicide (Caine, Lyness, & Conwell, 1996). Thus, there is a serious need for better preparation of physicians for screening and treatment of geriatric depression, and for screening and prevention of older adults at risk for suicide (NIH Consensus Panel on Assessment and NIH Consensus Panel on Depression in Late Life, 1992).

Armed with this knowledge of differential risk – particularly for White men over 80 – you ask Mr. Tinker about his current plans and perspectives:

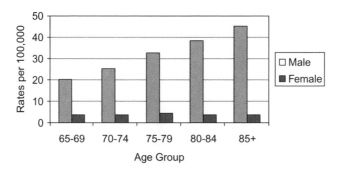

Figure 1.4 Suicide rates for ages 60 to 85+.
Source: American Association of Suicidology based on raw data from CDC. Retrieved from http://www.suicidology.org/c/document_library/get_file?folderId=232&name=DLFE-158.pdf.

> "It sounds like you're feeling pretty blue. Have you ever thought about ending things?"
> "I may be down, but I'm not crazy!"

Mr. Tinker quickly gives you a sense of his own perspective on his problems, allowing you to follow up with specific questions regarding intent. The conversation could have gone in a different direction:

> "It sounds like you're feeling pretty blue. Have you ever thought about ending things?"
> "Every now and then I get that feeling."
> "How would you do it?"
> "Well, I'd use that shotgun that I keep loaded next to the door – just head out to the barn, clear out the cows, and pull the trigger ..."

This conversation confirms your fears – he has motivation, a way to achieve that purpose, and seemingly very little concern about the consequences.

These two resolutions to the inquiry highlight the theme of variability among and between older adults. This variability is a hallmark of aging: As we get older, we get more distinct from our age-mates. This diversity among older adults (often called inter-individual differences) is the result of the complex patterns of both biological and biographical functioning across the life span.

The biographical elements may play a key role in two different ways: the history of the disorder and the history of the individual. In the case of Mr. Tinker's suicide potential, for example, we will want to know something about his previous experience with suicidal ideation: Has he been suicidal for many years and now grown older? Has he grown older and now become suicidal? These two divergent paths both arrive at suicide in later life, but they offer very different suggestions for treatment attempts, the availability of social and emotional resources, and the likelihood of successful intervention.

In summary, we will want to know more about several key elements of Mr. Tinker's history: his social and economic resources, his current and past physical health, his current and past mental health, and his functional abilities (NIH Consensus Panel on Assessment, 1988). Approaches to these issues will be presented in Part II of this book.

The Context of Clinicians and Clients: Now What Do We Do?

Thus far, we have had one conversation with Mr. Tinker and we have gathered information about his current functioning, his previous history, and his future ability to continue to cope on his own. What will we do next?

Our approach to Mr. Tinker is a function of several, inter-related elements: our sense of his strengths and weaknesses (e.g., how acute is his crisis; is he a threat to himself or others; how has he handled personal challenges in the past; etc.); our assessment of his capacity to be involved in health care decision-making as an active participant in developing the treatment plan; and the service setting and context that we work within. These issues are discussed in Chapter 12.

The context of mental health services for older adults has changed substantially during the last three decades. As part of a larger public policy of deinstitutionalization, there were increases in both institutional and outpatient services. In the institutional sector, inpatient services were shifted from state mental hospitals to private psychiatric hospitals, psychiatric units in general hospitals, and "swing beds" in general hospitals. As pointed out earlier, one other setting became increasingly important as a receiving site for mentally disordered older adults: nursing homes (Gatz & Smyer, 1992; Grabowski et al., 2009).

Access to mental health services is another important issue (Pepin, Segal, & Coolidge, 2009). According to the American Psychological Association (2003), about 63 percent of older adults with a mental disorder do not receive the services they need, and overall, only 3 percent of older adults report seeing a mental or behavioral health professional. In inpatient settings, older adults represent 11 percent of the population receiving inpatient care in specialty institutions and general hospitals (Rosenstein, Milazzo-Sayre, & Manderscheid, 1990). However, older adults represent 90 percent of the mentally ill population in nursing homes (Lair & Lefkowitz, 1990). This pattern reflects an over-reliance on nursing homes as a treatment setting for mentally ill older adults. Recently, Pepin et al. (2009) examined the kinds of barriers that prevent younger and older adults from accessing mental health services, finding that stigma was at the bottom of the ranked list of barriers for younger and older adults alike. Instead, more practical issues such as concerns about paying for treatment and difficulty finding an appropriate mental health service provider were perceived as greater barriers. A further understanding of barriers is an important avenue for further research study.

These patterns of care – with a substantial bias toward inpatient, medically oriented services – are only one of two major elements that shape the availability of and access to mental health care for older adults. The second is the combined priorities of major funding sources for geriatric mental health: Medicare, Medicaid, and private insurance plans (Smyer & Shea, 1996).

In 2003, the core costs of health care for mentally ill older adults were $15.1 billion (Mark et al., 2008). These costs included the direct costs of care, plus the indirect costs of associated morbidity and mortality. Thus, from an economic perspective, geriatric mental health care is worthy of attention – if only to foster cost-containment efforts.

Medicare is a federal health insurance program for older adults. Its eligibility criteria and scope of covered services are standardized throughout the United States. Unfortunately, Medicare coverage, although improved in recent years, is still somewhat restrictive. For example, in 2010 Medicare covered only 55 percent of outpatient mental health services (e.g., psychotherapy) provided by psychologists or other mental health professionals while it covered 80 percent of comparable physical health services provided in an inpatient setting (Centers for Medicare and Medicaid Services [CMS], 2010). Recent legislation has addressed this unfair practice but it will take several years for the changes to phase into the program, with full parity for outpatient mental health services (80 percent coverage) completed by 2014.

Medicaid is the US national health insurance program for the indigent. It is funded through a combination of state and federal funds and coverage varies from state to state. Medicaid has emerged as the payer of last resort in nursing home care for older adults, covering 6 out of every 10 nursing home residents. Medicaid pays for more than 40 percent of nursing home and long-term care coverage in the United States (Kaiser Family Foundation, 2009). Private insurance plans also provide some assistance for mentally ill older adults. The primary private options available for older adults consist of either supplemental insurance policies, often called "Medigap" policies, that cover the co-payment portions of original Medicare part B for a monthly premium or privatized "Medicare Advantage Plans" that function more like a health management organization (HMO) and are run by private insurance companies approved by and under contract with Medicare. These plans provide hospital and outpatient coverage but can charge different out-of-pocket co-payments for different services as well as the monthly premium.

These contextual factors – institutional patterns of service provision, insurance coverage, fee structures – affect the choices for services for Mr. Tinker. To work effectively with him, you will need to understand the coverage of mental health services that he has, the availability of services in your local community, and the range of services for which you can be reimbursed. These issues will be further discussed in Chapter 12 in this book.

Summary and Conclusions

In this chapter, we have introduced several themes that will re-emerge throughout the book. First, we have highlighted the importance of philosophical assumptions regarding normal and abnormal functioning in shaping our assessment strategies, targets for intervention, and definitions of therapeutic success. Next, we have emphasized the importance of individual differences in shaping our understanding of the etiology and presentation of mental health problems or disorders in later life. Finally, we have discussed briefly the fiscal and political context that shapes the availability of mental health services for older adults. These themes – ranging from individual functioning to social policy – illustrate the complexity of the task of providing mental health services to older adults. We hope that these themes also reflect the excitement inherent in trying to bring order out of the chaos of needs and services, of trying to both understand the older client and match her needs with the services available.

The last point we wish to emphasize in this introduction is that the DSM-IV-TR (American Psychiatric Association, 2000) is an *evolving* classification system. As such, at the time of this writing, the manual is undergoing revisions to the diagnostic categories including many specific mental disorders. These revisions are expected to be substantial for the next edition, which will be called the DSM-5. The interested reader can track progress of these developments at the website for the DSM-5 (http://www.dsm5.org), which is expected to be released in 2013.

2
Basic Gerontology for Working with Older Adults

Imagine that you have been hired as a consultant by a local nursing home. To prepare you for your first visit, the facility staff have developed two case descriptions:

> Max won't move. He used to be a successful accountant, but he hasn't worked in several years when he began to forget things. Now he barely allows himself to be nagged out of the bed or dressed ... He seems physically able to do things for himself but gently mumbles "I can't" when the nurses' aides encourage him to do anything. He looks very sad. When his photo album is brought to him he does spend some time mumbling and paging through it, but generally spends his time alone. He has been this way day in and day out, for as long as anyone can remember ... (Cohn, Smyer, & Horgas, 1994, p. 152)

> Molly collects spoons, both clean and dirty, from the dining room trays and stores them very carefully in her dresser drawer. She argues violently when the nurse tries to remove them. The nurse gives long explanations of why they need to go back to the kitchen, but Molly insists that the staff are stealing her things. (Cohn et al., 1994, p. 179)

Imagine that your consulting company has just landed a contract with a continuing care retirement community commonly called a life-care community. The head of social services calls with the following referral:

> Gloria has moved to the assisted living portion of the community, following hip replacement surgery. She had lived in her own apartment for four years before the surgery. During that time, she had been an active participant in the read-aloud program at a local school, a member of the "galloping gourmet" club (featuring dinners in each other's apartment every month), and an avid bridge player. Now

---

Aging and Mental Health, 2e. Daniel L. Segal, Sara Honn Qualls, and Michael A. Smyer
© 2011 Daniel L. Segal, Sara Honn Qualls, and Michael A. Smyer

Gloria is demanding to move back to her apartment. She complains that she wants more scheduling freedom, that she wants to cook her own meals again, and that she doesn't need any more "help." The social worker is concerned about Gloria's physical abilities and her capacity to make decisions on her own. Is Gloria's demand for "freedom" a sign of good mental health or a denial of her changed physical and mental abilities?

As any good consultant, you're immediately faced with a simple challenge: Do my knowledge and skills allow me to respond effectively? In these scenarios, the consultant also needs to ask herself: What do I need to know to work effectively with older adults?

This chapter is designed to provide an initial answer to that simple question. We begin with a brief depiction of the basic developmental issues necessary for a full understanding of aging and mental health. We end the chapter with a two-part question: How is clinical work with older adults similar to working with younger people? How is it different?

Developmental Issues in Mental Health and Aging

According to Schaie (1995), there are several key developmental issues that provide a useful foundation for clinical work with older adults. His suggested topics form an outline of mental health and aging: normal and pathological aging; individual differences in aging; age differences and age changes; changing person/environment interactions; and reversibility of age-related behavior changes.

Normal and pathological aging

As noted in Chapter 1, gerontology is the study of the process of aging. Geriatrics is the study and treatment of the diseases associated with aging. The boundaries between these two fields have become more and more blurred as researchers and clinicians question our basic assumptions about the course of development.

How can we differentiate normal from pathological aging? As noted in Chapter 1, if we take a statistical view, we might assume that chronic physical illness is part of normal aging. Consider arthritis, for example. Whereas more than 50 percent of older adults have some form of arthritis, the condition is not a *universal* part of aging and, therefore, is not part of the normal process of growing older. Rather, arthritis would be considered an *age-related illness*. This means that rates for arthritis increase with age, but arthritis is not directly caused by aging itself. An example of another age-related illness or disorder is dementia (described in detail in Chapter 7). Whereas the rates of dementia increase with age, even substantially so, becoming demented is still not a normal part of aging. Like arthritis, an underlying disease process causes the conditions.

Similarly, consider the epidemiological data on the prevalence of frequent mental distress and diagnosable mental disorders at different ages presented in Chapter 1 (see Figures 1.1 and 1.2). Several trends in these data are important: First, the percentage of adults experiencing frequent mental distress decreases as age increases. Second, older adults have the lowest rate of mental disorder of any age group. One notable exception to this pattern is cognitive impairment, which is relatively more common among older adults (discussed fully in Chapter 7). Third, at any age, and especially in later life, only a minority of adults have a mental disorder. Thus, mental disorder is definitely *not* a part of normal aging. Recent estimates suggest that approximately 20 percent of adults 65 years old and older meet the criteria for a mental disorder (Jeste et al., 1999). Even with mild cognitive impairment – presumably a marker for Alzheimer's disease and other dementias – it is a minority of older adults who are afflicted.

In sum, it is important to recall the distinctions among normal, optimal, and pathological aging. Equating age with disease is mistaking gerontology for geriatrics – a mistake in either research or clinical work.

Individual differences

Throughout life, three systems of influence work to assure that differences among people increase with age: normative age-graded influences, normative history-graded influences, and non-normative influences (Baltes, 1987; Marsiske, Lang, Baltes, & Baltes, 1996).

Normative age-graded influences are universal, time-ordered biological, psychological, and sociocultural processes that affect development. Age-norms or developmental tasks that are age-linked illustrate this type of influence. For example, in the United States most children enter first grade at age six or seven, representing a socially constructed influence. Some examples of biologically based normative age-graded influences include puberty, menarche, and menopause, all of which are events that usually mark a major change in a person's life.

Normative history-graded influences are events that most people in a specific culture experience at the same time. For example, the Great Depression (Elder, 1974), school desegregation (Clotfelter, 2004), and the impact of AIDS (Elwood, 1999) were major social developments anchored in particular historical conditions that affected the development of children and adults. A more contemporary example includes the terrorist attacks on the World Trade Center on September 11, 2001, which profoundly impacted the views about personal safety and national security among many people in the United States. Yet another example is the ongoing impact of the Holocaust on many older individuals (see Box 2.1).

The aging of our global society is another example of a normative history-graded influence on development (see Figure 2.1).

Demographic data portray two simple facts: over the coming decades we will witness increasing numbers and proportions of older adults in the United States and across the globe. At the global level, in 1950, 8 out of every 100 people were 60 years old and older. By 2050, it is expected that 22 out of every 100 people will be over 60 years old (United Nations, 2006). Moreover, by 2045 the global population of people 60 years old and older is expected to surpass, for the first time in history, the number of children under 15 years of age (United Nations, 2006). Like much

Box 2.1   Aging Holocaust survivors and PTSD

Every evening in nursing homes across the country, the staff assist wheelchair-bound residents to bed. One night, as Mrs. S was sitting in her wheelchair in the community room and the aide came over to take her to her room, she began to thrash her arms and legs. She refused to be moved, screaming what seemed like nonsense, that she wasn't going to allow the staff to take her away and kill her. For her, this nightly ritual of taking residents out of the room one at a time triggered memories of her experience during the Holocaust when those who were taken away never returned.

Mr. M was in the hospital for minor surgery. As it was anticipated that he would be weak during the first few days following the operation, an aide was assigned to assist him with bathing and grooming. The first morning the aide helped him into the bathroom and turned on the shower. Mr. M's face turned white and he refused to step into the showers. He took baths and used a hand-held shower head because for him the stand-up shower triggered memories of the showers of poison gas used in the concentration camps.

Mrs. F joined a bereavement group following the death of her husband. At the first meeting the members of the group introduced themselves and shared a bit about their recent losses. Mrs. F, however, did not speak at all of her husband. Instead she spoke at great length, and very emotionally, about her parents and her siblings who were killed by the Nazis. This was the first time she had ever spoken of this and once she started, she could not stop.

Although it has been more than 50 years, and the atrocities committed by the Nazis and their supporters during World War II continue to affect many of those who survived, Mrs. S, Mr. M, and Mrs. F are among the Holocaust survivors who suffer from post-traumatic stress disorder [PTSD] as it is defined in the DSM-IV: they were exposed to a traumatic event(s); they persistently re-experience the trauma; they persistently avoid stimuli associated with the trauma and experience numbing of general responsiveness; and they experience persistent symptoms of increased arousal. While this may not be such a surprise due to the magnitude of the trauma they survived, what is perhaps surprising is that Mrs. S, Mr. M, and Mrs. F were not diagnosed with PTSD until their later years. It seems that the experience of growing older, their normative aging superimposed upon their Holocaust experiences, triggered the start of these symptoms.

Retirement, physical deterioration and loss are a part of the aging process, yet each of these can force flashbacks to the war years, bringing unresolved issues from those traumas to the surface. Many survivors busied themselves in their careers not only to make enough money to support their post-war families, but also to distract themselves from the painful memories of what they had lost and what they had experienced. Retirement frees the older adult from the busy work schedule, yet the free time may allow the deeply buried memories to resurface.

For many, acknowledging illness during the war meant sudden death. Concentration camp inmates were taken directly to the gas chambers or tortured in medical

Continued

experiments instead of receiving treatment. Illness or physical deterioration even 50 years later can bring back fears of what happened during the war. For this reason, some survivors may, perhaps subconsciously, downplay poor health or their medical needs. They, and their families, may also disregard the seriousness of illness in old age, unwilling to believe that having survived in hiding, in the ghettos or in the concentration camps a survivor could succumb to "normal" diseases such as pneumonia, cancer or a heart attack. Alzheimer's disease, or other dementing illnesses, can be particularly difficult for survivors. As they lose their short-term memories and the ability to differentiate past and present, the pain of their long-term memories can be almost overwhelming. For those old enough at the time of the war to remember pre-war experiences, focusing them back to those very early days can actually be a blessing, but for others, the pain of the war years is their earliest memory.

The seemingly everyday sights, sounds and smells found in hospitals, retirement facilities and nursing homes can also bring back memories of ghettos and concentration camps. The antiseptic smells, white lab coats of doctors or uniforms of security guards, and sound of people crying or screaming from loneliness, sickness or fear may trigger reactions ranging from withdrawal to aggressive behavior. Other triggers include bright lights, sirens, dogs and people with heavy accents. ... Some concrete interventions can reduce the trauma that is triggered. For example, in the case of Mrs. S, the nursing home staff was able to calm her fears by bringing back one of the residents who had previously been taken to her room. This reassured Mrs. S that the residents were not being taken away to be killed, and she consented to be wheeled to her room in the company of this other resident. In another case, a resident was hoarding food, bringing something back to her room after every meal. Staff tried to reinforce the policy against food in the rooms, reminding her that three meals per day were served and there was always plenty of food. As this resident was responding to hunger pains from years ago at a time when sufficient food was not available, she did not respond to the staff's request to leave the food in the dining room. The facility feared spoiled food and bugs, while the resident needed the security of food in various hiding places in her room. To meet the needs of both, the resident was allowed as much canned foods and canned beverages as she wanted, instead of perishables like fresh fruit and milk. In both these examples, the flexibility on the part of the staff, and the awareness of the issues at play, enabled them to address the situations in a way that met the needs of the clients, even if it was not following standard policy.

... [T]he author certainly does not mean to suggest that all Holocaust survivors suffer from PTSD or react to the stimuli described above. However, for those who do, the awareness and sensitivity of clinicians can ease the pain of the return of the trauma.

Ann Hartman, MAJCS, MSW, LCSW, is coordinator of Hineinu, a program addressing the unique aspects of aging for survivors of Nazi persecution and their families, at the Council for Jewish Elderly in Chicago.

Reprinted with permission from Hartman (1997), pp. 3 and 5. Copyright © 1997 American Society on Aging, San Francisco, California. http://www.asaging.org.

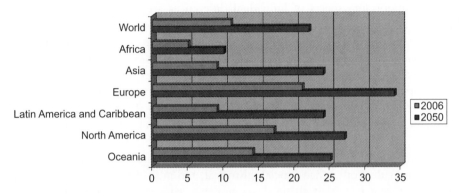

Figure 2.1   Percentage of population aged 60 years and older by major world region, 2006 and projected 2050.

of the rest of the world, the United States is in the midst of a longevity revolution, primarily due to the massive numbers of Baby Boomers marching into later life. Beginning in 2012, nearly 10,000 Americans will turn 65 every day and by 2030, more than 20 percent of the population will have passed their 65th birthday, representing over 71 million people (US Bureau of the Census, 2003).

The fastest growing sub-population of older adults is the oldest-old group (those 85 years old and older) who are also the frailest. In the United States, for example, the oldest-old group is projected to increase from the current 4.4 million people to 8.9 million by 2030 and to 19.4 million by 2050 (US Bureau of the Census, 2003). As of 2000, there were 70,000 centenarians in the United States. By 2050, this number is expected to increase by tenfold to over 800,000.

The culmination of these trends has generated a profound impact on modern society – for the first time in human history, surviving into later life is an expected part of the life cycle in all of the developed parts of the world. These demographic patterns influence the experience of aging across the life span.

Finally, *non-normative influences* are random, rare, or idiosyncratic events that are highly important to a specific individual person but are not experienced by most people. These unique events are neither age-graded nor history-graded influences. Some examples include the distinctive impact of genetic predispositions, family configurations, and individual life events, such as winning the lottery, being adopted, or surviving a plane crash (Martin & Smyer, 1990).

Importantly, all three types of influences interact continually across the life span. In addition, the same influence may affect individuals differently depending upon their age at the time (e.g., Elder's work on the differential effects of the Great Depression) or the interaction of influences. For example, Grundmann (1996) studied the impact of father absence on different cohorts of German men. Those who experienced father absence either before or after World War II, when such absence was socially non-normative, delayed their own transition to fatherhood. In contrast, those who experienced father absence linked to World War II, when such absences were socially normative, accelerated their own transition to fatherhood.

Other important aspects of individual differences are inter-individual variability and intra-individual variability. For example, variability is a hallmark of older adults with a mental disorder. We must differentiate among three patterns of older individuals with mental disorder: those who had a mental disorder early in life and maintained the same disorder into later life; those who grew old and experienced mental disorder for the first time in later life; and those who came to later life with a liability (e.g., genetic influence, life stress, etc.) that was exacerbated by the conditions of later life, producing mental disorder (Gatz, Kasl-Godley, & Karel, 1996; Gatz, & Smyer, 2001).

In sum, our clinical work must place older adults in a variety of contexts that produce individual differences: social, historical, and individual. We must understand the various influences that shape development across the life span producing the variability that accompanies aging.

Age differences and age changes

Understanding aging and its effects requires assessing several influences at once. Consider some of the basic questions of gerontology and geriatrics: Does intelligence decline with age? Is the risk of suicide greater in later life than in young adulthood? How would you investigate these questions?

One approach compares adults from different ages at one point in time. This *cross-sectional* approach confuses several elements at once, though: age differences, age changes, cohort effects, and time of measurement effects. A cross-sectional approach assumes that age *differences* reflect underlying age *changes*. This does not take into account the differences across the cohorts represented at any one point in time. It also does not consider the possible effect of when the study was done.

A second approach would follow the same people over a long period of time, measuring the group at several different ages. This *longitudinal approach* allows for observation and measurement of actual age changes in the individuals' functioning. This approach, however, has the limitation of following only one cohort of individuals. In doing so, one might mistake the characteristics of that particular cohort's experience for general patterns of aging.

Data on intellectual functioning across the life span offer a compelling demonstration of the difference between cross-sectional and longitudinal views (see Figure 2.2). These data represent performance on a verbal meaning test. The cross-sectional results represent age differences. If interpreted as age changes, we might think that verbal meaning performance peaks at around age 39 and then declines steeply starting around age 46. In contrast, when individuals are followed longitudinally, we see that their performance in fact increases until age 53 and then declines much more subtly than is suggested by the cross-sectional view. Thus, the age changes reflected in the longitudinal perspective are less dramatic and severe than suggested by the cross-sectional results.

The distinction between age differences and age changes is important for clinicians for several reasons. First, the client's current functioning needs to be compared with his or her own baseline, not solely in comparison to age-mates or to those in different age groups. Second, we place the person in context – in this case in a cohort context

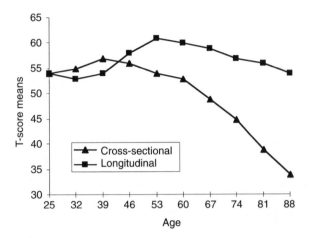

Figure 2.2 Comparable cross-sectional and longitudinal age gradients for verbal meaning. *Source*: Schaie and Willis (2002), Fig. 8.2, Chapter 8, "Cross-Sectional and Longitudinal Age Gradients for Verbal Meaning" © 2002. Reproduced by permission of Pearson Education, Inc.

of historical, educational, and social expectations, opportunities, and challenges. Consider the following example:

> The interview took place on a rural farm, a sharecropper's homestead. Mrs. Ella Smith, now in her late 80s, was surrounded by her children (in their late 50s and early 60s) and grandchildren. The multidimensional assessment began with a mental status test. Mrs. Smith did well until asked to perform "serial 7s": Please start at 100 and subtract 7, then 7 from that number, etc. She faltered and then explained: "I never was all that good at counting. I left school after third grade."

In Mrs. Smith's case, school was not one of the opportunities available to her rural cohort. Mrs. Smith was clearly educationally impaired. As it turns out, she was not also cognitively impaired. Her self-report reflected a comparison to her former functioning ("I never was good at counting"), a self-report confirmed by her children. In short, to equate her current inability with an age-related decline would have been off the mark.

Changing person/environment interactions

In his classic book, pioneering behavioral and social psychologist Kurt Lewin (1935) alerted us to the importance of concentrating on the interaction between the person and the environment more than 75 years ago. Since then, a number of scholars have concentrated on the importance of the environment for the continuing functioning among older adults.

Table 2.1   A balance sheet of losses and gains in later life

Losses	*Gains*
• Physical deterioration	• Verbal skill
• Speed of cognitive processing and capacity of working memory	• Social judgment
• Income	• Emotional balance and self-regulation
• Risk-taking	• Values clarity
• Declines in vision and hearing	• Family and role choices
• Social network	• Expertise and wisdom
• Roles	• Personality complexity

Several themes are important in conceptualizing the interplay between person and environment in later life. Some suggest that the optimal environment provides the best "fit" to the older person's changing abilities (e.g., Kahana & Kahana, 1996, 2003). For some, the concept of fit includes the notion of an optimally challenging environment – a context that demands that the older person stretch a bit and use her abilities to the utmost (e.g., Lawton, 1980, 1982).

Baltes and his colleagues (e.g., Marsiske et al., 1996) suggest that the basic dynamics of later life reflect two subtle and profound shifts: First, there is a changing balance between gains and losses, with increasing social, psychological, and physical losses; second, there is an increasing investment of the individual's reserve capacity toward maintenance functions, rather than toward growth. These generalizations, of course, provide a framework for assessing an older individual's unique combination of gains and losses, her idiosyncratic combination of physical, psychological, and social growth and maintenance. An overview of the "balance sheet" of losses and gains in later life is presented in Table 2.1.

We wish to emphasize that neither an overly pessimistic or negative view of aging (e.g., associating later life with decrepitude, loneliness, and melancholy) nor an overly positive view of aging (e.g., the image of a sweet old grandmother baking cookies all day) serves the clinician and researcher well. Rather, a realistic perspective of aging is necessary to fully appreciate the challenges and opportunities experienced by a specific older person, appreciating fully that later life is characterized by incredible diversity, and that in general there are more dissimilarities among older adults than similarities.

Gatz and her colleagues (1996) describe the mental health impact of the changing dynamics between the environment and older adults' vulnerabilities. They expand upon the diathesis-stress model of Zubin and Spring (1977) to emphasize three inter-related elements: biological vulnerability (including genetic influences); stressful life events (including physical and social losses or challenges); and psychological vulnerability or diathesis (including pessimistic thinking and poor coping skills). Gatz and her colleagues suggest that the changing interplay among these elements produces the curvilinear pattern of depressive symptoms and age often reported in the literature (see Figure 2.3).

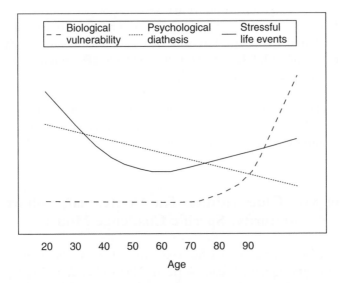

| Biological vulnerability | Psychological diathesis | Stressful life events |

20 30 40 50 60 70 80 90

Age

Figure 2.3 Depiction of developmental changes in the magnitude of influence on depressive symptoms exerted by biological vulnerability, psychological diathesis, and stressful life events across the adult life span.
Source: Gatz, Kasl-Godley, and Karel (1996). Adapted by permission of Academic Press.

For our purposes, the lesson is simple: Understanding the interaction between an older person and the social, physical, and psychological environment is essential for successful assessment and treatment of mental disorders in later life. Viewing the individual out of context will lead to an incomplete understanding of the person's difficulties and subsequent ineffective treatment.

Reversibility of age-related behavior change

How inevitable are the losses associated with aging? Can you teach an old dog new tricks? Is there anything we can do about the most common mental disorders in later life? In the 1950s and 1960s, much of the research and clinical lore focused on depicting the expectable losses of old age, with an emphasis on prompt treatment of excess disability.

More recently, however, attention has shifted to preventive interventions and effective strategies for coping with the most common problems of later life. A common theme has emerged: The "plasticity" of behavior in later life (Baltes & Baltes, 1990b). In short, results from a number of areas confirm that there are a variety of strategies and approaches that can be effective in reducing some of the deficits commonly associated with later life.

Consider the area of intellectual decline with age. Several studies have documented the impact of training interventions designed to improve the functioning of older adults. In either small group or individual sessions, Schaie and his colleagues have documented the impact of five-hour training programs on older adults' cognitive functioning on laboratory tests. Moreover, they have documented the lasting impact of such interventions with follow-ups seven years later. (For summaries of this work, see Schaie, 2005; Schaie & Willis, 2002, 2005.)

A variety of approaches can mitigate some of the losses of later life. The challenge for both the clinician and the older adult is to assess realistically the rewards of improvement likely to come from an investment of time and personal attention. These issues will be considered in more detail throughout Part III of the book.

Working with Older Adults: The Contextual, Cohort-Based, Maturity, Specific-Challenge Model

Most mental health practitioners who work with older adults are not geriatrics or gerontology experts (Qualls, Segal, Norman, Niederehe, & Gallagher-Thompson, 2002). Many have come to the issues of later life after working with other populations. Even those who have specialty training in geropsychology must focus on a simple question when working with older adults: Are the basic approaches to assessment and treatment different when working with older adults or are they the same as when working with other adult populations? Our answer is similar to the advice attributed to Yogi Berra: When you come to a fork in the road, take it. Working with older adults is both different from and similar to working with other age groups. In this section, we will briefly review both aspects. Our discussion is guided by the template provided by Knight (2004), who has proposed the *contextual, cohort-based, maturity, specific-challenge model* (CCMSC) to guide psychotherapeutic work with older adults. An overview of this model is presented in Table 2.2.

Table 2.2   An overview of the contextual, cohort-based, maturity, specific-challenge model (Knight, 2004)

Elements of maturity	Specific challenges	Cohort effects	Contexts
Cognitive and emotional complexity	Chronic physical illnesses and disability	Cognitive abilities and education	Age-segregated communities
Expertise	Grieving for the loss of loved ones	Word usage	Aging services agencies
Areas of competence	Caregiving	Values	Senior recreation sites
Multiple family experiences		Normative life paths	Medical settings and long-term care settings
Accumulated interpersonal skills		Social-historical life experiences	Age-based laws and regulations

Source: Adapted from Knight (2004).

Differences

The differences in therapeutic approach to working with older adults stem from changes over time in the older adult herself, differences between the contexts of older people and younger people, cohort differences, specific challenges commonly experienced in later life, and potential differences in the therapeutic alliance.

Interpersonal qualities and maturation Two aspects of older adults' functioning may differentiate them from younger adults: an increasing cognitive maturation and a changing sense of time.

Knight (2004; Knight & Qualls, 1995) has suggested that older adults develop increasing expertise in family, work, and social relationships across the life span. In addition, older adults may show increasing emotional complexity, with a greater understanding and control of their affective states. From a therapeutic perspective, this may offer an opportunity to collaborate with the older client in reflecting on the current problem within a perspective of past problem-solving successes: "How have you handled similar challenges in the past?"

Another frequently differentiating aspect of working with older adults is their sense of time. First, there is the obvious difference that more time has passed for older adults – giving them both more experience and the opportunity for greater perspective, an opportunity unfortunately missed by some.

A frequent benchmark used by one of our older friends reflects this greater perspective. When faced with a problem, he routinely asked: "Will it matter a year from now?" If the answer was no, he would not worry too much about that particular problem.

A second aspect of time reflects a subtle change in older adults' temporal calculus: Oftentimes there is a shift from focusing on time lived to concentrating on the time left to live (e.g., Carstensen, Isaacowitz, & Charles, 1999). These important differences in the perception of time left in life lead younger adults and older adults to differ in the types of goals they pursue. Whereas younger people tend to pursue goals that expand their horizons and provide new social networking opportunities, older adults tend to pursue goals that are more emotionally meaningful (Carstensen, Fung, & Charles, 2003; Carstensen et al., 1999). For some, shuttling between these two represents one of the therapeutic challenges – how to keep focused on the present and the future, without either denying or being consumed by the past.

Contextual complexity Working effectively with older adults requires recognizing the complexity of their lives and the impact of their contexts. We discussed the potential impact of the physical environment earlier. Here, we focus on the complexity of two aspects of the social, interpersonal environment: family members and those who provide care and support to the older client.

Knowing a person's age can provide some information about the historical time and cohort experiences to which she has been exposed. Knowing her generational position can also tell us much about the resources and demands presented by family members, about the give and take of family members and friends (Bengtson, Rosenthal, & Burton, 1995). Consider two men:

> Bryce is a 67-year-old CEO of a billion-dollar-a-year company. He is a middle generation adult, with caregiving concerns for his 89-year-old mother and his two children in their 20s.

> Charles is a 38-year-old professional. He also is a middle generation adult who divides his time and resources among his 80-year-old mother and his children who are in elementary school.

Whereas these men differ in age and life stage, they share a generational position that affects their psychological well-being. Focusing solely on their ages would over-look the psychological and social complexity of their generational positions.

Family members provide the majority of assistance to older adults who need help because of physical or mental health problems. Oftentimes, however, the family car-egivers are complemented by formal and informal services provided by physicians, social agency staff members, and friends. Again, to understand effectively the life context of the older client, the therapist must assess the availability of two types of support: emotional support in the give and take of daily interactions; and support that would be available in a time of crisis. In addition, the mental health professional must understand the affection and support that the older client provides to other family members.

The older population is also becoming more ethnically and racially diverse, yet another factor that impacts the contextual complexity of work with older people. In many cases, the task of the therapist is one of trying to leverage gerontological exper-tise. This requires sharing problem-solving approaches with those who have the most frequent contact with the older client: family members, friends, and other service providers, especially primary care physicians. Collaboration is a keystone in effective assessment and treatment of mentally ill older adults.

Cohort differences   Each of us carries with us the imprint of the culture and time in which we live. Think of today's oldest old: Born 80 or more years ago; witnesses to almost unimaginable technological changes; participants in world war and cold war; survivors of economic upheavals; among the earliest beneficiaries of Medicare and Medicaid. These experiences affect the ways that older adults encounter the challenges of later life. Consider, for example, one of our older clients who for the past 20 years wore a fresh pair of socks every day, donating the "old" socks to a charity at the end of each month. At first blush, this behavior may appear unusual until one considers the context: as a young boy growing up during the Great Depression, he and his family were extremely poor and could not afford clothing for the children, even socks to wear to school. In his later years, he "treated himself" to fresh socks each and every day as a reminder of the early struggles he had overcome.

Members of different cohorts, for example, may use different language to describe similar reactions.

Hazel reported that she was "frustrated" when the hospital social worker reported that Medicare would not pay for her medications.

The mental health professional probed Hazel's frustration. It became clear that younger clients might have used another word: angry.

Cohorts may also differ in their patterns of help-seeking and problem definition. When faced with a mental health problem, today's older adults might first seek out a primary care physician, a minister, or a neighbor – but not a mental health professional. Indeed, many older adults in the current cohort grew up with especially pejorative and stigmatized views of mentally ill individuals and mental health treatment. Indeed, "treatment" at that time was reserved only for the most severe forms of mental disorder (e.g., a psychotic disorder like schizophrenia) and usually meant long-term stays in locked units of state psychiatric hospitals. Effective psychiatric medications, such as major tranquilizers for the treatment of schizophrenia and other forms of psychosis, were not developed until the 1950s, meaning that treatments prior to that time for people with severe mental disorders were notoriously ineffective. Tomorrow's older adults, in contrast, are likely to be much more comfortable with mental health treatment, perhaps changing the profile of where mental health treatment is provided for older adults. Another important aspect that interacts with cohort is diversity, including the impact of race, culture, ethnicity, gender, and sexual orientation on the older person's lived experience as part of a specific cohort. Aspects of culture and diversity impact, sometimes in profound ways, the ways individuals express, experience, and cope with feelings of distress, the stigma associated with mental health treatment, and the preferences for and barriers to treatment for mental health problems (US Department of Health and Human Services, 2001). At the very least, mental health professionals should reflect on the role that the older adult's cohort experience and cultural background might play in problem identification, patterns of help-seeking, and expectations for change.

The specificity of challenges in later life   In sharp contrast to the increased maturity associated with normal development throughout the life span discussed earlier, it is equally important to be aware of the serious challenges of growing older. According to Knight (2004), there are several problems that, although not unique to later life, are commonly experienced by older adults. These areas include chronic physical illness and disability, grieving the loss of loved ones, and caregiving for an ill family member. An important premise of the CCMSC is that these problems are conceptualized as "challenges" that can be overcome with rehabilitation, psychotherapy, or other types of intervention. This perspective helps us recognize that it is not normal to become clinically depressed, severely anxious, or have difficulty managing one's day to day activities at any stage of the life span and that when signs of mental disorder are recognized, appropriate treatments should be offered.

Chronic illness, disability, and medication use. The majority of older adults come to late life with a variety of physical challenges and comorbidities: At least 80 percent of older adults in the United States are living with at least one chronic condition, and 50 percent have at least two (National Center for Health Statistics, 2003). These chronic medical conditions include arthritis, osteoporosis, cataracts, diabetes, asthma, prostate enlargement, hypertension, and heart disease. Moreover, whereas older adults make up about 13 percent of the US population, they account for 34 percent of all prescription medications and 30 percent of all nonprescription medications. Besides taking more medications, older adults also metabolize medications more slowly than younger adults and it is common for them to take numerous medications prescribed by multiple providers. As a consequence, older adults are at a much greater risk for adverse reactions to a medication or combination of medications than younger adults.

Apart from a modest developmental change of central nervous system slowing, the major physical challenges for the mental health professional and the older client involve the inter-relationship of physical and mental health. As noted in Chapter 1, there are four paradigms for examining the links between physical and mental health, reflecting the complexity of physical and mental interactions for older adults:

- psychological or psychogenic stress may lead to physical health problems;
- a physical disorder may lead to a psychiatric disturbance;
- coexisting physical and psychiatric disorders may interact;
- and social and psychological resources can affect the course of a physical disorder.

These complex interactions of physical and mental health for older adults require clinicians to monitor closely the older client's physical well-being. Thus, clinicians must have a solid understanding of the various kinds of chronic medical illnesses common in later life and the psychological impact of these illnesses, pain control techniques, and strategies to increase medication adherence (Knight, 2004). Close collaboration is needed among the range of people who interact with the older client: family members, friends, the primary care physician, and other health care and social service providers. (We will return to this collaborative theme shortly.)

Grieving losses. A sad reality of aging is that with advanced age we will inevitably outlive some if not many of the people whom we have loved. As an example, one of our older family members (a grandmother to DLS) had a prized possession of a photo of 20 couples who were present at her wedding in 1936. Many of the individuals depicted had remained lifelong friends. On her 90th birthday, she realized that she had outlived everyone in the photo including her husband of 65 years. Thus, a common theme in psychotherapy with older adults involves grief work (Knight, 2004), in many cases, multiple losses over a period of time. Besides helping an older client come to grips with the loss and accept the loss, the focus of therapy also typically turns to the future, helping the older person craft a meaningful existence despite the loss of loved ones.

Caregiving. Given the high rates of physical illness in late life, many relatively healthy older adults find themselves providing care for a family member who is physically frail, cognitively impaired, or in many cases, failing both physically and cognitively (Knight, 2004). Due to the caregiving demands, many caregivers become overwhelmed and experience high levels of emotional distress (Knight, 2004). Specific forms of psychotherapy have been developed and tested to help caregivers manage extremely difficult and taxing caregiving situations, with promising results (e.g.,

Gonyea, O'Connor, & Boyle, 2006; Knight, Lutzky, & Macofsky-Urban, 1993; Qualls & Zarit, 2009). We will return to the theme of caregiving throughout this text, especially in the context of caregiving challenges for an individual with cognitive impairment (Chapter 7).

Countertransference issues   Encounters with older adults as clients likely elicit a range of responses from the therapist, including stereotypical assumptions, fantasies, and projections about aging and older adults (Knight, 2004). At times, the countertransference issues raised may be either current issues in the therapist's own relationship with his or her parents or grandparents, or future issues on the horizon in the therapist's own family. Similarly, working with older adults may raise concerns about one's own aging, dying, and death. In each instance, the therapist must first be aware of the potential for countertransference processes and then depend upon supervision or collegial support to help differentiate the therapist's projections from the client's reality.

Similarities

Although Knight's CCMSC model describes many important aspects of later life that should be thoughtfully considered and understood in clinical work, working with older clients is not entirely different from working with other groups. Throughout this book we will be discussing approaches to assessment and treatment that build upon techniques developed and used with other age groups. In some cases, there have been modifications to accommodate age-related changes (e.g., large print versions of assessment instruments). In other cases, there has been a relatively straightforward application of previously developed approaches to the problems of later life (e.g., cognitive-behavioral therapy). Important findings from psychotherapy outcome studies with older adults have demonstrated unequivocally that psychotherapy with older adults is effective, roughly equivalent to the psychotherapy with younger adults and to the effects of psychiatric medications with older adults (see reviews by: APA Working Group on the Older Adult, 1998; Ayers, Sorrell, Thorp, & Wetherell, 2007; Engels & Vermey, 1997; Gallagher-Thompson & Coon, 2007; Gatz et al., 1998; Pinquart & Sörensen, 2001; Powers, 2008; Satre, Knight, & David, 2006; Scogin & McElreath, 1994; Scogin, Welsh, Hanson, Stump, & Coates, 2005). A note of caution about these findings, however, is that there is very little research on the efficacy of various psychotherapies among the oldest-old group (i.e., 85+ years). Our working assumption is that the essential skills that contribute to an effective clinician are also necessary for working effectively with older adults – necessary but not sufficient. In addition, the therapist must also call upon an appreciation of the developmental influences at work in later life.

Summary and Conclusions

In this chapter, we have attempted to provide the reader with a broad overview of the major concepts and themes of gerontology, highlighting aspects of aging that are critical for the further understanding of mental health and mental disorder. Clinical work with older adults requires knowledge about normal age-related changes, disease processes, cohort effects, specific challenges associated with aging, and the distinct social environment of older adults in our society. In working with older adults, knowledge about individual differences and the diversity of the experience of the aging process is also necessary. Throughout the life span, theoretical perspectives of the etiology, assessment, and treatment of disorders mold the therapist's approaches. In Part II, we will introduce several models, emphasizing those aspects that are most salient in each. Our working assumption is that the therapist's implicit and explicit models shape problem identification and treatment, regardless of the age of the client. The challenge, therefore, is to identify the strengths and shortcomings of each model. We turn to this challenge in Part II.

Part II
Models of Mental Health in Later Life

Discussions about the mental health of any population often begin with disclaimers about the ambiguity of the construct of mental health or mental disorder. A serious conversation with your peers focused on the task of defining mental health would generate quite diverse ideas and not just a small amount of controversy. Conceptions of health and disorder are varied, at least in part, because of the variety of assumptions made concerning the nature of human beings and their interactions with the environment.

Introductory chapters in abnormal psychology textbooks (e.g., Halgin & Whitbourne, 2010) typically summarize the major strategies for defining normal or abnormal behavior using a core set of definitions of abnormality that includes statistical definitions (i.e., what is non-normative), moral definitions (i.e., what is socially and culturally unacceptable), definitions of disability or dysfunction (what impairs social or occupational functioning), and definitions based on what is personally distressing. The current edition of the *Diagnostic and Statistical Manual of Mental Disorders* (DSM-IV-TR, 4th edition, text revision) defines mental disorder as:

> A clinically significant behavioral or psychological syndrome or pattern that occurs in an individual and that is associated with present distress (e.g., a painful symptom) or disability (i.e., impairment in one or more important areas of functioning) or with a significantly increased risk of suffering death, pain, disability, or an important loss of freedom. In addition, this syndrome or pattern must not be merely an expectable and culturally sanctioned response to a particular event, for example, the death of a loved one. (American Psychiatric Association, 2000, p. xxxi)

These definition alternatives can be used to examine the absence of mental health of older persons. Each provides some insights, but each also runs into conceptual conundrums. If a disorder process or organ deterioration is normative among 85-year-olds, does that mean it is normal? Can we talk meaningfully about what might be

---

Aging and Mental Health, 2e. Daniel L. Segal, Sara Honn Qualls, and Michael A. Smyer
© 2011 Daniel L. Segal, Sara Honn Qualls, and Michael A. Smyer

normal for 85-year-olds that would not be normal in 25-year-olds (i.e., is age *per se* a moderator of our definition of normal)? Perhaps we might acknowledge differences based on age in the area of memory or attention, but what about depression or anxiety?

Mental health or well-being is no easier to define than abnormality. Definitions may focus on competence, maturity, responsibility for actions, or freedom to love and work. Jahoda (1958) provided six highly cited criteria of positive mental health: positive self-attitudes, growth and self-actualization, integration of the personality, autonomy, reality perception, and environmental mastery. We appreciate the qualitative richness of the definition offered by Birren and Renner (1980) that, at any age, mentally healthy people "have the ability to respond to other individuals, to love, to be loved, and to cope with others in give-and-take relationships" (p. 29). Qualls (2002) draws on Ryff and Keyes' (1996) empirically supported theoretical framework for psychological well-being in later life with the following definition.

> A mentally healthy person, therefore, accepts the current self, with its strengths and weaknesses, uses the strengths available to him or her to maintain maximum autonomy by mastering their environment, and maintains positive relations with others, all with the overarching purpose of enacting personal meaning in life and personal growth. (p. 12)

Clinical work with older persons is sometimes challenging simply because it forces us to articulate our conception of normal mental health, and then adjust it (as needed) for older persons. As Birren and Renner (1980) acknowledge, the conceptual dichotomies implicit in most distinctions of mental health and mental disorder become even more complicated when applied to older adults. "The conceptual dichotomies ... – health and illness, competence and incompetence, and intrapsychic and interpersonal processes – seem, in the minds of the present authors, to have rather different implications for older adults in which there can be many coexisting features" (p. 7). The person described in the following case study pushes the clarity of our definitions of normality.

Joan Rankin is a 74-year-old woman who lives in her home in a small rural community. Her husband, Jim, died two years ago, following a five-year bout with cancer. Now that she is alone, Joan is tempted to move closer to her children, but cannot quite make up her mind. Her house is paid for, and she is not sure she could buy a comparable house in a city with the proceeds from a sale of this house. She has a modest pension that will be sufficient unless she needs major medical care. Sometimes she worries about not having enough money to carry her through. She chooses to live frugally with an occasional indulgence.

Joan belongs to the local garden club, but is not a particularly active member. She does enjoy working in her own small flower garden during the nice weather seasons. She also attends church almost weekly. Joan has a few close friends, but many of those friendships were strained by the period of Jim's illness. Even two years after his death, she is not sure how to fill her days. Her nights are usually tolerable although sometimes she lies awake for long periods in the middle of the night. At those times she feels overwhelmingly alone and scared.

Joan is generally healthy, although she has high blood pressure and some difficulties with thyroid and arthritis. She takes Tylenol for the arthritis, propanolol for blood pressure, and synthroid to regulate her thyroid.

Joan's two children live 300 miles away in major cities. Her daughter, Jeannie, is married, has three children (ages 4, 7, and 10), and teaches school. Her son, John, a very successful realtor, is currently engaged to be remarried. He was divorced four years ago from his wife of 18 years, who has custody of their two children, ages 8 and 13. Jeannie and John have never been very close. Nor was John close to his father, although he confided his troubles and joys to his mother privately.

Joan has two younger sisters still living, and two older brothers who died more than five years ago. Her sister Betty lives only two blocks away from Joan, and calls her daily. Sometimes Joan even resents the call because Betty is so perky and enthusiastic about life. Betty insists that Joan get out to social events regardless of how tired or sick Joan is feeling. Betty has always been the cheerful one, encouraging all those around her to enjoy life. Recently she has hinted that she might like to move in with Joan to share expenses.

Her other sister Vivian lives with her husband 30 miles away on a farm. They stay busy with farm responsibilities, and with their children and grandchildren. Joan sees them only at family gatherings on holidays. Vivian has always been the quiet, solid one in the family. Joan would like to spend more time with her, but can see that she is too busy with daily responsibilities to socialize.

Her brothers, Elwood and Milt, were in business together in a city 150 miles from Joan's home. They died of heart attacks exactly one year apart. They left their families quite well off financially, and their children and grandchildren have continued their business. Joan only visits with her sisters-in-law or their offspring at the annual family reunion each summer.

Is Joan mentally healthy? Clinicians would readily recognize several symptoms in this brief description of Joan that might be clinically meaningful. For example, she has difficulty with decision-making, worries, has mild insomnia, and is socially withdrawn. Could she be diagnosed with a mental disorder? Is her current distress caused by her recent widowhood, her health, her struggle to create meaning, the family and social systems conflicts, or some inadequacy in her personality that inhibits her coping? Given her circumstances, what would mentally healthy look like? Where would you begin to look for additional information to help you understand Joan's well-being?

A systematic examination of conceptualizations of the mental health of older persons leads us to examine the broader paradigms of psychology. A paradigm is a framework used to construct our understanding of the world. Such frameworks make basic assumptions about the nature of human beings, including assumptions about motivation, cognition, emotion, personality, and behavior. Built on those assumptions are postulates or theories that attempt to explain particular behavior patterns, including patterns defined as mental health and mental disorder.

In the section that follows, a series of chapters describes four basic paradigms used often by psychologists: the psychodynamic, cognitive-behavioral, stress and coping, and family systems paradigms. Each chapter will review the basic assumptions and core theoretical contributions of one paradigm. Specifically, descriptions are offered of the assumptions about what well-being looks like and how disorders are defined and conceptualized. Because approaches to assessment and intervention are rooted in the assumptions about mental health and mental disorder, each chapter also includes a description of the major approaches to assessment and intervention that have arisen from each paradigm.

Gerontology has not produced totally new paradigms for defining and examining human lives. It has instead applied existing frameworks to the unique and common problems of older persons. There is no single way to answer the questions raised at the beginning of this introduction regarding Joan Rankin. As will become evident, each paradigm produces a different (although perhaps related) explanation of Joan's mental health.

Regardless of paradigm or theory, gerontologists have developed a profound respect for the influence of culture and cohort experience on well-being. Subcultures offer specific definitions and mechanisms for demonstrating mental health and disorder. These definitions and mechanisms for experiencing well-being also vary by the historical period in which individuals are born and live (birth cohort). If Joan Rankin were Chinese, German, or Cherokee, how would that influence your understanding of her behavior and your analysis of her well-being? How would her experience be different and what different meanings would be embedded in her behavior if she lived in the seventeenth, twentieth, or twenty-first century?

As you study the chapters in Part II, engage yourself in the challenge of creating meaningful models for mental health and disorder in older adults. What paradigms explain behavior most adequately and parsimoniously? What tenets from each paradigm seem most credible? As you read, you may find it useful to write an analysis of Joan Rankin's story from each paradigm. When you have completed all four chapters, consider writing an integration essay that articulates your personal model of mental health and disorder in older adults.

3

Psychodynamic Model

The psychodynamic model of psychological functioning is one of the earliest comprehensive models of psychological well-being and disorder, but a relatively late
contributor to models of mental health in later life. The progenitor of this line of
theory was Sigmund Freud's psychoanalytic model. Subsequent contributors (e.g.,
Jung, Erikson) developed varied approaches to the inner dynamics of personality, but
stayed true to core assumptions about the importance of intrapsychic functioning,
the balance of genetic and environmental influence on personality, and the key role
of relationships in normal and abnormal development. The interpersonal school
shifted focus to the social contexts in which the personality structures were formed
and maintained (e.g., Horney, Sullivan). Thus, although the theories covered in this
chapter offer a wide range of constructs and explanations, they share a common focus
on the motivational and personality aspects of human beings whose social contexts
have powerful effects.

Maria Jiminez is increasingly isolated because she often just does not feel like
getting out. Up until a few years ago her home was the constant gathering place
of the extended family. After her husband's death, the nieces and nephews quit
coming around. Her children and grandchildren visit, but seem to resent it. The
entire family continues to mourn the death of Juan, the warm, generous, and
fun-loving patriarch of the family. Although Maria had always cooked for the
family, she was not known for a generous spirit. In family gatherings she usually
kept to herself, portraying a rather quiet person who waited for others to notice
what she needed or wanted. Her daughters feel obligated to care for their mother,
but it is a fairly joyless relationship on both sides. The "girls" can never quite get
it right – if they make apple pie, she wanted peach. If they clean the kitchen, she
laments about the dirt in the bathroom. The doctors don't pay enough attention
to her, the home health aide "is just working for money" and doesn't genuinely

Aging and Mental Health, 2e. Daniel L. Segal, Sara Honn Qualls, and Michael A. Smyer
© 2011 Daniel L. Segal, Sara Honn Qualls, and Michael A. Smyer

like Maria. Everyone recognizes Maria's depression and encourages her to seek help from a mental health professional. She resists because "any woman would feel depressed if she had a life like mine," but has made it to your office to tell you her sad story. She obviously likes having you listen to her, but tells you that she is sure you can't help her.

Introduction to the Model

How does the psychodynamic model describe and explain Maria's distress? As with any model, basic assumptions about human beings are the core constructs used to explain behavior. In the case of psychodynamic theory, the basic personality, developmental processes, and interpersonal relationships are the main foci of the theory.

The psychodynamic view of human beings emphasizes the complex interrelationships among cognition, emotion, and motivation in the formation of personality. The complexity into which these highly evolved structures are organized gives humans a tremendous advantage over other species of animals in the task of managing their basic needs (e.g., food, shelter, procreation). However, the struggle to survive, along with the knowledge that survival is tenuous, generates anxiety.

Managing anxiety is a primary task of the executive function of the personality, the ego. Freud initially postulated that anxiety was generated by conflict between the primitive life energy (libido) that resides in an animalistic structure called the id, and the societally imposed conscience structure called the superego. The ego's task, according to Freud, is to modulate the inevitable conflict between the two structures. Later, ego psychologists emphasized the interpersonal contexts in which the developing capability of the ego or Self emerges and forms a distinctive style. Other theorists postulate that the process of creating meaning is a key potential of the ego. What is shared in common by psychodynamic theorists, however, is their attempt to describe the organization and functioning of the basic structures of personality and suggest ways to assist humans to gain insight into the functioning of those structures so individuals can make more conscious choices regarding their motives, emotions, behavior, thoughts, and values.

Basic personality structures are established very early in life as the infant and very young child experiences its basic needs and the external world's response to them. The primary relationships for infants are known as their attachment relationships (Bowlby, 1969). Attachment figures are the persons who teach infants and toddlers about the external world (e.g., its safety, trustworthiness, and availability of nurturance) through their interactions. Because all humans begin as helpless, dependent creatures, the early experience of helplessness generates very basic survival anxiety.

Strong nurturing caretakers who teach the child that Others are trustworthy are internalized as parts of the Self that will be experienced as sharing those characteristics. Conversely, Others whose behavior increases anxiety or rage will not only teach the child about an unreliable, unsafe external world, but are also internalized as representations of the world as an unsafe, unreliable Self. These early experiences shape the form of the child's cognitive schema, emotional response patterns, and motivations. The resulting personality structures subsequently serve the function of buffering individuals from the core anxiety about living life and facing death. Thus, early relationships are where basic linkages are forged between thoughts, feelings, and motivations that culminate in an external world view. Similarly shaped by early relational experiences, internal self-protective structures, called *defense mechanisms*, are the human's primary ways of managing basic anxiety about life and death.

The development and evolution of these structures was once solely the purview of child psychologists interested in the initial structuring of personality during the first five years of life. Certainly, the experiences of childhood continue to be recognized as particularly profound because the early experiences establish styles or strategies for managing internal conflicts and adapting to external changes that have lifelong effects. For example, childhood attachment styles link to subsequent patterns of adult relationships (Shemmings, 2006). In adulthood, secure attachment styles would be expressed as mutuality in the processes of caregiving, intimacy, and sexuality. Avoidant attachment styles, in contrast, constrain the individual's subsequent ability or willingness to give or receive care, or to emotionally connect within a sexual relationship (leading to distancing or promiscuity). Most current theorists recognize the potential for growth and development across the life span as intrapsychic processes evolve in response to life experience as well as the critical importance of childhood experiences.

Adult Development: The Context for Aging

Developmental processes of adulthood provide new opportunities to mature in the course of responding to the many tasks and crises faced by all adults in the course of normal adulthood. Colarusso and Nemiroff (1979) offered seven hypotheses regarding the nature of development in adulthood that can be viewed as basic postulates of psychodynamic views of adult development (see Table 3.1). These statements claim that there is more continuity than discontinuity between child and adult developmental processes, with distinctions primarily in form and content. The basic structures through which development is evoked and expressed remain the same.

Thus, aged adults come to the last part of their lives heavily influenced not only by childhood events, but also by adult events and adaptations.

The individual enters late life with a personality structure that reflects a long history of life experiences. Idiosyncratic means of managing internal sexual and aggressive impulses and of coping with external stresses have been established, a well-engrained sense of self has been formed and shaped, providing an internalized representation that guides behavior and experiences, and child, adolescence, and adulthood disappointments and traumas have marked the individual with particular areas of psychological strength and weakness. In late life, the adult confronts age-correlated events (retirement, physical changes and illness, loss through death of friends and family) and internal psychological changes that can re-evoke long-unresolved but defended against internal conflicts, undermine the sense of self, and increase demands on ego resources and defense mechanisms thus requiring a new level of integration and development or resulting in depression, anxiety, or psychotic disturbance. (Newton, Brauer, Gutmann, & Grunes, 1986, p. 208)

Table 3.1   Psychodynamic model of adult development

Hypothesis I	The nature of the developmental process is basically the same in the adult as in the child.
Hypothesis II	Development in adulthood is an ongoing, dynamic process.
Hypothesis III	Whereas childhood development is focused primarily on the *formation* of psychic structure, adult development is concerned with the continuing *evolution* of existing psychic structure.
Hypothesis IV	The fundamental developmental issues of childhood continue as central aspects of adult life but in altered form.
Hypothesis V	The developmental processes in adulthood are influenced by the *adult* past as well as the *childhood* past.
Hypothesis VI	Development in adulthood, as in childhood, is deeply influenced by the body and physical change.
Hypothesis VII	A central, phase-specific theme of adult development is the normative crisis precipitated by the recognition and acceptance of the finiteness of time and the inevitability of personal death.

Source: Adapted from Colarusso and Nemiroff (1979).

The effects of a lifetime of experiences are embedded in the internal structures of personality. Despite the importance of external events to the adjustment to aging, the personality is considered a primary mediator of adaptation in later life.

Adult developmental processes have been outlined in terms of the tasks that provoke change (e.g., marriage, entry of children), the effects of adult events on development of the Self (e.g., Kohut, 1971), or the development of internal structures such as defense mechanisms (e.g., Vaillant, 1977). A popular framework for conceptualizing development is to divide the life span into stages. Stage theorists attempt to divide the life span into discrete phases that are characterized by common life tasks, especially those related to family development and work roles (Gould, 1978; Levinson, Darrow, & Klein, 1978).

Erik Erikson's (1963) early model of development across the life span (Figure 3.1) is one of the most influential stage models. Adults have opportunities to mature in response to the major tasks of the life course by restructuring internally. In the last formulation of his model, Erikson, Erikson, and Kivnick (1986) describe specific life themes that, although present throughout the life span, are most salient at the point in the life cycle when internal and external pressures highlight one particular theme. These themes are experienced within the dynamics of the personality as children and adults struggle with the use of their personality strengths and weaknesses to address life tasks. For example, the theme of autonomy that emerges so powerfully in toddlerhood as the child first experiences the power and frustration of the will, is again significantly addressed in adolescence, and again in old age. The substantive issues that generate the struggle vary, but the thematic focus on autonomy is similar. The struggle with the opposing alternative responses to life challenges is what produces the potential for growth of character or virtues. A balance between the alternatives generates growth toward maturity.

Older Adulthood	57	58	59	60	61	62	63	64 Integrity & Despair WISDOM
Middle Adulthood	49	50	51	52	53	54	55 Generativity & Self-Absorption CARE	56
Young Adulthood	41	42	43	44	45	46 Intimacy & Isolation LOVE	47	48
Adolescence	33	34	35	36	37 Identity & Confusion FIDELITY	38	39	40
School Age	25	26	27	28 Industry & Inferiority COMPETENCE	29	30	31	32
Play Age	17	18	19 Initiative & Guilt PURPOSE	20	21	22	23	24
Toddlerhood	9	10 Autonomy & Shame / Doubt WILL	11	12	13	14	15	16
Infancy	1 Basic Trust & Basic Mistrust HOPE	2	3	4	5	6	7	8

Figure 3.1 Psychosocial themes and stages of life.
Source: Adapted from Erikson et al. (1986).

The basic principles of Erikson's model are shared by most psychodynamic theorists: People use the styles and strategies consistent with their personality structure to address the psychosocial tasks of their life stage. The tasks or crises of adulthood challenge the familiar styles and strategies, however, creating an opportunity for development of more complex and mature personality structures. In the course of responding to life challenges, heightened anxiety may result if the task is not being managed well using familiar methods. Increased anxiety sets the stage for either growth within the personality or a breakdown in functioning (regression), perhaps even to the ultimate level of psychosis.

Development in the Second Half of Life

What new potentials for growth exist in later life that are not possible early in the life cycle? Beginning in mid-life, humans alter their perspective on their own life span.

Neugarten (1979) hypothesized that people begin to count time in terms of time until death rather than in terms of time since birth, a perspective that impacts relationship priorities, for example (Carstensen, Isaacowitz, & Charles, 1999). Having achieved a stable life structure, and given increased awareness of the limits of their life span, humans are prompted to re-examine their life for unused opportunities and unknown aspects of the self.

Jung (1933) noted the tendency for men and women to become androgynous by exploring characteristics of the other gender during the second half of their life. Men explore their feminine side while women are drawn to explore their underdeveloped masculine characteristics. Beginning in late mid-life, then, adults are drawn to explore new interests, skills, and interpersonal styles. For example, high-powered business executives may choose to paint, garden, and build close ties to family. Extroverts may explore their introverted side through journaling, meditation, or interests that draw upon the inner resources of creativity. Gutmann (1987, 1992) expanded on this theme by arguing that parenting is the organizing life structure of early adulthood that is sufficiently demanding that couples organize their work into constraining but efficient roles, traditionally along gender-based lines. Once the "chronic parental emergency" ends, individuals are free to resume the full range of their development, both masculine and feminine.

Erikson (1963) argued for the potential for wisdom in later life, as the individual makes peace with his or her life as it was lived. Like all of the other Eriksonian themes, the basic polarity of ego integrity versus despair is present in all stages of life. Yet a special perspective is available at the end of life.

> Throughout life, the individual has, on some level, anticipated the finality of old age, experiencing an existential dread of "not-being" alongside an ever-present process of integrating those behaviors and restraints, those choices and rejections, those essential strengths and weaknesses over time that constitute what we have called the sense of "I" in the world. In old age, this tension reaches its ascendancy. The elder is challenged to draw on a life cycle that is far more nearly completed than yet to be lived, to consolidate a sense of wisdom with which to live out the future, to place him- or herself in perspective among those generations now living, and to accept his or her place in an infinite historical progression. (Erikson et al., 1986, p. 56)

Mental Health in Later Life

A developmental approach to personality dynamics would imply that positive mental health requires a richer definition than merely the absence of pathology. Is it positive mental health when a frail elder maintains basic personality integrity despite the decline of physical abilities? Or when an older adult adapts to tremendous loss with only modest regression? Psychoanalysts have focused on pathology or maintenance of function in the face of loss and deterioration far more than on positive potentials, with rare exceptions. Emotional integration or deepening of personality is described by some developmentalists as a positive developmental potential in old age (Butler, Lewis, & Sunderland, 1998; Ryff, 1982). Kivnick (1993) suggests that vitality reflects the infusion of meaning into daily activities.

Throughout the life cycle, everyday mental health may be described as an attempt to live meaningfully, in a particular set of social and environmental circumstances, relying on a particular collection of resources and supports. Simply said, we all try to do the best we can with what we have. Part of this effort involves developing internal strengths and capacities; part involves identifying and using external resources; part involves compensating for weaknesses and deficits. (p. 24)

Yet another proposed component of mental health is deriving meaning. Meaning must be worked out for the entire life cycle in the form of a coherent *narrative* that explains the continuity of an individual life in the face of interruptions and adverse events (Cohler, 1993; Schiff & Cohler, 2001).

Development of Psychopathology

Psychoanalytic theorists who focus on developmental tasks unique to each life stage typically link later life to themes of loss such as: (1) grief over loved ones within one's intimate circle, (2) loss of roles, (3) loss of physical capacity and resulting dependency, and (4) loss of opportunity to alter one's life course. The belief that the loss theme dominates the aging experience often leads newcomers to the field of aging to assume that depression rates are particularly high in older adults. Surprisingly, however, older adults report lower rates of clinical depression than most adult populations (see Chapter 8). Clearly, the tasks of later life alone do not explain the emergence of psychopathology.

Psychodynamic theory points to internal rather than external causes of psychopathology because the external events or challenges associated with aging are experienced by far more older adults than those who develop psychiatric symptoms. Explanations of the etiology of psychopathology presume one or more of the following causal factors: (1) losses of later life re-enact significant childhood losses; (2) an underdeveloped self or immature defense mechanisms provide insufficient strength for handling the psychological challenges of later life; (3) loss of physical, cognitive, and emotional strengths with advanced old age undermine the functioning of the ego; and/or (4) the personal narrative cannot integrate with meaning the events and transitions of later life. As outlined below, each of these explanations are evident in the brief description of Maria Jiminez at the beginning of the chapter.

Losses

Classic psychoanalytic theory proposes that loss is particularly threatening to older adults if it evokes strong unresolved grief over a childhood loss. The model emphasizes the critical negative impact of childhood loss on formation of intrapsychic structures. Specifically, loss of an attachment figure evokes extremely powerful grief that overwhelms the young child's adaptive capacity. More recent research examines the role of childhood trauma and post-traumatic stress disorder on subsequent physical and mental health problems (Rosenzweig, Prigerson, Miller, & Reynolds, 1997; Shaw & Krause, 2002). The legacy of childhood experiences of death or trauma is anxiety about living in a profoundly unstable, unprotected world. Early experiences are significant wounds that may never heal, or may produce significant emotional scar tissue that is embedded in the organization of the brain. Defense mechanisms may protect an individual from severe depression, until such time as the defense mechanisms themselves are taxed by a life event or task too momentous for adaptation by the current psychological structures. The significant losses of later life leave a person particularly vulnerable to re-experiencing the feelings evoked during the childhood grief experience. When the grief over significant attachment figures re-enacts the childhood loss, this model predicts a regression in functioning into some form of psychopathology. However, the loss model may only address the latest phase of the life span when social and physical losses are pervasive (Gutmann, 1987).

> The fact that Maria Jiminez was unable to give much nurturance during her adult life would lead a psychodynamic clinician to suspect that she failed to receive sufficient nurturance in her own childhood to have a fully functioning ego. It turns out that Maria was the sixth of nine children in a very poor and busy household. Her mother was very ill for several months after her birth, leaving her in the care of her eight-year-old sister. This type of chronic, pervasive loss of parenting at a critical period limited her potential to engage in rich attachment relationships. Always seeking a caregiver, Maria had limited care to give.

Underdeveloped self or immature defenses

Throughout the life span, developmental tasks are most challenging to those who lack internal structures sufficient to support adaptation. In his model of successive tasks, Erikson (1963) noted that those who have not mastered previous developmental challenges when faced with adult tasks are considerably handicapped in their efforts to adapt. One study that attempted to examine the idea of maturation across the life span was a study of Harvard University sophomores that was launched in the early 1940s. Although containing an obviously limited sample (e.g., bright, well-to-do White men selected by the Deans at Harvard for being academically and emotionally strong, and who were not involved in World War II), the longitudinal nature of the study has offered an opportunity to examine change in personality structures over time through in-depth clinical interviews. Twenty-five years later, interviews illustrated the themes of stability and change as changes in defensive styles were studied. One question guiding the research was whether these men, who experienced society's most ideal developmental conditions in young adulthood (financial and educational resources, social status, and personality strength), would continue to mature throughout adulthood. Under what conditions would they mature, and what would stunt the maturational process? Specifically, would the men mature through a hierarchy of defense mechanisms as they experienced the challenges of adulthood? (See Table 3.2 for a listing of the defenses within the hierarchy.) Results of the clinical interviews when the men were 25, 30, 47, and 57 showed that there was a tendency for the men to use increasingly mature defense mechanisms with increased age, and those who failed to mature in defensive style have the worst outcomes (Vaillant, 1977; Vaillant & Vaillant, 1990).

Table 3.2 Schematic table of adaptive mechanisms

Level 1	Psychotic mechanisms	Denial
		Distortion
		Delusional projection
Level II	Immature mechanisms (common in severe depression, personality disorders, and adolescence)	Fantasy
		Projection
		Hypochondriasis
		Passive-aggressive behavior (masochism, turning against the self)
		Acting out (compulsive delinquency, perversion)
Level III	Neurotic mechanisms	Intellectualization (isolation, obsessive behavior, undoing, rationalization)
		Repression
		Reaction formation
		Displacement (conversion, phobias, wit)
		Dissociation
Level IV	Mature mechanisms	Sublimation
		Altruism
		Suppression
		Anticipation
		Humor

Within the loss model described above, it is postulated that early childhood trauma inflicts permanent personality scars that become points of vulnerability in old age. Gutmann (1987) uses an immune system analogy to describe the relationship between personality defenses and loss. The pathogen (loss) is powerful only to the extent that the immune system (personality structure) is vulnerable to that pathogen. Later life losses are particularly lethal to persons whose personality structures adapted to early losses in immature ways. Thus, an underdeveloped self exacerbates the power of loss to evoke psychopathology in late life.

Incomplete development can result from less traumatic sources as well. Gutmann's model suggests that the demands of mid-life are sufficient to limit the full range of individual development. Once the chronic parental emergency is past, adults can continue with their development in a wider range of domains. Young-old adults may experience the urges and drives to continue that development by exploring the unknown parts of the personality. As wishes and urges surface, the young-old find their personal myths (or self-stories) threatened by parts of the self that have not previously been integrated into the myth. Anxiety over the need to learn about new parts of the self and integrate them into the myth can spawn pathological reactions such as anxiety, depression, or more primitive psychotic reactions.

Maria used primitive defense mechanisms to protect her from the terror of being unnurtured in a dangerous world. She commonly projected her feelings onto other family members and neighbors, was a noted hypochondriac, and dealt with her anger consistently in passive-aggressive ways. The children knew not to ever confront her version of reality directly, or she would withdraw for days at a time, after which she always had a new illness "because of the stress of this family." Prior to her husband's death she had fared considerably better because she had managed to marry a nurturer who doted on her with tremendous amounts of warmth and affection. As the children perceived it, he was the "giver" and she was the "receiver" throughout their lives. Juan never complained, but the children could see his frustration at her constant manipulation of circumstances to ensure that her desires were met. After his death, Maria obviously was bereft of her primary caretaker and often behaved like a lost child.

Compensation for lost ego strength

Self psychologists describe the devastating impact on the self of the many age-correlated experiences such as loss of physical strength, cognitive abilities, and energy. Diminished capacity and energy are postulated to undermine self-esteem, forcing the person to find restitution for the loss. If the environment is insufficient to maintain the ego functions, a frail older adult may use compensatory mechanisms that appear pathological, such as recounting past glories or blaming others for lost items.

After her husband's death, Maria's environment clearly lacked sufficient structure and caretaking to maintain her highest possible level of functioning. Her constant blaming of the daughters for not doing enough was insufficient to make her feel better, but protected her from the reality that a perfect caretaker was simply unavailable. If she could just keep at them, the daughters could take care of her well enough, she was sure.

Inability to preserve or build a coherent narrative

Later life is the period in which each individual is particularly challenged to integrate a meaningful ending to his or her life narrative that is also internally consistent with the entire story (Cohler, 1993).

From this perspective, the so-called wisdom achieved in later life consists of the ability to maintain a coherent narrative of the course of life in which the presently remembered past, experienced present, and anticipated future are understood as problems to be studied rather than outcomes to be assumed. The question is not whether older adults are able to realize wisdom but rather how these older adults are able to continue to experience a sense of coherence while confronting factors associated with the loss of personal integrity, as well as feelings of fragmentation and disruption of the life story across the course of their lives. (Cohler, 1993, pp. 119–120)

Cohler postulates that the life constructs from earlier adulthood may not be adequate to integrate the experiences and expectations of later life into the personal narrative, necessitating a true developmental shift. If the shift cannot be made, the individual is vulnerable to psychopathology characteristic of personal fragmentation. Even events as traumatic as the Holocaust are rewritten with multiple, and at times para-doxical, meanings for the human life (Schiff & Cohler, 2001).

> Maria's adolescence and young adulthood were a Cinderella story. Raised doing the hard labor of women in a poor family, Maria was rescued by Prince Charming who was the only person who truly recognized her for the princess that she really was. Unfortunately, he took her to a blue-collar subsistence in a small town rather than a true castle, a failing for which she never quite forgave him. The world could never know just what she could have become if the circumstances had been right, and now it never would. Not only is it hard to be an aging princess, but her prince is gone. No one else treats her like she deserves; if she doesn't demand good work, they will all do just the minimum. Maria sees herself as stuck in a bad fairytale that won't force the wicked stepsisters to recognize the true beauty of a princess. The narratives of old age that describe contentment from a life lived well and making peace with lost opportunities and the limited accomplishments of a human life are a foreign language to Maria.

Assessment

Psychodynamic theorists and clinicians focus assessment on internal personality struc-tures: beliefs, narratives, emotional responses, values, meanings, and behavior pat-terns. A developmental history of the individual life cycle is a key starting point, including developmental stages, tasks, and themes (Nemiroff & Colarusso, 1990). Early childhood experiences hold obvious importance within this model, which pre-sumes that early development constrains later developmental styles. Of particular importance are the critical events or traumas, and the attachment relationships within which the earliest experiences were processed.

Important for treatment is assessment of the capacity for insight. Psychodynamic treatments rely upon the patient's insight into his or her own personality to make conscious the structures and processes that influence behaviors and self-perception. To bypass the requirement for insight, projective techniques can be used to elicit information about personality structure and function. For example, Thematic Apperception Test cards allow respondents to project their basic assumptions about relationships into the stories they tell about standardized pictures. The Projective Assessment of Aging Method (Starr, Weiner, & Rabetz, 1979), a Thematic Apperception Test designed specifically for assessing dynamics of later life, depicts older adults during reflection and social interaction. Projective tests continue to be used for a variety of clinical and research purposes, although their use is declining (Norcross, Hedges, & Castle, 2002), and there is a current debate and significant controversy about the empirical justification for projective tests (see Wood, Nezworski, Lilienfeld, & Garb, 2003).

Kivnick (1993) developed an interview schedule for eliciting information specifi-cally about life strengths. Drawing on her interview experience with older participants in the longitudinal study reported by Erikson, Erikson, and Kivnick (1986), she designed this instrument to reflect the language and themes relevant to the psychological work typical of old age. The interview is designed to solicit primarily positive aspects of development.

Treatment

The goal of psychodynamic treatment with older adults is to (1) provide direct support to a fragile ego, (2) modify personality structure, or (3) strengthen the psychosocial functioning of the person. Psychodynamic psychotherapy engages clients in an intensive and often long-term revisitation of the experiences of childhood during which the core self was constructed from experience with parental caregiving styles. The therapeutic relationship offers the opportunity for reworking the interpersonal experience base for defining the self.

Brief psychodynamic psychotherapy is one of the therapeutic approaches that has a sufficient empirical research base to categorize it as an evidence-based treatment for depression in older adults (Scogin, Welsh, Hanson, Stump, & Coates, 2005). Other psychodynamic therapeutic approaches also are now being applied to older adults (e.g., interpersonal psychotherapy and narrative therapy) with interesting results. Supportive psychotherapy represents a less directive low-intensity approach that may also be appropriate when the capacity for insight that is necessary to produce personality change is limited.

Interpersonal psychotherapy

Interpersonal psychotherapy (IPT) was developed to treat major depression (Klerman, Weissman, Rounsaville, & Chevron, 1984) by addressing the interpersonal difficulties that often lead to depression. IPT has now been formally structured in a treatment manual for depression (Weissman, Markowitz, & Klerman, 2000) and has been the focus of clinical trials for a very wide range of client populations. Four particular interpersonal problem areas are addressed in IPT: grief, interpersonal role disputes, role transitions, and interpersonal deficits. Clients are assessed for symptom intensity as well as for difficulties in these four areas. Assessment findings are shared with clients, and one or two problem areas are chosen by therapist and client together as a focus of therapy. The time-limited treatment approach begins with an assessment and education phase in which the therapist explains to the client how depression was created by the interpersonal difficulties. The middle phase of therapy is when the therapist applies well-elaborated strategies to address very specific problems identified in the interpersonal life of the client or patient. The approach is essentially collaborative and hopeful as the therapist points to the array of options that can be used to address each problem. The final phase addresses the termination process, including review of progress as well as remaining challenges, feelings about ending the relationship, and possible need for additional treatment. Although rooted in the interpersonal school of psychiatry and thus broadly construed as a psychodynamic model, the focus is on the here-and-now and behavior change, which represents a significant departure from traditional psychodynamic psychotherapy and also shares much in common with problem-solving therapy (covered in Chapter 4).

IPT has been demonstrated to be effective in treatment of depression (Mello, Mari, Bacaltchuk, Verdeli, & Neugebauer, 2005). IPT also shows probable effectiveness with depressed populations of all ages, including adolescents and older adults for whom the limited research literature offers less powerful support than with adults generally (David-Ferdon & Kaslow, 2008; Scogin et al., 2005). Trials of IPT for other disorders, including anxiety disorders, post-traumatic stress disorder, and eating disorders, have also been conducted in recent years, with growing evidence of the value of the approach for preventing and treating a range of psychological problems. Older adults may be particularly well situated to benefit from IPT because of the significance of social losses in later life (Hinrichsen, 2008).

Narrative therapies

Narrative therapies build upon the tendency of humans to write and rewrite their autobiography throughout the life span. Indeed, humans construct their core self through stories that define identities, interpersonal positions, and create meaning (White & Epston, 1990). The telling of a narrative inevitably involves the selection and discarding of information that is relevant to the immediate story or stories through which meaning is created. Therapists using this approach focus on the process of telling, inviting clients to tell and retell the stories, reframing experiences in ways that open possibilities for creating change in behavior, meaning, and identity.

Erickson claimed that life review is a natural developmental process that must be embraced in order to achieve a sense of ego integrity in old age when decline and loss become themes. His approach emphasized the importance of proactive self-management of ego functioning in later life when the salience of limited time left to live constrains the urge to revise one's life mistakes. Furthermore, the assaults on the sense of the integrity of one's life are not only internal. Ageism and negative stereotypes of aging have powerful effects on the day-to-day functioning and well-being of older adults (Levy, 2003). Narrative therapies provoke conscious reflection on a life lived, inviting an active re-examination of the meaning of the particular life one lived.

Reminiscence therapy is one of the earliest psychotherapies developed for older adults, drawing upon the power of narrative to combat depression or the loss of purpose or identity. At its simplest level, reminiscence engages an older adult in revisiting pleasant periods of life as a reminder of what has been. At a far more complex level, life review reminiscence offers the option of reassigning meaning to events and relationships through which the core self has been created and interpreted. Reminiscence and other narrative therapies offer older adults the option of exploring how a long developmental history intersects with immediate life challenges to shape the meaning of a life. Evidence of the effectiveness of reminiscence therapies suggests they may be useful in treating depression (Scogin et al., 2005).

Supportive therapy

Although non-directive supportive psychotherapy shows somewhat less effectiveness than other psychotherapies (e.g., for depression; Cuijpers, van Straten, Andersson, & van Oppen, 2008), there may be clients for whom it remains the only available treatment approach. Later life may challenge the personality structures of older adults through cognitive impairment or by stripping away psychosocial supports, leaving few psychological resources to engage in psychotherapy. If environmental enrichment is not possible, or is insufficient to rebuild the ego functions, supportive psychotherapy may be all that is appropriate. In such cases, support is provided until the ego or core self is shored up or the environment is enriched to provide more external support for basic ego functioning. For example, supportive therapy might be used with personality disordered older adults or those with more primitive defense mechanisms that are too well defended for insight. Given the intensity with which the ego functioning can be undermined by the losses of later life, there are occasions when it is most appropriate to begin with supportive therapy and progress to insight-oriented therapy only when it is evident that the ego has regained sufficient strength to tolerate depth work (Gutmann, 1992). On the other hand, therapists should not assume that aging or frailty keeps a person from engaging in anything other than supportive psychotherapy. Many therapies now have been demonstrated to be effective with older adults, and therapists should resort to supportive therapy only when other therapies clearly did not work yet the person shows capacity to benefit from supportive therapy.

> Maria Jiminez would likely be considered an appropriate candidate for supportive psychotherapy. Likely, her capacity for insight is quite limited. She has used immature defense mechanisms her entire life, and is only now in exceptional distress because the environment no longer supports her sufficiently. As she becomes more physically dependent on others, she will likely become more depressed unless given sufficient support. Supportive therapy may focus on helping her adjust to being an unrecognized princess in a foreign land. Given enough nurturance from the therapist, Maria's ego strength may be sufficient to engage in less destructive interpersonal relationships. For example, although the therapist's nurturance may be perceived as her due, Maria may be sufficiently gratified that she reduces her verbal abuse to her daughters.

Psychotherapy process

As with younger adults, the patient–therapist relationship is a primary tool for treatment. Indeed, Newton et al. (1986) acknowledge the potency of the relationship in particular for persons who live isolated, lonely lives. Such persons experience tremendous validation of the self merely from interaction with an empathic, caring figure. For most older clients, however, the relationship is experienced through the transference and the therapy process. Transference is the process by which a client projects onto the therapist characteristics of significant persons (e.g., parents) whose interactions with the client shaped his or her basic beliefs about human beings and interactions. These projections are not based on the real interactions of client and therapist, but on projected assumptions about how the relationship functions. Countertransference is the therapist's own process of projecting onto the client or the interaction with the client perceptions that are not based on the real interaction or person, but on the therapist's own conceptual and emotional framework.

Transference processes can be particularly complex, because a lifetime of powerful relationship experiences is available for projection onto the therapist of an older client. The therapist may become a lover of 40 years ago, a parent, a child, a grandchild, or a significant mentor. The therapist is encouraged to identify the patient's "secret inner age" that holds the key to the transference projection (Berezin, 1972).

Countertransferences are also complex because therapists are generally younger than their elderly patients and thus have not personally experienced either the historical period or the developmental stages (Knight, 2004). Novice younger therapists are likely to experience a reaction to aging itself. The effects of biological aging (e.g., physical limitations, reduced energy, changing physical appearance) and the functional consequences of aging (e.g., limited autonomy, social stigma, reduced activity level) must be acknowledged and experienced empathically by younger therapists for whom such experiences are "off time." A certain amount of courage is needed to tolerate handling the psychological work of another developmental period, even after the younger therapist comes to understand it (at least cognitively).

Less emotionally powerful but equally important is the knowledge that younger therapists need of the historical contexts in which their older patients have lived their lives. As Knight (2004) describes, the terminology, customs, idioms, and preferences of birth cohorts vary systematically. Therapists must be familiar with the ways in which emotions are expressed and described by the children of the Great Depression, for example. Thus, real differences between therapists and clients are typical of therapy process with older adults, and must be acknowledged as real. In addition, projections distort perceptions of the immediate interaction, complicating efforts to track the process of psychotherapy.

The psychotherapy process uses a variety of techniques to prompt insight into the developmental processes described above. Life review or reminiscence is commonly used to assist the patient's integration of life experiences into a coherent narrative, and as an assessment strategy. The life review may rewrite the story several times during the course of psychological work. Traditional strategies such as interpretation of dreams and exploration of ambivalence are also used with older adults.

As with any developmental task unfamiliar to a patient, it is often useful to educate the older patient about the aging process. Distortions and cultural myths can lead to inappropriate expectations or service underutilization. For example, the belief that memory loss with age is normal may keep an older woman from recognizing an organic disease process in her husband. Similarly, the belief that it is inappropriate to ask one's children for assistance can leave an older adult quite vulnerable to isolation and feeling excessively overwhelmed in the face of significant caregiving responsibilities.

Confirmation of the patient's strengths in the face of mounting deficits is an important role for therapists working with frail older persons (Gutmann, 1987; Newton et al., 1986). The battered ego may need to be supported by a therapist who can hold up a mirror to the patient's life so it is easier to see the full array of strengths and resources that have sustained the person throughout the life span. The therapist helps regain perspective on the entire life as it was lived, a process that gives courage to a fragile ego whose capacities have diminished. At times, therapists need to encourage particularly depleted clients to engage in self-enhancing behaviors, just to regain some semblance of experienced strength.

In general, the process of therapy with older adults does not vary dramatically from that used with adults of any age. Knight (2004) recommends that therapists modify the process somewhat for older adults. For example, therapists should take a more active role in therapy, be less formal in the structuring of the role, and be more flexible with the termination process. The other differences relate primarily to the transference and countertransference components of the relationship, recognition of normal aging processes, and the unique historical context in which older persons have lived.

Summary and Conclusions

In summary, the psychodynamic model can have useful applications across the life span. By alerting the therapist to the continuing impact of early events, current losses, and contemporary therapeutic relationships, the framework provides a coherent focus for assessment and treatment of older adults. Psychodynamic models invite us to examine the ways inner processes shift over the life span. They maintain a strong focus on development or maturation of strategies for coping with inevitable tensions between inner life and outer world. Interpersonal dynamics continue in later life to influence the quality of life, building on a lifetime of experience of self in the context of other people.

4

Cognitive-Behavioral Model

The nursing home staff are very annoyed at Anna Tweed because she constantly stands at the nurse's station asking them questions. Even if they answer her queries, Anna simply won't go away. When the staff try to involve her in something else, she returns to the nurse's station within a few minutes. Nurses and certified nursing assistants (CNAs) complain that they get headaches from trying to write their notes or answer phones while Anna is constantly talking. Staff understand that she has a severe memory problem but they don't know how to get her to stop asking the repeated questions.

Joanna Jenkins came to the mental health clinic because her daughter insisted that she do so. Her daughter is worried and frustrated that her mother is so lethargic and uninterested in life. Joanna doesn't believe you can do anything for her because nothing in particular is wrong with her. She is just old, and she is waiting to die.

Introduction to the Model

As the chapter title suggests, the cognitive-behavioral model is actually a combination of two important but distinct approaches in psychology. The behavioral model was founded in the 1920s by American psychologist John Watson as a reaction to the predominant psychodynamic approach and its emphasis on introspection and the unconscious, topics that were difficult to quantify and measure clearly. The cognitive model was developed in the 1960s based on the work of two pioneers, psychiatrist Aaron Beck and psychologist Albert Ellis, who highlighted the primary role of thought processes in mental health, mental distress, and psychotherapeutic treatment strategies. Despite their distinct origins, the two approaches have been largely unified

Aging and Mental Health, 2e. Daniel L. Segal, Sara Honn Qualls, and Michael A. Smyer
© 2011 Daniel L. Segal, Sara Honn Qualls, and Michael A. Smyer

into the cognitive-behavioral model, which places emphasis on the internal cognitions or thought patterns experienced by individuals and the specific measurable observable behaviors they exhibit. The type of psychotherapy associated with this approach is called *cognitive-behavior therapy* (CBT). This is not to say that there are no behaviorists or cognitive therapists who focus heavily on the primary domain of interest, but rather that the vast majority of clinicians and researchers who identify in the cognitive and behavioral areas appreciate the impact of overt behaviors and internal thought patterns on psychological functioning. As a learning tool, let us next describe the cognitive and behavioral aspects of the model separately with the full appreciation that in modern-day practice, the two models are not only compatible but also synergistic in their combination.

Cognitive Aspects of the Model

Cognitive theory focuses on the contributions of thoughts and beliefs to maladaptive behaviors and negative emotions. As neuroscience evolved, the complexity of the brain/behavior relationships required more explanatory variables than were provided by the theories of learning. Several different cognitive-behavioral approaches emerged to describe how various cognitive processes influenced the acquisition and performance of behaviors. For example, expectancies, internalized rules, performance standards, self-instruction, and imagery all influence behavioral performance (Bandura, 1977). At the most general level, all cognitive theories share three fundamental hypotheses (Dobson & Dozois, 2001; Dozois, Frewen, & Covin, 2006):

1 that cognition affects emotion and behavior,
2 that cognition can be monitored and changed, and
3 that by altering cognitions, one can exert desired emotional and behavioral changes.

 To elaborate, cognitive theory suggests that an event, in and of itself, is not the cause of one's emotional response, but rather it is how one *interprets* or *perceives* that event (i.e., it is the accompanying cognitive processes) that causes one's emotional reaction. Consider the death of a loved one as an example. It might be assumed that this death would automatically make someone sad and despondent, but that is not always the full picture. The death of an older person that ends the person's struggle with a long, painful, and debilitating disease might result in other feelings in the survivors such as relief, as well as some normal degrees of sadness. Indeed, in this example, the extent to which one feels intense despair or relief (or sometimes combinations of various feelings) depends on the *meaning* that one attaches to the death. Thus, according to the theory, our attitudes and beliefs about an event give rise to our emotions and not the events themselves.

 Indeed, this central idea that thought processes are an important determinant of emotions and behaviors is, in fact, quite old. Centuries ago, Phrygian Stoic philosopher Epictetus (c.101 AD) expressed his view in *The Enchiridion* that "Men are disturbed not by things, but by the view which they take of them" (Epictetus, c.101/1955). Direct application of cognitive-behavioral principles to mental health problems has been made by cognitive therapy theorists, including Aaron Beck and Albert Ellis. Beck's approach focuses on the role of thought distortion in the production of mental health problems such as depression and anxiety (Beck, Emery, & Greenberg, 1985; Beck, Rush, Shaw, & Emery, 1979). These theorists and clinicians identified a specific set of inaccurate core world view assumptions and related thought distortions that produce and maintain mental disorders. Beck and others developed interventions that restructure cognition patterns to produce more adaptive and realistic appraisals of self, the world, and the future than are typical of depressed and anxious persons' ways of thinking.

Beck's theory emphasizes three levels of cognition. The first level is called *schemata* or core beliefs. Schemata or schemas are often expressed as unconditional evaluations about the self and others. Some examples include beliefs that: "I am incompetent," "I am defective," "I am unlovable," "I am special," "Others are hurtful and not to be trusted," "Others need to take care of me," and "Others must love and admire me." Schemas are generally thought to be formed early in life and tend to persist if no conscious effort is made to identify, examine, and challenge them (Dozois et al., 2006). Schemas are believed to influence perceptions and thoughts at a more conscious level.

The second level is called *information-processing biases*, which are represented as dysfunctional beliefs (sometimes called cognitive distortions) that many people can learn to recognize. Some of the commonly occurring cognitive distortions include: all-or-none thinking (seeing personal qualities or situations in absolutist "black and white" terms, and failing to see shades of gray in between), catastrophizing (perceiving negative events as intolerable catastrophes, commonly referred to as "making mountains out of molehills"), labeling (attaching a global label to oneself [e.g., I am a loser] instead of referring to a specific action or event [e.g., I did not handle that particular situation very well]), magnification and minimization (exaggerating the importance of negative characteristics and experiences while discounting the importance of positive characteristics and experiences), personalization (assuming one is the cause of an event when other factors are also responsible), and "should" statements (using *should* and *have-to* statements to provide motivation or to control behavior).

Finally, the third level of cognition in Beck's model is *automatic thoughts*, which refer to the stream of cognitions that people have throughout the day. Such thoughts stem directly from core beliefs (schemas), cognitive distortions, and current life events.

Consistent with Beck's model, the methods developed by Albert Ellis are based on the premise that when people are faced with unfortunate life circumstances, they make themselves feel miserable, frustrated, and upset, and they behave in dysfunctional ways because they construct irrational beliefs about themselves and their situations (Ellis, 1991; Ellis & Dryden, 2007). More adaptively, people can craft adaptive feelings and behaviors by adopting more reasonable and rational thoughts.

An important aspect of Ellis' approach is the ABC model, which purports that emotional and behavioral consequences (C) are not directly precipitated by an activating event (A) or life stressor such as becoming physically ill or becoming a widow, but rather that one's beliefs about the event (B) mediate the relationships (Ellis & Dryden, 2007). Like Beck, beliefs, emotions, and behaviors are viewed as inter-related processes, although beliefs are given primary importance in causing psycho-logical problems. A final important aspect of the cognitive approach is its emphasis on education about the client's symptoms and about the cognitive therapy model so that the process is transparent, fully understood by the client, and collaboratively carried out with the therapist and client as active and equal participants.

Behavioral Aspects of the Model

The classic behavioral model focuses attention on *behavior* rather than emotion, motives, or biological factors (Kazdin, 2001). An individual's behavior results from the interaction between the person and his/her environment. In general, adaptive and maladaptive behaviors function in the same way. They evolve as a function of the interaction between behavior and environment. Behaviors are believed to be under the direct control of environmental events and cues that influence the acquisi-tion, performance rate, and termination of specific behaviors according to principles of learning theory. The focus is primarily on observable behaviors, although some private events (e.g., thoughts and feelings) are considered to be equally under the influence of learning principles (discussed in more detail below) and thus modifiable by behavioral techniques.

The behavioral model emphasizes the benefits of empirical scientific research, and organizes its assessments and interventions accordingly. Behavioral mental health providers draw heavily from the empirical literature that reports on the efficacy of interventions whose impact has been evaluated according to rigorous scientific criteria (i.e., with research designs that control for alternative explanations). Training in single subject designs (Barlow, Nock, & Hersen, 2008) as well as group designs is considered imperative for effective implementation and evaluation of behavioral interventions.

The literature on behavioral interventions with older adults covers a wide range of behaviors, including self-care, social interaction and participation, memory and language, health maintenance, anxiety, depression, and disruptive behaviors (LeBlanc, Raetz, & Feliciano, in press). The empirical results are clear: Many behaviors previ-ously believed to be a normal product of aging have been demonstrated to be modifi-able by changes in the environmental context. Perhaps most dramatic are the effects of behavior modification programs in institutional settings with particularly low-functioning ill older persons (e.g., Allen-Burge, Stevens, & Burgio, 1999; Teri, Logsdon, Uomoto, & McCurry, 1997) and behavioral interventions for depressed caregivers of individuals with dementia (Gitlin et al., 2003).

Assessment and intervention generally focus on observable variables – what people do. As we discuss more thoroughly below, cognitive-behavioral clinicians include self-reports of cognitive activity or thought processes in the category of observable variables. The focus on observable characteristics from the behavioral model can be contrasted with other models whose domain of work is motives, drives, traits, or unconscious processes that are inferred from patient behavior but cannot be observed directly. There are many specific behavioral techniques used by clinicians to help people change maladaptive behavior to more adaptive behavior. At its core, however, the behavioral aspects of CBT focus on helping clients increase access to reinforcing and positive experiences (e.g., the identification and subsequent scheduling of pleasant events) and training in specific skills (e.g., assertiveness, communication, relaxation, problem-solving, and coping skills).

Behaviorists observe human behavior in context because behavior is believed to be an adaptive response to help individuals meet their needs in a particular environment. The principles used by behaviorists to describe human behavior link the behavior to the information available to the person in the environment, especially information contiguous in time with the behavior. *Antecedents* refer to the information available to the person immediately prior to the target behavior, whereas *consequences* refer to the information available immediately following the behavior.

Traditional learning theory offers three primary learning mechanisms to explain the acquisition and maintenance of human behavior: classical conditioning, operant conditioning, and modeling. Notably, the same learning mechanisms are thought to account for adaptive behavior as well as maladaptive (abnormal) behavior. Classical conditioning occurs when a previously neutral stimulus elicits a response that is reflexive or automatic in the presence of a stimulus. Drawing from his famous experiments in which dogs learned to salivate to the sound of a bell that immediately preceded the presentation of their food, Russian psychologist Ivan Pavlov created labels for the natural and conditioned stimuli. The reflexive or automatic response to a natural (Unconditioned) stimulus was called an Unconditioned Response. Classical conditioning occurs when the Unconditioned Stimulus (UCS) is paired with a previously neutral stimulus (now the Conditioned Stimulus; CS) to produce the target response (e.g., salivating) without the UCS ever being presented. When Pavlov's dogs salivated to the sound of the bell (CS) alone, the target response was called a Conditioned Response (CR). Classical conditioning theory explains behavior that occurs in the presence of an apparently neutral stimulus by demonstrating that the behavior is under the control of the antecedent conditions.

Operant learning theory maintains that the acquisition and performance of behavior are controlled by the consequences of behaviors (Skinner, 1953). The principle of reinforcement states that behaviors will increase in frequency if they are followed closely in time by positive events (e.g., being praised by someone after doing a kind deed; receiving a good grade on an exam after studying hard for the exam). The positively experienced event is called a reinforcer if it reliably increases the rate of behavior. Negatively experienced events that decrease the rate of behavior are called punishers. Older nursing home residents have learned to increase the rate of self-care behaviors when staff pay attention or provide other positive consequences that are contingent on the performance of the targeted behaviors (see Baltes & Wahl, 1996).

The third form of learning, modeling, is defined as learning new behaviors by imitating the behavior of another person. The new wrinkle here is that people do not have to receive consequences themselves to learn new behavior, but that they can learn by observing the consequences that others experience. Consider, for example, a newly admitted resident to a nursing home who sees that another resident gets a great deal of attention, albeit some of it negative attention, when she complains vociferously to the staff. The new resident begins to complain more having imitated the behavior from the other resident. As an exercise, consider the types of behaviors you have learned by watching others. Can you identify some positive behaviors that have been modeled? Can you identify some less adaptive ones? Finally, we should emphasize here that the mechanisms of learning frequently co-occur. For example, both modeling and operant principles are in play when a person tries a new behavior because of observing another person model it, and receives a reward following the new behavior.

Mental Health from the Cognitive-Behavioral Model

From the behavioral perspective, adaptation is defined as the capacity to meet one's own needs effectively within the environment, a preferred alternative to the term "mentally healthy." Behaviors that meet an individual's physical, social, and emotional needs within the particular relevant environment are considered adaptive. Persons who cannot meet their needs effectively are viewed as having problems in living that occur because of one of the following:

- they have learned maladaptive behavior or frameworks;
- they failed to learn effective or appropriate behavior or frameworks because of a poor learning environment or because of their particular learning history;
- they are responding to the wrong environmental contingencies or are self-regulating poorly.

In contrast to the pure behavioral perspective, cognitive-behaviorists use adaptation and subjective distress to measure well-being. Distress is experienced when an individual is unable to meet his or her own goals, including internalized goals in the form of standards or expectations, which are cognitive constructs. For example, a common problem for depressed persons is negative self-evaluation that occurs when a perfectionistic standard cannot be met. A reasonable goal for treatment in this case might be to reduce the person's perfectionistic standards, allowing the person to be less self-critical, and thus less distressed. As another example of a cognitive goal, a depressed person may want to increase her sense of hope. Hope is her own goal, and exists solely in her mind as a cognition, but is a perfectly legitimate goal for a cognitive-behaviorist. Cognitive-behaviorists must balance the individual's subjective sense of distress with some objective judgment about adaptability to the immediate environment.

The two cases presented at the beginning of the chapter show the value of using multiple criteria for defining disorder. Anna Tweed is not particularly distressed, but her behavior is not adaptive in that environment. Or is it? Her constant questioning may gain her additional staff attention, interpersonal interaction, and cognitive stimulation that may be lacking elsewhere in the nursing home. Her behavior is disruptive for staff more than for her, although over time Anna will probably receive negative attention from frustrated staff members. Of course, the ethics of intervening with an individual's behavior for the good of the institution must be examined carefully. Joanna Jenkins is distressed but does not seek help because she does not believe there is help or that there is hope for change. Her behavior is also not adaptive because she is no longer attempting to meet her own social needs due to her lethargy and her learned helplessness.

Mental Health in Older Adults

The CBT definition of mental health for older persons would be the same as for any other population – a pattern of thoughts, beliefs, values, and behaviors that lead to healthy adaptation and adjustment to one's environment and a lack of significant personal distress or impairment in one's functioning. However, some changes commonly associated with aging may make the processes of adaptation and adjustment more challenging. For example, changes with age may occur in the array of available antecedents and consequences, the contingent relationships among antecedents-behaviors-consequences, and the needs of the individual. In the young-old years (sixties and early seventies), adults are likely to live within environments and contingency patterns similar to those of middle adulthood. With advanced age, physical impairments may limit mobility, dull sensation, and may force changes in the environments within which older adults live and meet their needs.

Changes in the living environment may simply alter the array of antecedents and consequences, or may enrich or deplete the available options. For example, moving from one's suburban home to a senior high rise apartment complex may significantly enrich the array of social stimuli, or may simply change which social relationships are available while holding steady the amount and reinforcement value of the relationships. On the other hand, the presence of 100 other residents of a high rise may not compensate for the loss of access to close friends in the former neighborhood.

Physical illnesses characteristic of old age are likely to restrict the range of activities in which some very old persons can engage. Limited mobility, restricted vision and hearing, or cognitive impairment may alter the older adult's ability to respond to environmental contingencies. Yet freedom from some demanding roles that are characteristic of young and mid-life adulthood (e.g., raising a family, maintaining a career) may enhance older people's responsiveness to environmental stimuli. For example, a recent retiree may experience the freedom to be much more socially responsive to neighbors and friends.

Baltes and Baltes (1990b) suggest that older adults show high rates of adaptability or *behavioral plasticity*. Recall that early behavioral research demonstrated that behaviors commonly thought to be typical of old age were actually under the control of environmental contingencies. Baltes and Baltes go a step further to argue that older adults naturally modify their behavior in predictable ways to adapt to changing capabilities and changing environments, a process reflecting the role of adaptability in mental health. Specifically, they suggest that older adults draw upon their areas of competence to compensate for areas in which they have lost function or in which the environment is more impoverished. The process of adaptation involves "selective optimization with compensation."

Despite this natural process of adaptation, certain environments are clearly more challenging than others. For example, nursing home life presents a serious challenge to the mental health of many older residents (Molinari, 2000; Rosowsky, Casciani, & Arnold, 2008; Snowden, Sato, & Roy-Byrne, 2003). Although only 5 percent of older adults live in a nursing home at any one point in time, the effects of the institution on mental health warrant comment. Institutions such as traditional nursing homes provide few natural reinforcers because the institution regiments so many aspects of daily life, including bathing, dressing, sleep schedules, food schedules and selection, and may even structure social interaction. Residents of nursing homes are typically physically very frail and often cognitively impaired, which limits further the sources of pleasure available to them and their capacity to respond to environmental contingencies. The rates of mental disorders are particularly high in nursing homes, as might be predicted by the environmental contingencies, although environment is only one factor in the high rates of mental disorders (physical illness and cognitive disorders are two other important factors). Behavioral techniques have been suggested as one effective strategy for mental health treatment in nursing homes (Burgio, Stevens, Burgio, Roth, Paul, & Gerstle, 2002; Cohn, Smyer, & Horgas, 1994; Meeks, Looney, Van Haitsma, & Teri, 2008; Meeks, Shah, & Ramsey, 2009; Molinari, 2000).

Assessment

Refer back to the case scenarios presented at the beginning of the chapter. Consider yourself a consultant to these two women. What kind of assessment needs to be done to design the best intervention to help Anna Tweed and Joanna Jenkins? Take a moment to review the principles we have presented, and develop a conceptualization and hypothesis for the two cases. Your framework for the problem will, of course, determine where you begin with assessment. In both cases, you will obviously need considerably more information than was given initially. What do you need to know, and how will you gather the information (e.g., from whom?, in what format?)?

Purposes of assessment

Assessment from the cognitive-behavioral model focuses on the two important domains identified within the model: cognitions and behaviors, which are often intertwined. Assessment focuses on clarifying behavior patterns and identifying cognitive and environmental variables that mediate behavior. The primary purpose of assessment is to assist with the design and evaluation of interventions. Assessment for the purpose of a richer understanding of the client, or even to formulate an accurate diagnosis, is most valuable to the extent that it directly benefits the intervention. Although cognitive-behaviorists do not necessarily ascribe to the medical model of diagnosis on which the DSM-IV is based, they support the use of diagnostic categories if they are used for scientific purposes of producing homogeneous client groups in which to test interventions. Indeed, an active and growing research base on cognitive and behavioral interventions for a broad array of mental disorders is an important strength of the cognitive-behavioral model.

Assessment also serves as a baseline for determining progress in treatment. Assessments are used as feedback for the therapist and the client regarding the impact of particular interventions. Clients often begin to change simply because of the clear feedback about their own behavior that is provided by cognitive and behavioral assessment (i.e., the assessment may function as an intervention itself).

Principles of cognitive-behavioral assessment

Cognitive and behaviorally oriented mental health providers follow general practice guidelines for older adults by initially examining the medical data available to ascertain if the problem could be caused by disease or medication. For example, whereas the therapist would recognize that Joanna Jenkins' scenario matches the general profile of a depressed person, the description is also consistent with physical illness (including medication-induced delirium) or even an organic brain disorder. If Joanna Jenkins has not received a thorough physical examination to rule out potentially reversible medical causes of the symptom profile, such an evaluation would be the first order of business. Only after physical causes of the symptoms have been ruled out would a strictly cognitive-behavioral approach to assessment and intervention be appropriate. For the sake of clarity, let us presume that an appropriate medical evaluation has been completed and that Ms. Jenkins is physically healthy and on no medications that could produce this behavior profile.

With the strong commitment to gathering empirical data regarding behavior, a cognitive-behaviorally oriented mental health provider would focus assessment on *specific problem behaviors*. If staff or family members have framed the problem as "she's manipulative" or "her life has no purpose," the therapist would ask questions about specific behaviors until the exact behaviors that are problematic are defined in terms that render the behavior directly observable. Exactly what does Joanna do, and when does she do it? How is this different from one or five years ago? How much distress does she report or show? What self-care behaviors does she do for herself? In the Anna Tweed scenario, exactly when and for how long does Anna stand at the nurse's station? How many questions does she ask? What is the content of her questions? What happens when staff answer them? Careful questioning of the exact behavior patterns observed by staff will give a mental health consultant enough information to form hypotheses about the reinforcement contingencies. Other methods for obtaining behavior information are described below.

The assessment also focuses on the *context* of the problem behavior. Exactly when and under what conditions does Anna leave the desk? What is the exact context when she asks questions (e.g., who is present; are others also talking or does she wait for a break in conversation)? What time of day does the questioning either intensify or reduce? The behavioral assessment will show the contextual variables that serve as reinforcers and punishers (increasing or decreasing the frequency of specific behaviors).

The assessor would also want to identify times when the problem behavior is not present. When does Anna Tweed leave the nurses' station? Are there ever occasions when she maintains attention focused on something other than the nurses' station? Do alternative behaviors exist within the client's behavioral repertoire that are not being used to meet her goals? How sensitive is she to social cues? She may have appropriate behaviors, but they are not being controlled by appropriate cues and contingencies. In the case of Joanna Jenkins, one might ask when she shows the most animation and energy. Are there days or hours when she feels better than other times?

The process of obtaining a full assessment from the cognitive-behavioral model typically requires several methods of data collection. Self-reports of distress may be obtained from the clients and the involved care providers. For example, Anna Tweed may be asked about the goal of her questioning behavior because her behavior may be explicitly goal directed. In this particular case, Anna Tweed is actually experiencing a dementia that produces such severe memory impairment that she is unaware of how frequently she asks questions in her attempt to try to orient herself to time, place, and purposive activity.

Joanna Jenkins has more obvious subjective distress and thus she would likely be asked to complete a self-report depression scale as part of a diagnostic evaluation. Data on the severity of depression would also serve as a baseline against which treatment progress can be evaluated. Several self-report inventories on depression are described in Chapter 8. The responses of Ms. Jenkins to a popular one, the Geriatric Depression Scale (GDS; Yesavage et al., 1983), are shown in Figure 4.1. As you can see, she has scored 21 out of 30, indicating a severe range of depressive symptoms.

Take a moment to look at the specific symptom description you get from this instrument. Now look back at the initial description of her problem in the first lines of this chapter. Based on the GDS data, you know that Ms. Jenkins is experiencing boredom and a sense of emptiness. She reports having trouble with concentration and worry that disturbs her. She also reports feeling worthless. A clinical interview would be done to follow up on this valuable type of data to elicit further details about each symptom. For example, what kind of worry? How much difficulty with concentration? Brief self-report symptom inventories are used throughout the intervention to track progress. A graph like that shown in Figure 4.2 would provide evidence of the effectiveness of an intervention.

More objective data may be requested to clarify the actual frequency and context of specific behaviors. For example, Joanna Jenkins may report her activities and mood in a mood and behavior log. For Anna Tweed, the staff at the nursing home may be asked to keep a record of the frequency of questions asked during each hour of the day to identify variations in the frequency pattern during the course of a day. A behavioral observer may collect descriptive data regarding the frequency, content, and context of the questions over the course of a day. A typical behavior recording chart of a scenario like Anna Tweed's is shown in Figure 4.3.

You will note that there is a pattern evident in this record of behavior. Ms. Tweed's question asking is more intense when more persons are present. When the staff leave the nursing station, so does Ms. Tweed. What hypothesis might you form about the reinforcement contingencies for Ms. Tweed's question-asking behavior? Further assessment may be needed to determine how she meets her information goals when staff are not available at the nurses' station. As noted above, the recording of specific details is what made a pattern evident. Staff might have stated, "she's there all of the time," a fact that matches their experience while they are at the nurses' station, but was not the whole picture.

	Client's response	Scoring	
		Yes	No
1. Are you basically satisfied with your life?	N	0	1
2. Have you dropped many of your activities and interests?	Y	1	0
3. Do you feel your life is empty?	Y	1	0
4. Do you get bored often?	Y	1	0
5. Are you hopeful about the future?	N	0	1
6. Are you bothered by thoughts you can't get out of your head?	N	1	0
7. Are you in good spirits most of the time?	N	0	1
8. Are you afraid that something bad is going to happen to you?	N	1	0
9. Do you feel happy most of the time?	N	0	1
10. Do you often feel helpless?	N	1	0
11. Do you often get restless and fidgety?	Y	1	0
12. Do you prefer to stay at home, rather than going out and doing new things?	Y	1	0
13. Do you frequently worry about the future?	Y	1	0
14. Do you feel you have more problems with memory than most?	N	1	0
15. Do you think it is wonderful to be alive now?	N	0	1
16. Do you often feel downhearted and blue?	N	1	0
17. Do you feel pretty worthless the way you are now?	Y	1	0
18. Do you worry a lot about the past?	N	1	0
19. Do you find life very exciting?	N	0	1
20. Is it hard for you to get started on new projects?	Y	1	0
21. Do you feel full of energy?	N	0	1
22. Do you feel that your situation is hopeless?	N	1	0
23. Do you think that most people are better off than you are now?	N	1	0
24. Do you frequently get upset about little things?	Y	1	0
25. Do you frequently feel like crying?	N	1	0
26. Do you have trouble concentrating?	Y	1	0
27. Do you enjoy getting up in the morning?	N	0	1
28. Do you prefer to avoid social gatherings?	Y	1	0
29. Is it easy for you to make decisions?	N	0	1
30. Is your mind as clear as it used to be?	N	0	1

Total = 21

The GDS is in the public domain and available for free from the following website:

http://www.stanford.edu/~yesavage/GDS.html.

Figure 4.1 Geriatric Depression Scale responses for Joanna Jenkins.

The role of assessment in designing an intervention is illustrated in the treatment of Joanna Jenkins. As described in more detail in Chapter 8, the cognitive-behavioral model for treating depression postulates that depression is caused and maintained by a deficiency in the amount of response-contingent positive reinforcement as well as

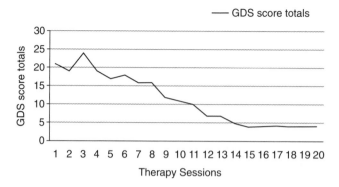

Figure 4.2 Geriatric Depression Scale scores for Joanna Jenkins.

Date	Time Start	Time End	Who was Present?	Content of Questions	How Questioning Ended?
3/16	0830	0840	Nurse, CNA, Activity Director	When is lunch?	Activity Director took to room
	0915	0930	Nurse,CNA	What to do next?	Nurse took to day room
	1110	1145	Nurse, QA Staff	When is lunch?	CNA took to lunch
	1430	1450	Nurse, Social Worker, CNA	Where is her daughter?	Activity Director took to activity
	1500	1530	2 Nurses	Where is her daughter?	CNA took to activity
	1600	1620	Nurse, family member	When is dinner?	CNA took to dinner
	1730	1740	CNA	Where is daughter?	Volunteer took to day room
	1820	1845	Nurse, family member	What happened to sweater?	Nurse took to room
3/17	0840	0850	Nurse, CNA	When is lunch?	CNA took to bath
	0955	1005	Nurse, Activity Director	What to do next?	Activity Director took to activity
	1050	1100	Nurse, Activity Aide	When is lunch?	CNA took to lunch
	1320	1330	Nurse, CNA	What to do next?	CNA took to room and turned on TV
	1610	1625	Nurse	Where is daughter?	Activity Aid took to hairdresser
	1730	1745	Nurse, family member	Where is daughter?	CNA – TV in Day room
	1930	1950	Nurse	Needs pill	Nurse took to room

Figure 4.3 Record of questioning behavior by Anna Tweed.

negative thought patterns that contribute to the negative views of self, the world, and the future. The deficiency may be caused by several factors, the most common of which are a low rate of engagement in pleasant activities, high levels of anxiety that interfere with actually experiencing the pleasantness, high rates of unpleasant activities, or cognitive schemas that are pervasively negative.

Therapists begin detailed assessment with daily mood monitoring. Depressed clients tend to believe that they always feel bad and that nothing ever happens to make them feel good. They do not believe the depression is under their control, or even under the control of environmental factors (e.g., pleasant events). Daily mood monitoring demonstrates to the client that although her mood may never be great, it does indeed fluctuate, indicating that some days are better than others, or, as the depressed client would report, some days are worse than others. Figure 4.4 shows Ms. Jenkins' first week of mood monitoring. Typical of persons who are depressed, she reports that her mood fluctuates along the lower end of the mood scale. Can you see any pattern in the days that are better versus those with the lowest mood scores?

Joanna Jenkins would also be asked to complete a Pleasant Events Schedule on which she would indicate the frequency with which she engages in a set of different activities that many older persons find pleasant. The Older Adult Pleasant Events Schedule (Teri & Lewinsohn, 1982) contains activities commonly enjoyed by older adults. On this scale Ms. Jenkins would also rate each activity as to its subjective pleasantness for her. A few items from Ms. Jenkins' scale are recorded in Figure 4.5. Specific items that she rated low in frequency but high in pleasantness would then be selected for daily monitoring. She would be asked to indicate whether she engaged in that activity each day. The therapist would begin graphing her mood and the rate at which she engaged in pleasant activities. This is both an assessment and an intervention tool, because in a short time Ms. Jenkins would be able to see quite clearly the relationship between mood and certain activities.

Cognitive aspects of Ms. Jenkins' depression would become the focus of therapy as well. Interviews are often used to identify thought patterns, assumptions, and world views with a specific focus on those cognitive patterns that produce negative affect (e.g., depression or anxiety). One popular instrument used to identify the specific thought patterns and their relationships to mood states is the Dysfunctional Thought Record. A sample record for Joanna Jenkins is shown in Figure 4.6.

Many other specific tools can be created to assist cognitive-behavioral therapists in measuring and recording subjective experiences, thoughts, and behaviors. Furthermore, older adults respond well to use of cognitive-behavior therapy self-help books, even without the assistance of a therapist (Floyd, Scogin, McKendree-Smith, Floyd, & Rokke, 2004). When used with a therapist or on one's own, CBT assessment tools provide rich data about the frequency, intensity, and context of problem behaviors, thoughts, and feelings. These data serve as excellent prompts for behavior change because the problem is so clearly defined.

The cognitive-behavioral model provides a straightforward, easily understood framework within which a behavior problem can be analyzed. Individualized assessment tools are frequently developed to facilitate tracking of specific targeted thoughts, feelings, and behaviors for a particular client.

Treatment

CBT is a time-limited, learning-based approach and is considered a short-term psychotherapy. The goal of CBT is indeed to modify behavior, whether overt action,

Daily Mood Rating Form

1. Please rate your mood for this day; i.e., how good or bad you felt, using the nine-point scale shown below. If you felt good put a high number on the chart below. If you felt "so-so" mark five, and if you felt low or depressed mark a number lower than five.

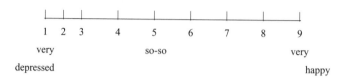

2. On the two lines next to your mood rating for each day, please briefly give two major reasons why you think you felt that way. Try to be as specific as possible.

Date	Mood Score	Why I think I felt this way
Monday, 5/10	1	1. Bored. Watched TV 2.
Tuesday, 5/11	1	1. Worried about daughter 2.
Wednesday, 5/12	3	1. Son and children stopped by 2.
Thursday, 5/13	2	1. Neighbor took a walk with me 2.
Friday, 5/14	1	1. Worried about checkbook balance 2.
Saturday, 5/15	4	1. Grandchildren brought new puppy to visit 2. Old friend called and we had a long talk
Sunday, 5/16	5	1. Church and lunch with friends 2. Neighbor stopped by for tea after dinner
		1. 2.
		1. 2.
		1. 2.

Figure 4.4   Daily mood rating form for Joanna Jenkins.

thoughts, or feelings. CBT is highly instructional and clients are frequently given homework assignments outside of the therapy sessions which can also shorten the therapeutic process. The process is designed to be highly collaborative – that is, the therapist and client set goals together, and they work together to monitor progress

	Frequency Rating			Pleasantness Rating		
	Often	Sometimes	Never	Very Pleasant	Somewhat Pleasant	Not at all Pleasant
Listening to music	3	2	(1)	(3)	2	1
Shopping	3	(2)	1	3	2	(1)
Smiling at people	3	2	(1)	3	(2)	1
Arranging flowers	(3)	2	1	3	(2)	1
Solving a problem, puzzle, or crossword	3	2	(1)	3	(2)	1
Baking a new recipe	3	2	(1)	3	2	(1)
Going to church	3	2	(1)	3	(2)	1
Thinking about people I like	3	2	(1)	(3)	2	1
Listening to birds sing	3	2	(1)	3	(2)	1
Having a clean house	3	2	(1)	(3)	2	1
Looking at stars or moon	3	(2)	1	3	(2)	1

Figure 4.5 Older Adult Pleasant Events Schedule completed by Joanna Jenkins.

toward the goals. Its flexibility is ideally suited to the complex nature of problems experienced by many older adults seeking treatment (Knight & Satre, 1999; Satre, Knight, & David, 2006).

Behavioral aspects of CBT

The principles by which behavior can be changed are typically quite simple and straightforward (Kazdin, 2001). Behavior therapy has been applied in numerous settings with a wide variety of populations, including older adults (Laidlaw, Thompson, Dick-Siskin, & Gallagher-Thompson, 2004).

Alter reinforcement contingencies to engage in pleasurable activities Altering the contingencies for behavior involves changing or adding reinforcers to produce the

Cognitive-Behavioral Model

Daily Record of Dysfunctional Thoughts

	SITUATION	EMOTION(S)	AUTOMATIC THOUGHT(S)	RATIONAL RESPONSE	OUTCOME
Date	Describe: 1. Actual event leading to unpleasant emotion, or 2. Stream of thoughts, daydreams or recollection, leading to unpleasant emotion	1. Specify sad/anxious, angry, etc. 2. Rate degree of emotion 1–100	1. Write automatic thought(s) that preceded emotion(s) 2. Rate belief in automatic thought(s) 0–100%	1. Write rational response to automatic thought(s) 2. Rate belief in rational response 0–100%	1. Re-rate belief in automatic thought(s) 2. Specify and rate subsequent emotions 0–100
5/11	*Worry about daughter*	*anxious = 85* *sad = 70*	*She is going to be an unhappy lonely old woman now that she is divorced 95%*	*Divorce doesn't have to mean she is lonely. She might not be unhappy forever. My worrying about her does not help her and only makes me miserable. 60%*	*40% – still anxious but I can't worry forever and worrying won't do her any good; anxious = 50 sad = 40*

Explanation: When you experience an unpleasant emotion note the situation that seemed to stimulate the emotion. (If the emotion occurred while you were thinking, daydreaming, etc., please note this.) Then note the automatic thought associated with the emotion. Record the degree to which you believe this thought 0% – not at all, 100% – completely. In rating degree of emotion 1 = a trace, 100 = the most intense possible.

Figure 4.6 Dysfunctional Thought Record for Joanna Jenkins.

desired behavior more often or adding disincentives to decrease the frequency of undesirable behavior. To change the reinforcement contingencies, a true reinforcer must be identified. Pleasant events or rewards for good behavior may be experienced as positive, but are not considered to be a reinforcer unless they actually change the rate of the targeted behavior. Similarly, an aversive consequence of a behavior is only a true punishment contingency if it decreases the rate of behavior.

A pleasant events reinforcement intervention might be appropriate for Anna Tweed. The first step would be to identify the desired behavior. The goal in this case is to decrease the frequency of a behavior that is noxious to staff (asking questions at the nurses' station), so a desirable behavior that is incompatible with the undesirable behavior must be identified. The goal behavior might be engaging in pleasant activity in the day room. The next step would then be to identify a reinforcer for her, that is, some event or item that is so valuable to her that she increases the frequency of the desired behavior in order to obtain or experience it. Nursing staff may have noticed that when one of them talks with Anna in her room she does not engage in the constant questioning behavior, nor does she seek to return to the nurses' station. Staff attention is likely to be a reinforcer for her that could be administered contingent on the targeted behavior. A behavioral program might be designed in which staff talk with her in the day room contingent on her engaging in a certain period of appropriate behavior that does not include questioning. Staff attention is being used to reinforce her for engaging in activities away from the nurses' station. Punishments are unlikely to be used to decrease this particular behavior because it is generally considered unethical to use punitive strategies in an institutional setting to control behavior that is not harmful to self or others.

Apply differential reinforcement Often, the desired behaviors are occurring, but in an inappropriate context. Perhaps the behavior occurs where it is annoying to others, or perhaps the behavior is simply not reaping the desired effects for the older person. For example, a perfectly appropriate question asked to a person with severe hearing impairment may yield no effect. The questioning behavior was appropriate, but the context was not appropriate to yield the desired effects. Interventions can be established to differentially reinforce the behavior in one context but not another. For example, Anna Tweed might be given attention for asking questions of staff if the behavior occurs in her room, but not at the nurses' station.

Generalization (of stimuli and responses) While new behavior patterns are being established, reinforcement contingencies and eliciting stimuli are tightly controlled to maximize the efficiency with which the behavior is learned. Typically, however, the desired outcome is for the client to be able to perform that behavior in a variety of appropriate settings. Stimulus generalization refers to the process by which a person learns to perform the desired behavior in the presence of a wider variety of stimuli. If a reinforcement training program were established for Anna Tweed, it might be implemented by one or two staff initially. Eventually, however, the goal would be for Anna to be able to distinguish between a broader category of "busy staff" and "staff available to talk." This latter discrimination requires her to generalize her initial learning about talking with staff only in the day room and never at the nurses' station to a much broader set of cues that staff are busy.

Response generalization refers to the fact that reinforcement of one response may increase the probability of other responses that are similar (Skinner, 1953). Reinforcing Anna Tweed's conversations with staff who enter the day room may not only increase her rate of interaction with staff, but may lead her to increase her interaction with other people. Combined with stimulus generalization, the effects of response generalization would create for Ms. Tweed a more appropriate, active social life away from the nurses' station.

Extinction Behaviors decrease if the positive reinforcement contingencies are removed. The gradual elimination of behavior following the removal of reinforcement contingencies is called extinction. Many behaviors are maintained by positive social consequences such as attention or praise. Removal of attention in response to the performance of the targeted behavior will result in a lower frequency of that behavior. This principle is particularly useful when working with behaviors that are either self-defeating or aversive to others. For example, Anna Tweed's behavior at the nurses' station may be inadvertently reinforced by social interaction from nurses during the time she stands at the station and asks questions. An extinction intervention would require all staff to ignore consistently Anna's presence and her verbalizations while she is standing at the nurses' station. Unfortunately, nursing home residents are often on an extinction paradigm for behavior the staff actually desires.

Shaping and chaining   Desired behaviors do not always occur spontaneously in the environment in which we want to reinforce them. The procedure of shaping involves reinforcing tiny steps toward the desired behavior. In the classic animal paradigms, pigeons were initially reinforced for turning toward the stimulus with which they were to interact. Once they were consistently turning toward the stimulus, they were reinforced only if they took steps toward the stimulus. Eventually, they had to complete the full behavior of turning, walking, and pecking the stimulus (the desired behavior) to be reinforced. The pecking behavior was shaped through reinforcement of small successive approximations of the desired behavior. As long as Joanna Jenkins is depressed, she may never spontaneously behave in a way that would elicit positive social reinforcement for her in a natural environment. A therapist or family member might establish a shaping procedure in which she is initially reinforced for behaving in a slightly less negative way that is typical for her. Increasing standards of positiveness would be required in her behavior in order to elicit the stimulus over time, until she is behaving in ways that will more naturally elicit positive social reinforcement from her natural social network.

Chaining refers to the process by which a person learns to emit a series of behaviors in a particular sequence. Reinforcement is initially given for a single behavior. Later, another behavior is required before the reinforcer is given. Finally, the full series of behaviors must be accomplished prior to reinforcement. Older adults who have experienced a stroke may need to relearn how to dress. Dressing is a long series of discrete behaviors that must be accomplished in order. A chaining procedure might be created to teach the steps of dressing oneself.

Exposure   Exposure techniques are typically applied to a wide array of anxiety-based problems or disorders. The nature of exposure therapy is to repeatedly expose a person to the thoughts, events, objects, activities, and situations which are causing the person intense anxiety. The idea is that after being exposed to the anxiety-provoking stimuli on a regular basis, and seeing that they pose no real threat, the person will eventually become desensitized to them and experience less anxiety. Relaxation training is often combined with exposure so that the person learns to relax in the presence of the feared object or situation and no longer has to rely on avoidance (which is sometimes inadvertently reinforced and keeps the fear and anxiety going).

Cognitive aspects of CBT

In a nutshell, the cognitive therapy approach involves the recognition of distorted, illogical, or unhelpful thoughts with the goal of replacing such thoughts with less distorted and more logical and adaptive ones. Indeed, a therapeutic outcome occurs when clients learn to identify unhealthy thinking patterns and then alter their thoughts accordingly (Reinecke & Clark, 2004). In practice, cognitive therapy is highly pragmatic and strongly emphasizes individualized effective treatments. The identification of the client's particular pattern of misperceptions, attitudes, assumptions, core beliefs (schemas), and interpersonal strategies is crucial for cognitive therapy to proceed. Cognitive therapists, therefore, emphasize the recognition of irrational and harmful thinking and the learning of self-counseling skills (Reinecke & Clark, 2004).

Cognitive therapy has been adapted for older adults and widely applied to diverse types of problems common in later life (see excellent resources by Gallagher-Thompson, Steffan, & Thompson, 2008; Laidlaw et al., 2004). Indeed, the individualized treatment approaches that cognitive therapists have developed adapt well to the unique challenges experienced by many older adults, contrary to some pejorative earlier reports that older adults would not be able to do much cognitive work due to the rigidity of thinking that was associated with later life. This notion is clearly a myth that has been debunked. It certainly is possible to "teach old dogs new tricks," and much research data attest to the positive impact of cognitive therapy among older clients (see Laidlaw et al., 2004; Satre et al., 2006). Some of the specific strategies used to help clients (of all ages) learn and apply methods of challenging negative thinking are described next.

The first step in the process is to help the client identify his or her own automatic negative thoughts. Because some people confuse thoughts and feelings (e.g., "I feel like a failure" rather than "I think I am a failure"), use of the Dysfunctional Thought Record can help people pinpoint the beliefs that mediate between a life event and an affective state. This often takes some practice but the vast majority of cognitively intact people of all ages can learn to identify their own thought processes. Once unhelpful thoughts are identified, the therapist then teaches the client a set of specific skills to combat, defeat, or neutralize the negative thinking. The typical strategies include:

1 Examining the evidence – what information or data is there to support the negative belief?
2 Examining the consequences of maintaining the belief – to what extent does holding the belief make the person miserable, depressed, anxious, scared, etc.? Is it worth it to continue to hold the belief?
3 Examine how somebody else would see the situation – would a friend or family member look at the situation in the same way that the client does and draw the same conclusion that the client has drawn? Often people are able to recognize the dysfunctional nature of their beliefs by stating that a friend would not agree with their perspective or conclusions.
4 Considering alternative beliefs – what are some other possible ways to view the situation that are backed up by some data and would have some potential benefit to the person to adopt the new way of thinking? Once a series of alternative thoughts are generated, each one can be scrutinized more fully to determine the validity or usefulness of the new way of thinking.

Problem-solving therapy

An important offshoot of traditional CBT is problem-solving therapy (PST). The underlying core premise of PST is that one's mental and physical health can be enhanced by learning how to use a step-by-step process to find solutions to different types of problems that arise in life (D'Zurilla & Nezu, 2007). The PST approach consists of teaching clients two major strategies. The first is applying a *problem-solving orientation to life*, which involves appraising problems as challenges to be solved, believing that problems can be solved, and understanding that effective problem-solving requires time and systematic efforts. The second component of PST is learning *rational problem-solving skills*. The specific skills include:

1   attempting to identify a problem when it occurs;
2   defining a problem;
3   attempting to understand the problem;
4   setting goals related to the problem;
5   generating alternative solutions to the problem;
6   evaluating and selecting the most promising alternatives from the list;
7   and, finally, evaluating the effectiveness of the effort at problem-solving.

The process of PST is structured and intensive, involving written and oral presentations of the problem-solving steps by the clinician, guided practice in applying the model in session, and homework assignments to apply the model to real problems. PST has been found to be effective for major depression in younger patients (Nezu & Perri, 1989), adult medical patients (Mynors-Wallis, Gath, Day, & Baker, 2000), and developmentally disabled adults (Nezu, Nezu, & Areán, 1991; Nezu, Nezu, & Dudek, 1998). The model has also been applied successfully to diverse groups of older adults including depressed older adult outpatients (Areán et al., 1993), depressed medically fragile, home-bound older adult patients (Gellis, McGinty, Horowitz, Bruce, & Misener, 2007), depressed older adult primary care patients (Areán, Hegel, Vannoy, Fan, & Unuzter, 2008), and depressed older adults with comorbid executive dysfunction (e.g., impaired initiation, perseveration, and response inhibition) (Alexopoulos, Raue, Kanellopoulos, Mackin, & Areán, 2008), a group known to be especially resistant to conventional pharmacotherapy for depression. Further application of this model will hopefully extend the suitability and effectiveness of PST with caregivers of individuals with a cognitive disorder. These studies as a whole suggest that PST is an important and viable therapeutic option for many older adults with clinical depression.

Additional Comments about the Cognitive-Behavioral Model

The power of classical and operant conditioning to develop and maintain behavior in older adults has been illustrated in several naturalistic settings with older adults (Wisocki, 1991). One illustrative research program has examined the effects of antecedents and consequences for controlling behavior in nursing homes in the United States and Germany. Baltes and colleagues have demonstrated that staff in nursing homes reinforce dependency behavior from residents, but extinguish (fail to reinforce) independent behavior from residents (Baltes, 1988). Staff tend to interact with residents most, and most warmly, when the residents are receiving hands-on care. In other words, if residents want warm social contact with staff, they must "need" care from staff. Obviously, this line of research illustrates several principles of cognitive-behavioral theory. Staff appear to extinguish independent behavior by not providing even an intermittent reinforcement schedule. At the same time, they are reinforcing dependent behavior. Altering staff behavior so it reinforces the desired independent behaviors has also been shown to be effective (e.g., Burgio, Burgio, Engel, & Tice, 1986; Cohn et al., 1994).

Interventions to alter cognitions and behavior always require careful examination of ethics. When designing interventions for frail persons who either cannot collaborate in the establishment of treatment goals (e.g., cognitively impaired persons) or whose power to refuse the intervention is compromised (e.g., in a nursing home), cognitive-behaviorists must be particularly careful to examine the ethical implications of their decision to intervene (Carstensen & Fisher, 1991). For example, when is family or staff displeasure a sufficient reason to intervene? How much understanding must be present for informed consent to be truly informed? Cognitive-behaviorists must respect the burden of ethical consideration that is placed on them by the very power of their tools.

Summary and Conclusions

In summary, the cognitive-behavioral model is rooted in a scientific approach to investigating efficiency and effectiveness of interventions. As such, the amount of evidence supporting the utility of this model to explain mental health problems and to design interventions is impressive (e.g., Gallagher-Thompson & Coon, 2007; Satre et al., 2006; Scogin, Welsh, Hanson, Stump, & Coates, 2005; Stanley et al., 2003). CBT practitioners working with cognitively intact persons have demonstrated significant impact with challenging problems like depression, anxiety, health behaviors, and insomnia. Many interventions, especially more behaviorally focused ones, have been successful even with cognitively impaired individuals (e.g., incontinence programs and self-care programs), suggesting robust application of the model to older individuals with diverse levels of functioning.

5

Stress and Coping Model

Consider the following example:

> Mrs. C is an 80-year-old African American woman whose adaptation in late life is plagued by disruptive relocation and very poor health. Not surprisingly, she exhibits severe psychological distress, and her medical chart includes a diagnosis of clinical depression. She is currently surviving on the barest social, economic and health resources. She is also socially isolated. "My family – they're all dead, my mama, my papa, everyone." She had been married in her late teens and widowed before thirty – "so long ago I can hardly remember it." Her son and a grandson died many years previously, and she subsequently lost contact with a second grandson.
>
> Before retiring because of illness, she worked as a domestic for forty years. Currently she subsists on SSI. Compounding her many losses, she was recently evicted from an apartment where she had resided for 30 years. This event was especially traumatic because it removed her from a familiar neighborhood, proximity to her church, and friends of long standing. Following her eviction she rented a room from an "odd" landlady. "I won't say nothing. I might get kicked out." The waiting list for senior housing is long and she has resisted moving to general public housing. "That's where all the bad folks are." She has one male friend whom she sees every Saturday, when they go out for breakfast and then to his place to watch ball games on television. She has no friends living near her current residence and spends her days by herself reading the Bible and singing hymns. She complains of loneliness and believes that her doctor is her only confidante. Her declining physical health is a serious factor in her current distress. According to her medical charts, she was recently diagnosed as having cervical cancer and nodular shadows were seen on her chest X-ray. She and her doctors were most troubled about the possibility of a serious systemic disease. (Johnson & Johnson, 1992, p. 233)

Aging and Mental Health, 2e. Daniel L. Segal, Sara Honn Qualls, and Michael A. Smyer
© 2011 Daniel L. Segal, Sara Honn Qualls, and Michael A. Smyer

Mrs. C's situation challenges her and those who are working with her. How do we conceptualize her problems? What can we do for her and with her? Not surprisingly, Mrs. C has multiple problems with which she is struggling: cancer, a disrupted living situation, limited economic resources, dwindling social resources, and a personal wariness that may keep her from seeking help.

Introduction to the Model

This chapter outlines a stress and coping perspective that may be useful for working with older adults like Mrs. C. We draw upon research and clinical work from several different disciplines to help sketch an understanding of the stress and coping process and its implications for assessment and treatment.

Well-being

Have you ever been "stressed out?" How do you know?

In developing your answer, you worked from an implicit model of what stress is and how it works. For some, stress is experienced as a physical reaction: sweating, chills, quickened heart beats, upset stomach, neck pain. For some, stress is experienced as a combination of feelings: worry, fear, apprehension. For others, stress is identified with external problems: problems in paying bills, too much work and too little time, conflict with a friend or family member.

Consider a softball player. Her team is tied in the bottom of the last inning. She is at bat with two strikes called against her. Is this situation stressful? Is it unhealthy for her? Your answer depends upon your implicit model of the stress process and its implications for well-being. A more formal definition of stress is in order. Stress may be defined as a physical, mental, or emotional response to events that makes you feel threatened or upsets your balance in some way. In small amounts, stress can be positive in that it may motivate you to perform well. In contrast, high levels of chronic stress are usually unhealthy for the mind and body.

Let's return to the case example. Is Mrs. C stressed out? Again, your answer depends on your implicit model of stress and differences between "normal" stress and abnormal or unhealthy levels of stress. Aldwin (2007) outlined an integrative perspective on stress, coping, and development. She suggested that it is useful to think of stress and coping as a process with three key elements: an internal state of the person, called *strain*; external events or *stressors*; and an experience that derives from the interaction of the person and environment, called *transactions*.

Strain

The concept of strain encompasses reactions that are physiological (e.g., sympathetic activation; parasympathetic suppression; neuroendocrine changes; immune function changes) and emotional (e.g., negative feelings; positive feelings; emotional numbing). Growing interest in the connection between the mind and the body spurred the development of the relatively new field of psychoneuroimmunology (PNI). PNI is the study of the interaction between psychological processes and the nervous and immune systems of the human body (Daruna, 2004; Vedhara & Irwin, 2005). Indeed, the links between stress and immune system functioning have received a great deal of research and clinical attention (Kiecolt-Glaser, 2009). In their review of this literature, Herbert and Cohen (1993) highlighted several important themes: First, both objective stressful events and subjective reports of stress are related to immune changes; second, objective events have a greater impact than subjective reports; and, third, the nature of the events (e.g., interpersonal stress vs. non-social events) affects the type of immune response.

How does this help us understand Mrs. C's situation? To begin with, we might attend to the objective stressful events that have occurred for her, and their likely impact on her physiological functioning. For example, consider only two aspects of her situation: depression and cancer. There is a substantial link between clinical depression and compromised immune system functioning (Gruenewald & Kemeny, 2007) and these effects are greatest among older and hospitalized patients. Similarly, there is a clearly established link among the stress of cancer diagnosis and treatment, other life stresses, and subsequent health or illness (e.g., Penedo & Dahn, 2005). Thus while depression and cancer are not directly related, they both relate to poorer health outcomes.

In short, there is good reason to suspect that the stresses of clinical depression and a cancer diagnosis and subsequent treatment regimen – apart from any of the other objective stressors or subjective perceptions – put Mrs. C at risk for suppressed immune functioning and poor disease prognosis.

Stressor

Examples of external events or stressors include traumatic experiences (e.g., being a victim of crime; undergoing a contentious divorce; death of a parent), aversive physical environments (e.g., being too hot, too cold, in pain), chronic role strain (e.g., simultaneously having to care for an ill older parent and younger children), and daily hassles (e.g., facing traffic each day on the way to work). These stressors cause the experience of stress. A distinction between strain and stressors is that strains are generally chronic whereas stressors are generally acute.

The concept of stressor shifts our attention to the social, historical, and physical context that surrounds older adults. As noted in Chapter 2, three types of influences shape the individual's life course: age-graded, history-graded, and non-normative events. Age-graded influences are associated with a specific chronological age, for example, entering school or graduating from high school are usually linked to a narrow age band. History-graded influences are linked to the particular historical period in which the individual has lived (e.g., the Great Depression; the Vietnam War; the Oklahoma City Bombing; the 9/11 attacks; Hurricane Katrina). Non-normative events are influences that occur at any time in the life span but are not part of the "expected" life pattern (e.g., death of one's parents at an early age; winning the lottery). As we discussed earlier, these influences vary across the life span.

In the case of Mrs. C, we might use these frameworks to consider both the history-graded, age-graded, and non-normative influences that have shaped her development.

An 80-year-old, she was born in 1930. She experienced the Great Depression as young child, married after World War II, and was widowed during the Korean War. She has had several other non-normative events befall her: death of a grandson and eviction from her home.

The deaths of her family members remind us that Mrs. C's life events are interwoven with the events of her family members and friends. Pruchno, Blow, and Smyer (1984) call these "life event webs" as a way of reminding us of interdependent lives. Potential sources of support for Mrs. C are denied her through the deaths of her husband, son, and grandson.

Mrs. C has also coped with another chronic stressor: financial strain. Her career as a domestic suggests that she has not been highly paid, and her current subsistence on SSI confirms this suspicion. Krause (1995a) summarized the impact of chronic financial strain on older adults' social and mental well-being, noting that financial strain has a significant impact on depressive symptoms – second only to the impact of a physical illness. In Mrs. C's case, we might ask what the impact of this chronic stressor has been for her depressive symptoms (Krause, 1995a): Has it caused depression to occur for the first time in later life? Has it prolonged an already-existing depressive episode? Has it caused a relapse of a previously diagnosed disorder? These are leads that we may want to pursue in our history-taking with Mrs. C.

Transaction

The third element of the stress process is transaction, the interaction between the person and the environment. The basic assumption is that the person's *perception* of the stressor affects his or her coping response, highlighting a cognitive dimension to the stress process. For example, imagine that you are taking an important course and a final exam is coming up. You might view this impending stressor in at least two different ways: a threat to your mental health and educational well-being or a challenge to your intellectual skills and an opportunity to hone your knowledge on the course topics. How you view the stressor may very well affect what you do about it. An appraisal of the intensity of the stressor (e.g., weak, moderate, strong, ambiguous) is another aspect of the stress process. Stressors appraised with stronger intensity typically yield stronger emotional and physiological responses.

Lazarus and his colleagues have highlighted two basic approaches to coping that are linked to the perception of stress: *problem-focused coping* and *emotion-focused coping* (Folkman, Lazarus, Pimley, & Novacek, 1987; Lazarus & Folkman, 1984). Problem-focused coping is aimed at managing or altering the problem that is causing distress, whereas emotion-focused coping is aimed at regulating distressing emotions. Both styles of coping include behavioral and cognitive strategies. The type of coping utilized depends upon an individual's appraisal of the situation, namely, whether or not the stressful problem is perceived as being amenable to change. In general, problem-focused coping is directed at conditions that are assessed as amenable to change whereas emotion-focused coping is directed at conditions where nothing ostensibly can be done to alter the challenging situation (Lazarus & Folkman, 1984). Typically, use of problem- or emotion-focused coping does not preclude the other; rather, individuals use some combination of both when handling a stressful problem.

Indeed, the type of coping that is used in response to a particular stress is a function of the individual's perceptions, the specific types of stress, and the context for coping.

A central element of perception is the individual's sense of control over the event (Skaff, 2007). In a classic study in this area, Zautra, Reich, and Newsom (1995) focused on the links between sense of control, loss of autonomy, and mental health among older adults. They found that it is important to assess the individual's sense of control that derives from experience with the possibility of shaping the events of life – both positive and negative. They focused on mental health and adaptation in the face of a loss of autonomy because of either physical disability or conjugal bereavement. Their results were impressive: A sense of personal control over events was associated with positive mental health and adaptation in the face of increased disability or decreased autonomy. In general, the consensus of recent literature suggests that entering later life with a strong sense of control is highly adaptive (see review by Skaff, 2007).

What about Mrs. C? How does she view the stressors in her life? How much control does she perceive herself to have? Her comments about her landlady ("I won't say nothing. I might get kicked out") suggest that she feels little sense of control over her living situation.

Stress and Coping: Normal and Abnormal Adaptation

Is Mrs. C's profile of strain, stressors, and transactions normal for older adults? Although a great deal of knowledge about stress and its impact on older adults has been synthesized (Aldwin, Park, & Spiro, 2007), much remains unknown. We simply cannot chart the normal ebb and flow of stress and coping across the life span for all older adults. A more pragmatic approach might be to ask about the individual's own development, and deviations from her own baseline of functioning. For each individual, successful coping with stress is a function of three elements: the individual's level of vulnerability, the stress that the individual encounters, and protective factors (Gatz, Kasl-Godley, & Karel, 1996). Individual vulnerability includes genetic influences, acquired biological vulnerabilities, and psychological factors that affect the individual's adaptation (e.g., a tendency to be pessimistic or think negatively; poor problem-solving skills; poor communication skills). Stress incorporates psychosocial elements, environmental elements, and the individual's perception of these. Protective factors include biological, psychological, or social elements that can either buffer the older adult from stress or moderate its impact, for example being physically active, having effective coping skills, and relying on a solid social support network.

With Mrs. C, we might begin by asking how her current adaptation compares to her earlier situation. We know that many of her social supports are no longer available – her son, grandsons, previous neighbors. We also know that the familiar physical environment has changed (after she was evicted). Her medical status is threatened (with the cancer diagnosis) and her current psychological adjustment is poor (with a diagnosis of depression).

As we review her history and consider her current adjustment, we have an implicit view of the interaction between Mrs. C and her interpersonal, social, and physical environment. This perspective is consistent with Lewin's (1935) classic emphasis on the interaction between person and environment and seminal work in geropsychology focusing on the interaction between the individual's capacity and environmental characteristics that may affect the development and course of disorders (e.g., Lawton, 1980, 1982). As described in Chapter 2, Gatz and her colleagues, for example, used this framework to depict the factors that affect the probability of developing a depressive disorder in later life (see Figure 2.3 in Chapter 2). The important element is the interaction among the individual's biological vulnerability or predisposition, the situational stressors of life events or life circumstances, and the individual's psychological coping mechanisms. This conceptualization provides a framework for assessment and subsequent intervention.

Assessment Strategies

Assessment within the stress and coping framework focuses on the individual's vulnerabilities, the stresses to which she is exposed, and the protective factors that may mitigate the stress process.

Assessing individual vulnerabilities

One of the key elements for assessment is Mrs. C's biological vulnerability. Two aspects are particularly important when getting Mrs. C's history: her experience of chronic illness, and previous episodes of mental disorder, in this case depression.

The interaction of physical and mental well-being in later life is a complex, interdependent process. From the brief case description, we know that Mrs. C is currently coping with cervical cancer and the possibility of other health problems. It will be important to assess Mrs. C's history of coping with chronic illness since this chronic strain is a robust predictor of poor mental health in later life (Krause, 1995a). Thus, we need to understand where in the coping process we encounter Mrs. C as she faces the chronic illness of cancer and its treatment.

Another focus of assessment should be the history of the mental disorder itself: Is this Mrs. C's first bout of depression? Is it a recurrent pattern? Did Mrs. C have significant depression earlier in life, only to have it vanish until recently? Each of these patterns would have different implications for treatment and the likely course of the disorder.

Assessing life stresses

Two aspects of life stresses should be assessed: the individual's subjective perception of the stress; and the "objective" indicators of stress. Each component must be understood as distinct and in interaction with the other (Aldwin, 2007).

Assessing Mrs. C's subjective perception of stress focuses us on a simple question: What is Mrs. C's assessment of how stressful, upsetting, or overwhelming her situation is? Cohen, Kamarck, and Mermelstein (1983) developed a set of 10 self-report questions for this purpose, the Perceived Stress Scale (PSS). Some sample items of the PSS include the following:

- In the last month, how often have you been upset because of something that happened unexpectedly?
- In the last month, how often have you felt that you could not cope with all the things that you had to do?
- In the last month, how often have you felt difficulties were piling up so high that you could not overcome them?

Cohen et al. found that perceived stress was associated with illness, illness symptoms, and a range of health behaviors. The PSS illustrates the usefulness of a standardized inquiry into the individual's perceptions.

Objective assessments of stress have typically focused on checklists of life events. A classic example of this type of measure is the Social Readjustment Rating Scale (SRRS; Holmes & Rahe, 1967), which asks respondents to rate the degree to which a large number of life events are stressful. The SRRS considers both positive and negative events as stressful, because even positive events (e.g., getting married; having a baby) require an adjustment that may be perceived as stressful. Most stress, however, comes from a series of little stressors, or daily hassles, that include irritations and demands that occur in daily life. In general, the number of daily hassles that are reported on a weekly basis tend to decrease with age, most likely due to the fact that as social roles decrease with age, so do the hassles associated with those roles (Aldwin, Yancura, & Boeninger, 2007).

A good example of an elder-specific stress checklist is the Elders Life Stress Inventory (ELSI; Aldwin, 1990), which includes 31 items that measure whether or not the respondent has had specific stressful experiences over the past year. A helpful aspect of the ELSI is that it encompasses both stressful events (e.g., death of a spouse; death of a child; major personal illness or injury; retirement) and stressful processes (e.g., deterioration of relationship with a child or spouse) that affect older adults.

However, there are some limitations to checklists. If Mrs. C merely endorses an item (e.g., indicating the death of a spouse or a son), it tells us little about the impact of that event on her subsequent adjustment and it reveals little about the specific context in which the event occurred.

Instead of checklists, a structured interview or a clinical interview may be used to assess current stresses. For example, a structured approach designed to understand age-specific stressors is the Louisville Older Persons Stress Scale (LOPES; Murrell, Norris, & Hutchins, 1984), which includes 54 items that are administered in an interview format. For each stressful event that is identified as having occurred in the past six months, the interview evaluates salient characteristics of the stressful event including information about the degree of change required by the stressor, desirability of the changes, novelty of the stressor, preoccupation with the stressor, and the exact date of the occurrence. According to Murrell et al., the most frequent stressful life events among adults were health problems whereas the most undesirable life events were the loss of a home and the death of a loved one.

Emphasizing a clinical interview approach to understanding stressors, Krause (1995b) listed life stresses under the major roles that older adults play, such as spouse, parent, or grandparent. In addition to a standardized list, it is helpful to ask an open-ended question at the end of each section. For example, under the section on the parental role, it is useful to ask whether anything else had happened with their children (Krause, 1995b). Another follow-up inquiry may focus on whether the life stress was desirable or undesirable. In short, by using an interview format, the clinician can gauge three elements of the older adult's life stresses: their frequency, their perceived saliency, and their desirability. In Mrs. C's case, the interview might reveal the importance of her role as a church volunteer and the impact that losing this role has had on her well-being.

Assessing protective factors

Two types of protective factors will be important to assess: the individual's own coping capacity and the environment that can either help or hinder coping.

Individual coping There are two basic approaches to assessing an individual's coping: a trait approach or a state approach (see Aldwin, 2007 for a thorough review). The trait approach assumes that the individual's coping style is fairly stable, regardless of the particular type of stress that she encounters. In contrast, the state approach assumes that the process of coping may vary across time, depending upon the particular stressor encountered. These different assumptions have different implications for assessment strategies.

Those who focus on coping styles as traits use standardized questionnaires to assess the individual's general pattern of coping, often called dispositional coping. A popular dispositional measure is the Coping Orientations to Problems Experienced Scale (COPE; Carver, Scheier, & Weintraub, 1989), which consists of 60 self-report items. The COPE provides scores on three main clusters of strategies (Problem-focused Coping; Emotion-focused Coping; Dysfunctional Coping), with each cluster containing five specific scales (see Table 5.1 for a full description of the COPE scales and a sample item for each scale). Notably, a brief version of the COPE containing only 28 items is available (Carver, 1997).

Cross-sectional research has documented that individuals of different ages use dissimilar dispositional coping strategies. For example, Folkman and colleagues (1987) found that older adults used more positive reappraisal and distancing as coping strategies whereas younger adults tended to seek social support more often and used more confrontive coping styles. Diehl, Coyle, and Labouvie-Vief (1996) found that older adults used a combination of coping strategies indicative of greater impulse control and they tended to evaluate conflict situations more positively than younger adults. Segal, Hook, and Coolidge (2001) used the COPE to examine coping styles in younger and older adults and they found that older adults used dysfunctional coping strategies at lower levels than younger adults. Specifically, older adults were less likely to use focusing on and venting of emotions, mental disengagement, and alcohol or drugs to cope with their problems. In the problem- and emotion-focused clusters, older adults were more likely to use restraint coping and religion, but less likely to use humor.

In contrast to dispositional measures of coping, the process-oriented measures focus on the individual's reaction to a specific stressor or type of stressor. The most widely used process measure of coping is the Ways of Coping Questionnaire (WCQ;

Table 5.1 COPE clusters, specific scale definitions, and sample items

Strategy type	Definition	Example
Problem-focused cluster		
Active coping	Taking active steps to try to remove or circumvent the stressor or to ameliorate its effects	I concentrate my efforts on doing something about it.
Planning	Thinking about how to act upon a stressor	I try to come up with a strategy about what to do.
Suppression of competing activities	Putting other projects aside or trying to avoid becoming distracted by other events	I keep myself from getting distracted by other thoughts or activities.
Restraint coping	Waiting until an appropriate opportunity to act presents itself	I restrain myself from doing anything too quickly.
Seeking social support for instrumental reasons	Seeking advice, assistance, or information	I try to get advice from someone about what to do.
Emotion-focused cluster		
Seeking social support for emotional reasons	Seeking moral support, sympathy, or understanding	I get sympathy and understanding from someone.
Positive reinterpretation and growth	Reappraising a stressor in positive terms	I try to see it in a different light, to make it seem more positive.
Acceptance	Recognizing the reality of a stressful situation	I learn to live with it.
Turning to religion	Utilizing religious beliefs	I pray more than usual.
Humor	Taking a light-hearted approach to a stressful situation	I laugh about the situation.
Dysfunctional cluster		
Focus on and venting of emotions	Focusing on the distress one is feeling and ventilating those feelings	I let my feelings out.
Denial	Refusing to believe that the stressor exists or trying to act as though the stressor is not real	I say to myself, "this isn't real."
Behavioral disengagement	Reducing one's effort to deal with the stressor	I just give up trying to reach my goal.
Mental disengagement	Reducing one's thoughts about the stressor	I turn to work or other substitute activities to take my mind off things.
Alcohol/drug use	Using alcohol or drugs in response to a stressor	I use alcohol or drugs to make myself feel better.

Source: Adapted from Carver et al. (1989).

Table 5.2 WCQ factors, definitions, and sample items

Scale name	Definition	Example
Confrontive coping	Aggressive efforts to alter the situation and suggests some degree of hostility and risk-taking	I stood my ground and fought for what I wanted.
Distancing	Cognitive efforts to detach oneself from the situation and to minimize the significance of it	I went on as if nothing had happened.
Self-controlling	Efforts to regulate one's feelings and actions	I tried to keep my feelings to myself.
Seeking social support	Efforts to seek informational support, tangible support, and emotional support	I talked to someone to find out more about the situation.
Accepting responsibility	Efforts to acknowledges one's own role in the problem with a concomitant theme of trying to put things right	I criticized or lectured myself.
Escape-avoidance	Wishful thinking and behavioral efforts to escape or avoid the problem	I hoped for a miracle.
Planful problem-solving	Deliberate problem-focused efforts to alter the situation, coupled with a rational approach to solving the problem	I made a plan of action and followed it.
Positive reappraisal	Efforts to create positive meaning by focusing on personal growth	I changed or grew as a person in a good way.

Source: Adapted from Folkman and Lazarus (1988).

Folkman & Lazarus, 1988). The WCQ is designed to identify the thoughts and actions an individual has used to cope with a *specific* stressful encounter, and as such, it measures coping processes, not coping dispositions. It contains 50 self-report items and provides scores on eight empirically derived factors (see Table 5.2 for descriptions of the factors and sample items).

In Mrs. C's case, we might focus on how she has coped with depression in the past, perhaps using the Self-Help Inventory (Burns, Shaw, & Crocker, 1987), which consists of 45 items that include behavioral strategies (e.g., "get busy"), cognitive strategies (e.g., "remind myself that my upset will pass and I will feel good again"), and interpersonal strategies (e.g., "talk to a friend or relative that I like").

The coping environment   It is also important to assess the individual's coping environment: Does it present additional challenges in the face of impairment? Does it facilitate her adaptation? Consider Mrs. C's situation: She has recently moved from a familiar physical environment (her home of 30 years) and she reports a dwindling social environment (only one friend whom she regularly sees).

We should not focus solely on her friends and family, however. It is also important to gauge the range of institutional and organizational resources that Mrs. C can call upon (Smyer, 1995). For example, we know that Mrs. C receives SSI. Is she also linked to the "aging network" in her community? Does she receive meals-on-wheels? Does she attend the programs at her local senior center? Because many older adults do not receive formal services from agencies or organizations but rather obtain informal help from friends and family members, both informal and formal elements of support must be gauged when assessing the coping environment. Assessing these resources often leads directly to the development and implementation of a treatment plan.

General Treatment Strategies and the Emergence of Health Psychology

The field of *health psychology* is strongly associated with the stress and coping model. Health psychology is the branch of psychology that investigates the psychological factors related to wellness and illness, including the prevention, diagnosis, and treatment of medical problems. In recent years, clinical health psychology (and clinical health geropsychology) has come of age and flourished due to the mounting evidence for effectiveness of interventions used by psychologists to help medically ill patients and growing opportunities for reimbursement (Qualls & Benight, 2007). Health psychology has also expanded as the traditional dichotomy between mind and body has been replaced by the more integrative biopsychosocial framework that considers each area important to mental and physical health. Many clinical health psychologists focus their work on psychophysiological disorders, which are medical problems caused by an interaction of psychological, emotional, and physical difficulties (Molton & Raichle, 2010) and on the management of chronic illnesses (e.g., diabetes, cardiovascular disease, arthritis).

An important policy development for the practice of health psychology is the creation and development in 2002 of health and behavior (H&B) codes, which allow psychologists to bill Medicare for services provided to help older adults manage chronic medical problems. Qualls and Benight (2007) summarized the variety of services covered by these codes, including assisting patients with:

- adherence to medical treatment
- symptom management (e.g., pain management)
- reduction of negative health behaviors (e.g., smoking)
- adjustment to the medical disorder

These codes provide validation for the important role that psychologists can play in the management of health problems as part of a multidisciplinary team and they also will likely provide the impetus for the critical expansion of psychology's role in health care.

Treatment Strategies

As in the other frameworks, treatment within the stress and coping paradigm follows from the assessment approaches. A comprehensive assessment should highlight those areas needing prompt intervention and those that form longer-term objectives. A comprehensive treatment plan should include social, physical, and mental well-being. Throughout, realistic goals should be established, focusing on those elements that are controllable. Finally, the initial assessments should be viewed as a baseline against which to judge the impact of treatment at follow-up.

Five major treatment strategies are consistent with a stress and coping theoretical framework (Gatz, 1992):

- eliminating stressors
- modifying the physical and social environment
- teaching coping skills
- providing social support
- improving health practices

As this list suggests, often the therapist must pursue several simultaneous intervention strategies, depending upon the client's life history and life circumstances. Each strategy is discussed next.

Eliminating stressors

If life stress is a major contributing factor to mental disorders, then one effective intervention may be to eliminate (or reduce) as many stressors as possible. The clinician can use the assessment information regarding the client's perceptions of stressors to target specific stresses for elimination. In Mrs. C's case, for example, a major stressor seems to be her recent relocation from her familiar neighborhood, with its links to friends and the church. One intervention strategy, therefore, might be to explore the possibility of relocating Mrs. C back into her old neighborhood, in a setting that she can afford.

Modifying the environment

Within the interactionist perspective on stress and coping, the context directly affects the individual's well-being. Therefore, intervention strategies can target aspects of the physical or social environment that work against the client. For example, the physical environment may act as a barrier to the older client's active social involvement. (See Box 5.1.)

Consider the case of an older woman with deteriorating arthritis in her knees. She lives on the second floor of a duplex, with steep stairs. She enjoyed gardening for many years, but she can no longer bend or stoop in the garden. She refuses to change apartments to the ground floor: "It's too dangerous. You never know who's going to break in and knock you in the head." Yet she complains that there's nothing left for her to do. The solution? Consider a window garden, or involving her in a local gardening program that can bring gardening enthusiasm and aid to her apartment. The specifics will vary by location and the resources available. The universal element, however, is that the therapist broadens the therapeutic role to consider the ecology of the coping that the client brings with her, the fit between

Box 5.1   Prevention starts at home: eliminating potential problems in the physical environment

The physical environment may present additional stresses for an older adult. Several areas are important as potential sources of trouble:

1   Medications: Are they stored and labeled in easy-to-read letters?
2   Stairways: Are they free from clutter? Are there gates to prevent falls?
3   Water temperature: Is the water heater set to 120 or lower? Are hot water pipes insulated or exposed?
4   Is the kitchen safe? Is there clutter near the stove? Are the knobs on the stove or the settings clearly indicated?
5   Is the bathroom safe? Are there grab bars near the toilet and the shower or tub? Is there a bath mat that might slip? (Could it be replaced with bathroom carpeting?) Is there a skid-resistant mat in the shower or tub?

Source: Adapted from Mace and Rabins (2001).

the client's capacities and the demands of the physical and social environment (Lawton, 1980, 1982).

Teaching coping skills

A third strategy focuses on improving the client's skills for coping with current and future stressors. Consider the case of mild to moderate depression. A skill-based approach has been developed focusing on the client's skills in identifying the proximal causes of negative and positive mood changes, the link between daily events and mood, and the client's control over these elements (Lewinsohn, Munoz, Youngren, & Zeiss, 1992). This approach has been extended to older adults, with impressive results (Gallagher-Thompson & Thompson, 2010; Thompson, Dick-Siskin, Coon, Powers, & Gallagher-Thompson, 2010).

Similarly, interventions have been designed to increase older clients' sense of control over positive events and mastery of negative events (e.g., Reich & Zautra, 1989, 1990). In this case, the focus was not solely depressed older adults. The target audiences were recently bereaved or disabled people. The common element, however, was a skill-building emphasis on increasing self-initiated positive events and responding effectively to negative events. Mindfulness meditation is another skill that has recently garnered empirical support for the treatment of health problems including pain, depression, and anxiety (see review by Davis, Zautra, Johnson, Murray, & Okvat, 2007).

In Mrs. C's case, we might try to increase her skill at controlling her depressed mood by helping her identify what she can do to give herself some pleasure in her day, as well as what she can do to avoid the negative stresses of the day, and by increasing her awareness of positive moods. By giving her skills to manage moods, we may improve her adaptation, even in the face of chronic, challenging stresses (Gallagher-Thompson & Thompson, 2010).

Providing social support

A common strategy for those encountering life stresses is to find others who are coping with similar problems. For many older adults, however, this is easier said than done. Consider the case of a 90-year-old widow who has outlived her older friends, her age-mates, and even many of her younger friends. Her children are in their late sixties, coping with the challenges of their own aging. Mrs. C, our 80-year-old, reflects this situation in her lament: "My family – they're all dead, my mama, my papa, everyone." Perhaps one tack for the therapist is to engage others as social supports for Mrs. C.

Two challenges quickly arise, however: What type of support and how? Two major types of support are emotional support and instrumental support. The timing of these, however, may vary depending upon when we encounter the client:

> the needs of clients may vary depending upon where clients are located temporally in the natural history of an event. Early in the history of a stressor, emotional support may be most useful, but later on tangible assistance may be more helpful as the client becomes more willing to take concrete steps to reconstruct his or her life. (Krause, 1995a, p. 213)

In Mrs. C's case, for example, she may need emotional support in coping with the recently discovered cancer diagnosis. A support group that can provide a shared sense of experience and understanding may be an important first step of linking her to outside help. Later on, she may call upon group members for their advice on how to handle the details of chemotherapy and its accompanying unpleasant side effects.

All social support is not the same, however, and the context in which support is offered is critical to determining its perceived effectiveness (Uchino, 2009). Some peers may encourage you to "lean on me – let me share your burden." Others might encourage you to "pull yourself up by your bootstraps." This advice is fairly common from relatives and friends of clients with depression. Which type of support is best?

Evidence suggests that the effectiveness of each strategy depends upon the timing of the support in relation to the impairment:

> It comes as no surprise that healthy individuals gain in mental health with a social network that encourages self-reliance. For those with an established impairment, these types of messages may also ease feelings of helplessness. It is during the time of loss that the social network messages of self-reliance are incongruent with the person's experience and his or her needs. During this period of crisis, receiving messages that you can rely on others, the "lean on me" message, appears to play a valuable part in limiting the damage caused by the crisis events, perhaps by providing ways of maintaining a sense of control. (Zautra et al., 1995, pp. 167–168)

In Mrs. C's case, she may be in need of emotional support that allows her to rely on others, as she copes with the recent diagnosis of cancer. Thus, the nature of the support group that she joins may be very important.

Improving health practices

The interaction of physical and mental well-being in later life makes working with older adults a challenge. Chronic stress can adversely affect the client's immune system functioning and health status (e.g., Gruenewald & Kemeny, 2007; Penedo & Dahn, 2005). For example, the chronic stress of caregiving for an ill relative adversely affects cardiovascular, metabolic, and immune system functioning (Vitaliano, Zhang, & Scanlan, 2003) and also causes increases in depressive and anxiety symptoms, helplessness, social isolation, and perceived loss of control (Fortinsky, Tennen, Frank, & Affleck, 2007). In contrast, psychosocial interventions (e.g., cognitive restructuring, relaxation, hypnosis, exercise) can positively affect immune system functioning (Penedo & Dahn, 2005), and, perhaps, health. In short, the interaction of physical and mental well-being requires the therapist to work closely with the client's medical team.

In Mrs. C's case, for example, we may want to assess her current nutritional status, assure that the cancer treatments are undertaken, and coordinate with her doctor, upon whom she relies.

Summary and Conclusions

The stress and coping model is an important complement to the other models presented earlier in this section of the book because, at some level, all mental health practitioners help their clients cope with whatever difficult experiences they are facing. This chapter reviewed the three key elements of the stress and coping process, namely, strain, stressors, and transactions, and discussed the assessment and intervention approaches associated with the model, with applications to older adults. Whereas excitement for this growing area of research and practice is understandable, caution is also necessary because our understanding of life stresses, coping, and aging is far from complete. Despite these limitations, however, the stress and coping framework can be a useful way of thinking about older clients and their challenges.

6

Family Systems Model

Why consider a family model of mental health and aging? Aren't older adults often abandoned by family members and left to live isolated, lonely lives in an institutional setting? We have chosen to include a family systems model for conceptualizing mental health of older persons precisely because the myth of the isolated, abandoned elder is just that – a myth. Indeed, older adults nearly always are in frequent, close contact with their families (Fingerman, Miller, & Seidel, 2009; Shanas, 1979). Because of the close interrelatedness of older adults with their later-life families, we believe it is important to consider ways in which to support positive mental health of older persons by supporting family functioning, and also to explore the possibility that family dysfunction might deleteriously affect the mental health of older family members. The systems model for examining family relationships is a useful guide in those two endeavors, and will be described below. Before examining the conceptual model, however, a brief description of later-life families may help dispel a few other myths regarding relationships between older adults and their families. The following two family situations will be used to illustrate points throughout the discussion.

Jason Martinez, age 21, lives with Ruth and James Jones, his grandmother and her second husband in the San Francisco Bay area. Jason's parents live by a rule that all of their children must move out on their own at age 18. Jason found it difficult to earn enough money to maintain an apartment, a car, and have a social life. After two failed roommate arrangements, he asked Ruth and James if he could live in their basement for a few months until he could get back on his feet. They agreed readily, hoping to be of some help to a grandson they viewed as floundering. Ruth and James have a long-standing conflict with Jason's parents, Nancy and Reuben, over what Ruth views as "mean rules that don't help the kids grow up." Although the entire family typically gathers for the major holidays, no one has initiated a gathering since Jason moved in with Ruth and James, a loss that

Aging and Mental Health, 2e. Daniel L. Segal, Sara Honn Qualls, and Michael A. Smyer
© 2011 Daniel L. Segal, Sara Honn Qualls, and Michael A. Smyer

Ruth mourns but accepts because she believes they are just doing "what they have to do, and if Nancy can't understand that then it's her loss."

Jillian Jarvis insists vehemently that she will never leave the family farm in rural Nebraska. Last month when her daughter, Jean, came to visit from Chicago, she was appalled to see the unkempt house, lack of food in the refrigerator, and Jillian's obvious dishevelment. Jean immediately drove her mother to a major medical center in a nearby city for a full evaluation. The initial evaluation showed that Jillian was malnourished, had significant bruising on several parts of her body, and that her vision and hearing were significantly impaired. Despite Jillian's protests, Jean made arrangements to place her mother in a nursing home in the city. Before the hospital social worker could accomplish the placement, John and JoAnn, Jean's brother and sister, arrived on the scene and insisted on taking Jillian back home "where she wants to be and where she belongs." They angrily demanded that the social worker produce evidence of their mother's incompetence "before she just goes and puts her away for all time." Jillian kept wringing her hands and saying she was sure that if Ed were only alive he would know what to do to keep the kids from fighting. The physician and social worker decided to hold Jillian in the hospital two more days to try to resolve the family disagreement, despite the fact that insurance was no longer paying for the hospital care.

Introduction to the Model: Aging Families

When you think of family, what do you picture? Do you picture children with parents whose task it is to rear them? Do you picture aunts, uncles, grandparents, and cousins? Family theorists traditionally have referred to the first kind of family as a *nuclear family* and the second set of relationships as *extended family* (Parsons, 1949). The implication is that the nuclear family is more important to individual development than is the extended family. Theory and data, however, suggest that the extended family is intimately involved with daily life functions of persons of all ages (Antonucci & Akiyama, 1995). Grandparents rear grandchildren with increasing frequency. Sibling relationships are powerful relationships in adulthood just as they are in childhood. Parenting does not end when children go off to college or even when they create their own nuclear families. In essence, a model of family development, like models of individual development, cannot presume development ends when children enter adulthood. Family development is truly a life-cycle phenomenon. Thus, the primacy of nuclear family relationships should not be presumed.

Marriage is an obvious form of daily family contact experienced by most older men (72 percent) and some older women (42 percent) over the age of 65 (US Bureau of the Census, 2007). Although over half (50 percent) of older adults are married, the rates decrease with advanced age, resulting in much lower rates of marriage for older women in particular (14.5 percent of women over age 85 are married compared with 56.5 percent of men). Generally, older persons report high rates of satisfaction with their later-life marriages (Gilford & Bengtson, 1979; Levenson, Carstensen, & Gottman, 1993), a phenomenon that appears to be at least partially a function of the tendency of the current older adult cohort to prize marital longevity, commitment, and contentment.

Contact with children occurs regularly for the vast majority of older persons. In contrast to the myth that our mobile society has limited face-to-face contact between adults and their aging parents, several studies report that even among very old (85+) adults, the vast majority maintained weekly face-to-face contact with at least one child and very high rates of telephone/letter/gift contact with children (Troll & Bengtson, 1993). Even those living far away are involved in older persons' lives through contacts, photographs, and memories.

Sibling relationships are also highly valued by older adults despite the generally weaker ties of obligation than parent–child relationships (Bedford, 1995). The sibling relationship evolves across the life span with lower rates of contact and investment in early adulthood that increase into old age. Siblings are not often the primary care providers, but maintain ties of mutual assistance and emotional connection that gain in meaning and salience across the life span.

Most older adults are grandparents (over 75 percent) and many are great-grandparents (50 percent) (Shanas, 1980). Grandparents are known to be involved in the socialization of younger family members, the exchange of goods and services within families, and to assist their children in times of crisis (e.g., divorce, serious physical illness) (Robertson, 1995). The meaning of the grandparent role varies, however. Kivnick (1985) describes five dimensions of meaning that mid-life and older adults may derive from the role: role centrality, valued eldership, immortality through clan, reinvolvement with personal past, and indulgence. As with other family relationships, the timing and sequencing of grandparenting within the life course of the specific older person will shape the role definition and meaning.

Other family ties certainly exist as well, but much less is known about them. Nieces and nephews, cousins, in-laws, and the variety of blended relationships that occur as a consequence of divorce and remarriage also are part of the relationship network of older adults. The structures of families vary across racial and ethnic groups, partnership structures (gay and straight), rural and urban, and social class. The size of families, the age at marriage or partnership, and patterns of divorce and remarriage are among the many family characteristics that are shaped by cultural identity and socialization.

What do people do in these relationships? A popular image is that of a frail older person being cared for by children and grandchildren. And this image is accurate – caregiving and care receiving are important functions of families of all ages, including later-life families (Fingerman et al., 2009). Aging increases the probability that care recipients will be parents rather than children, but does not guarantee it. Older adults provide a significant amount of childcare services to their children, grandchildren, and great-grandchildren. They also give care to adult children who need assistance because of disability, injury, or illness. Typically, only in the very last years of the life span do aging individuals need assistance from family members.

Families serve a variety of functions other than providing care for frail or disabled persons (Fingerman et al., 2009). As is true at any age, family relationships support the development of family members in a myriad of ways. Families often celebrate individual developmental milestones, provide mutual support in periods of stress, and share decision-making. Families are also the context in which values are socialized, a sense of personal lineage is created, and the most powerful individual developmental tasks are accomplished (Hagestad, 1986). For example, family relationships are the context within which individuals struggle with the dialectics between autonomy and dependency, connectedness and separateness, and continuity and change (Bengtson & Kuypers, 1984).

Individual developmental tasks and the events of later life often affect other family members. Three later-life transitions usually force a restructuring of family relationships: (1) the emptying and re-emptying of the "nest"; (2) retirement; and (3) onset of chronic physical illness. Several key aspects of family relationships are affected by individual life transitions: time structure, roles, communication, power balance, and nurturance (Qualls, 1995a). Families are primary components of the "life event web" in which the ripple effects of major life changes are felt (Pruchno, Blow, & Smyer, 1984).

Despite the familiar normative patterns of family contact among generations across the life span, families often find themselves organized in complex new structures. Recent decades have witnessed profound changes in the structure of Western populations that also affect family functioning. Among the demographic changes that alter family life are increased life expectancy, declining fertility, increased participation of women in the work force, increased rates of divorce, and ethnic diversification (Kinsella, 1995). The separate and cumulative effects of these shifts alter the structure and functioning of families. For example, families are far more likely to contain three or more generations. Family members tend to spend far more years in each relationship (e.g., perhaps 80–90 years as a sister and 60–70 years as a mother), but have fewer sisters or aunts or cousins from which to choose models or special relationships (Hagestad, 1988).

In summary, families are an active, powerful interpersonal context for older adults. Family contact is frequent and meaningful. Like younger persons, older adults meet many basic social needs within the family context and thus are vulnerable to the rippling effects of major life events in the lives of many family members. Deaths, divorces, marriages, births, retirement, illness, injury, misfortune – all occur in the families of older persons and alter the ways in which older persons' needs are met.

Family Dynamics: A Systems Model

How do families interact to accomplish their tasks? What causes conflict? Distress? What family interactions might play a role in the development of mental disorders in older persons? What impact do mental disorders have on the families of older persons and on their efforts to provide care?

As applied to behavioral sciences, the systems model emphasizes the social context in which human beings live (Whitchurch & Constantine, 1993). Problems are conceptualized as residing in the social unit, rather than in the individual. Systems theory acknowledges that there are indeed organically based problems (e.g., Alzheimer's disease), but the problems are experienced as particularly distressing or problematic when the social unit cannot manage them effectively.

As a primary social unit, families are usually the focus of systems theorists' conceptualizations of mental health (Whitchurch & Constantine, 1993). The family of an older adult is highly likely to be an idiosyncratically defined extended family constellation. In other words, it is not perfectly obvious who is "the family" that is relevant to a systems analysis. Spouses, adult children, nieces and nephews, siblings, and neighbors may be among those who are involved in significant ways in the life of the older person seeking assistance. The systems model would suggest beginning with those whose regular contact is important to the daily functioning of the older person. Other key persons may be included later if their interaction patterns are demonstrated to be significant to the functioning of the unit (e.g., in Jillian Jarvis' family the hospital social worker found that she was not dealing with all of the relevant members of the system). In the case of institutionalized older adults, the social unit might include key staff (e.g., the nurse aides who tend to the resident regularly, the charge nurse, the social worker, and perhaps a dietitian or administrator, depending on the nature of the problem) plus relevant members of the family (Norris, 2009).

The system is considered to be a complex interactive unit whose members are directly and indirectly affected by each other continually. Each member of the unit is both actor and reactor. In traditional social science frameworks, cause and effect relationships are conceptualized as if they occur in linear sequences (e.g., A causes B; his remark made me angry). In contrast, systems theory argues that complex systems such as families are better conceptualized in terms of circular causality. Events are related through multiple interacting cycles in which it is arbitrary to identify one event as the cause and one as the consequence because if one interrupted the cycle at another moment, those same events might be conceptualized differently. For example, a common scenario in which one person's angry remark provokes an angry response might be interpreted by those using linear causality as a two-point sequence in which the first angry remark caused the second. Systems theorists would point out that there was some preceding event that provoked the first angry remark that is just as relevant to understanding the sequence as either of the two recorded remarks. So Person A's perception that Person B put him down might be another point in the chain that warrants attention. Person B's quiet leering look that preceded Person A's perception of the put-down might add further information. In other words, human interactions tend to consist of complex cycles of ongoing communication via behavior, expectations and beliefs about behavior, and reactions to behavior. Thus, in families, every person's behavior is believed to be related directly or indirectly to every other person in the system.

Given the importance of understanding the circular causal sequences in human interactions, behaviors are observed carefully for their communication function (Watzlawick, Beavin & Jackson, 1967). The vast majority of communication is accomplished nonverbally. In familiar social settings, an even greater percentage of communication occurs at the nonverbal level. Words are certainly used to communicate, but the context of the words creates the meaning of the communication. Actors make their living by learning the subtleties of communicating very different messages with the same text by altering tone of voice or body language. Relationship structures form an even more powerful context within which communication is structured.

Relationships are structured with specific power dimensions and hierarchical link-ages. A faculty member's casual inquiry to a student, "So, did you go partying last night?" may elicit a defensive response simply because the student hears the question within the context of his or her salient awareness of the power differential in their relationship. A peer asking the same question may elicit a long excited description of the events of the previous evening. In the first family described above, the parents of Jason Martinez (Nancy and Reuben) may be withdrawing from contact with Ruth and James because the parents perceive the invitation for Jason to live with his grand-parents as a direct insult. The previous relationship between Nancy and her mother and step-father is the context in which Jason's living arrangement will be interpreted by all parties involved.

Family relationship structures are similarly powerful factors influencing family interactions. Generational hierarchies are among the most prominent structures, but gender roles, favorite son and daughter designations, or family scapegoat roles will also set the context for interpreting all interactions. The term "rules" is used to articulate the typically unspoken observations of behavior patterns that not only describe, but usually prescribe behavior. For example, "One must never show anger" is a family rule that will constrain behavior of family members. The very presence of this rule prescribes masking attempts, and establishes a family member as a rebel or a problem if he or she expresses overtly his or her anger. A family with such a rule may very well label a child as behaviorally disturbed if he acts out anger, even if the behavior would be considered appropriate by society at large or by mental health professionals. This example suggests that the child's "problem" may actually be a family system problem. In Jason Martinez's family, the unspoken rule may be, "If you believe someone has insulted you, don't talk to that person."

Ironically, older family members who are identified as problems within a family may have invested considerable effort earlier in life enforcing family rules that they find unacceptable later in life. For example, an older person who decides to co-reside with a partner without marrying may find him- or herself experiencing outrage from adult children who were taught by this elderly parent that such behavior was immoral. Even behavior that is caused by a cognitive or dementing disorder can be particularly upsetting to family members if it goes against the family rules (e.g., angry, combative behavior; sexual behavior). Any older person whose behavior changes from previously established family norms is particularly likely to elicit strong emotional responses from other family members because the elder him- or herself had participated in generating or maintaining the very rules he or she is now breaking.

Boundaries are the rules that define who participates in what roles and which forms of participation are acceptable (Minuchin, 1974). The purpose of boundaries is to differentiate members within a family. For example, there are boundaries that define who makes financial decisions, who provides emotional support, and who disciplines children. Many systems theorists believe that the clearer the boundaries, the greater the probability that the family is healthy. However, family dysfunction may occur with boundaries that are too rigid as well as too diffuse. Therapists refer to families with extremely rigid boundaries as *disengaged* (the boundaries keep them from being flexible in roles when adaptation is needed) and to families with diffuse boundaries as *enmeshed* (everyone engages in all possible roles). Most families are believed to fall somewhere between these polarities. Formal measurement tools are available to assess these characteristics (e.g., Olson, 1996), but clinicians commonly apply this framework from clinical observations.

Later-life families seldom share the same immediate household membership or residents as is characteristic of childrearing nuclear families, but can nonetheless be conceptualized as functioning systems whose interaction patterns are governed by rules. Interactions consist of verbal and nonverbal behaviors that occur in repeating cycles. For example, when a decision must be made about the housing and medical care of Grandma, her oldest daughter and son-in-law typically decide what they believe is best and then call her other two children to get their approval. The rule in this case could be stated, "oldest daughter and son-in-law decide what is best, and inform other siblings who are expected to approve." If a brother were to disapprove, he might be labeled a troublemaker. Or, if the oldest daughter and son-in-law were to be gone on vacation when a crisis in care occurred, the family might be confused about how to proceed because the familiar rule could not be enacted. Think back to the conflict among Jillian Jarvis' children over how to decide about her care. The siblings probably have not ever had to negotiate explicitly their rules about how to make decisions about their mother. Neither has Jillian had experience letting her children decide, so her fantasy is to go back to the original nuclear structure in which her husband Ed ruled over all of them.

Each member of the system carries a set of beliefs about what the rules are, why they are structured in that way, and what would be the consequences of breaking them. Attributions for the rules may be based on the personality of the persons involved (e.g., "she has to keep control over Grandma," or "he won't help so I don't bother asking"). Such personality-based attributions are focused on traits that appear to be unalterable and are likely not to generate task-focused problem-solving efforts. Indeed, many family difficulties arise from failed attempts to solve problems (Herr & Weakland, 1979). Personality-based attributions for family rules may generate attempts to change the personality of a person, an effort that is likely to be resisted by the target of the change efforts. Jillian Jarvis' children are possibly locked in a personality-attribution model that undermines their ability to cooperate to address the task at hand effectively.

Members of systems can generate many more solution alternatives when they work from behavioral descriptions of the behavior sequences (e.g., "when a problem arises in Grandma's care I decide what to do, arrange for it, and then place telephone calls to my three siblings in which I describe what has been done; I do not expect or solicit any input and am surprised and insulted if my siblings want to participate in the decision with any communication except statements of approval"). Behavior descriptions offer multiple points for intervention and usually make it evident that a variety of interventions initiated by any one person in the sequence would alter its pattern and outcome.

The hospital social worker in the Jarvis case will need to help the adult children define the task at hand behaviorally. Rather than framing the question as, "Does Jean have a right to place her mother in a nursing home?," the family needs to work to meet Jillian's needs. Instead of focusing on the differences between the personalities of Jean, whose style is to "get the job done," and John, whose style is to "consider every option before acting," the siblings need to focus on the task. First, they need information. Exactly which of Jillian's capabilities are compromised? Which housing options are congruent with her level of functioning? The children's values and preferences about their mother's housing can be examined in the context of which options best serve her needs. Likely, all of the children want her to be safe and well cared for, yet as autonomous as possible. The task they need to accomplish is to identify the set of options that meet those values.

Family members are often bound to one another in particular kinds of ties that shape the dynamics of the family. Three kinds of relational ties that are often tracked in family systems are alliances, triangles, and coalitions. *Alliances* involve two persons who share a common interest not shared by a third person. In other words, two persons ally together "against" another. *Triangles* describe the relationship that occurs when two persons manage conflict by funneling it through a third person. The classic paradigm for triangles in childrearing families shows a child with behavior problems (the "identified patient") who is triangulated between parents experiencing serious marital unhappiness or conflict. In aging families the structure of the triangle is more variable (i.e., it is less likely to involve a married couple triangulating a child in their conflict). A prototypical scenario might involve two siblings with a long-standing conflicted relationship who enact their conflict by taking incompatible approaches to caring for a parent. The parent's care becomes a huge problem that deflects focus from the underlying sibling conflict, as appears to be the case in the Jarvis family. Many other family structures also can triangulate. A mother and daughter conflict can be deflected by their mutual concern over the father. In other words, triangles can cross generational lines and sibling, parent, cousin, aunt/uncle, grandparent structures in diverse ways. Nancy and Reuben Martinez likely experience Jason's move into Nancy's mother and step-father's home as indicative of a coalition being formed against them. In this case, Jason is triangulated between two couples – his parents and his grandparents.

Mental Health Within a Systems Model

Systems that meet members' needs are considered functional and those that inhibit one or some members from meeting needs are considered problematic. Mental health, therefore, is not conceptualized as an individual-level construct. An older adult whose self-care capacity, social needs, or self-esteem needs are not met would not be labeled "mentally ill." Rather, the systems model would argue it is more appropriate to examine the interpersonal context that elicits or supports this behavior. The specific interpersonal system relevant to an individual older person's problem would be examined to identify the circular causal loops that maintain the problematic behavior.

The current interpersonal interactions that are maintaining the problem behavior are the most important behavior sequences to track. Finding the historical cause of the behavior may help the members of the system understand how the circular loop evolved, but the immediate interpersonal interactions are far more important. Herr and Weakland (1979) point out that a family system's first attempts to solve a problem are often unsuccessful, yet the same strategy may be maintained over time because the family cannot identify an alternative approach. The failed solution is likely to create another behavior problem (often the one for which help is sought) as a consequence of the ongoing failure experience. Thus, failed solutions are often functioning to maintain the current problem.

Systems with poorly functioning structures will encounter difficulties meeting members' needs throughout the life span, including later life. Families that are enmeshed or have poor boundaries around decision-making units (e.g., a marriage) are likely to encounter difficulty adjusting to the normative as well as the non-normative life events. The structures themselves inhibit flexibility needed to adapt well or to communicate clearly about changing needs and preferences.

Even well-functioning families may be challenged by particular events if they lack knowledge about how to meet members' needs or choose a poor strategy for adapting. For example, families with a demented member need a basic understanding of the impact of the disease on the patient and family in order to make appropriate care decisions and to support caregivers adequately. Families who functioned well through previous life events but who lack knowledge of dementia may solve problems ineffectively, and may even become stuck in a failed solution that harms one or more family members. The underlying structure may be functioning well except in one problem area. As such, a limited psychoeducational intervention may be sufficient to solve the problem. Assume for the moment that Jillian Jarvis has a vascular dementia that renders her too confused to eat properly and unsteady in gait so she falls often. Jean's decision to place her in a nursing home may be appropriate. John and JoAnn may lack information about the diagnosis or nature of the cognitive disorder, and are primarily concerned to protect their mother's autonomy. A family meeting in which the cause and nature of the disorder are carefully described may be sufficient to engage the three children in shared problem-solving.

Some families bring to later life a long history of poor adaptation with poorly functioning family structures. Even an adequate knowledge base regarding dementia care is unlikely to engage the family in a collaborative caregiving experience. If John and JoAnn have long-term unresolved conflicts with Jean that lead them to ally against her on any issue, then a common information base about their mother's needs may be only the first of several steps needed to resolve the family conflict that threatens Jillian's care.

Assessment

Assessment may be conducted with only one family member, or with many, depending upon who seeks services. Clinicians may only have the opportunity to work with the primary caregiver of an older adult or may ask that person to bring in other family members whose roles are important to the focus of concern. The care recipient may or may not participate in a family assessment or intervention. In cases of cognitive impairment that interferes with the person's ability to recognize the range or impact of cognitive deficits on daily functioning, participation in the room may be very limited. In other cases, the older adult is a key participant. Clinicians become skilled

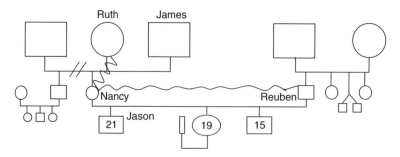

Figure 6.1   Genogram depicting Jason Martinez's family.

at deriving a relatively objective view of family functioning from careful interviews of individual family members using strategies described below. In cases of family conflict, however, engagement of multiple members in the therapy room or even through email interchanges provides important clinical insight into the sequences of interaction.

What should be assessed? The answer to that question depends on the nature of the problem, of course. There are a few general categories of information a mental health worker would want to know if doing a family systems intervention.

Family structure

A graphic depiction of family structure, called a genogram, is a very useful way of organizing efficiently information about several generations of family members (McGoldrick, Gerson, & Petrie, 2008). Figure 6.1 shows an example of Jason Martinez's family.

In addition to depicting the membership of the family according to generational lineage, a genogram can include information about the alliances, bonds, and conflicts in the family. The relationship between Jason and his grandmother is very strong, but his relationship with his mother and father is highly conflicted. The mild conflict between Nancy and Ruth in the past is blossoming into major warfare as they react to Jason's efforts to leave home.

Family development

Another way to describe families is in terms of their stage in the family life cycle. A model of the family life cycle in shown in Figure 6.2 (Rodgers & White, 1993). Although not universal, the stages as sequenced in this figure illustrate a common pattern of family development stages. The stages are marked by the entry and exit of members from the nuclear family. Obviously, the stage can only be labeled relative to one particular member. That is, a 50-year-old woman is perhaps in the "Launching" stage while her daughter is establishing her family and her mother is in the final stage. Obviously, the life cycle is not a simple linear or even a simple circular sequence. Many complications in family development shape the life cycle of a given family.

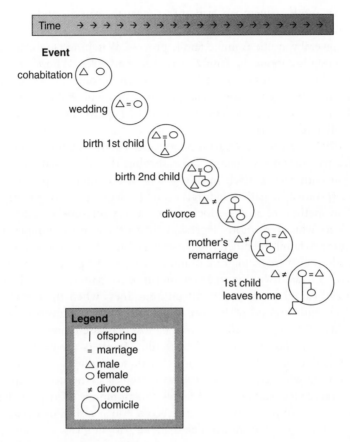

Figure 6.2 Family stages and events.
Source: Adapted from Rodgers and White (1993).

Divorce, chronic illness, death of a child, and job loss are just a few of the life experiences that might alter the sequencing or meaning of various life stages (Carter & McGoldrick, 1988).

Mental health professionals can use the knowledge of each member's stage to identify ways in which the life tasks of various family members may be interfering with each other. For example, a young adult who is attempting to establish autonomy and independence may resist the desires of her grandmother to knit the family more closely. The family life cycle is a method of identifying the developmental tasks appropriate to each family member that will inevitably affect the family's style of functioning.

Family functioning

Systems approaches want to understand how a family meets members' needs. The structure of the family often becomes apparent by examining closely the patterns of interaction that result as members attempt to meet their needs and accomplish their developmental tasks.

There are several ways to examine family process. Watching family members interact verbally tells a lot about the family's structure and roles. Whose words are heard by everyone? Who expresses emotions? What happens if someone contradicts a family member in a different generation? Who gets the final word? Who is blamed or left out? The bonds, alliances, and conflicts described above become evident as one observes family interactions.

Shields (1992) observed interactions between family members and a depressed caregiver to a patient with Alzheimer's disease while they discussed a salient issue the family was currently facing. Each small segment of the interaction was given a code for emotion (positive, negative, neutral), and the sequencing of the segments was analyzed. This method of analysis documented a very interesting pattern of interaction. Caregivers who were more depressed than others in the sample were highly likely to respond to family members' negative emotion-laden comments with empathy. In other words, they were taking care of more than just the patient. Caregiver depression was also correlated with another counterintuitive pattern. "Family members of more depressed caregivers respond with more sadness when the caregivers express negative affect, and respond with more anger when the caregivers express positive affect" (Shields, 1992, pp. 25–26). When the most depressed caregivers in the sample are able to generate positive affect, their family members are likely to respond to them with anger! Obviously, the dynamics in these families are far more complex than is often acknowledged when we think of families as sources of support.

Another strategy for learning about family functioning is to identify the sequence of behaviors that family members use to accomplish a task. For example, when a physician calls a caregiver to inform her that the patient's lab tests show some disturbing information, what does that caregiver do? Whom does she call? Does everyone get the same amount of information? Who is involved in decisions? How do family members respond to the caregiver's distress? Which behaviors are experienced as supportive or interfering? Do those match the actor's intention? Herr and Weakland (1979, pp. 103–112) describe a case that illustrates the ways in which behavior that is intended to be supportive may actually reinforce dependency. They describe a mid-life woman caring for her father in the home she shares with a husband and two boys. The father has become excessively dependent on the family to do tasks he could do for himself if he would. She has tried several strategies to encourage him to perform activities on his own (e.g., pleading, cajoling, demanding). When the family therapist began to elicit a detailed picture of the sequence of behavior interactions, it became evident that the daughter's behaviors were reinforcing her father's dependent demands. Her threats that she would not serve him were always met with efforts by her father to prove he needed help, to which she responded by "giving in" because it seemed cruel to let him suffer. Only by very carefully eliciting a detailed picture of behavior sequences could the clinician identify this pattern. This analysis is similar to that generated by a behaviorist because her "giving in" behavior is viewed as reinforcement in both models. However, a systems analysis emphasizes the reciprocal patterns of reinforcement rather than viewing the interaction as a linear Antecedent-Behavior-Consequence sequence that relates solely to the father's behavior.

A systems assessment also needs to examine outcomes of family activity: Are members' needs being met and are developmental tasks being accomplished? Families have a myriad of ways of structuring themselves to accomplish the task of supporting members' development. Thus, the methods of accomplishing tasks are primarily relevant to examine when some members' needs are not being met. For example, a family may be able to meet the needs of young children, but be unable to support the needs of adolescents to launch themselves. Or in later life, a family may adjust beautifully to the "empty nest," but may be unable to adapt to the severe illness of an aging family member whose dependency needs exceed the children's skill or expectations. This functional deficit may become apparent through one member of the family whose behavior is problematic; this person is generally known as the *identified patient* (IP). The IP's abnormal functioning simply signals that the family is unable to meet all members' needs (rather than signaling some form of psychopathology in the IP), and thus a thorough assessment of the family would be useful.

Family history

Two aspects of family history may become relevant: How previous generations dealt with aging-related challenges, and how this particular family constellation adapted to previous life transitions. Systems theorists emphasize the importance of intergenerational transmission of family rules, values, interaction patterns, and even anxiety (Boszormenyi-Nagy & Spark, 1984; Bowen, 1978). A current systems problem may become simpler to solve when compared with the ways in which previous generations managed similar developmental tasks. Given that previous generations were less likely to live until advanced old age, many families are struggling to manage current problems without the benefit of the experience of previous generations. Idealized images may be serving as a proxy for real family experiences with some of the particular challenges and events of old age. On the other hand, families with clear rules for handling aging-related problems may find that those rules do not work well when applied to the needs of a particular aging relative in a particular context.

Although families may experience aging-related challenges to be novel and unfamiliar, in many cases the family's strategies for adapting to previous life events will apply directly to the current difficulties. Families who successfully managed previous family transitions often have resources and strategies for interacting that would be useful to the current dilemma if they are reminded of their previous successes.

Intervention

When working with families, the first task for any professional is to join the family. Professional helpers are obviously not members of the family, so joining the family is in itself an intervention. A common role families create for professional helpers is the "expert consultant." The consultant is expected to know something about aging and the adaptations required of families, and is expected to support the family as it adapts. Creating this role requires the family to acknowledge formally that there is a problem and also to open themselves somewhat to education. The process of joining and assessing the family is often an intervention itself, so the intervention process cannot be readily differentiated from assessment.

Systems models distinguish between interventions that are targeted at first-order change and those targeted at second-order change (Watzlawick, Weakland, & Fisch, 1974). *First-order change* is that which modifies behavior patterns without altering substantially the basic structures and functioning patterns of the family. *Second-order change* alters structures to create a new kind of system. Generally, the principle used by mental health professionals is to begin with interventions targeted at first-order change to see if they are sufficient to solve the problem, and proceed to second-order interventions only if the less intrusive interventions did not work.

Later-life families are often dealing with new challenges they simply do not understand. A common first-order intervention is education about the challenge (e.g., an illness, retirement, grief) and about the resources available to assist the family's adaptation and coping. Functionally, education about the problem takes the focus off of the IP and onto the underlying problem. Education usually includes not only information about the life event or developmental task, but also about the importance of obtaining support, and the resources available in the community for assisting the family.

Second-order change efforts are explicitly targeted at altering the family's structure and familiar ways of functioning. One strategy commonly used is to reorganize the smaller units of the family system that are responsible for particular roles in the family. For example, a family therapist might direct the family to reorganize its decision-making structure if the current structure cannot function well. Or a therapist might encourage the family to break rules that make it taboo for adult children to tell a parent directly when they do not want to discuss a matter in a case where a widowed woman and her daughter appear to be engaging in constant conflicts primarily because they do not have any other ways of maintaining appropriate separateness.

Another strategy for accomplishing second-order change is to alter the interaction patterns. Therapists may ask family members to alter where they sit in the therapy room in order to force an immediate restructuring of an alliance. Therapists also may direct the sequencing of an interaction, interrupting familiar and nonproductive patterns to allow new interaction patterns to form. In essence, systemic factors can create the stress experienced by later-life families, including caregiving family members, and interventions that address family structures can be helpful (Mitrani et al., 2006).

One case that illustrates these principles is that of a 66-year-old woman who brought her 68-year-old husband and 42-year-old daughter to see a family therapist. The therapist immediately recognized a father–daughter alliance against the mother. An obvious enactment of the alliance against the mother was evident in the very way the three members chose their chairs when they walked into the therapist's office: The father and daughter sat next to each other on the couch, leaving the mother the chair across the room next to the therapist. As the family explained to the therapist their reasons for coming, the mother suggested that she was worried about her daughter who seems to lack initiative. The father interrupted her with "That's crazy!" and immediately contradicted his wife by naming all of the activities the daughter did this week. The daughter sat silently, leaning against her father as if for support.

The father and daughter were allied in their shared view that the daughter's inability to live independently is not a problem. However, the father–daughter alliance is interfering with the intimacy of the father and the mother in their marriage (a structure problem), and impeding the daughter from launching into independent adulthood (a developmental problem). Asking father and mother to move their chairs close to one another and hold hands while discussing their perceptions of their daughter's strengths might force recognition of the marital bond that would be ignored if father and daughter were allowed to enact their alliance.

Once the bond is made salient, the parents' discussion of their concerns about their daughter is much more likely to be productive. The therapist might alter the interaction sequences by creating first a conversation between the mother and the father that the daughter is not allowed to enter, then setting up a conversation between mother and daughter that father is not allowed to enter. If the father's typical role is to deny the problem or run interference for the daughter, then the mother and the daughter will each feel anxious about interacting in a more direct and vulnerable way. This anxiety creates the opportunity for a new pattern of interaction to form, one that is more likely to handle directly the developmental tasks at hand. Families will attempt to maintain homeostasis, so therapists must engage actively and creatively with the family to create second-order change in the family structures (Qualls & Noecker, 2009).

Other approaches to work with aging families focus more at the level of family values, obligations, and balances in reciprocity (Hargrave & Anderson, 1992). Families pass across generations not only values statements about how it "should" be done (that may or may not be relevant to current social and familial conditions), but also pass along rules and obligations from the families' unique history and lineage (Boszormenyi-Nagy & Spark, 1984). Family conflict over parent care may be rooted in conflicted values or the sense of being trapped to fulfill obligations. Dialogue to increase awareness of the unspoken forces shaping the family members' interactions with each other is another intervention strategy.

The majority of published research on interventions with aging families has been conducted with one family member, the primary caregiver, for the purpose of assisting him or her care for another, ill elderly family member (Zarit, 2009). Researchers have now identified which interventions show the strongest effects (Gallagher-Thompson & Coon, 2007; Pinquart & Sörensen, 2006).

The majority of interventions focus on first-order interventions such as education, support, and problem-solving about specific illness-generated difficulties, yet growing evidence shows that systems analysis and intervention are helpful. Scharlach (1987) involved daughters who served as primary care providers to elderly mothers in one of two intervention conditions. Part of the sample was given information about caregiving and about community resources while encouraging the daughters to focus on meeting their mothers' needs for assistance. The other intervention group involved daughters in modifying unrealistic expectations of responsibility to their aging mothers, and encouraged them to promote self-reliance in their mothers while enhancing their own well-being. Daughters in the second group reported less burden and better relationship quality while their mothers reported less loneliness than the first group (or a control group). Although only the daughters were involved in this intervention, this study could be interpreted as an intervention to teach daughters to set boundaries and take on different roles, thus altering family structure.

Flexible family interventions use a variety of intervention strategies and whichever family members can be most helpful in creating the necessary change. Mittelman and colleagues, who have conducted the longest-running family intervention in which they offer a combination of individual and family counseling to primary caregivers of demented relatives, delayed nursing home placement with their family intervention (Mittelman, Ferris, Shulman, Steinberg, & Levin, 1996). When compared with caregivers who received only support group interventions, the families receiving ongoing counseling reported more involvement from the family network in support of patient and caregiver, increased caregiver satisfaction with the support network, as well as delayed rate of institutionalization. Furthermore, the family intervention had beneficial effects even when placement ultimately had to occur (Gaugler, Roth, Haley, & Mittelman, 2008).

Even technologies show potential to impact family functioning and well-being. Eisdorfer and colleagues (2003) found significant benefits to primary caregivers of persons with dementia from placing a conference-type telephone in the home. Other technologies are also used to help families remain supportive of one another, congruent in their approaches to care, and, quite simply, connected (Blechman, 2009; Williams & Lewis, 2009).

Unfortunately, the research base demonstrating the utility of the systems model with later-life families is limited. However, preliminary results of clinical cases (e.g., Gallagher & Frankel, 1980), clinical analysis (Qualls & Noecker, 2009; Shields, King & Wynne, 1995), descriptive research (e.g., Shields, 1992), and outcome research (e.g., Gaugler et al., 2008; Mittelman et al., 1996) are promising. The need for both more theoretical and more empirical research is apparent, but the value of a model for mental health and aging that explicitly incorporates families as a system is also clear.

Summary and Conclusions

The mental well-being of older adults is often heavily influenced by characteristics of their families. Family systems theory offers a rich framework for examining the interpersonal environment of the family. The family systems model explains how the interpersonal context influences observable behavior as well as subjective well-being. Interventions with the family system can improve the well-being of older adults as well as their family members. Interventions can focus on family structures, processes, and dynamics that are as relevant in later life as during childrearing years.

Part II

Summary and Commentary
Choosing Among Models of Mental Disorders in Later Life

In this section we have described several different models of mental health and mental disorder. Before we consider the treatment of specific disorders in more detail in Part III, it may be useful to consider a simple question: How do you choose among the various models?

Let's begin to answer this question by reflecting on what we want from a model of mental health or mental disorder. Remember, a model is a representation, something like a map that draws our attention to certain aspects of the terrain while allowing us to find our way. Similarly, models cannot fully represent the complexity of an older adult's life situation. Instead, they focus our attention on the most salient elements of the older adult and his or her environment. In doing so, all models provide answers to several basic questions (see Table S1.1). Each model emphasizes certain elements for understanding mental health. By focusing our attention on certain aspects of the individual's functioning, the model explicitly and implicitly asserts that other elements are less important.

Similarly, the model's explanation of what changes in mental disorders and in aging implicitly alerts us to the potential targets of therapeutic intervention. For example, in psychodynamic perspectives, the focus of attention is personality structures. As outlined in Chapter 3, structural change is often viewed as a desirable therapeutic goal, but often beyond the capacity of either the therapist or the client.

Models also differ in the *type* of change they predict for the older adult: quantitative (different in degree) or qualitative (different in kind). For example, the cognitive-behavioral models focus on differences in quantity of behaviors, behavioral excesses, or deficits. In contrast, systems perspectives focus on differences both in quantity and in quality of interactions among the system's components.

Finally, the models also differ in how they explain change. This set of assumptions provides the clearest set of suggestions for therapeutic intervention. For example, the cognitive-behavioral perspectives emphasize the chain of antecedents and

Aging and Mental Health, 2e. Daniel L. Segal, Sara Honn Qualls, and Michael A. Smyer
© 2011 Daniel L. Segal, Sara Honn Qualls, and Michael A. Smyer

Table S1.1   Choosing among models

Model elements	Psychodynamic	Cognitive-behavioral	Stress and coping	Family systems
• What is studied?	• Motivation and personality	• Thought patterns and overt behaviors	• Strain, stressor, and interactions	• Interactions among elements of the system
• What changes with age or with mental disorder?	• Personality structure	• Cognitive and behavior patterns	• Individual adaptability or stressors or the interaction	• Developmental tasks and systems interactions
• What kind of change occurs?	• Qualitative change	• Quantitative change (behaviors) and qualitative change (cognitions)	• Qualitative and quantitative change	• Qualitative and quantitative change
• How is change explained?	• Structure/ functional relationships	• Changes in thought patterns combined with changes in reinforcement patterns	• Interaction of the person and the environment	• Interaction among the elements of the system

consequences that develop and maintain specific behavior patterns. To alter behavior requires changing this chain by affecting either the antecedents or the consequences of behavior. Similarly, theorists from the stress and coping model assess the interaction of the individual's coping repertoire (including, perhaps, the immune system's stress reactivity) and the stressors that confront him or her.

Applying Models to Individual Life Circumstances

With this understanding of models and their underlying assumptions, let's return to the cause that opened Part II, that of Mrs. Rankin.

> Joan Rankin is a 74-year-old woman who lives in her home in a small rural community. Her husband, Jim, died two years ago, following a five-year bout with cancer. Now that she is alone, Joan is tempted to move closer to her children, but cannot quite make up her mind. Her house is paid for, and she is not sure she could buy a comparable house in a city with the proceeds from a sale of this house. She has a modest pension that will be sufficient unless she needs major medical care. Sometimes she worries about not having enough money to carry her through. She chooses to live frugally with an occasional indulgence.

Joan belongs to the local garden club, but is not a particularly active member. She does enjoy working in her own small flower garden during the nice weather seasons. She also attends church almost weekly. Joan has a few close friends, but many of those friendships were strained by the period of Jim's illness. Even two years after his death, she is not sure how to fill her days. Her nights are usually tolerable although sometimes she lies awake for long periods in the middle of the night. At those times she feels overwhelmingly alone and scared.

Joan is generally healthy, although she has high blood pressure and some difficulties with thyroid and arthritis. She takes Tylenol for the arthritis, propanolol for blood pressure, and synthroid to regulate her thyroid.

Joan's two children live 300 miles away in major cities. Her daughter, Jeannie, is married, has three children (ages 4, 7, and 10), and teaches school. Her son, John, a very successful realtor, is currently engaged to be remarried. He was divorced four years ago from his wife of 18 years, who has custody of their two children, ages 8 and 13. Jeannie and John have never been very close. Nor was John close to his father, although he confided his troubles and joys to his mother privately.

Joan has two younger sisters still living, and two older brothers who died more than five years ago. Her sister Betty lives only two blocks away from Joan, and calls her daily. Sometimes Joan even resents the call because Betty is so perky and enthusiastic about life. Betty insists that Joan get out to social events regardless of how tired or sick Joan is feeling. Betty has always been the cheerful one, encouraging all those around her to enjoy life. Recently she has hinted that she might like to move in with Joan to share expenses.

Her other sister Vivian lives with her husband 30 miles away on a farm. They stay busy with farm responsibilities, and with their children and grandchildren. Joan sees them only at family gatherings on holidays. Vivian has always been the quiet, solid one in the family. Joan would like to spend more time with her, but can see that she is too busy with daily responsibilities to socialize.

Her brothers, Elwood and Milt, were in business together in a city 150 miles from Joan's home. They died of heart attacks exactly one year apart. They left their families quite well off financially, and their children and grandchildren have continued their business. Joan only visits with her sisters-in-law or their offspring at the annual family reunion each summer.

How would each model approach Mrs. Rankin's life situation?

As outlined in Chapter 3, the psychodynamic perspective assumes that Mrs. Rankin's symptoms will resolve if she comes to terms with the normal developmental tasks of later life. Erikson and his colleagues, for example, argue that the primary conflict to be resolved in later life is between ego integrity versus despair (Erikson, Erikson, & Kivnick, 1986). Clearly, Mrs. Rankin has spent much time and energy in the earlier developmental conflict (generativity vs. self-absorption), providing care for her ailing husband. Within this perspective, much attention would initially focus on her beliefs and values and the meaning that she attributes to her life, the coherence of the personal narrative that she has developed in thinking about her life. A major goal of treatment within the dynamic perspective might be to provide supportive therapy for

Mrs. Rankin as she re-evaluates her experience in later life. In doing so, the therapist would begin with an assessment of her capacity for insight, her ability to reflect upon her experiences, and her aptitude for engaging in the therapeutic process.

In contrast, a cognitive-behaviorally oriented professional would not focus on the underlying structure of Mrs. Rankin's personality or the "coherence" of her personal narrative (see Chapter 4). Instead, someone working within the cognitive-behavioral perspective would focus on assessing specific thought patterns and problem behaviors, including the context for the development and continuation of those behaviors. In Mrs. Rankin's case, for example, the focus might fall on her periods of sleeplessness at night. Exactly when and under what conditions does this occur? Conversely, are there conditions under which the sleeplessness does not occur? The therapist might ask Mrs. Rankin to keep an activity log or a record of her sleep pattern and context for several days, trying to identify the pattern of antecedents and consequences that affect the sleep disruption. The cognitive-behavioral treatment would focus on altering the contingencies within Mrs. Rankin's context. First, it would be important to identify the desired outcome, which in this case is uninterrupted sleep. Next, attention would focus on one of two strategies: expanding the conditions that have led to a full night's sleep in the past or eliminating the conditions that are associated with the current bouts of sleeplessness. For example, if it were found that Mrs. Rankin slept better on the days that she had talked with one of her children, the therapist might enlist the children in a schedule of calls or contact. Similarly, if it were discovered that Mrs. Rankin had disrupted sleep on days that Betty called after 4 p.m., the therapist might work with Betty to change the schedule of her contacts. In addition, the therapist might also focus on Mrs. Rankin's own thoughts regarding being alone (i.e., her report of feeling "alone and scared"). To what extent does she have catastrophic or hopeless thoughts about the future? Specific negative thought patterns would be identified and she would be helped to replace them with more adaptive thought patterns.

A therapist working in the stress and coping framework might try a variety of strategies targeting several key aspects of Mrs. Rankin's experience: chronic strains, social resources, Mrs. Rankin's own vulnerabilities and resources, and her physical well-being (see Chapter 5). For example, the therapist might begin by targeting assessment and treatment for two chronic strains that are currently affecting Mrs. Rankin: her concerns about her financial well-being and her coping with her chronic health problems (e.g., arthritis, high blood pressure, and thyroid problems). Another target for assessment and treatment might be Mrs. Rankin's social resources. Here, the emphasis might shift to first assessing her current levels of social involvement and then enlisting effective social support for her. A third element of assessment and treatment might emphasize Mrs. Rankin's own approach to appraising her situation and the attributions she makes about her current life circumstances. Again, an initial step might be an assessment of her current and previous coping strategies. Treatment would then explore either application of previously successful coping attempts or development of new coping skills to fit her current life context. Finally, someone working within the stress and coping framework might focus on improving Mrs. Rankin's health practices, perhaps by focusing on a relaxation training or meditation program to decrease her anxiety.

A mental health professional working within a family systems perspective would emphasize other aspects of Mrs. Rankin's situation: her family's structure and function (see Chapter 6). For example, a therapist working within a systems perspective might start by asking Mrs. Rankin to complete a family genogram, including information about the alliances and bonds among various members of the family. Similarly, the therapist might be interested in the family stages represented by the various members (e.g., her daughter's children are all under 10; her son's children are also in the school age years, etc.). This information helps the therapist to be aware of other family members' developmental tasks that may be competing with Mrs. Rankin's own challenges. Another focus of assessment would be how this family works: To whom does Mrs. Rankin turn in times of crisis? Whom does she call first for everyday help? For major assistance? Whom does she avoid? Treatment within this framework might require both "first-order" and "second-order" change. At the very least, the mental health professional should be clear whether the goal is to change the behavior patterns of the family or to alter the basic structure of the family. Either goal might require the active involvement of several family members in the treatment process.

In summary, each of the therapeutic models offers directions for assessment and treatment. Each has explicit and implicit assumptions about the salient contributors to mental health and mental disorder in later life. Each focuses therapeutic attention and effort to specific aspects of Mrs. Rankin's life and circumstances.

If models differ substantially in their basic elements, how do we choose among them? Each of the four models presented in Part II is both precise and capable of explaining a wide scope of functioning in older adults. Each of the four models has also proven itself useful from clinical and research perspectives. The challenge for the practitioner working with older adults is to assess which perspective will be more helpful in understanding and intervening on behalf of a particular older client. Another important factor is which perspective most closely matches the values, beliefs, and personal style of the practitioner.

There are two different approaches that clinicians may follow: the single lens or the kaleidoscope. Some prefer to become an expert within a single framework, knowing its strengths and limitations in depth. For example, a practitioner may focus on dynamic approaches exclusively or cognitive-behavioral strategies exclusively. The clinician comes to learn the precision afforded by the theoretical and practical aspects of the framework in detail. He or she also comes to learn and respect the scope of clinical utility of the framework, respecting that it probably will not be adequate for all clients and all conditions.

Most clinicians, however, report that they are "eclectic," which means that they use techniques from a variety of perspectives. In contrast to someone who uses one framework exclusively, these clinicians may emphasize aspects of several different frameworks, as if turning the kaleidoscope to see different facets of the same scene.

In the end, the clinician must ask a differential diagnostic question: Which assessment and treatment approaches for which types of geriatric mental disorders will produce which types of outcomes? Answering this question will force you to detail the precision and scope of your implicit or explicit frameworks.

Part III

Introduction to Mental Disorders

Consider the following letter Dr. Smyer once received from a client:

Dear Dr Smyer:

I have toyed with the idea of writing you ever since I heard you speak at the Presbyterian Church a couple of years ago. The occasion was one of a series of brown-bag lunches sponsored, I think, by the Area Agency on Aging. You may remember me, since I'm sure you were embarrassed when I substituted one word for another in trying to ask a question about the part inheritance plays in senility. My question made no sense, and you tactfully said, "I don't believe I understand your question," and I repeated it, correctly, saying, "You can see I'm senile already." (I was trying to be funny, but I was not amused.)

The question I asked is one that has haunted me all my adult life (I've just turned 78), and I think I have always known the answer. My father's father, my father, and the three sisters who lived long enough were all senile. I am obviously following in their footsteps, and have discussed the matter with Dr Klein, who became my physician last year. I have told him that I have never taken much medication and have been opposed to "pain-killers," tranquilizers, etc., but that the day may come when I will accept medical help as the lesser of two evils. He assures me that there are new drugs which may help.

My question, Dr Smyer, is this: Since I'm sure there must be ongoing research into the problem of senility, would it be of any value to such research if I volunteered as a test subject? At this point my memory is failing so rapidly, and I suffer such frequent agonies of confusion, that I am at the point of calling on Dr Klein for the help he has promised. But I don't want to do so yet if my experience can be of value to someone else, and particularly to the nine daughters of my sisters, ranging in age from 58 to 70, and to my own daughter, 42, who must be wondering if they too are doomed.

Aging and Mental Health, 2e. Daniel L. Segal, Sara Honn Qualls, and Michael A. Smyer
© 2011 Daniel L. Segal, Sara Honn Qualls, and Michael A. Smyer

Is there any merit to this proposal? I will be most grateful for any advice you can give me.

Sincerely,

Mrs. Rose

How would you respond? Immediately, you have to make a clinical judgment about the seriousness of this older woman's concerns. Are her complaints a part of normal aging? Are they part of a pattern of significant mental disorder? How do you make sense of her use of the term *senile*, which is no longer used clinically? Your answer implicitly combines information from developmental epidemiology, psychiatric epidemiology, clinical investigations, and the psychology of adult development and aging. If you decide that Mrs. Rose has a severe mental disorder, what would you do? Your answer reflects your assumptions regarding the cause of the disorder and how effective you can be in altering that cause.

The chapters in Part III are designed to describe the patterns of specific mental disorders along with effective methods for assessment and treatment of the disorder. In preparing these chapters, we face the same dilemmas as clinicians: How do we know that specific symptoms are part of a picture of pathology? How can we identify specific treatments that are effective with older adults?

It is now apparent that the earlier models of psychology and psychiatry for describing patterns of disease, causation, and treatment were too simplistic. We would like to reduce the complexity of assessment and treatment to a simple focus on the individual, or perhaps even on one aspect of the individual (e.g., biological functioning). However, an effective understanding of mental disorders in later life requires an understanding of the ecology of interactions of several levels of influence, from the molecular to the molar, from genetic predispositions to the social environment, that either protect or exacerbate the individual's vulnerability.

A Summit was sponsored by the Institute of Medicine (IoM) in 2009 at which health care leaders explored the challenges, opportunities, and imperatives for shifting to an integrative care approach to health care. The report from that summit, *Integrative Medicine and the Health of the Public* (2009), calls for a broadening of the lens used by health care providers to encompass multiple domains of human lives. Rather than focusing on diseases, leaders called for patient-centered care that assessed the mental and behavioral health, environmental and social contexts, and beliefs and motivations as well as biomarkers and disease states. Fifteen years ago, the IoM developed a research agenda aimed at preventing mental disorders (Mrazek & Haggerty, 1994) by examining multiple points of possible intervention in a model that presaged the current call for integrative care. That IoM report on prevention suggested that we need to consider a new spectrum of mental health interventions for mental disorders. The spectrum includes three major classes of intervention: prevention, treatment, and maintenance. A central element in the scheme is the concept of risk for a disorder. Formerly, risk might be thought of as solely an individual characteristic, indentified by individual indicators (e.g., genetic history, age, sex, socioeconomic status). However, recent work in epidemiology and clinical investigation suggests that risk for developing a disorder is an interaction of several systems and levels of influence, including aspects of the individual's setting, the individual's own characteristics, and characteristics of the broader culture. The multiple sources of risk suggest multiple options for intervention as well.

Susser and Susser (1996) put it this way:

> Systems also relate to one another; they do not exist in isolation. A metaphor may serve to illuminate this ecological perspective. We liken it to Chinese boxes – a conjurer's nest of boxes, each containing a succession of smaller ones. Thus, within localized structures, we envisage successive levels of organization, each of which encompasses the next and simpler level, all with intimate links between them...
>
> ... The outer box might be the overarching physical environment which, in turn, contains societies and populations (the epidemiological terrain), single individuals, and individual physiological systems, tissues and cells, and finally (in biology) molecules. (pp. 675–676)

Gatz and her colleagues (1996) also stressed the interaction of three types of influences on the development and presentation of mental disorders among older adults: the individual's level of vulnerability, which is a product of biological vulnerabilities and psychological factors affecting risk; stress, both environmental and social; and protective factors that can serve as psychological, biological, or social buffers. They argue that the combination of protective and risk factors affects the individual's susceptibility of developing a mental disorder.

To be effective, then, the clinician must understand the context of the individual and the patterns of interaction among several levels of influence (Qualls, 2005). This multilayered ecological perspective will affect how symptoms are labeled, how clinical syndromes are defined, and, ultimately, case identification. It will also affect strategies that are developed for assessment and treatment.

For example, consider Mrs. Rose's complaint about memory problems. If we look solely at her individual situation, we may miss important information about the social stresses that may be presenting a challenge for her. Optimally, we would like to place her current functioning in a larger context: Does she have a history of memory problems and complaints? Does she have a family history of such problems? Has she been treated for these difficulties in the past? What is the context of this most recent complaint (e.g., changes in her own functioning, her social context, her physical well-being)? Have her medications changed recently? Have there been any recent physical illnesses? In short, we would be assessing the three key elements of the scheme proposed by Gatz et al. (1996): individual vulnerability, stresses, and protective factors.

At the same time, we focus on just two types of history: the history of the individual and the history of the disorder. Again, consider Mrs. Rose. We want to know much more about her personal history and about the history of her memory complaint. Epidemiologists focus on incidence and prevalence rates: patterns of development of new episodes and rates of overall presence of the disorder, regardless of when it began. On the clinical level, we might envision different treatment strategies for two different patterns: Some might grow old and get memory problems; others might develop memory problems and grow old (Kahn, 1975). These different life histories and different problem histories would suggest different approaches.

The chapters in Part III take the following elements as a starting point: an ecological perspective that acknowledges several layers of interacting influences that produce risk for the various mental disorders and the patterns of those disorders; individual life history and individual history of the specific mental disorder experienced by the person, both of which affect assessment and treatment of the disorder; and the necessity for an integrated approach to assessment and treatment of mental disorders that acknowledges individual vulnerability, assesses sources of stress, and builds upon current effective sources of social support. The chapters also emphasize effective case identification and treatment for the mental disorders. In doing so, they draw from the models of mental health and mental disorder described in Part II. The assessment and treatment approaches outlined in Part III embody causal models of each disorder and, therefore, assumptions regarding effective clinical approaches.

7

Cognitive Impairment

Cognitive impairment is a broad term indicating some degree of deterioration in cognitive function that alters daily functioning. Common causes of cognitive impairment (CI) in later life include delirium, dementia, and depression, although a myriad of other factors can also lead to reduced cognitive functioning. Because of its devastating effect on the autonomy of older adults, CI warrants aggressive assessment and interventions to support the maximum possible level of functioning. Anyone working with older adults must have some familiarity with the causes, consequences, and remedies for CI. This chapter addresses the extent to which cognitive decline is a part of normal aging, and describes impairments due to delirium, mild cognitive impairment, dementia, and depression. Strategies for assessing cognitive functioning and for designing interventions to enhance the functioning of cognitively impaired persons are also described. Consider the following three cases that describe some of the challenges faced by persons with CI.

Jane Winthrop is an 85-year-old widow who is experiencing increasing difficulty living alone. Her daughter visits every Saturday to write out bills, set up medications for this week in a pillbox, and take her shopping. Jane has trouble figuring out how much of her favorite foods to buy, and typically purchases prepared meals that can be heated in the microwave. Her daughter leaves reminder notes on the microwave about how to work it, and on the entry door to the apartment about what security measures should be taken before bedtime. On the bathroom mirror is a reminder to brush teeth, and on the kitchen table is a reminder to take medications after meals. Jane stays in her apartment most of the time because the hallways and elevator confuse her. Friends in the apartment complex check in on her daily.

Noni Smith's daughter was alarmed when she visited her mother last weekend. Within a week's time her mother had changed! She had a vacant look in her eyes,

Aging and Mental Health, 2e. Daniel L. Segal, Sara Honn Qualls, and Michael A. Smyer
© 2011 Daniel L. Segal, Sara Honn Qualls, and Michael A. Smyer

was not interested in talking, was dressed in mismatched clothing, and her hair was not combed. The neighbor shared the daughter's concern, indicating she had not seen Noni out walking this week as was her custom. The daughter called Noni's physician who asked to see her immediately to check whether the new medications he initiated two weeks ago could be causing the problem.

Jim Hunt complains constantly about his poor memory. He is so disturbed by his inability to concentrate and remember things that he has quit two of his favorite hobbies – woodworking and reading about politics. He no longer has the showcase yard of the neighborhood because he only seems able to do the minimum. His family is growing concerned that he may have Alzheimer's disease.

What Jane, Noni, and Jim share in common is a perceived or real loss of abilities to think, remember, solve problems, and handle the affairs of everyday life. Indeed, CI is one of the most feared aspects of aging. Although there are changes in cognitive functioning that are normative with old age, these rarely affect daily functioning. However, the expectation for normative cognitive decline can keep older people and those around them from seeking assessment. Family and friends often compensate for deficits in cognitive functioning by assisting with tasks, similarly to how they have done across the life span. Families and even professional staff often fail to recognize the extent of cognitive impairment (Knopman, Donohue, & Gutterman, 2000; Nichols & Martindale-Adams, 2006). The risks of CI are well documented in both hospitalized and community-dwelling older adults. For example, the risk of hospitalization and a longer length of stay in the hospital are higher in older adults with CI than those with intact cognitive functioning (Binder & Robbins, 1990). The cost of services correlates directly with the level of impairment (Zhu et al., 2006).

What is the range of cognitive functioning that is of interest to mental health providers? Cognition is usually examined within broad areas such as attention, language, memory, visuo-spatial skills, problem-solving, decision-making, and executive functioning. Within each domain are many specific functions. Neuropsychologists organize their analyses of cognitive functioning within a hierarchy that ranges from the simplest functions (e.g., attention) to the most complex (e.g., abstract thinking and problem-solving), as illustrated in Figure 7.1. This hierarchical organization reflects the foundational role of the simpler functions for all complex cognitive activities that rank higher in the hierarchy. In other words, if basic processes like attention are impaired, all higher-order processes will be negatively affected. As a general rule, more complex functions are the most easily disrupted by illness, brain dysfunction, or potentially toxic agents like medications.

Is CI Normal for Older Adults?

The answer to this question is actually a qualified, "clearly yes and no." On one hand, tests of cognitive functioning consistently show age-related decrements in many

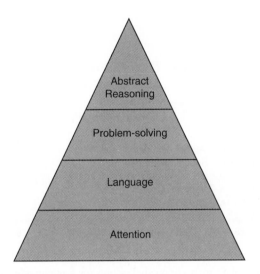

Figure 7.1 Hierarchy of cognitive functions.

cognitive functions that begin during middle adulthood (Foster, Cornwell, Kisley, & Davis, 2006). On the other hand, the normative decrements in functioning that are evident in laboratory tests rarely make an impact on daily functioning.

Several factors make it possible for age decrements to be normative, but to result in few effects of those changes in everyday life. First, laboratory tests of cognition push the limits of skills in ways that rarely occur in daily life. Age-related normative cognitive declines are relatively subtle, becoming visible primarily when functioning is pushed to its limits. Second, there is tremendous variability among older adults in the degree of decline experienced in any specific function. Thus, although mean scores may decline, the highest functioning older person may still be functioning above the average for younger adults. Third, humans are highly adaptive creatures who adjust their behavior to compensate for deficits (Baltes & Baltes, 1990b). Decrements in cognitive impairment may not be evident in daily life because the individual is skilled at compensating for deficits with external aids (e.g., written grocery lists), or by drawing upon an intact skill to compensate (e.g., relying on a cognitive map to drive to a friend's house when verbal memory for directions is impaired). In this chapter, CI refers to impairments that are substantial enough to affect daily functioning, that is, those that are caused by some serious disease or dysfunction that warrants intervention.

Before discussing clinically significant CI, the types of cognitive deficits that are normative with age will be described. Detailed summaries of findings on normative cognitive changes with age can be found elsewhere (Foster et al., 2006; Schaie & Zanjani, 2006). A graph depicting the typical longitudinal picture of cognitive decline with advancing age is presented in Figure 7.2, taken from the Seattle Longitudinal Study of Intellectual Abilities (Schaie, 1994). Note that most abilities depicted in this

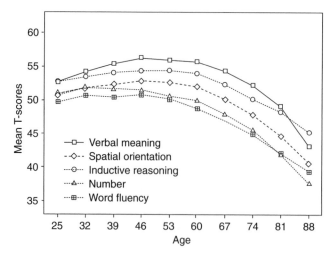

Figure 7.2 Longitudinal estimates of mean T-scores for single markers of the primary mental abilities, from seven-year within-participant data.
Source: Schaie (1994).

graph remained stable or actually improved throughout middle adulthood. In the sixties and seventies declines in functioning begin to be apparent in some functions, and by the eighties all functions show some degree of deterioration.

Although aging affects all of the skills in the pyramid in Figure 7.1, its greatest effects are evident in performance of complex skills illustrated at the top of the figure. Generally, simple attentional processes are maintained well into advanced old age, as are most language abilities. Language abilities are generally preserved intact until well into the seventies, at which time some deficits are evident in semantic linguistic abilities (e.g., verbal meaning). Performances on complex laboratory tasks (e.g., selective attention) typically show some age-related decrements that ultimately relate to performance on complex tasks such as driving.

Memory functions have been the focus of more research than any other cognitive function. Reducing a complex field to a broad summary, we can say that age has a negative effect on memory. Younger adults perform better than adults older than age 50 on most tasks. By age 70, performance within several domains is quite impaired. Of course, the extent of deficit is influenced by the method of assessment and the memory task (e.g., with and without cues, meaningful vs. non-meaningful stimuli, visual and verbal stimuli). Intervention research has demonstrated that some of the deficits seen in long-term memory can be ameliorated by providing additional structure to the memory tasks (e.g., providing cues, instructions in encoding strategies, or use of recognition rather than recall tasks), although memory skill remains lower, on average, for older adults than younger adults even under enhancement conditions. Not all memory processes are affected equally by age. Generally, sensory memory (e.g., very, very short-term memories of visual or auditory sensory data) and primary memory (or very short-term memory of a few seconds of duration) are least affected, whereas learning and retaining information over time (secondary memory) are where the greatest declines with aging are evident.

Abstract reasoning and complex problem-solving abilities also appear to decline by the sixties and seventies (Foster et al., 2006). Tasks such as the Wisconsin Card Sort, the Block Design subtest on the Wechsler Adult Intelligence Scales (now in its fourth edition), and explaining proverbs all elicit lower performances in older adults than in young adults. As is true of most cognitive functions, the method of assessment and the type of task produce variations in the results, although the picture that emerges is essentially consistent.

Knowledge of what is normative within healthy older adults is critical to the formation of appropriate expectations about performance on tests of cognitive functioning in clinical populations. The clinical assessment of CI requires either baseline data on the individual's previous functioning or normative data on older adults within an appropriate comparison group. The importance of age-appropriate norms will be discussed further in the section on assessment below.

The most common causes of CI are delirium, dementia, and depression. In recent years, an interim condition between normal aging and dementia has also been defined, called *mild cognitive impairment* (MCI), which appears to be a transitional state in the progression of brain deterioration due to dementia. Each of these four common causes of CI are discussed below.

Delirium: A Common, Reversible Cause of CI

A delirium is "a disturbance of consciousness that is accompanied by a change in cognition that cannot be better accounted for by a preexisting or evolving dementia" (APA, 2000, p. 136). Delirium develops rapidly over the course of hours or days, and often fluctuates during the day. At times, delirium is referred to as an *acute confusional state* or *reversible dementia*. The case of Noni Smith described above is typical of a case of delirium. The onset is rapid, and the person's behavior is disorganized in ways that are not typical for her. By definition, the cognitive disturbance is caused by physiological factors.

The DSM-IV-TR (APA, 2000, pp. 143–147) criteria for all types of delirium, regardless of etiology, are outlined in Table 7.1. In addition to the criteria that require

Table 7.1   Diagnostic features for delirium, regardless of etiology

- There is a disturbance of one's consciousness (i.e., reduced clarity of awareness of the environment) with impaired ability to focus, sustain, or shift attention

- There is a change in the level of one's cognition (e.g., a memory deficit, difficulty speaking or understanding language, disorientation) or there is the development of a perceptual disturbance that is not due to some type of dementia

- The disturbance develops quickly (usually over several hours to days) and the symptoms tend to fluctuate throughout the day

Source: Adapted from the American Psychiatric Association (2000).

a disturbance in cognition, persons experiencing delirium are also likely to report a disturbed sleep–wake cycle and unpleasant affect (e.g., fear, depression, anger). Attentional processes are particularly disrupted, leading to impairment in higher-level cognitive functions (e.g., memory, problem-solving).

Older adults are especially at risk for delirium because of their increased likelihood of chronic illness and the increased use of medication to manage those illnesses. Within the community, approximately 0.4 to 1.1 percent of adults over age 55 met diagnostic criteria for delirium (Folstein, Basset, Romanoski, & Nestadt, 1991). Common medical causes of delirium include acute illnesses (e.g., urinary tract infections), central nervous system disorders (e.g., stroke), cardiovascular disorders, dehydration, and metabolic disturbances. As many as 30 percent of all hospitalized older adults, and up to 47 percent of post-operative patients (Noimark, 2009), are diagnosable with delirium. Older adults show high rates of delirium during hospitalizations primarily due to factors related to the hospitalization (e.g., infection, medication changes, cardiovascular conditions), but risk is also increased among those with pre-existing cognitive impairment. Although reversible, delirium is a serious risk factor for illness and mortality rates among older adults, and increases the risk of long-term care placement (Saxena & Lawley, 2009).

Medications are among the first possible sources of delirium that need to be investigated. Almost any medication, including the most apparently innocuous over-the-counter medications, can cause delirium if the right conditions are present. One reason for vulnerability is that the process by which drugs are distributed, metabolized, and excreted is altered significantly with age (Hutchinson & O'Brien, 2007). Changes in several physiological systems contribute to the reduced capacity to metabolize, break down, and excrete drugs from the body. Thus, adverse drug reactions or drug toxicity are significant risk factors for older adults. Older adults are also more vulnerable to medication-induced delirium because of their high rate of medication use. Community-dwelling older adults are on an average of five medication prescriptions and two over-the-counter medications. In addition, almost half of older adults take vitamins and minerals along with herbal supplements (Kaufman, Kelly, Rosenberg, Anderson, & Mitchell, 2002). The average nursing home resident is on over nine medications, at least one of which is likely to be a psychotropic medication (Avorn, Soumerai, Everitt, & Ross, 1992). The potential for drug interactions is obviously extraordinarily high. Taken together, physiological changes result in altered responsiveness to medications such that even very small doses can produce delirium.

Environmental conditions can also add to the probability of delirium, although deliria in older adults only rarely result solely from environmental conditions. Psychosocial factors, sensory deprivation, and sleep deprivation may contribute to the development of delirium when other causal factors (e.g., toxic or metabolic factors) are present (Rabins, 1991).

Dementia: The Most Devastating Cause of CI

Dementias are the class of brain disorders characterized by irreversible declines in cognitive functioning that interfere with social and occupational functioning (APA,

Table 7.2   Common diagnostic features for dementias

- The development of multiple cognitive deficits manifested by a clear impairment in one's memory (e.g., difficulty recalling previously learned information or difficulty learning new information) and at least one of the following cognitive disturbances: aphasia (language disturbance), apraxia (impaired ability to carry out motor activities), agnosia (failure to recognize or identify objects), or disturbance in executive functioning (e.g., problems with organizing, planning, or sequencing)

- The cognitive deficits noted above cause significant impairment in the person's social or occupational functioning and represent a significant decline from the person's previous level of functioning

---

Source: Adapted from the American Psychiatric Association (2000).

2000). Dementias produce memory impairment along with other cognitive disturbances that are sufficient to disrupt functioning. The course of the decline in cognition typically is gradual and progressive, meaning that the trajectory downward will continue until death. The diagnosis of dementia is made according to the diagnostic features listed in Table 7.2. The specific diagnostic categories for dementias link the deficits outlined above with particular physiological etiologies (APA, 2000, pp. 157–171).

Persons with dementia are usually aware of some degree of deficit (although not always), but they typically underestimate the level of deficit (Lopez, Becker, Somsak, Dew, & DeKosky, 1994), and thus are unlikely to have considered that the cause could be a serious disease (Elson, 2005). Family members are often the first to pick up on the problem. Yet even as they watch their loved one lose capacity to function at the level the person had previously enjoyed, families are slow to recognize the very early signs until a significant safety risk forces their attention to the amount of change that has already occurred (Knopman et al., 2000; Nichols & Martindale-Adams, 2006). Ironically, prior to the onset of dementia, older adults prefer to be told their diagnosis, even if it is Alzheimer's disease (Elson, 2005). Unfortunately, older adults who previously said they wanted to know their diagnosis are later likely to be unable to accept that they have serious CI. Regardless, physician practice guidelines recommend that they share the diagnosis.

Dementias are found in 14 percent of the population over age 71 (Plassman et al., 2007). Advanced age clearly adds to the probability of dementia, with the risk doubling approximately every five years after age 65 (Jorm, Korten & Henderson, 1987). One recent epidemiological study found that 24 percent of persons ages 80–89 and 27 percent of persons over age 90 are diagnosable with dementia (Plassman et al., 2007). These data are considered conservative.

Due to the rapid aging of the population, dementia prevalence is expected to double in the next 20–30 years. These percentages translate into very large numbers of real people, of course. As of 2009, approximately 5.3 million people have a diagnosis of Alzheimer's disease (AD), a rapidly growing figure because every 70 seconds someone is diagnosed with the disease (Alzheimer's Association, 2009b). Keeping in mind that AD is only one of many forms of dementia, the problem is growing very rapidly.

Dementia can be produced by 50 or more different causes, although neurodegenerative diseases make up the vast majority of dementias. The most prevalent dementia is Alzheimer's disease, accounting for 70 percent of dementias, while vascular dementias account for another 17 percent and all other dementias make up the remaining 13 percent (Plassman et al., 2007). However, autopsy data present a far more complex picture that suggests multiple etiologies are common (Schneider, Arvanitakis, Bang, & Bennett, 2007).

The greatest risk factor for dementia is advancing age. Gender and education are also risk factors, with women showing higher lifetime risk (even after accounting for their longer life expectancy) than men (Seshadri et al., 2008), whereas education has a buffering effect on incidence (Alzheimer's Association, 2009b). Genetics plays a strong role in only a small number of cases (genetics appears more important in early-onset dementia, defined as onset before the age of 65 years, rather than late-onset dementia), although a genetic allele (apolipoprotein E-e4; APOE-e4) enhances risk of late-onset AD. Cardiovascular disease and the lifestyle patterns associated with risk for it (e.g., diet, exercise, obesity) are also risk factors for dementia. Brain injuries and infections from earlier life also create risk for dementias, a fact of growing concern to athletes for whom concussions are relatively common. To date, no cause has been identified that suggests a cure.

The pathophysiology of each dementia is somewhat distinct. AD includes unusually high rates of neuronal cell loss, along with unusual concentrations of amyloid, and an increased prevalence of neuritic plaques and neurofibrillary tangles in the cortex, amygdala, and hippocampus areas of the brain. Decreased levels of acetylcholine, the neurotransmitter involved in learning and memory, as well as other neurotransmitters further compromise brain function. Lewy body disease is commonly associated with Parkinson's disease because it often disrupts motor functioning when abnormal protein deposits deplete dopamine, a neurotransmitter involved in movement as well as cognition. These descriptions of the pathology do not truly explain the dementias, whose etiologies are still a mystery. Despite evidence of a genetic base for some dementias, the cause of the vast majority is still unknown.

Dementia progresses slowly and continuously, leading to declining functional capacities over time but without specific markers of decline. Functional deterioration occurs in approximately the opposite sequence to the gains made early in childhood neurological development. The Global Deterioration Scale (Reisberg, Ferris, De Leon, & Crook, 1982) outlines that sequence in a series of seven stages ranging from normal cognitive functioning to severe dementia (see Table 7.3).

Vascular dementias are caused by loss of neuronal tissue as a result of occlusions of vessels or small infarctions (i.e., hemorrhages) in the brain. Diagnosis of vascular dementia requires the presence of the cognitive signs of dementia described above, as well as the documented presence of cerebrovascular disease or the presence of focal signs and symptoms that appear to be caused by localized damage to the brain (APA, 2000). Vascular dementias can be either cortical or subcortical or mixed, depending upon location of the vascular damage.

Vascular dementias can present with a step-wise progression of small losses of functioning that result from the small infarcts, although those steps may be so small that observers describe the changes as continuous. Vascular dementias can follow a

Table 7.3 Global Deterioration Scale

Stage	Clinical phase	Clinical characteristics
1 No cognitive decline	Normal	• No subjective complaints of memory deficit or evidence during clinical interview.
2 Very mild cognitive decline	Forgetfulness	• Subjective complaints of memory deficit with appropriate levels of concern, but no objective evidence of memory deficit on clinical interview, in employment, or in social situations.
3 Mild cognitive decline	Early confusional	• Earliest clear-cut deficits appear, with manifestations in multiple areas of daily life and objective evidence of memory deficit during an intensive interview conducted by a trained geriatric psychiatrist or neuropsychologist. • Decreased performance in demanding employment and social settings. • Denial begins to become manifest and mild to moderate anxiety accompanies symptoms.
4 Moderate cognitive decline	Late confusional	• Clear-cut deficit is apparent on careful interview. Deficit manifests in multiple areas (e.g., decreased knowledge of current and recent events, difficulty remembering personal history, concentration deficits, and decreased ability to travel, handle finances, and so on). • Frequently, no deficit is apparent in orientation to time and person, recognition of familiar person and faces, and ability to travel to familiar locations. • Inability to perform complex tasks, but denies or lacks awareness of deficits. • Flattening of affect and withdrawal from challenging situations occur.
5 Moderately severe cognitive decline	Early dementia	• Person can no longer survive without some assistance. • Inability to recall a major relevant aspect of their current lives (e.g., their addresses or telephone numbers of many years, the names of close members of their families such as grandchildren, or the names of the high schools or colleges from which they graduated). • Frequently, some disorientation to time (date, day of week, season, etc.) or to place is present, but may retain knowledge of major facts regarding themselves and others. They invariably know their own names and generally know their spouse's and children's names. • They require no assistance with toileting or eating but may have some difficulty in choosing the proper clothing or dressing.
6 Severe cognitive decline	Middle dementia	• They will be largely unaware of all recent events and experiences in their lives, but may retain some knowledge of their past life. • They are generally unaware of their surroundings, the year, the season, and so on. • They will require some assistance with activities of daily living. • They almost always recall their own names, but may occasionally forget the names of the spouse on whom they are entirely dependent for survival. • Personality and emotional changes occur.
7 Very severe cognitive decline	Late dementia	• All verbal abilities are lost. Frequently, there is no speech at all – only grunting. • They require assistance with the most basic self-care (e.g, toileting and feeding). • They lose basic psychomotor skills (e.g., ability to walk).

Source: Adapted from Reisberg et al. (1982).

stroke, and share increased risk of stroke. The prognosis for vascular dementia is similar to that of Alzheimer's disease: slow, progressive deterioration in a broad range of cognitive functions. Certainly, dementias can co-present within a patient, such that, for example, vascular dementia and Alzheimer's dementia are both diagnosed.

Subcortical dementias, a category containing many distinct diseases (e.g., Huntington's disease, Wilson's disease, Parkinson's disease, progressive supranuclear palsy), have effects on cognitive functioning that differ from dementias whose early, primary impact is in the cerebral cortex (Kaufer & Cummings, 2003). In contrast to the dementias that attack the cerebral cortex early (e.g., Alzheimer's), subcortical dementias tend to show memory retrieval rather than learning deficits, speech difficulties, and motor impairments. Similarities between cortical and subcortical dementias are in the areas of problem-solving deficits, and visuo-perceptual and constructional deficits. The explosion of research in the neurosciences during recent decades has made it possible to understand the finest of neurological distinctions among these diseases, and to discriminate often among these diseases pre-mortem with the careful application of thorough assessment techniques. Knowledge of the specific diagnosis can be particularly helpful when designing behavior management interventions that need to draw upon the available cognitive abilities to compensate for deficits and behavior problems.

The impact of dementia on daily life progresses from modest effects on self-management of daily affairs to nearly complete devastation of all self-care skills, as illustrated in the case of Jane Winthrop described at the beginning of this chapter. Independence is most threatened by the loss of ability to provide basic self-care functions that are usually measured as Activities of Daily Living (ADLs, including bathing, dressing, eating) and Instrumental Activities of Daily Living (IADLs, including management of finances, transportation, telephone use). Early in the disease progression, IADLs become challenging for the person, who may attempt to hide the level of difficulty experienced. Later, as the disease progresses, even the most basic ADLs require assistance as the person forgets how to eat or walk.

Problem behaviors also often occur, adding burden to the care of persons with dementias. Common behavior problems include depression, sleep disturbances, and agitated behavior, all of which can be as disturbing of daily functioning and personal well-being for the person as the cognitive impairment itself. Severe behavioral disturbances are very disruptive to the person with dementia as well as the caregivers, so require a systematic approach to reducing the disturbance that often ends up involving non-pharmacological interventions as well as medications (Salzman et al., 2008). Not surprisingly, the costs of care for persons with dementia accelerate with both the decline in cognitive functioning and the presence of clinical characteristics such as depression (Zhu et al., 2006).

Mild Cognitive Impairment (MCI)

The past decade has witnessed increased interest in a milder form of cognitive impairment in older adults who do not meet the criteria for dementia but whose cognitive deficits are greater than would be produced by normal aging. Various categories for non-dementia CI have been proposed and evaluated, with mild cognitive impairment (MCI) emerging as a term that is commonly used in clinical settings. The cognitive changes associated with normal aging overlap with those associated with MCI, suggesting a continuum of deterioration that may progress into a dementia for at least a portion of the population (Smith & Rush, 2006). Although evolving, the definition of MCI requires exclusion of dementia along with the presence of impairment in at least one domain of functioning. Three subtypes of MCI have been identified. Amnestic MCI shows memory impairment for age along with memory complaints. Single non-memory-domain MCI involves impairment in one of the following domains: attention/concentration, executive functioning, language functioning, or visuo-spatial functioning. Multi-domain MCI has impairment in two or more domains, often including memory.

Part of the interest in non-dementia CI is driven by the high prevalence rates (over 22 percent of persons over age 70 and rates as high as 13.7 percent in 60–64-year-olds), and high rates of conversion to dementia (over 12 percent per year, with variability across subtypes) (Kumar et al., 2005; Plassman et al., 2008). Causes of these non-dementia CIs include chronic medical conditions such as heart failure and diabetes as well as incipient dementia in very early pre-disease stages.

Do older people want to know if they are developing CI at this mild level? Recent research makes it clear that older adults want to know about CI in themselves or in a close family member (Dale, Hougham, Hill, & Sachs, 2006). They also report being willing to be screened for MCI (Dale et al., 2006), although families anticipate resistance and anger at any suggestion that an evaluation is needed (Nichols & Martindale-Adams, 2006). Persons with MCI also appear more capable of reporting their functional abilities than are persons with a dementia (Farias, Mungas, & Jagust, 2005).

Although families say they want to know about MCI, Whitehouse and colleagues have voiced concern that very early clinical labeling of cognitive impairment can have deleterious effects on well-being (Whitehouse & Moody, 2006). These researchers question the reliability and validity of the category that does not yet have strong predictive validity for diseases. Thus, very early medicalization of brain aging primarily may benefit the pharmaceutical industry whose stake in early intervention is great. In contrast to medical frameworks for mild cognitive decline, social constructions of aging processes present powerful reasons not to use clinical language for a relatively ambiguous phenomenon. Among the negative effects of using clinical language for MCI is the establishment of an expectation of decline that can serve as a self-fulfilling and other-reinforcing prophecy. Very early diagnosis of cognitive decline prior to the time when its predictive validity is clear creates a medical framework that can easily dominate the meaning and structures of a person's life. Further research may render this debate moot, if cognitive testing improves in predictive validity, but for today, Whitehouse and Moody remind us that the power of diagnostic labels to shape social constructions warrants thoughtful dialogue on the establishment of diagnostic criteria.

The mainstream of care, however, reflects the belief that early detection of MCI has the same value as early detection of dementias of any type, including Alzheimer's disease. Patients have time to plan proactively for their future care, and families have time to anticipate future needs and care strategies. Many barriers exist to early detection, however, despite patients' and families' interests in obtaining it. Primary care appears to be an obvious choice of a site for routine screening, but Medicare reimbursement for cognitive screening requires established medical necessity (i.e., it cannot be reimbursed for an entire population), so the time and expertise invested in obtaining screening results is lost revenue. The cognitive screening tools that are in common use are particularly ineffective with detection of the specific symptom profile of MCI (Lonie, Tierney, & Ebmeier, 2009; Trenkle, Shankle, & Azen, 2007). The available screening tools detect difficulties in a limited set of domains, and are rarely able to predict transition from MCI to dementia (Lonie et al., 2009). Full neuropsychological evaluations are needed to produce a diagnosis while more effective screening tools, including those that require less labor (e.g., computerized screens), are developed for primary care and other settings where elders routinely receive services.

Care for persons with MCI requires an appreciation for the experience of the person with the condition (Lingler et al., 2006). The impairments caused by MCI are by definition mild in intensity and scope, and thus not readily discernible by others in surface-level interaction. Thus, the person with the disorder lives suspended between his or her status as a normal, high-functioning-yet-impaired person and someone with deficits significant enough to be diagnosable with a disease. Those living with, and caring for, persons with MCI observe subtle but important changes that alter their relationships (Blieszner, Roberto, Wilcox, Barham, & Winston, 2007). Although not as overtly impairing as dementia, MCI provides individuals and families with substantial challenges in daily life, and a likely prognosis for declining functioning in the future.

Depression and Cognitive Impairment

Individuals with depression sometimes express concerns about their memory and/ or actual functional deficits in daily cognitive functioning as reported by a family member or other informant. The negative cognitive set associated with depression produces excessively negative self-appraisals in many areas, including cognitive functioning. The case of Jim Hunt, offered at the beginning of the chapter, is a typical presentation of depression. He is very concerned about his own deficits and is withdrawing from activities that bring him pleasure. Obviously, a thorough evaluation is needed to rule out cognitive impairment, but the presentation is also typical of a depressed person.

Although depressed adults complain about memory deficits even if no objective memory performance deficit is evident, depression is associated with actual cognitive deficits under two circumstances. First, depression is associated with deficits in actual cognitive performance, as is anxiety (Bierman, Comijs, Jonker, & Beekman, 2005). By definition, the CI can be attributed to depression only if it remits with successful treatment of the depression. CI due to depression sufficiently mimics dementia that it was previously referred to as *pseudodementia*, a misnomer because the CI is not false. Second, depression and dementia can, and often do, coexist (Teri, 1996).

Approximately 30 percent of demented patients meet the criteria for diagnosis of depression, most often in the early stages of the disease (Teri & Wagner, 1992). Similarly, depression is comorbid in MCI (Gabryelewicz et al., 2004). Other factors that are often present in older adults also can produce depression and dementia-like symptoms that further complicate matters. For example, disrupted sleep, anxiety, or physical illness can produce concentration deficits or personality changes that are common in either depression or dementia.

Summary of Four Types of Cognitive Impairment

Differential diagnosis of delirium, depression, dementia, MCI, and other sources of cognitive impairment is a common challenge to the geriatric mental health provider. The disorders present with similar symptoms, the symptoms can co-occur, and the symptoms can be misidentified (e.g., passivity in dementia may be described as depression; impaired attention due to delirium may be described as dementia). Further complications are suggested by research documenting that late-onset depression is often a predictor of the onset of dementia within three years (Gatz, Kasl-Godley, & Karel, 1996), suggesting that the disorders may actually present sequentially. A task force of the American Psychological Association (APA) currently is revising recommendations for discriminating the disorders, updating the original recommendations by an APA Presidential Task Force published in 1998. The most recent guidelines can be found at the website of the Office on Aging within the American Psychological Association (http://www.apa.org/pi/aging).

Assessment

In order to discriminate among the various potential causes of CI in older adults, multidisciplinary evaluations of medical, pharmacological, neuropsychological, and daily functioning are necessary. Multiple disciplines must be involved to gather a picture of the full range of functional abilities and deficits, and to examine all possible causes of deficits. The medical evaluation includes a thorough history and physical, examination of the medical history, and review of current medications. Social workers provide a social history that includes occupational and social functioning and evaluates family functioning. Psychologists evaluate cognitive, emotional, and personality functioning, and neuropsychologists provide an in-depth examination of cognitive and memory functioning. Pharmacy consultants and psychiatrists often contribute to the evaluation of the effects of illnesses and medications on psychological functioning (cognitive as well as mood). Other health professions such as physical therapy, dentistry, or occupational therapy may be involved in the evaluation if problems in posture, range of motion, movement safety, oral health, or functional capacity to fulfill daily tasks are in question.

The medical aspects of the evaluation are particularly critical because reversible causes of CI must be ruled out immediately. Left untreated, reversible causes of CI can produce permanent deficits. The functional components of the examination (e.g., evaluation of ADLs and IADLs) are key to determining the level of independent functioning that is possible and safe. In the case of patients with dementia, evaluation of family functioning is also important. Family caregivers maintain responsibility for patient well-being, and are often highly stressed.

Neuropsychological examinations often begin with screening tools that evaluate mental status and depression, and proceed to a full evaluation only when needed. Commonly used mental status exams include the Folstein Mini-Mental State Examination (FMMSE; Folstein, Folstein, & McHugh, 1975) and the Mattis Dementia Rating Scale-2 (Mattis, Jurica, & Leitten, 2001), although newer screening tools have been recommended based on their greater effectiveness (Trenkle et al., 2007). A good example is the Montreal Cognitive Assessment (MoCA), which is designed to detect mild cognitive impairment (see the MoCA website for further details: http://www.mocatest.org/). Each screening tool assesses functioning in several domains, but with little depth of examination in each area. Any indication of deficit leads to more rigorous examination of cognitive functioning. Diagnosis cannot be made on the basis of any screening measure!

A full neuropsychological examination includes tests of specific domains of functioning that can portray a rich picture of the strengths as well as the deficits of a particular patient's functioning. Test data are compared with norms from age-matched older adults living in a similar setting (e.g., community dwelling, nursing home) to determine whether one individual's performance varies from what would be normative for a person that age in that setting. An example of a neuropsychological battery that is used at a major clinical research center to assess the full range of functions (e.g., attention, memory, problem-solving, language, visuo-spatial abilities, and motor abilities) is listed in Table 7.4 (Fillenbaum et al., 2008; Morris et al., 1989).

A neuropsychological test report provides detailed information on the patient's performance on each test, compared to national norms for healthy older adults, and, if available, persons with various dementias. Test performances are interpreted within the context of the patient's past educational and occupational experiences. In highly educated persons, an average score may not appear to be deficient if compared against national norms, but may be well below that person's historical capacity to function. The test report concludes by addressing any specific questions (e.g., capacity to function safely within current living environment or decision-making competency) and summarizing cognitive strengths that can be used to compensate for any deficits. Some neuropsychologists provide personalized feedback to patients and families in a face-to-face session (Green 2006), or therapists may provide a written report that translates the neuropsychological findings into practical advice for family adaptation (Qualls & Noecker, 2009).

In addition to diagnostic evaluations, assessment is used to evaluate the existence of distress in persons with dementia and in their caregivers, and to determine the extent of problem behaviors. Common forms of distress are depression and anxiety, which are often comorbid in this population just as they are in the general population. Assessment of depression in dementia is effective but anxiety assessment tools need further refinement (Beaudreau & O'Hara, 2008). A thorough evaluation should include assessment of family stress due to the burdens of managing care and the

Table 7.4 Example of dementia battery: Core battery of the Consortium to Establish a Registry for Alzheimer's Disease (CERAD) and ancillary materials

---

Neuropsychology Tests (available in Chinese, French, Hindi, Korean, Spanish, and Yoruba)
   Verbal Fluency – Animals
   Boston Naming Test – 15 words from low, moderate, and high frequency occurrence in
     everyday language
   Mini-Mental State
   Word List Memory Test – 3 trials of a 10-word list
   Constructional Praxis – drawn copies of four geometric figures
   Word List Recall – delayed recall for the Word List Memory
   Word List Recognition – provides the 10 words with 10 distractor words to test retention
Clinical Battery: Demographics, clinical history, cognitive and behavioral screening tools
Neuropathology Battery: Demographics, history, gross examination, findings on structural
   and vascular findings from imaging
Behavior Rating Scale for Dementia: Presence and frequency of behaviors characteristic of
   depression, inertia, vegetative symptoms, irritability/aggression, behavioral dysregulation,
   psychotic symptoms
Family History Assessment: 1st and 2nd degree kin map of likely presence of Alzheimer's
   disease, Parkinson's disease, and Down syndrome
Services Assessment: In-home and community-based service use and need

---

Source: Fillenbaum et al. (2008); Morris et al. (1989).

behavior problems that often accompany CI. The Revised Memory and Behavior Problems Checklist (Teri et al., 1992) is a commonly used tool that identifies significant behavior problems and the degree of distress each problem evokes in the caregiver. Family members should also be evaluated for depression, a distressingly common consequence for caregivers whose sources of pleasure are usually disrupted at the same time that they are dealing with challenging health and behavior problems.

Assessment of problem behaviors often engages the caregiver in recording behaviors, including the time, location, and social context of the behavior. Behavioral observations may be used to gather accurate records of behavior, especially in long-term care settings, but informant reports are generally accurate enough to suggest reliance on their more efficient approach (Cohen-Mansfield & Libin, 2004).

Finally, an emerging field of assessment of persons with dementia focuses specifically on their decision-making capacity (Moye & Marson, 2007). Very important legal and ethical issues arise as a person's cognitive abilities decline, especially when awareness of the decline is absent. Persons may be at substantial risk of self-neglect or abuse, or exploitation and fraud, if their capacities are lower than required to remain safe within their environments. The American Psychological Association and American Bar Association have collaborated on a series of handbooks to guide lawyers, judges, and psychologists through the process of evaluating a person's capacity for decision-making in a variety of contexts (e.g., health, financial, and legal contexts) (ABA/APA, 2008).

Interventions

A thorough assessment can be considered the first and most important intervention for CI. If the cause of the CI is reversible (e.g., delirium or depression), then the evaluation should lead to aggressive treatment of the underlying condition, which will partially or completely resolve the problem. When the CI is determined to be caused by a non-reversible etiology, such as a dementia, the focus of intervention turns toward management of the disease, with the goal of preventing excess disability and rapid decline. Planning, environmental interventions, behavioral interventions, and education and support for those who will provide care for the impaired person are all useful management strategies. Direct intervention to improve cognitive functioning may be beneficial in certain cases.

Families of demented persons have too often lamented that they were told by their physician something like, "I'm sorry, but your husband has Alzheimer's disease and there's nothing that can be done." The hopelessness and despair produced by such pronouncements of doom are substantial, and truly unnecessary. Furthermore, the statement is only true in the sense that no treatment reverses the damage caused by the disease. Indeed, many interventions can be useful.

Management of progressive, intractable CI focuses on maximizing independent functioning while anticipating the consequences of current and future levels of impairment on the patient and the caregivers. The case of Jane Winthrop with which the chapter opened is an example of intensive management to maintain independence in her living environment. Early in a dementing process, families often begin to implement small supportive interventions that allow the person with the disease to maintain independence in his or her own home. For example, a son or daughter may initially "check in" on a mother to make sure she is OK. Later, the adult child may handle complex financial transactions such as taxes, even though the diseased person continues to manage the monthly budget. Later, the checkbook may be handled by an adult child, and eventually even routine grocery shopping may have to be done by a caregiver. In Jane Winthrop's case, the family was using external memory aids so Jane could maintain basic safety in her own home. The implied sequence of increasing care services is illustrated by the continuum of family roles *vis-à-vis* a demented person that is presented in Figure 7.3.

Planning

Ideally, a person with CI has the opportunity to make significant decisions about how legal, financial, housing, and health care decisions will be made prior to significant CI, when there are sufficient cognitive abilities intact to make sound decisions. For example, adults with early-stage dementia are encouraged to work with an attorney and family members to determine appropriate financial, legal, and health care decision-making arrangements for the future when the impairment will disable their decision-making capacity (see Chapter 12).

In recent years, several legal tools have been developed to help adults state their intentions for handling their affairs once they are incapacitated. For example, a

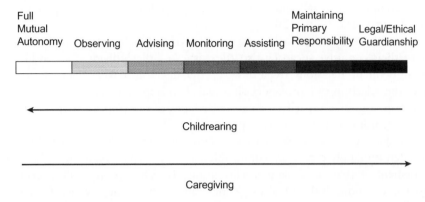

Figure 7.3 Family involvement with members.

durable health power of attorney identifies and sanctions a legal decision-maker to handle health care decisions once an individual is incapacitated. A *living will* identifies the level of medical intervention desired by the individual when he or she is both incapable of stating his or her own needs and when heroic measures might be used to sustain life in the face of death. Housing options, such as life-care communities that guarantee provision of the level of care needed by the older adult who purchased the life-care services ahead of time, allow an individual to select the housing for the future. Advanced planning for finances and other needs ensures that the individual's own desires will be the basis for decisions once capacity to decide is compromised.

When cognitively impaired individuals have not legally stated their wishes for how things should be handled after they are incapacitated, surrogate decision-makers are called upon to make the key decisions. State statutes define who is the surrogate decision-maker of choice for health care decisions, with a sequence of alternative persons in a specific order. Typically, a spouse is the first person of choice, followed by a parent or an adult child, with specific assignments of priority thereafter. For other decisions (e.g., housing or finances), a similar strategy is typically supported by the legal system even though it may not be defined by statute.

Even a cognitively impaired individual is his or her own legal decision-maker, except when decisions would generate a threat to someone's welfare, or the court appoints a guardian. Guardianship is a dramatic step that strips an individual of basic rights and liberties. The decision to appoint a guardian is made by a judge, based upon evidence that relates to the specific state statutes that define the basis for incompetency. No national standard has been established for competency determinations – neither a standard definition of competence and incompetence, nor a standard procedure for determining competency – but consensus has grown as to the appropriateness of assessing functional abilities for specific capacity domains (Grisso, 2003). In most states, partial or limited guardianships can be granted to cover only domains in which the individual's incapacity is sufficient to warrant an alternative decision-maker (e.g., finances but not housing). Indeed, the determination of competency is a highly complicated legal field that rests upon significantly complex psychological and legal constructs (Grisso, 2003).

Legal and health professionals consistently encourage adults to plan ahead for the event of their cognitive incapacity so the wishes of the individual are available to guide subsequent decisions, regardless of the decision-maker. Planning typically involves the selection of a proxy decision-maker to step in at the point at which the person loses cognitive capacity for particular types of decision, as well as statement of values regarding the types of care preferred under particular conditions.

A considerable evidence base exists to show that interventions can reduce stress and burden on family caregivers whose roles will often span many years for persons with dementias (Coon, Gallagher-Thompson, & Thompson, 2003; Gallagher-Thompson & Coon, 2007; Qualls & Zarit, 2009). The point at which families seek help will shape the selection of interventions from a wide range of options, making assessment a critical component in caregiver interventions (S. H. Zarit, 2009). Almost all interventions include education, problem-solving, and efforts to increase social support for the caregiver. Two large multi-site studies that were funded by the National Institute on Aging demonstrate that multiple interventions may be effective if selected for caregivers based on assessment results. These studies, referred to as REACH 1 and REACH 2 (Resources for Enhancing Alzheimer's Caregiver Health), generated a diverse set of approaches that were tested in multiple regions of the country with multiple culturally diverse populations (Belle et al., 2006; Wisniewski et al., 2003). REACH 2 produced positive results with a tailored intervention approach that constructed a personalized treatment plan from common, empirically supported core intervention strategies. Family counseling studies have also generated positive effects on caregivers as well as a delay in nursing home placement (e.g., Mittelman, Roth, Coon & Haley, 2004). Interventions with caregiving families are powerful tools for reducing the burden and stress on the caregivers, improving the care for the care recipients, and delaying the need for intensive institutional care.

Environmental Interventions

Individuals with CI are more vulnerable to the impact of the environment on their capacity to function than are non-impaired individuals (Lawton & Nahemow, 1973). As illustrated in Figure 7.4, lower levels of competence limit the range of environments in which the individual can competently function. Thus, the selection of an appropriate environment can profoundly affect, positively or negatively, an individual's capacity for independent functioning. Effective management of cognitively impaired individuals requires the caregivers to identify the level of environmental prosthesis that will support independent functioning maximally, by providing sufficient challenge to require the individual to use available cognitive capacities without generating frustration or excess disability.

Persons with mild CI may be able to live alone in a familiar home or apartment with minimal support. However, substantial CI usually requires at least one move from independent living to a more supportive level of housing. Meals, janitorial, maintenance, and housekeeping services may be sufficient to maintain a state of rela-

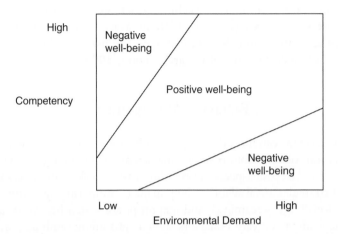

Figure 7.4   Relationship between environmental press, competency, and well-being.
Source: Adapted from Lawton and Nahemow (1973).

tive independence. Nursing homes provide the most intensive levels of health-supportive services, including medication dispensing, nutrition monitoring, and skilled nursing services. The high rate of CI in nursing homes noted earlier in this chapter reflects the negative effects of institutional life as well as the increased likelihood of needing the full array of support services once one is cognitively impaired.

Architectural features of a living environment can profoundly impact behavior, especially of the cognitively impaired (Lawton, 1979), and are thus appropriate targets for intervention. Among the numerous environmental characteristics that affect the behavior of normal as well as impaired older adults are factors such as privacy, availability of small group spaces, opportunities to facilitate family–resident interactions, support for way-finding, and focused and appropriate stimulation (Cutler, 2007). The arrangement of public and private spaces can affect the frequency and value of social interaction to residents of senior housing. Environmental richness (sounds, sights, and tactile stimulation) affects rate of activity and socializing. For demented and depressed individuals with CI, environmental interventions that increase the rate of stimulation without requiring initiation on the part of the impaired individual can produce significant improvements in functioning as long as the stimuli are paced in frequency and intensity.

Facilities designed for persons with Alzheimer's disease use creative design features to foster desired behavior. For example, colored blocks inlaid into the surface of a table to look like a placemat have been used to help demented persons identify the territory within which their food is served. Pictures of a resident as a young person as well as a current picture of the aging person may be used instead of a name or number outside the door to enhance the likelihood that the resident can identify his or her own room.

Environmental technology to support independence is another area of rapid development. Technologies now exist for monitoring and prompting, structuring tasks, and simplifying access to computers. Technologies targeted at caregivers offer assistive devices to assist with practical care (e.g., bathing) as well as communication technologies that facilitate interaction. Not surprisingly, the use of technology in dementia care is a very hot emerging area of research (Topo, 2009).

Behavior Management

Cognitive impairment can limit the range of behavior as well as produce problematic behaviors that can benefit from behavior management. Handling behavior problems is one of the most stressful aspects of providing care to a demented person. Behavior management strategies are available to help manage wandering, incontinence, disruptive vocalizations (e.g., screaming), and inappropriate sexual behaviors, as well as to enhance independent self-care behaviors such as grooming, ambulation, and eating (Logsdon, McCurry & Teri, 2007). Agitated behaviors are some of the more complex behaviors to manage (Cohen-Mansfield & Libin, 2004), but several strategies have been demonstrated to be effective (Kong, Evans, & Guevara, 2009; Logsdon et al., 2007). Daily care providers such as family members or certified nurse aids (CNAs) in nursing homes must be trained to implement evidence-based behavior management protocols in order to achieve successful results. In contrast to medications that are sometimes used to sedate individuals whose agitation is extremely disruptive to their environment, behavior management programs rarely produce side effects. Physicians generally prefer non-pharmacological interventions and federal regulations discourage use of antipsychotic and other sedating medications unless used in the presence of psychiatric diagnosis, but physicians often view lack of resources and knowledge as a barrier to using behavioral interventions in long-term care settings (Cohen-Mansfield & Jensen, 2008). Ethical concerns about altering the behaviors of persons who are not capable of consenting to treatment always warrant careful consideration.

The burden of caring for cognitively impaired individuals falls heavily upon family members. Problem behaviors associated with CI provoke the most adverse emotional and physical consequences for caregivers (see review by Pinquart & Sörensen, 2007). The disruptive and odd behaviors that often accompany serious CI can significantly interfere with sleep, daily routines, and social contact. However, the burden of care tasks and social loss also falls on families. Interventions for families usually focus on education about the disease, problem-solving assistance, encouragement to maintain strong social support, and, when needed, family therapy to resolve serious family dysfunction (Gallagher-Thompson & Coon, 2007; Qualls & Noecker, 2009).

Interventions to Enhance Cognitive Functioning

Efforts to reverse or slow deterioration in CI include pharmacological interventions and cognitive retraining. Medications to enhance cognitive functioning in dementia (especially AD) patients show short-term benefits (6–12 months) in about half of individuals (Alzheimer's Association, 2009b). These effects are primarily produced by increasing the concentration of specific neurotransmitters in the brain. Unfortunately, currently available medications can neither cure nor stop the development of dementias.

In laboratory settings, older adults have been demonstrated to be capable of benefiting from training to use memory aids and strategies such as spaced retrieval (Camp, 2006; Unverzagt et al., 2007). Rarely does that training generalize to behaviors outside the behaviors that were targeted in the training, which limits its utility. Emerging medications, herbs, technologies, and games that claim to improve cognitive fitness in older persons have generated concern among scientists about verifying the claims some make to have a cure for dementia, a way to slow cognitive decline, or at least a way to improve memory. A cadre of top international cognitive psychologists specializing in aging reached consensus regarding the current state of research on cognitive fitness interventions (Stanford Center for Longevity & the Max Planck Institute for Human Development, 2009). Key points on which they agree include:

- There are reasons to be optimistic, including the improvement of cognitive functioning across historical cohorts such that current cohorts of older adults have lower rates of cognitive impairment compared with earlier-born cohorts.
- Dietary supplements lack support for their claims that natural herbs such as gingko biloba can enhance cognitive functioning or reduce decline in functioning over time.
- Software training programs designed to improve cognitive performance can improve functioning on the tasks involved in the training, but those skills do not translate into everyday life tasks.
- Consumers need to be savvy about investigating claims for impact on cognition, seeking information about research to support claims. Consumers should be particularly leery of claims related to curing either symptoms or underlying pathology of dementias.
- Physical exercise, especially regular aerobic exercise, increases blood flow to the brain with demonstrated impact on attention, reasoning, and some components of memory.

Summary and Conclusions

Cognitive impairment is one of the most dreaded changes associated with aging because of its profound negative impact on autonomy and the very identity of the person experiencing the disorder. Reversible causes of CI are sufficiently prevalent among older adults to warrant aggressive evaluation of CI. Irreversible causes of CI in older adults are primarily caused by dementias, which produce devastating, progressive, and long-term effects on cognition. A thorough assessment requires the involvement of multiple disciplines in a coordinated effort to identify a multidimensional picture of the person's physical, psychological, social, and self-care functioning. Based on the assessment, many interventions are possible to assist the impaired person and those caring for him or her.

8

Depression

Jenny Miller's husband of 46 years died three years ago from a sudden heart attack. She keeps thinking she will get over it and get on with life, but she somehow can't seem to figure out what life is anymore. Her children call her every week, and each one flies out to visit a couple of times each year, but they haven't been able to help her get over her grief. Unfortunately, she feels like she has no energy to handle daily routines, let alone try new things. Every morning she wakes up about 4 a.m. and is unable to get back to sleep. It is so frustrating for her that she is irritable much of the time, and is sure that other people won't want to be around her anyway. She rarely calls her friends, and complains that most of her "couple" friends obviously don't want to see her now that she is a widow. Although she has enjoyed sewing and needlework all of her life, she hasn't started a project in a couple of years because she just doesn't care that much about it any more, and frankly no longer believes she has the mental capacity to do it. She is convinced that her memory is failing and complains that she can't concentrate on anything anymore. Much of her day is spent watching soap operas and game shows, dozing off occasionally because she is so tired.

Jenny Miller is experiencing what clinicians define as a Major Depressive Disorder (MDD). As described below in more detail, Jenny reports many characteristic symptoms of depression, including insomnia, fatigue, irritability, social withdrawal, difficulty concentrating, memory difficulties, and a lack of interest in almost all aspects of her life. She is not particularly dysphoric or sad, nor does she cry excessively, so some people might think she is not depressed. Unfortunately, her experience is what some people imagine is normal for later life, leading the general public and even some health professionals to believe that depression is so common among older adults that it is almost expected. Although depression is indeed among the more common mental disorders experienced by older adults, it is also the case that fewer older adults than young adults suffer from diagnosable depression.

Aging and Mental Health, 2e. Daniel L. Segal, Sara Honn Qualls, and Michael A. Smyer
© 2011 Daniel L. Segal, Sara Honn Qualls, and Michael A. Smyer

Definition of Depression

The *Diagnostic and Statistical Manual of Mental Disorders*, 4th edition, text revision (DSM-IV-TR; American Psychiatric Association, 2000) classifies depression within the broad category of mood disorders because a disruption in mood is the most salient characteristic. There are actually several depressive disorders that vary by intensity and duration. Table 8.1 shows the DSM-IV-TR classifications for three disorders with significant depressive symptomatology, including the symptom and duration diagnostic features for each disorder. The most intense depressions are classified as Major Depressive Disorder whereas the most chronic are termed Dysthymic Disorder. In addition to the depressive disorders recognized by the DSM-IV-TR, minor or subsyndromal depression is currently being espoused as a major clinical concern for older adults that may warrant its own diagnostic code. There appear to be some consistent differences in the presentation of depressed older adults compared to depressed younger adults, with depressed older adults showing less affective symptoms (e.g., feelings of sadness or guilt) but more cognitive symptoms (e.g., complaints about memory; executive function deficits), somatic symptoms (e.g., fatigue, sleep disruption), and loss of interest in activities and living.

Epidemiological studies consistently find high rates of clinically significant depressive symptoms in older adults (about 15–25 percent) compared to the relatively low rates of diagnosable MDD. That is, there are high rates of symptoms in individuals who do not meet the diagnostic threshold for one of the formal depressive disorders in the DSM. These *minor depressions* are receiving increasing attention because of their clinical importance to physical and mental health. Minor depression is technically diagnosed as Depressive Disorder Not Otherwise Specified within the DSM classification system, but it is recognized as a distinctive problem within the research literature. Specifically, Blazer and colleagues (1989) analyzed symptom clusters in an effort to identify variant forms of depression. One symptom cluster that emerged from their analysis was found almost exclusively in older adults. The symptoms included depressed mood, psychomotor retardation, difficulty concentrating, and problems performing on the mental status examinations. In addition, these individuals described themselves as having poor health. Although they would not meet criteria for MDD, these older adults were obviously struggling with significant depressive symptoms that were associated with physical illness and cognitive impairment. In another study of the symptom patterns of minor depression, Oxman, Barret, Barret, and Gerber (1990) found that the common symptoms included worry (84 percent), blaming self (79 percent), decreased energy (79 percent), everything an effort (68 percent), irritability (63 percent), disturbed sleep (53 percent), crying (53 percent), and feelings of hopelessness (53 percent). Once again, physical as well as psychological symptoms characterized the minor depression.

Prevalence of Depression in Older Adults

Recall from the introductory comments to this section that prevalence rates for disorders are reported in a variety of ways. One way of examining population patterns

Table 8.1 DSM-IV-TR diagnostic features for Major Depressive Disorder, Dysthymic Disorder, and Adjustment Disorder With Depressed Mood

Type of depression	Diagnostic features
Major Depressive Disorder	A. Five or more of the following symptoms have been present during the same 2-week period and represent a change from previous functioning: At least one of the symptoms is either (1) depressed mood or (2) loss of interest or pleasure. (1) depressed or sad mood experienced most of the day, nearly every day (2) diminished interest or pleasure in previously enjoyed activities (3) meaningful unintended weight loss or weight gain, or meaningful decrease or increase in appetite (4) insomnia or hypersomnia (5) psychomotor restlessness or slowing (6) low energy or fatigue (7) feelings of worthlessness or excessive or inappropriate guilty feelings (8) reduced ability to make decisions or concentrate (9) having thoughts of death, suicidal ideation, a plan for completing suicide, or a suicide attempt B. The cluster of symptoms cause meaningful personal distress or an impairment in social, occupational, or other areas of functioning.
Dysthymic Disorder	A. Depressed or sad mood for most of the day, for more days than not, lasting at least 2 years. B. Presence, while depressed, of at least two of the following: (1) poor appetite or overeating (2) insomnia or hypersomnia (3) low energy or fatigue (4) low self-esteem (5) reduced ability to make decisions or concentration (6) having feelings or hopelessness During the 2-year period of the disturbance, the person has never been without significant symptoms for more than 2 months at a time.
Adjustment Disorder With Depressed Mood	A. The development of emotional or behavioral symptoms in response to a specific stressor occurring within 3 months of the onset of the stressor. B. These symptoms or behaviors are meaningful as shown by either of the following: (1) distress that is in excess of what would be expected from exposure to the stressor (2) meaningful impairment in social, occupational, or academic functioning.

Source: Adapted from the American Psychiatric Association (2000).

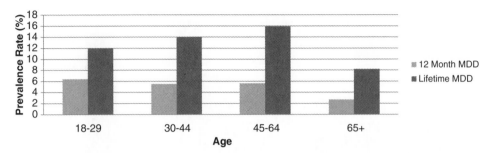

Figure 8.1 Prevalence of Major Depressive Disorder (MDD) by age, 12-month rates and lifetime rates.
Source: Adapted from Hasin et al. (2005).

of disorders is in terms of the rates of disorder among a specific population within the past year, referred to as 1-year prevalence rates. Lifetime prevalence rates describe the percent of a population who have ever experienced the disorder. The prevalence rates reported in this section are drawn from the recent reviews of the literature written by Fiske, Wetherell, and Gatz (2009) and Blazer (2003), who describe the epidemiological literature in considerable detail.

Community-dwelling older adults living in the United States as well as around the world show generally low rates of diagnosable MDD, with rates ranging from 1 to 5 percent. As shown in Figure 8.1, 12-month prevalence rates for MDD are highest in the 18–29-year-old group, the rates are slightly lower for the 30–44-year-old group and 45–64-year-old group, and are the lowest for the 65+ group. Lifetime rates for MDD show a slightly different picture, with rates peaking in the 45–64-year-old group. Note, however, that for both 12-month rates and lifetime rates, older adults show the lowest rates of MDD, despite the fact that their advanced age has afforded many more years in which a disorder could develop (Hasin, Goodwin, Stinson, & Grant, 2005). These data speak to the resiliency developed by many older adults who are able to ward off clinical depression despite many of the challenges posed by growing older. Other explanations for the pattern include differential mortality rates for persons with depressive disorders or differences in recollections of depressive episodes.

Rates for dysthymic disorder are less than 2 percent for community-dwelling older adults. In contrast to the low rates for diagnosable depression, prevalence rates for subsyndromal depressions are quite high among community-dwelling older adults at about 15 percent (Blazer, 2003). Women consistently report more depressive symptoms than men throughout the full adult life span (at about a 2:1 ratio), although the gender gap appears to narrow somewhat in later life. The reasons for this narrowing remain unclear at present (Fiske et al., 2009). There are no differences in depressive symptoms with increasing age when confounding variables such as gender and functional status are controlled (Blazer, 2003). About half of older adults with depression have the first onset of depression in later life, called *late-onset depression*. The remaining half of older adults with depression had experienced prior episodes

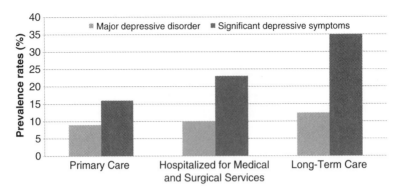

Figure 8.2 Prevalence of depressive disorders in older adults across settings.
Source: Adapted from Blazer (2003).

of depression, in some cases maintaining the disorder as they entered the later life stage (Fiske et al., 2009). In contrast, dysthymic disorder rarely begins in later life but may persist from midlife into later life (Blazer, 2003).

The prevalence of depression among older adults varies significantly across setting (see Figure 8.2). In sharp contrast to the low prevalence rates for community-dwelling older adults, institutionalized older adults (i.e., in long-term care settings) and hospitalized older adults show much higher rates of MDD and significant depressive symptoms. Similarly, older adults in primary care settings also report elevated rates of MDD and significant depressive symptoms compared to community-dwelling older adults. The importance of comorbidity of medical disorders with depression for older adults will be discussed in more detail below. What is particularly noteworthy is the much higher rates of depression among older adults in hospital and nursing home settings.

Theories of Etiology

Across the life span, depression is a mental disorder of biological, psychological, and social etiology. In this section, each of these aspects will be discussed, whereas approaches to assessment and treatment will be described in the following sections.

Biological factors

Biological models of the etiology of depression focus on genetics and on the chemical deficiencies of particular neurotransmitters. Studies of aging twins in the Swedish Twin Registry indicate that genetic heritability for lifetime major depression was moderate overall, but stronger for women (42 percent) than men (29 percent) (Kendler, Gatz, Gardner, & Pedersen, 2006). Several hypotheses regarding the structural and chemical mechanisms through which biological changes might create or enact depression have been offered and examined closely. The profile of neurotransmitters in the brains of adults with depression, and specifically older adults with depression, is different from that in adults without depression. The presence of higher or lower concentrations of particular neurotransmitters in persons with depression than without, along with the effectiveness of antidepressant medications that are intended to alter the concentrations of those same neurotransmitters, lead some researchers to conclude that depression has a biological etiology. However, the biochemical markers that characterize the brains of adults with depression are also found in other disorders, and thus lack the specificity to serve either as an assessment tool or as a clear causal link at this time. It is also difficult to determine if the neurotransmitter changes are the *cause* of depression or a biological *effect* of being clinically depressed. These biological factors (i.e., a genetic propensity toward depression; neurotransmitter changes) are probably best considered as risk factors for depression in later life but are probably not a direct cause of depression.

In older adults, depression is often associated with medical illnesses, medications taken to treat medical conditions, and other psychoactive substances that alter brain chemistry through various mechanisms, producing depression as a side effect. In cases where depression is a direct physiological result of a medical condition or of ingesting a psychoactive substance (whether legal or illegal in nature), the formal diagnoses, respectively, would be Mood Disorder Due to a General Medical Condition or Substance-Induced Mood Disorder. Table 8.2 provides a list of illnesses and

Table 8.2 Medical conditions and medications associated with depression among older adults

Medical conditions
Coronary artery disease
  Hypertension, myocardial infarction, coronary artery bypass surgery, congestive heart failure
Neurologic disorders
  Cerebrovascular accidents, Alzheimer's disease, Parkinson's disease, amyotrophic lateral
  sclerosis, multiple sclerosis, Binswanger's disease
Metabolic disturbances
  Diabetes mellitus, hypothyroidism or hyperthyroidism, hypercortisolism,
  hyperparathyroidism, Addison's disease, auto-immune thyroiditis
Cancer
  Pancreatic, breast, lung, colonic, and ovarian carcinoma, lymphoma, and undetected
  cerebral metastasis
Other conditions
  Chronic obstructive pulmonary disease, rheumatoid arthritis, deafness, chronic pain,
  sexual dysfunction, renal dialysis, chronic constipation

Medications
anesthetics, analgesics (used to relieve pain), anticholinergics, anticonvulsants (e.g.,
  carbamazepine), antihypertensives (used to relieve high blood pressure), anti-Parkinson
  medications, antiulcer medications, cardiac medications (e.g., digitalis; calcium channel
  blockers), psychotropic medications (e.g., antidepressants; benzodiazepines), muscle
  relaxants, steroids, sulfonamides

Source: Adapted from the American Psychiatric Association (2000).

medications that commonly produce depression among older adults. A thorough evaluation of depression in older adults should therefore include a detailed assessment of any current medical conditions and any current medications, whether prescribed or over-the-counter, and the nutritional status of the person.

Psychological factors

Each model of mental health and aging generates its own theory of depression. As described in Chapter 3, the psychodynamic model of depression in older adults describes several mechanisms through which an older adult may become depressed. One central theme revolves around the high rate of losses in later life that challenge the individual's ego functioning (Newton, Brauer, Gutmann, & Grunes, 1986). Losses of social roles, friends, family members, spouse or partner, and physical vitality and functioning, all must be grieved. The grief itself is a risk factor for depression, and the fact that the losses are often cumulative in a short period of time yields particular vulnerability to depression. Additional complications of loss may occur if the person experienced a highly significant loss in childhood (e.g., the loss of an attachment figure) that may establish a particular vulnerability for re-experiencing the highly intense grief as it was experienced when a child. Immature defense mechanisms always leave a person vulnerable to complications during significant life transitions because immature defenses offer less flexibility to adapt. Thus, individuals with lifelong patterns of immature coping are particularly vulnerable to poor adaptation to the many losses of later life (Vaillant, 2002).

Given that a major theme of later life is decline of physical strength and, in some, cognitive abilities, this diminished capacity is also viewed as a risk factor for depression by psychodynamic theorists. Such losses drain the strength of the ego to structure internal and external adaptation, thus leaving the individual vulnerable to feeling out of control, inadequate, and, ultimately, depressed. Finally, psychodynamic theorists describe the importance of integrating later-life losses into one's personal narrative in a manner that creates meaning and a coherent life story (Cohler & Hostetler, 2003). Narratives that cannot integrate loss themes in ways that sustain a strong sense of personal meaning can lead to despair and depression.

Behavioral theories relate depression to a loss of reinforcers. Individuals engage in lower rates of behavior and thus receive lower levels of positive reinforcement (Laidlaw, Thompson, Dick-Siskin, & Gallagher-Thompson, 2004; Zarit & Zarit, 2007). A vicious cycle develops in which the person, who may feel apathetic or blue, begins to isolate himself. This isolation leads to less contact with things/persons/events that were previously pleasurable, and serves to maintain depression. Another related theory is that there are decreased positive interactions between the person and his or her environment (Teri, 1996). The individual experiences a loss of ability to engage in previously enjoyed activities. This leads to an increased reliance on others to initiate and maintain activities. The loss of significant others due to death or withdrawal can also lead to a reduction in reinforcers, particularly if the significant other was one on whom the person relied to maintain activities. Finally, increased aversive interactions between the person and his or her environment can also lead to the development of depression (e.g., marital conflict, occupational problems). Effective treatment may improve the quality of life for the older person and also lead to a decrease in depression-associated problems for both the depressed older person and his or her caregivers (Teri & Wagner, 1992; Zarit & Zarit, 2007).

Another aspect is the strong contingent relationship between pleasant activities and depression in older adults and younger adults (Lewinsohn & Graf, 1973). Persons with depression engage in fewer pleasant activities and receive less pleasure from them than do persons without depression. Interventions have demonstrated the causal relationships between activities and mood. For example, reducing the frequency of pleasant events in a nondepressed person's life increases his or her risk of negative mood, whereas increasing the rate and pleasurableness of pleasant activities also reduces the rate of depression. Thus, behaviors and contingent relationships between behavior and reinforcers are viewed as causal agents for mood disorders, as described in more detail in Chapter 4.

Cognitive theories of depression implicate dysfunctional thought patterns as being causal, emphasizing the role of negative thinking in development and maintenance of depression. Although cognitions are given primary importance in the development of mood states, the model is best thought of as being more circular in nature, in which the effects of mood states on thought patterns are also important. Several specific cognitive distortions (or irrational beliefs) are common among depressed persons, including all-or-none reasoning, jumping to conclusions without first checking the evidence, using their emotional state to explain causal sequences, and the use of "should" statements (Laidlaw et al., 2004). As has been demonstrated with adults of all ages, specific cognitive distortions create depressed feelings (Beck, Rush, Shaw, & Emery, 1979). Depression, on the other hand, also maintains cognitively distorted perceptions of the self, the world, and the future, commonly called the "cognitive triad" for depression. In practice, the cognitive and behavioral models are typically blended into the CBT perspective.

Social factors

Social factors (that is, psychosocial stressors) are almost always involved in the onset of depression or in the deterioration of a person currently experiencing depression. People with depression can typically identify several stressors that are negatively affecting their mood, and sometimes the stressor is the precipitating event for treatment (e.g., retirement, death of spouse, divorce, diagnosis of a chronic illness, relocation to a care facility). A small minority of people with depression cannot seem to easily identify any specific stressor, but during a thorough clinical interview with the person, some relevant stressors typically can be uncovered. The point we are emphasizing is that depression usually does not occur "in a vacuum" outside of the context of a particular person's psychological and social environments.

Psychosocial factors that affect risk for depression among older adults have been organized by George (1994) into six categories that progress from distal to proximal factors (see Table 8.3). Demographic variables such as age, gender, and race/ethnicity affect prevalence rates of depression, although the correlation of these variables with depression is often weaker for older than younger adults. Category 2, events and achievements from childhood, such as deprivations (e.g., poverty or

Table 8.3 Social antecedents of depression

Category	Name	Illustrative indicators
1	Demographic variables	Age, sex, race, ethnicity
2	Early events and achievements	Education, childhood traumas
3	Later events and achievements	Occupation, income, marital status
4	Social integration	Religious affiliation, voluntary organization participation, neighborhood stability
5	Vulnerability and protective factors	Chronic stressors, social support vs. isolation
6	Provoking agents and coping efforts	Life events, coping styles and strategies

Source: Adapted from George (1994), p. 132.

parental separation and divorce) and educational attainment, predict depression throughout adulthood. Later events and achievements such as work and marital experiences also predict depression (category 3). For older adults, these characteristics often reflect past lifestyles more than current experiences, again offering less predictive power. Social integration (category 4) encompasses both individual-level characteristics (e.g., social networks) and aggregate-level characteristics (e.g., neighborhood disintegration).

The fifth and sixth categories of this model include the factors that have been studied most extensively in older adults. Category 5 includes factors related to chronic stress that render a person either vulnerable or are protective over time. Chronic financial problems, chronic physical illness, and caregiving responsibilities have all been shown to have negative effects upon mental health, and depression in particular. Social support is recognized to have very positive, protective effects against the impact of chronic stress. George (1994) summarizes three types of social support that have been demonstrated to affect mental health: (1) social network (size and structure of network of significant persons); (2) tangible support (e.g., instrumental and emotional services); and (3) perceptions of social support. The individual's *perceptions* of supportiveness appear to be more powerful buffers of stress than any objective characteristics of the network. As such, the understanding of perceptions of support systems is an important topic in a clinical interview with an older person with depression.

Category 6 includes the factors that are current and salient: life events and coping strategies. Several events are recognized to provoke adaptive behavior in the lives of older adults, including retirement, widowhood, death of friends, and onset of physical illness. Life events show a consistent relationship to depression, although it is a modest one. Clearly, most older adults experience the events of later life without becoming depressed.

The biopsychosocial model: Putting it all together

Whereas we have discussed biological, psychological, and social factors in depression separately, in the vast majority of cases, these three factors *interact* to cause depression in an older person. One biopsychosocial theory points to stressful life events as a trigger for depression. This is often referred to as a *diathesis-stress model*, in which the individual has some biological and/or psychological vulnerability to depression and a stressor (e.g., loss of loved one; physical illness or disability) precipitates development of the depression. Other psychosocial factors implicated include the meaning of loss to the person, a limited social support system, and poor coping resources (Zarit & Zarit, 2007).

Other Risk Factors for Depression

One of the life events most widely believed to be associated with depression in later life is the death of a loved one and the consequent bereavement and grief. Perhaps because social losses are common in later life, grief is an intuitively compelling predictor. Indeed, in some cases the grief process produces emotions, thoughts, and behaviors that are similar to those evoked by depression, a pattern called *complicated grief.* The loss of a relationship that in many cases is lifelong (exceeding 50 or 60 years together) can leave survivors with a deep sense of despair, loneliness, and other mood symptoms. The case of Jenny Miller described above illustrates the depression that can result from an unresolved or complicated grief process. Prigerson and her colleagues (e.g., Prigerson, Vanderwerker, & Maciejewski, 2007) have argued that the symptoms of complicated grief are associated with enduring functional impairments and appear to define a unique mental disorder (called prolonged grief disorder) that is deserving of specialized treatment.

Grief, however, typically proceeds forward to resolve the symptoms without the persistent, pervasive effects of depression. Indeed, from his series of well-designed studies, Bonanno (2004, 2009) concluded that most people are naturally resilient in the face of bereavement and other traumatic losses and that in many cases people cope with grief and loss in ways that seem at first blush to be counterintuitive, such as by experiencing joy, laughter, and a deepening of connections to others. Again, it is important to recognize that whereas loss, bereavement, and grief are normative in later life, depression is not.

Coping strategies may be one mediating variable that buffers individuals from the deleterious effects of negative life events. Two types of coping appear to be useful: problem-focused or instrumental coping, and emotion-focused or accommodative coping (Lazarus & Folkman, 1987). People use problem-focused coping to try to change the circumstances that produced the impact of the negative event. Emotion-focused coping, on the other hand, directs people to accommodate to the circumstances by reducing the emotional impact of the stressor. In contrast to the benefits of problem-focused coping and emotion-focused coping, it appears that a ruminative coping style, in which one repeatedly but passively thinks about one's distress, is associated with depression among older adults (Fiske et al., 2009). As discussed in Chapter 5, Aldwin has examined the effects of coping strategies on adjustment to the stressors of later life.

Personality variables may also place a person at risk for depression. In their investigation of depression as a trait in longitudinal studies of normal aging, Costa and McCrae (1994) report high levels of stability in the depression trait over a six-year period for adults of all ages. The personality trait of neuroticism is also robustly related to depression among older adults. Furthermore, the clinical evidence of comorbidity between personality disorders (discussed fully in Chapter 11) and depression also suggests an important role for personality as a risk factor for depression. As many as 50 percent of older adults with MDD also demonstrate significant personality disorder features (e.g., Thompson, Gallagher, & Czirr, 1988). Whether these disorders are risk factors, are simply comorbid, or are even consequences of depression is unclear, but the risk of a coexisting personality disorder in depressed older adults is substantial. Of course, more adaptive personality traits (e.g., optimism, extraversion) can also serve as buffers against depression.

Physical illness is a major risk factor for depression in older adults. About 30 percent of medical inpatients report high rates of depressive symptoms on self-report scales (Rapp, Parisi, & Walsh, 1988). Clinical depression occurs in medically ill patients at approximately 12 times the rate that it appears in community-dwelling older adults (Lichtenberg, 1998). Unfortunately, depression also can complicate healing and rehabilitation because persons with depression are far more likely to report "excess disability" or disability beyond their actual limitations. Excess disability reporting can lead to non-compliance with rehabilitative efforts that leaves the person vulnerable to reduced functional capacity and further illness. Even more concerning is the tendency of physicians to fail to detect depression (Rapp et al., 1988).

Institutionalization is another risk factor for depression. A high rate of nursing home residents are clinically depressed, with estimates ranging from 14 percent to 42 percent (see review by Fiske et al., 2009). Apparently, institutionalization itself places people at risk, in addition to the risks produced by their physical illnesses. The mechanism for this tendency for residents to become depressed is likely a combination of the increased disability due to illness, isolation from personally meaningful relationships and objects, reduced sense of control, and the tendency for staff to support dependent rather than independent behavior. Due to the high rates of depression in these settings, an expert interdisciplinary panel led by the American Geriatrics Society and the American Association for Geriatric Psychiatry (2003) recommended routine and regular screening for depression in every nursing home resident. Sadly, assessment and appropriate treatment of depression among nursing home residents are typically poor. Finally, interpersonal conflict and social stressors are other important risk factors for depression (Hinrichsen & Emery, 2005).

Vascular Depression and its Link to Dementia

In addition to the biopsychosocial etiological factors for depression we have just described, an emerging literature base has documented an important connection between cardiovascular disease and depression in some older adults. Specifically, the "vascular depression hypothesis" suggests that cardiovascular disease can *predispose, precipitate, or perpetuate* a depressive episode in many older adults with underlying neurologic brain disorders (Alexopoulos et al., 1997). This hypothesis is supported by the high frequency of depression in older adults with coronary artery disease, hypertension, diabetes, and stroke. The term *depression-executive dysfunction syndrome of later life* is currently utilized to describe this combination of depressive symptoms and cognitive deficits that may not be exclusively caused by vascular disease (Fiske et al., 2009).

A related issue is that the emergence of depressive symptoms in late life appears in most cases to be associated with greater cognitive impairments, especially executive function deficits such as planning and organizing behavior. Older adults with late-onset depression are also more likely to subsequently develop a cognitive or dementing disorder. This is particularly true for those with accompanying cognitive impairment or evidence of structural brain changes (e.g., from an MRI exam), suggesting that some types of late-onset depressions represent the prodromal or early precursor phase of dementia (Fiske et al., 2009).

Assessment

Assessment can serve four major purposes: screening for the presence of a problem, identifying the classification of the problem, establishing baseline information useful for planning intervention, and assessing the outcomes of the interventions (Futterman, Thompson, Gallagher-Thompson, & Ferris, 1995). Assessment tools are chosen to meet a specific purpose because each type of tool has its strengths and limitations. Generally, *self-report scales* are very useful for identifying clinical levels of depression, although they do not provide a diagnosis. *Structured and semi-structured interviews* are more useful for creating a reliable and valid diagnosis, although they typically take at least one to two hours to fully administer. Neither of those strategies is sufficient to serve as a basis for guiding intervention planning or measuring progress toward treatment goals. Treatment planning and evaluation require measurement of the specific domains of functioning targeted by the treatment (e.g., cognition or behavior).

Before describing a select set of tools that can address all three goals of assessment, some general comments regarding the assessment of older adults are needed. First, age-appropriate norms must be used to interpret any assessment scale scores. The norms for older adults are often quite different from those for younger persons. The differences in norms may be based on differences in how cohorts express their distress, the impact of physical illness on the symptom profile of mental disorders, or true differences in the phenomenon of late-life depression. Second, the medical conditions and medication usage of older adults are particularly likely to affect psychological functioning. Thus, assessment of depression in older adults must include a careful medical and pharmacological evaluation. Third, older adults who abuse substances are particularly unlikely to disclose their substance usage, making substance abuse an important focus of assessment in persons with depressed affect.

Refer back to the case of Jenny Miller at the beginning of the chapter. How would you proceed with an evaluation of Jenny? Although there are obvious psychosocial factors we might suspect to be involved in her depression, other factors such as medical illness, pharmacological agents, and substance abuse must be ruled out before proceeding with a psychologically focused intervention for depression.

Self-report measures are used primarily for screening purposes, and as a quick indicator of the intensity of clinical symptoms during the treatment process. Several short depression screening instruments are readily available for clinical and research use:

- The Center for Epidemiologic Studies – Depression Scale (CES-D; Radloff, 1977) consists of 20 self-report items that tap depressive symptoms experienced over the past week. Each item is rated on a 4-point Likert-type scale ranging from 0 (rarely/none) to 3 (most of the time). Traditionally, a total score is calculated by adding the ratings for all items. The possible range of total scores is from 0 to 60, with higher scores reflecting greater levels of depression. The CES-D was developed primarily as a research instrument for studies with adolescents and adults, although it has been used successfully with older adults due to its relatively low emphasis on somatic symptoms.

- The Beck Depression Inventory – Second Edition (BDI-II; Beck, Steer, & Brown, 1996) is a 21-item self-report questionnaire that is widely used in clinical research and practice as a screening device. Each item describes a specific manifestation of depressive symptoms, and the respondent reads four evaluative statements and indicates his/her current severity level for that item. Thirteen items assess psychological symptoms of depression, whereas eight items assess somatic symptoms. Potential scores range from 0 to 63, with higher scores corresponding to higher levels of depression. According to the BDI-II manual, scores of 0–13 denote minimal depression, scores of 14–19 denote mild depression, scores of 20–28 denote moderate depression, and scores of 29–63 denote severe depression. The main criticisms of the BDI-II are that it has many somatic items, which may not be reflective of depression in some older adults, and that the response format is not as simple as the other popular self-report measures, a particular detriment when working with individuals with cognitive impairment. A recent study reported excellent psychometric properties of the BDI-II among community-dwelling older adults (Segal, Coolidge, Cahill, & O'Riley, 2008), suggesting that these potential limitations should not preclude use of the BDI-II with older adults.

- The Geriatric Depression Scale (GDS; Yesavage et al., 1983) is a 30-item self-report measure designed specifically for use with older adults, making it by far the most popular screening inventory for clinical and research purposes with older adults. As shown in Figure 4.1 (Chapter 4), all of the items of the GDS are appropriate for usage with older adults. The GDS focuses on cognitive and behavioral aspects of depression, whereas somatic items are generally excluded, which prevents the possible spurious elevation in screening measure scores obtained by medically ill but not depressed older adults. Another useful feature of the GDS is the very simple "yes/no" response format for each item. In 20 of the 30 items, the answer "yes" indicates depression; in the remaining 10, the answer "no" indicates depression. The total GDS score consists of the sum of all items. The recommended cutoffs for the GDS include 0–10 for minimal to mild depression, 11–20 for mild to moderate depression, and 21 to 30 for severe depression. A short version of the GDS containing 15 items is also available and has been well validated as a screening measure (Sheikh & Yesavage, 1986). A potential drawback to the GDS is its limited validity for use with ethnically diverse older adults (Mui, Burnette, & Chen, 2001).

For more detailed reviews of the various tools available for the screening of depression, see Edelstein et al. (2008) and Fairchild and Scogin (2008).

Despite popularity of the self-report measures described previously, it should be noted that a definitive diagnosis of depression (or any mental disorder for that matter) should never be made on the basis of self-report inventories alone, which can be subject to response biases (e.g., social desirability) and generally can be easily faked. In practice, a two-step process is typical whereby elevated self-reported scores on the screening instrument are followed up by a clinical or structured interview to confirm presence or absence of the disorder.

Clinical interview is the most common method of assessing depression in everyday practice, typically in unstructured format. During the interview, the clinician gathers information about the person's current symptoms of depression, including a history of the depression and attempts at coping with the depression. Other topics are typically pursued to place the experiences with depression in the context of overall functioning, including an in-depth personal history, mental health history (including interventions), medical history, marital, family, social, and work history, and a mental status examination. Collateral interviews with concerned family members or caregivers are a common and usually informative component of the depression assessment. To facilitate rapport, clinicians should explain clearly the purposes and procedures of the assessment, address any concerns the person may have about the evaluation, and be especially flexible when engaging older persons and their family members (Segal, Coolidge, & Hersen, 1998). Being generous with warmth, support, and reassurance (when needed) also helps with rapport. During the interview it is important for clinicians to screen for cognitive disorders to rule out cognitive impairments that could be causing some or all of the depressive symptoms.

In contrast to an unstructured clinical interview, structured interviews provide increased clinical accuracy by structuring questions to elicit details about frequency and intensity of symptoms (Segal & Coolidge, 2007). Examples of structured interviews that are commonly used for clinical research and training include the *Diagnostic Interview Schedule for DSM-IV* (DIS-IV; Robins, Cottler, Bucholz, & Compton, 1995) and the *Structured Clinical Interview for DSM-IV-TR Axis I Disorders* (SCID; First, Spitzer, Gibbon, & Williams, 2002). Each of these has been demonstrated to be useful for older adults.

The focus and strategies of assessment for the purpose of treatment planning are shaped significantly by the theoretical model from which the therapist works. A cognitive-behavioral therapist may focus on assessing the frequency of participation in pleasant and unpleasant activities as well as the nature of the client's thought patterns, whereas a psychodynamic therapist may evaluate in detail the interpersonal relationship style with which the client engages the therapist. Treatment goals such as reducing depressogenic cognitive distortions require specific assessment of the types and frequency of cognitive distortions. Only by documenting the specific, operationalized instances of the distortions can a therapist design an appropriate intervention or measure the impact of the intervention on that specific problem.

Our original point about assessment bears repeating: Assessment tools need to be selected to be appropriate for the task at hand. For example, a screening instrument is insufficient to determine a diagnosis but useful for detecting problematic symptoms, and a clinical interview is insufficient to guide treatment planning but appropriate for diagnosis. Referring back again to the Jenny Miller case, an appropriate assessment strategy might begin with administering a self-report screening instrument such as the Geriatric Depression Scale to determine the intensity and range of symptoms experienced, followed by a clinical interview to identify the appropriate diagnosis. If she is indeed clinically depressed, assessment of her specific concerns may be used to formulate a treatment plan. Further assessments of her grieving process, family and friend relationships, daily activity schedule, cognitive framework, coping strategies, and mental abilities are all needed before treatment can be planned.

Interventions

More research and clinical case studies have focused on interventions with depressed older adults than any other older clinical population, highlighting clearly that various psychotherapeutic approaches and biological interventions *are effective* for late-life depression.

Biological approaches

The two main categories of biological treatments for depression include psychiatric medications and electroconvulsive therapy (ECT).

Most older adults seek treatment for depression from their primary care provider rather than from a mental health specialist. Thus, it is not surprising that a high percentage of mental health treatment for older adults is pharmacological. The vast majority of medications used to treat depression fall into one of three categories: tricyclic antidepressants (TCAs), monoamine oxidase (MAO) inhibitors, and selective serotonin reuptake inhibitors (SSRIs). These three classes of medications work on different aspects of the neurotransmitter systems of the brain. The tricyclic antidepressants work to increase the availability of norepinephrine and serotonin in the brain, and show the same effectiveness in older adults that are evident in young adults. Their primary disadvantage is the high probability of unpleasant side effects (e.g., weight gain, sedation, cardiovascular effects, postural hypotension, and confusion). The mechanism for MAO inhibitors is unclear. Their usage is complicated by the necessity of dietary and medication restrictions, but they are also effective with older adults.

SSRIs represent the newest class of antidepressant medications and increase the availability of serotonin. Whereas trials have demonstrated similar efficacy for SSRIs, TCAs, and MAO inhibitors (with moderate to large effect sizes), the SSRIs have the fewest side effects, and thus represent a first line medication choice for many older adults (Blazer, 2003; Shanmugham, Karp, Drayer, Reynolds, & Alexopoulos, 2005). Medications are chosen according to the following criteria: side effect profile, prior history of response to medication, history of first degree relatives' response to medication, concurrent medications and illnesses that may render one choice more risky than another, likelihood of adherence to the medical regimen, degree of interference with lifestyle, cost, and preference of patient or prescriber (Agency for Health Care Policy and Research, 1993).

ECT has been a highly controversial intervention used primarily for severe recalcitrant depression that has not responded to pharmacotherapy or psychotherapy and has life-threatening complications (e.g., severe suicidal potential). The literature on ECT suggests it is an effective, evidence-based form of treatment that is used disproportionately with older adults (Kelly & Zisselman, 2000). Improvement is seen in about 80 percent of patients (although relapse can be a problem) and evidence that it is used effectively with patients for whom other therapies have failed lends further credence to claims of its effectiveness (Kelly & Zisselman, 2000; Wilkinson, 2002). Potential complications for ECT among older adults include cardiac problems, confusion, memory loss (which is usually temporary), and delirium, suggesting that caution with this approach is advised (Fiske et al., 2009), particularly in individuals with cognitive impairment.

Psychotherapeutic approaches

The effectiveness of psychological interventions for clinical levels as well as subclinical levels of depression among older adults is quite high, indicating that several types of psychotherapy meet the benchmark for an evidence-based intervention. These interventions include behavioral therapy, cognitive-behavioral therapy, cognitive bibliotherapy, problem-solving therapy, brief psychodynamic therapy, and life review therapy (see reviews by Scogin & McElreath, 1994; Scogin, Welsh, Hanson, Stump, & Coates, 2005).

Therapy outcome studies find that pharmacotherapy and psychotherapy of various types are approximately equally effective, treating successfully between 50 and 70 percent of older adults with MDD within 12–20 sessions (Agency for Health Care Policy and Research, 1993). A recent meta-analysis comparing psychological and pharmacological interventions for depression indicated that effect sizes may even favor psychotherapy (Pinquart, Duberstein, & Lyness, 2006). The presence of a personality disorder or other complicating factors often reduces the success rate of psychotherapies (Thompson et al., 1988).

The conceptual and statistical analyses comparing the effectiveness of different therapies (including pharmacotherapy and the range of empirically tested psychotherapies) yield a consistent conclusion: No one empirically supported therapy is clearly superior to all others, but all of the empirically supported therapies are superior to no intervention or placebo. This pattern is helpful to clinicians who typically draw upon a variety of frameworks and techniques to effect change with a wide variety of clients. Of course, the full range of clients who are depressed is not included in research outcome studies, many of which are notably lacking in their inclusion of nursing home residents, ethnic minority older adults, and the very old (over 85 years of age). Researchers find it most useful to narrow the possible confounding variables in therapy outcome studies by limiting participation to older adults without other physical and mental health problems. Clinical work in other settings requires more flexibility in working with depression of many varieties combined with various other physical or mental health problems (e.g., arthritis, anxiety, or substance abuse). Thus, the therapy outcome studies provide very useful guidance, but the treatment protocols often must be adapted to meet the needs of complex clients.

CBT is the most thoroughly tested psychotherapy used with depressed older adults. CBT attempts to alter the cognitive frameworks of clients to eliminate depressogenic thought patterns and to change behavior patterns to include a higher rate of pleasant activities (Gallagher & Thompson, 1981; Laidlaw et al., 2004; Thompson, Gallagher-Thompson, & Dick, 1995). The essence of this treatment model is to alter the person's thought patterns and behavior simultaneously by engaging him or her in 12–20 structured therapy sessions and substantial homework activity between sessions. Therapists help clients to identify, plan, and increase pleasant events and to learn the connections between thoughts and feelings, identify cognitive distortions, and change negative thought patterns. To help clients increase pleasant events, the behaviorally based interventions involve identifying enjoyable activities through behavioral self-observations using an activity diary and a mood rating scale. Once mood-enhancing activities have been identified, the procedure entails increasing involvement in enjoyable activities that are realistic given the older person's current physical and cognitive abilities. These interventions may also include a component aimed at decreasing behaviors that lead to or maintain depressive symptoms (e.g., overdependence, passivity) (Laidlaw et al., 2004).

Methodologically rigorous outcome studies suggest that this form of therapy shows efficacy rates that are maintained over a two-year period, similar to the success rates of pharmacological treatments and psychodynamic psychotherapy (Pinquart et al., 2006). CBT has been used effectively with depressed caregivers of ill older adults, with depressed Alzheimer's patients, and with older adults experiencing major depression (e.g., Gallagher-Thompson & Steffan, 1994; Teri, Logsdon, Wagner, & Uomoto, 1994). CBT has also proven effective when offered in a group psychoeducational format using nonprofessional leaders as well as professional leaders to remediate minor depression (Thompson, Gallagher, Nies, & Epstein, 1983).

Cognitive bibliotherapy is a treatment wherein participants learn the principles and techniques of CBT by reading books about the topic, such as *Feeling Good* by David Burns (1999). In essence, cognitive bibliotherapy is self-administered CBT. Its educative and self-paced structure may be ideal for older adults, and the outcome data show it is an effective form of treatment (Floyd, Scogin, McKendree-Smith, Floyd, & Rokke, 2004; Scogin, Jamison, & Davis, 1990).

Problem-solving therapy (PST) has at its core a step-by-step process that clients learn to identify and implement solutions to problems they are experiencing (see Chapter 4 for a more thorough description of the PST model and specific problem-solving steps). PST therapy is known to be effective for a wide range of depressed older adults including outpatients (Areán et al., 1993), frail home-bound older adults (Gellis, McGinty, Horowitz, Bruce, & Misener, 2007), primary care patients (Areán,

Hegel, Vannoy, Fan, & Unuzter, 2008), and older adults with executive dysfunction problems (Alexopoulos, Raue, Kanellopoulos, Mackin, & Areán, 2008).

Two forms of psychodynamic therapies have been shown to be effective with depressed older adults. Brief psychodynamic therapy was tested by Gallagher and Thompson (1981) in their clinical trials. Psychodynamic therapies focus on working through grief and loss concerns that generate sufficient anxiety to impede the maturation of functioning. By addressing the anxiety directly, patients are able to proceed with their development toward more mature styles of coping and defense (see Chapter 3 for a more thorough discussion of this model). This form of treatment showed the same success rate as CBT in treating MDD (Gallagher-Thompson & Steffan, 1994).

Another psychodynamically based model that has generated considerable interest in its use with older people is interpersonal therapy (IPT; Weissman, Markowitz, & Klerman, 2000), which is a practical, focused, brief, manual-based therapy that has been adapted successfully for older adults (Hinrichsen, 2008; Hinrichsen & Clougherty, 2006). IPT focuses on disturbances in current relationships by addressing four themes considered core to the development or maintenance of depression: grief (e.g., the death of a loved one), interpersonal disputes (e.g., conflict with peers or children), role transitions (e.g., retirement), and interpersonal deficits (e.g., lack of communication or assertiveness skills). Using a semi-structured, time-limited approach (12–20 sessions), IPT employs a range of eclectic psychotherapeutic techniques intended to improve interpersonal communication, clarify emotional states, express affect, and support renegotiated role relationships. In combination with an antidepressant (nortriptyline), IPT has been shown to be an effective treatment for depression in older adults, both in the acute phase and for relapse prevention (Reynolds et al., 1999).

Life review therapy (also called reminiscence therapy) is another empirically supported therapy approach for depression in older adults. As one of the few therapeutic modalities that has arisen from clinical work with older adults, it warrants attention. Building on the theories of Erik Erikson, Butler (1974) proposed that conducting a life review is a normal developmental task of later life. The life review requires older adults to integrate the disparate themes of a given life. Persons who do not integrate their lives successfully are vulnerable to despair and depression. Many different forms of life review therapy have been used, although clinical trials have tended to structure the reminiscence around the themes Erikson believed to be salient (e.g., past accomplishments and failures, interpersonal conflicts, meaning). There is solid support for life review therapy as an evidence-based treatment (Areán et al., 1993; Serrano, Latorre, Gatz, & Montanes, 2004). Although not specific to depression, a recent meta-analysis (Bohlmeijer, Roemer, Cuijpers, & Smit, 2007) suggests that life review is a worthwhile intervention for enhancing psychological well-being in older adults with effect sizes comparable to CBT.

With the plethora of useful approaches available for treating depression in older adults, how does one decide which to use and for how long? Some groups have worked to develop algorithms for treatment decisions. For example, the Agency for Health Care Policy and Research (1993) published guidelines to assist primary care physicians in identifying, assessing, and treating depression. The guidelines initially recommended medications as the first line of attack, but more recent evidence resulted in the recommendation of either medications or psychotherapy depending on patient preferences (Schulberg, Katon, Simon, & Rush, 1998). Interestingly, when given a choice, older primary care patients seem to prefer psychotherapy approaches over medication (Gum et al., 2006). Sadly, despite the effectiveness of many treatments, depression is frequently not recognized, and thus not treated in older adults (Charney et al., 2003). Some reasons for this problem include biases of clinicians and older adults themselves (e.g., assuming it is normal to become depressed in later life; assuming that there are no appropriate treatments), misattribution of symptoms, the difficulty detecting depression due to the age differences in presentation described earlier, and the true complexity of diagnosing depression in medically ill or neurologically impaired older adults (e.g., Fiske et al., 2009; Karel, Ogland-Hand, Gatz, & Unützer, 2002).

Prevention of Depression

We have just provided an overview of treatments for depression in older adults, highlighting the point that several biological and psychological treatments for depression are evidence based, empirically supported, and as such known to be effective for older adults. However, one may wonder: What do we know about the *prevention* of depression in late life?

Prevention efforts for depression in later life may be aimed at three areas: to avoid a first onset of depression in later life, to prevent the recurrence of depression in older individuals with a prior history of MDD, and to prevent relapse after successful treatment for depression (Fiske et al., 2009). In their review of this topic, Fiske et al. note that targeting older adults who are at high risk for developing depression is an important and effective strategy. For example, treating older adults with subsyndromal levels of depression (before it becomes a full-fledged diagnosable mental disorder – i.e., secondary prevention) could prevent almost 25 percent of new cases in later life. Because insomnia is a known risk factor for depression in later life, treatment for insomnia (discussed in more detail in Chapter 10) may be another avenue to prevent the development of depression in older adults.

Other preventative efforts may also be directed at older adults at risk for depression due to physical illness and its consequences, bereavement, caregiving responsibilities for an ill person, and loneliness (Fiske et al., 2009). Finally, educational efforts directed at physicians, senior service professionals, and older adults in the community to help them recognize the signs and symptoms of depression and understand that depression is *not* a normal part of aging may also help with early detection and intervention (Fiske et al., 2009).

Suicide

Before completing a chapter on depression, one needs to consider the risk of suicide in older adults. Suicide is a topic that warrants special attention because of the alarmingly high rate of suicides among the older adult population. In the United States, older adults complete about 20 percent of all suicides whereas they comprise only about 13 percent of the population, reflecting a disproportionate risk in later life. Older adults also have the highest suicide completion (i.e., suicide death) rate of any age group at 14.7 per 100,000 people (Centers for Disease Control and Prevention [CDC], 2005). In particular, older European American men are at greatest risk at more than 32.1 deaths by suicide per 100,000 people (CDC, 2005). Even though European American men 50 years old and older comprise less than a quarter of the population, they are responsible for almost 40 percent of all suicides. Older adults tend to use more lethal means during a suicide attempt, having an attempt to completion ratio that is much lower than that of younger individuals.

The major risk factors for suicide in later life (besides male gender) include depression, hopelessness, substance abuse, previous suicide attempt, widowhood, physical illness, social isolation, family discord, financial strain, and stressful life events (e.g., Blazer, 2003; Duberstein, Conwell, Conner, Eberly, & Caine, 2004; Fiske et al., 2009). Institutionalization may also be a predictor of suicide, although residents of nursing homes tend to use more subtle forms of self-termination that may not be labeled officially as suicide. Unfortunately, the majority of older adults who complete suicide were experiencing their first episode of depression without substantial complications, a condition that would be readily treatable. More alarming, 75 percent of those persons were in their physicians' offices within a month prior to the suicide (Conwell, 1994). Obviously, suicidal thoughts and intent must be assessed in any depressed older adult. General queries about suicidal ideation should be followed up with probes about specific plans and intent.

There are several formal assessment measures for suicidal thinking and behaviors. The Scale for Suicidal Ideation (SSI; Beck, Kovacs, & Weissman, 1979) is a 19-item scale that is completed by a clinician following a semi-structured interview. The Geriatric Hopelessness Scale (GHS; Fry, 1986) is a 30-item self-report scale with a simple "yes/no" response format designed to assess pessimism and cognitions of hopelessness in older adults, which are theoretically related to suicidal behavior in Beck's model of depression. Recently, a specialized measure of suicidal ideation in older adults has been developed and validated. The Geriatric Suicide Ideation Scale (GSIS; Heisel & Flett, 2006) is a 31-item self-report multidimensional measure of suicide ideation with each item rated on a 5-point Likert scale. The GSIS assesses Suicide Ideation (e.g., "I want to end my life"), Death Ideation (e.g., "I welcome the thought of drifting off to sleep and never waking up"), Loss of Personal and Social Worth (e.g., "I generally feel pretty worthless"), and Perceived Meaning in Life (e.g., "I am certain that I have something to live for").

Clearly, if the assessment reveals that the older client is currently at risk for self-harm, the clinician must act to protect the client. If the client is in immediate and imminent danger of suicide and less restrictive treatments are not sufficient, the clinician is required to hospitalize the client. It is best if such hospitalization can be done collaboratively and with the older person's consent by explaining the benefits that may result from a hospital stay (e.g., stabilization with medications). In some cases, hospitalization needs to be done without the consent of the older person, and is called involuntary commitment. This is often stressful for the older person and mental health professional alike. Complications that can arise from involuntary commitments include the hospitalized patient's anger at the clinician and subsequent termination of therapy once released, and the incurred and unwanted financial costs for the hospitalization. As such, involuntary hospitalization is only considered after all other reasonable approaches are exhausted to keep the suicidal older person safe.

Summary and Conclusions

Although depression is a disorder commonly believed to be nearly normative with aging, the rates of clinical depressive disorders in older adults are generally lower than are found in younger adults. However, depression must be taken seriously when it is encountered in older adults, particularly in light of the higher risks of suicide and high degree of excess disability associated with depression. Methods of assessing and treating older adults are similar to those used with younger adults, with minimal alterations required, and they result in similar rates of effectiveness. Despite solid evidence of treatment efficacy, a significant problem is that many older adults with depression do not receive adequate diagnosis and treatment. Due to the high emotional and physical costs of depression, our understanding and increased effectiveness in preventing depression in later life are top priorities for researchers and clinicians.

9

Severe Mental Disorders in Older Adults
Schizophrenia and Other Late-Life Psychoses

Stephen J. Bartels, MD, MS*

As the number of older adults dramatically increases over the next 30 years, the nation's capacity to adequately care for an aging population with schizophrenia will be significantly challenged. Schizophrenia is among the most serious mental disorders, affecting nearly 1 percent of the population, and is associated with health care costs of approximately $40,000 per diagnosed person each year on average (Meeks & Jeste, 2008). In the broader context of improved health care services and extended life expectancy, the treatment of older adults with schizophrenia poses a serious health challenge as the population is expected to grow significantly in the coming decades.

Schizophrenia is a severe and persistent mental disorder that has a dramatic and debilitating effect on most aspects of life functioning, behavior, and personal experience. Early views of schizophrenia maintained that it always began in young adulthood and inevitably resulted in a progressive deterioration of function, thinking, and cognition. This perspective was reflected in the name "dementia praecox," first introduced by Kraepelin (1919/1971) to describe the disorder of schizophrenia (Reeves & Brister, 2008). This term reflected a belief that people affected by the disorder had permanent and progressive mental deterioration beginning at an early age.

Since the original description of dementia praecox, studies of schizophrenia and aging have challenged this view of the disorder. Studies of older populations have found that schizophrenia can begin in middle or old age (Reeves & Brister, 2008). More importantly, longitudinal research on schizophrenia over the life span has shown considerable variation in long-term outcomes. In contrast to the view that

* Director of the Dartmouth Centers for Health and Aging, Professor of Psychiatry, Community, and Family Medicine, and The Dartmouth Institute for Health Policy and Clinical Practice.

Aging and Mental Health, 2e. Daniel L. Segal, Sara Honn Qualls, and Michael A. Smyer schizophrenia results in inevitable cognitive and functional decline, many individuals with schizophrenia experience substantial improvement in symptoms and function as they age (Folsom et al., 2009; Jeste et al., 2003), including some who have full remission of the disorder. At the same time, other individuals have persistent symptoms and functional challenges throughout the life span (Palmer, Heaton, & Jeste, 1999). Common factors that complicate the course of schizophrenia in older age include medical comorbidity (e.g., obesity, diabetes, hypertension, heart disease, chronic obstructive pulmonary disease, hepatitis, and HIV), substance abuse, cognitive impairment, and premature nursing home admission and institutionalization (Andrews, Bartels, Xie, & Peacock, 2009; Bartels, 2004; Rystedt & Bartels, 2008). Advancements in the treatment of schizophrenia have affected the course and outcome of the disorder for many individuals. Modern treatment options include pharmacological therapy, psychosocial rehabilitation, vocational rehabilitation, and models of support for community-dwelling individuals. These treatment options have resulted in more individuals with schizophrenia surviving into old age (Cohen, 2000; Reeves & Brister, 2008).

This chapter contains an overview of schizophrenia over the life span including a description of symptoms, gender differences, course, and outcomes. This chapter first provides an overview of the difference between early-onset and late-onset schizophrenia, in conjunction with considerations in the assessment and treatment process, and concludes with a discussion of future challenges and areas of focus to advance treatment options for older adults with schizophrenia.

Overview of Schizophrenia throughout the Life Span

Schizophrenia is a syndrome characterized by disordered perceptions, thinking, and behavior that has a pervasive effect on personal, social, and vocational functioning. For some individuals, the earliest signs of the disorder may include problems in premorbid (pre-disorder) functioning such as difficulties in social adjustment and interpersonal relationships (Folsom et al., 2009). For others, there may be no signs of significant psychological problems until the onset of psychosis. The onset of schizophrenia generally develops over a period of months. Early signs typically consist of social withdrawal, unusual perceptions or thoughts, and declining interest and spontaneity. For example, a person may fail to show up for work or school and spend long hours in seclusion. Contacts with friends or family may be punctuated by hostile, paranoid, or bizarre comments.

There are a variety of symptoms that make up the syndrome of schizophrenia once it has fully emerged, including positive, negative, and affective symptoms. *Positive symptoms* consist of the primary active symptoms of psychosis. The most common positive symptoms include delusions and hallucinations. Examples of other positive symptoms include severe problems in thought processes such as illogical or poorly related thoughts or illogical or "loose" associations. Behavioral problems include bizarre behaviors, repetitive or ritualistic behaviors, and posturing. Exacerbations of positive symptoms are the most common signs of acute relapse and may require acute hospitalization.

Negative symptoms, or psychomotor poverty symptoms, consist of deficit symptoms including a lack of active or spontaneous behaviors, emotions, or thoughts. Negative symptoms were first used to describe the appearance of neurologically impaired patients who had traumatic brain injuries involving the frontal lobes of the brain (Jackson, 1984). These victims of traumatic brain injury were often passive, spoke few words, and lacked emotional responsiveness. This concept was subsequently applied to the subgroup of individuals with schizophrenia who often lacked prominent active positive symptoms of psychosis, but had severe deficits in social, emotional, and cognitive functioning. Common negative symptoms include the "five As" of negative symptoms in schizophrenia:

- blunted or flat affect (lack of emotional expression);
- alogia (reduced amount of speech or poverty of content);
- asociality (social withdrawal);
- apathy (lack of interest or spontaneity or psychomotor retardation);
- attentional impairment (difficulty concentrating or performing sequential tasks).

Severe negative symptoms are strongly associated with poor social functioning (Bellack, Morrison, Wixted, & Mueser, 1990) and are relatively stable over time (Mueser, Sayers, Schooler, Mance, & Haas, 1994).

In addition to positive and negative symptoms, *affective symptoms* such as depression are common in schizophrenia. Approximately 60 percent of adults with schizophrenia experience major depression during the course of their disorder, with post-psychotic depression occurring after 25 percent of acute schizophrenic episodes. Contrary to early clinical descriptions suggesting better prognosis, depression is associated with poorer outcomes including increased rate of relapse, longer duration of hospitalization, poorer response to pharmacological treatments, chronicity, and suicide. Approximately 50 percent of persons with schizophrenia attempt suicide at some time during their lives, with a 10 percent rate of mortality (Roy, 1986). Three broad subtypes have been described within depression in schizophrenia: depressive symptoms secondary to organic factors (e.g., medication side effects, alcohol and substance abuse, medical disorders); depressive symptoms associated with acute psychosis; and depressive symptoms in chronic states including secondary major depression, negative symptoms, chronic demoralization, and early signs of acute psychotic episodes (Bartels & Drake, 1988). Appropriate and effective treatment of depression in schizophrenia is dependent on identifying the subtype and implementing the appropriate treatment or intervention (Bartels & Drake, 1989).

Schizophrenia is a heterogeneous disorder with considerable variation in severity of symptoms and functioning across different individuals. However, a hallmark of the syndrome consists of impaired functioning in basic living skills, including initiating and maintaining meaningful interpersonal relationships, fulfilling major roles in society (e.g., education, employment), or engaging in basic self-care or community living skills (e.g., grooming, hygiene, managing finances). Many people with schizophrenia experience problems obtaining basic needs, including adequate housing and medical care (Drake, Wallach, & Hoffman, 1989; Koran et al., 1989).

Differences in the Onset, Course, and Outcome of Schizophrenia

Age

The onset of schizophrenia most commonly occurs in late adolescence or early adulthood, between the ages of 16 and 30 years old. However, for a minority of individuals schizophrenia can first occur in middle age, and less commonly, in old age (Jeste & Nasrallah, 2003). In a review of the literature, Harris and Jeste (1988) found that 23 percent of all individuals with schizophrenia have onset of the disorder after the age of 40. A population-based study by Castle and Murray (1993) found similar rates of late-onset schizophrenia, reporting that one-quarter (28 percent) of the new cases of schizophrenia in the Camberwell (London) catchment area from 1965 to 1984 occurred after age 44, and 12 percent occurred after age 64. Overall, the annual incidence rate for late-onset schizophrenia was 12.6/100,000, approximately half that for those aged 16–25.

Gender

Gender differences have been found in age of onset and the outcome of schizophrenia. The mean age of onset of schizophrenia in women is approximately five years later than in men (Lewine, 1988; Moriarty et al., 2001). Women with schizophrenia are more likely to marry (Aleman, Kahn, & Selten, 2003), are more likely to maintain contact with their children (Aleman et al., 2003), and, hence, tend to have better social networks compared to men with schizophrenia (Grossman, Harrow, Rosen, & Faull, 2006). Higher levels of social skills have been found in women with schizophrenia (Mueser et al., 1990), perhaps resulting in less social isolation and better function in the community. Male gender, by itself, may represent a risk factor to poorer outcomes in schizophrenia (Goldstein, 1988; Seeman, 1986). This increased risk may be due to biological causes such as structural differences in male and female brains (Lewine, Gulley, Risch, Jewart, & Houpt, 1990) or differences in protective hormonal levels, such as estrogen (Seeman & Lang, 1990).

Alternatively, secondary complications of schizophrenia that dramatically affect function and outcome may be less prevalent in women. For example, women with schizophrenia report significantly less substance and alcohol abuse than men (Drake, Osher, & Wallach, 1989; Mueser et al., 1990). Such abuse has been associated with a variety of poor outcomes including increased use of hospitalization and emergency services (Bartels et al., 1993), aggressive and hostile behaviors (Bartels, 1989), and housing instability and homelessness (Drake, Wallach, & Hoffman, 1989).

Factors Complicating Course and Outcomes of Schizophrenia

Medical comorbidity

As many as 75 percent of persons with schizophrenia have a co-occurring medical disorder (Rystedt & Bartels, 2008). Oftentimes these co-occurring disorders serve to complicate the course and outcome of schizophrenia over the life span. Several factors that complicate the course and outcomes of persons with schizophrenia include medical comorbidity, early mortality, early nursing home admission, and substance abuse. Collectively, these factors are associated with increased disability, diminished quality of life, and early mortality. This section reviews each of the complicating factors associated with schizophrenia and explores the impact they have on individuals over the life span.

Medical comorbidity, including diabetes and cardiovascular disease, chronic obstructive pulmonary disease (COPD), HIV-AIDS, and Hepatitis B and C, is more common among persons with schizophrenia compared to the general population (Folsom et al., 2002; Jeste, Gladsjo, Lindamer, & Lacro, 1996; Morden, Mistler, Weeks, & Bartels, 2009; Rystedt & Bartels, 2008). Some prevalence estimates indicate that one in six people with schizophrenia has diabetes and one in four has hypertension. Estimates also indicate that one in eight has cardiovascular disease while almost a quarter of persons with a serious mental disorder have COPD. Hepatitis B and C infections, including HIV, are more common in persons with schizophrenia than the general population.

Higher rates of medical comorbidity experienced by persons with schizophrenia are in part due to health behaviors associated with a chronic mental disorder including lack of exercise, poor diet, smoking, alcohol and drug abuse, and unsafe sexual activity. An important approach to reducing the risk of serious medical conditions resulting in disability and early mortality for persons with schizophrenia focuses on helping individuals implement healthy lifestyle changes. At the same time, many of the antipsychotic medications used to treat the core symptoms of schizophrenia are associated with weight gain, diabetes, and increased cardiovascular risk factors. Switching to alternative antipsychotic medications with a lower likelihood of causing weight gain can sometimes help to reduce the risk of medical disorders associated with obesity. Finally, improving health outcomes for persons with schizophrenia will be supported by efforts aimed at addressing the poorer quality of health care experienced by many persons with psychiatric disabilities.

Early mortality

A recent five-state study found that individuals with a serious mental disorder have a life span that is 25 to 30 years shorter than the rest of the population (Colton & Manderscheid, 2006). Of major significance, longevity for individuals with a serious mental disorder has actually declined over the past three decades (Saha, Chant, & McGrath, 2007) at the same time that overall longevity has increased to the longest average life span ever: approximately 79 years on average (US Census Bureau, 2009). Among major psychiatric disorders, schizophrenia is associated with among the highest risks of premature death (Brown, Inskip, & Barraclough, 2000). Mortality rates for persons with schizophrenia have been estimated at two to four times the rate in the general population (Cohen, 2000) and include both natural and unnatural mortality. According to the five-state study, the most common cause of early mortality is due to cardiovascular disease (Colton & Manderscheid, 2006). Overall, increased mortality is largely due to heart disease, diabetes, and respiratory disorders, as well as unrecognized medical disease (Jeste et al., 1996). Other factors associated with poor health outcomes include alcohol and substance abuse (Drake, Osher, & Wallach, 1989; Kelly & McCreadie, 1999) and poor treatment compliance for medical issues including problems with health care coverage, lack of transportation, and other financial limitations (Rystedt & Bartels, 2008). There is also a slightly increased mortality rate associated with antipsychotic treatment (Mortensen & Juel, 1990), especially second-generation antipsychotic medications (Saha et al., 2007).

Recommendations for addressing early mortality in schizophrenia include considering policy reforms related to integration of medical and physical health care. To date, the community mental health system of care has been physically, financially, and organizationally separate from general health care. For example, mental health services have been financially "carved out" in health insurance plans. Since most accounts of early mortality are linked to medical causes, current reforms need to consider how to bring together physical and mental health services for persons with schizophrenia. Current initiatives include developing integrated models of medical care and psychiatric services, including models of chronic disease care management, as well as providing primary health care within community mental health settings (NASMHPD, 2005, 2006). Additionally, efforts are needed that encourage, support, and sustain health promotion and prevention, specifically addressing smoking, alcohol use, diet, and other mitigating lifestyle factors at the community level for persons with schizophrenia (Brown et al., 2000).

Premature nursing home admission

Premature nursing home admission is another factor that complicates the course and outcomes for persons with schizophrenia. In a 2009 study that tracked nursing home admissions over a 10-year period, persons with schizophrenia were more likely to enter a nursing home earlier (median age 65) than persons with no mental disorder (median age 80) (Andrews et al., 2009). The largest disparity arises between the ages of 40–64 years, when risk for admission is three and one-half times more for persons with schizophrenia than for persons with no mental disorder (Andrews et al., 2009).

Premature nursing home admission for persons with schizophrenia may significantly diminish quality of life, including hindering opportunities to interact with family and friends, to engage in meaningful work, and to build a fulfilling life. The United States Supreme Court formally recognized the potentially deleterious impact of unnecessary or avoidable nursing home admissions in the 1999 Olmstead Decision. This ruling determined that preventable residence in a nursing home for persons with disabilities is a violation of the Americans with Disabilities Act when a community-based alternative is preferred (Bartels, Miles, Dums, & Levine, 2003; Bartels & Van Citters, 2005). In addition to diminished opportunities that result from being segregated from community living, premature admission increases overall health care costs due to the expense of skilled nursing home care compared to less intensive community-based options. Overall, the costs of medical and psychiatric care for individuals with schizophrenia are among the highest of any single group, with a substantial cause of Medicare and Medicaid expenditures due to nursing home care (Bartels, Clark, Peacock, Dums, & Pratt, 2003).

The Aging Person with Schizophrenia: Early-Onset Schizophrenia (EOS)

Historical overview

Schizophrenia is a heterogeneous disorder with a variety of clinical presentations and outcomes. The term early-onset schizophrenia (EOS) commonly refers to individuals who first manifest the symptoms of schizophrenia in adolescence or early adulthood, although "early onset" is technically defined as occurring any time before the age of 45 (Jeste et al., 1995). EOS is characterized by positive symptoms (e.g., hallucinations, delusions), negative symptoms (e.g., apathy and deficiencies in emotional responses), and significant psychosocial functional impairment (Reeves & Brister, 2008). Of note, the long-term course of schizophrenia over the life span has been marked by considerable debate and controversy.

The earliest descriptions addressing the life course of schizophrenia assumed a persistent, chronic, and gradual deterioration of psychosocial and cognitive functioning. Kraepelin's (1919/1971) original description of schizophrenia used the term "dementia praecox," underscoring the assumption that early onset of schizophrenia was associated with an inevitable progressive decline in functioning and premature syndrome of dementia (Palmer et al., 1999). However, early treatment methods for schizophrenia were limited to chronic institutionalization, which was highly correlated with a decrease in functioning over time. Despite this pessimistic view of the disorder, longitudinal outcome studies have found half or more individuals with schizophrenia experience substantial remission of symptoms in older age, including, for some, complete recovery (Ciompi, 1980; Harding et al., 1987a,b). Age is associated with remission of symptoms in more than half of individuals with schizophrenia (Harding, Brooks, Ashikaga, Strauss, & Breier, 1987a, 1987b), suggesting that some older individuals may be spared the risks of continued exposure to antipsychotic medications. Jeste, Lacro, Gilbert, Kline, and Kline (1993) reviewed six double-blind studies of antipsychotic drug withdrawal that included older adults with schizophrenia followed for a mean of six months and found an average relapse rate of 40 percent, compared to a relapse rate of 11 percent for those who continued on medication. The authors concluded that stable, chronic outpatients without a history of antipsychotic discontinuation should be considered for a carefully monitored trial of antipsychotic withdrawal.

It is highly likely that better long-term outcomes can be attributed to treatment methods that have improved over the years, emphasizing community integration, psychosocial rehabilitation, supported employment, and integrated treatment of substance use disorders and medical care. At the same time, a subgroup of older adults with schizophrenia have persistent impairment of functioning and suffer from significant cognitive impairment in older age, including those who have experienced long-term residence in institutions (Davidson et al., 1995; Palmer et al., 1999). The following sections provide an overview of these two cohorts of individuals with schizophrenia, including the "oldest-old" subgroup of adults with EOS who lived in an era marked by extensive long-term institutional care, and a "younger-old" subgroup of individuals with schizophrenia who lived during a time of "deinstitutionalization" with an emphasis on community-based integration and services.

The "oldest old" with EOS and long-term institution-based care

A subgroup of the "oldest old" with EOS developed the disorder prior to the introduction of antipsychotic medication, at a time when long-term institutionalization was the rule for psychotic disorders. This cohort is known to have had significant exposure to living in institution-based settings, including state mental health hospitals and nursing homes. In general, individuals in this subgroup have impaired independent living skills, have poor social skills, and depend on a structured supervised setting to meet their needs. Older individuals with extensive histories of institutional care represent a specific age and treatment cohort with substantially different exposure to rehabilitative treatments and limited opportunities for developing independent living skills. As a cohort they also have different risk factors for adverse outcomes. Following the first wave of deinstitutionalization in the 1960s, there has been a progressive closure of state-funded institutions including long-term psychiatric hospital settings and nursing homes dedicated to caring for persons with psychiatric disorders. Unfortunately, early infusions of funding for home and community-based alternatives have eroded. These concurrent trends over the last two decades have been associated with alarming increases of homelessness for persons with serious mental disorders (Folsom et al., 2002; Olfson, Mechanic, Hansell, Boyer, & Walkup, 1999), exposure to crime and victimization (Eisenberg, 2005), institutionalization in the criminal justice system (Fazel & Danesh, 2002), exposure to public health epidemics such as HIV infection (Baillargeon et al., 2008), and high rates of substance use disorder (Olfson, Sing, & Schlesinger, 1999).

The following case study describes an older adult with EOS who spent over three decades residing in state psychiatric hospital with minimal exposure to contemporary models of community-based psychosocial rehabilitation. In addition, this case study describes physical health complications that can occur with psychiatric medication treatment requiring ongoing health care management that is integrated into the overall delivery of mental health services. The case study highlights the risk factors associated with EOS and illustrates the importance of assessment and treatment with regard to positive outcomes.

> Mr. K is a 78-year-old man with a long history of multiple hospitalizations dating back to his early twenties. As a teen he was somewhat isolated and had few friends. At the age of 19 he became withdrawn and reclusive, quitting his job as a factory worker based on a belief that his foreman had tried to poison him. Thereafter, he began to report to his family that voices were telling him that Satan had placed a "spell" on the family. During a gathering over the Christmas holidays, he became acutely agitated, screaming at his parents that they were "doomed" and ran out of the house partially clothed. He was picked up by the local police authorities who brought him to the local hospital. After a brief evaluation, he was mandated to the state psychiatric hospital, where he was hospitalized for most of the following 30 years. He was placed on a variety of trials of "first-generation" antipsychotic

medications including chlorpromazine and haloperidol, and his delusions and hallucinations decreased. However, he remained withdrawn and lacked basic self-care skills. He also developed neurological side effects including tremors due to antipsychotic-induced Parkinson's syndrome. Attempts to reduce his antipsychotic medication to a lower dose were not pursued due to concerns that he would experience a symptomatic relapse. At the age of 50, he was transferred to a board and care home when the long-term care unit at the state hospital was closed. For the following decade he resided in the board and care home, spending most of his time in his room with little involvement in the surrounding community.

At the age of 65 he was moved to a different room when the board and care home was remodeled. He became acutely agitated and paranoid, refusing to take his medications. After being hospitalized, he was started on olanzapine with the goal of treating his psychosis with a second-generation antipsychotic medication with fewer neurological side effects. He subsequently became less withdrawn and began to voluntarily take his medications once again. He returned to the board and care home where he continued to need supervision and assistance with basic living and self-care skills. His tremors dramatically decreased on olanzapine, but he also began to gain weight. In addition, he continued to smoke two packs of cigarettes per day.

Over the subsequent five years, Mr. K's weight increased from 190 to 255 pounds. More recently (over the past year), Mr. K complained that Satan put a snake in his abdomen creating intermittent pain and cramping. He complained that the snake in his stomach was constantly thirsty, and consumed large amounts of fluids. The manager of the board and care home attributed these symptoms to his long-standing religious delusions, and his antipsychotic medication was increased by his local physician by an order given over the phone. His physical status continued to decline until he eventually stopped eating altogether and was admitted to the hospital acutely dehydrated, weak, and acutely confused. On admission, Mr. K was found to have dangerously high blood glucose levels and a diagnosis was made of adult-onset diabetes. He was also found to have high blood pressure and high blood lipid levels. With medical treatment, his blood glucose levels and blood pressure decreased, and his pain and dehydration were addressed. His confusion resolved, and he was discharged back to his board and care home with orders for a visiting nurse to monitor his medications (including insulin treatment, glucose testing, and lipid-lowering medications required by his medical physician) as well as diabetes education. His psychiatrist successfully switched Mr. K to an alternative antipsychotic with less likelihood of causing weight gain and increased blood lipids. Once his diabetes had stabilized, the case manager and visiting nurse collaborated on supporting a plan for physical exercise and worked with the group home to provide a balanced diabetic diet in the group home. Finally, a smoking cessation program was initiated.

This case illustrates several key points in the assessment and treatment of the aging person with schizophrenia. First, Mr. K has an extremely severe disorder with persistent negative symptoms and limited functional abilities, and he belongs to a generation of individuals who were chronically institutionalized. He is representative of the oldest and most severely ill individuals with EOS who first became ill before the development of antipsychotic medication, at a time when treatment generally consisted of long-term institutionalization. Like many, he remained in institutions for most of his adult life, first residing in a state psychiatric hospital, followed by discharge to a board and care home, and then finally, admission to a nursing home. The years of institutional care have left Mr. K with few (if any) social supports outside of the institutional setting, poor social skills, and severe limits in functional abilities. Without adequate independent living skills, he is largely dependent on care providers for basic needs. Due to these limitations, Mr. K initially experienced his transfer to a board and care home as a disorienting and traumatic event, resulting in an acute depression and decompensation.

This case also illustrates the significant interaction of psychiatric disorder and medical illness in the older adult with a severe mental disorder: the psychiatric disorder affecting medical symptoms, and the medical disorder affecting psychiatric symptoms. In the first instance, Mr. K's psychiatric disorder was associated with worsening of his physical health. In a state of depression and agitation following his transfer to a board and care home, he stopped taking medications that were essential to his physical and mental health. His anticonvulsant medications had controlled his seizure disorder for years, yet on stopping these medications he once again suffered from uncontrolled seizures. After resuming his medications in the hospital, he recovered. Several years later he developed another medical disorder, insulin-dependent diabetes, yet this time this severe condition went undiagnosed. In this instance, his medical condition directly influenced his psychiatric status, causing severe confusion, withdrawal, and physical symptoms that were mistaken for delusions.

Co-occurring medical disorders are a common complication of the aging process and are often undiagnosed and undertreated in individuals with a serious mental disorder. Factors which may contribute to this poor physical health include a high prevalence of health-damaging behaviors such as smoking (Hughes, Hatsukami, Mitchell, & Dahlgren, 1986) and substance abuse (Drake, Osher, & Wallach, 1989), limited access to good health care because of financial constraints, and a delay in seeking medical treatment as a result of the high pain threshold found in many persons with schizophrenia (Dworkin, 1994). The physical health of individuals with schizophrenia in late middle age or early old age may be more typical of the health status of individuals without a mental disorder who are much older (Bartels, 2004; Rystedt & Bartels, 2008). The high rate of medical comorbidity in persons with schizophrenia underscores the need to include a thorough medical evaluation and ongoing general health care services as an integrated component of comprehensive psychiatric services to older persons with a severe mental disorder (Morden et al., 2009).

This case also illustrates the development of co-occurring cognitive impairment. In addition to the complication of medical illnesses that often accompanies the aging process, older individuals with a serious mental disorder are also vulnerable to the development of comorbid cognitive impairment. Older adults with EOS and LOS (late-onset schizophrenia) both have global cognitive deficits when compared to normal controls, although these deficits are stable in most individuals, and have been described as a static encephalopathy following the initial onset of the disorder (Goldberg, Hyde, Kleinman, & Weinberger, 1993; Heaton et al., 1994). However, several studies suggest that a subset of individuals with schizophrenia progress to states of dementia (Davidson et al., 1995; Lesser et al., 1993). For individuals like Mr. K, the symptoms of dementia can overshadow the psychosis and become the primary source of functional impairment in late life. At this point a supportive, supervised setting becomes even more of a necessity and nursing home care may be unavoidable. Comorbid cognitive impairment is one of the most significant differences between older adults with a severe mental disorder in nursing homes compared to those living in the community (Bartels, Mueser, & Miles, 1997b). Overall, degree of cognitive impairment may be one of the most important clinical factors associated with level of care and level of function among older persons with schizophrenia (Bartels, Mueser, & Miles, 1997a).

The case of Mr. K illustrates an era of institution-based treatment that is coming to an end. A growing number of aging individuals with a severe mental disorder have received much of their treatment in the community following deinstitutionalization and have different levels of functional ability and treatment needs.

The "younger old" with EOS and community-based services

In contrast to the chronically institutionalized cohort of individuals with EOS, a more recent and younger group of aging individuals with a severe mental disorder have spent most of their adult life in community treatment settings following the deinstitutionalization movement of the 1960s. This group of individuals with schizophrenia is known as the "community-dwelling" cohort of individuals. Community-dwelling individuals are more likely to have social supports in the community, to have used community resources, to have developed community living skills associated with more favorable outcomes, and to have been treated earlier in their disorder with newer (and more effective) antipsychotic agents. At the same time, however, this group is also more likely to have experienced the negative consequences of declining public funds for community mental health services over the last two decades (Druss et al., 2008).

The following case describes an older person with schizophrenia who has benefited from a community support program and medication management.

Mrs. M is a 62-year-old woman with schizophrenia residing with a companion in a senior housing apartment in the community. She was married at the age of 19 and had her first psychotic episode at age 20. She then underwent a series of psychiatric hospitalizations, at first returning to live with her husband, until her husband eventually became overwhelmed by her recurrent paranoid episodes and pursued a divorce. Thereafter, she moved in with her parents, and received outpatient treatment at the local community mental health center.

Mrs. M continued to have severe paranoid symptoms over the early years of her disorder requiring episodic hospitalizations. Her parents worked closely with the mental health case managers to develop the needed supports and monitoring of symptoms to keep Mrs. M in the community as much as possible. This included notifying treatment providers of the early symptoms of relapse, as well as assuring that Mrs. M regularly took the appropriate dose of her antipsychotic medication.

During periods of relative remission of symptoms, Mrs. M was able to hold down a part-time job and regularly went out for dinner and to cultural events with her parents. Although her psychiatric symptoms were relatively well controlled with her antipsychotic medication (haloperidol), Mrs. M had long-standing side effects. These included episodes of muscle stiffness and slowed movement (drug-induced Parkinson's syndrome) and tardive dyskinesia manifested by significant abnormal involuntary movements (twitching and writhing movements) of her face, arms, fingers, and trunk. Attempts to substantially reduce her dose of medication to minimize side effects resulted in psychotic relapse.

When Mrs. M turned 55, her father had a stroke and was placed in a nursing home. Shortly thereafter, Mrs. M's mother had a sudden heart attack and died. Mrs. M stopped taking her medication, became acutely psychotic, and was admitted to a psychiatric hospital. Due to her long-standing difficulties with neurological side effects to the haloperidol, Mrs. M was started on a second-generation antipsychotic medication, clozapine. Mrs. M recompensated and returned to her former level of function. In addition, she no longer had medication-induced Parkinson symptoms and had a decrease in her symptoms of tardive dyskinesia. The discharge planning team recognized her reliance on others for social support and monitoring of medications and symptoms, and recommended that Mrs. M be discharged to a senior housing apartment with a roommate, complemented by frequent visits by her case manager from the geriatric mental health outreach team. With active support by the mental health team, Mrs. M made this transition without major difficulties and resumed many of her former activities. She successfully switched to an alternative antipsychotic medication (aripiprazole) that is easier to monitor and has fewer side effects. Over time, she joined the local senior center and is engaged in volunteer work at the local hospital.

This case illustrates several important points. First, Mrs. M belongs to a different treatment cohort than Mr. K. Most of her treatment occurred in community-based programs with episodic acute hospitalizations. Thus, she was able to reside in the community and developed community living skills. Older adults with severe mental disorders residing in the community have substantial difficulties in many areas of functioning compared to those with disorders such as depression (Bartels et al., 1997a). However, comprehensive support services can overcome many of these problems and facilitate living in the community. Her treatment included services that sought to minimize institutional dependence (unlike Mr. K) and to maximize her ability to live in the least restrictive setting. She was able to develop and maintain social skills and supports. Unfortunately, the severity of her disorder resulted in substantial stress to her marriage, resulting in an eventual divorce. Although this was a significant loss, she was able to fall back on the support of her family of origin, moving back to live with her parents.

Secondly, this anecdote illustrates the importance of social supports. One of the major differences between older individuals with a severe mental disorder residing in the community compared to nursing homes and other institutions is the presence of family members who are able (and willing) to provide assistance with daily activities and needs. Compared to a person without a psychiatric disorder, persons with schizophrenia are less likely to marry, they are less likely to have children, and less likely to work. In the community, their social networks are often constrained to members of their families of origin, and a few friends. In this respect, family supports are especially crucial to community tenure. The family members who provided a stable and supportive environment helped to facilitate Mrs. M's ability to remain in the community. This aspect underscores a vulnerability of the individual with a severe mental disorder who is aging. Many individuals with a severe mental disorder reside with family members (often parents). The aging, disorder, and eventual death of parents who are key supports place these individuals at risk for loss of ability to continue to reside in individual placement in the community. When the parent becomes ill or dies, the child, then frequently in his/her forties, is left to cope with the emotional impact of losing a parent and a primary source of social contact and support. At the same time, the individual must quickly adjust to a dramatic reduction in financial and social support, which may also coincide with a loss of residence.

This case also illustrates that older persons are especially sensitive to the adverse side effects of medications, and thoughtful attention to choosing the appropriate type and dose of medication can be extremely important. Mrs. M had medication-induced Parkinson's syndrome caused by extrapyramidal nervous system side effects (EPS) from haloperidol. Aging is associated with an increased prevalence of EPS due to biological changes in neuroreceptor sensitivity and a declining amount of dopamine occurring with age. Clozapine and other second-generation or "atypical" antipsychotic agents are associated with little or no EPS. However, agents such as clozapine may require particularly close monitoring of potential side effects that may impair function, such as sedation and weight gain.

Finally, this case illustrates the different characteristics of older individuals with EOS from different age and treatment cohorts or groups. Many of the oldest individuals with EOS have spent most of their lives in institutional settings, as illustrated in the first case example. More recently, a different group of EOS older individuals has emerged. These individuals are the "young old" (in their sixties) and are among the first wave of severely mentally ill individuals who became ill when states were closing their long-term wards and shifting treatment into the community. This historical cohort of younger individuals with schizophrenia includes individuals who have developed independent living skills and are more likely to continue to live independently in the community in late life.

Course and outcomes of early-onset schizophrenia

The long-term course of early-onset schizophrenia is highly variable. A minority of individuals experience poor outcomes and marked impairment. Factors associated with worse outcomes include preadolescent onset, poor premorbid adjustment, poor cognitive functioning, cerebral asymmetry, and negative symptoms during prodromal and post-onset phases (Malla & Payne, 2005). For example, individuals with these risk factors are more likely to experience high rates of occupational impairment of at least moderate severity (44 percent), financial dependence on parents (51.6 percent) or public assistance (30.9 percent), and low rates of independent living (16.5 percent) (Malla & Payne, 2005).

However, many individuals experience gradual improvement, and in some cases total remission, later in life (Ciompi, 1980; Harding et al., 1987a, 1987b). Neuropsychological studies of schizophrenic individuals in their third, fourth, fifth, sixth, and seventh decades of life do not suggest progressive dementia or deterioration (Goldberg et al., 1993). Long-term studies of the natural history of schizophrenia suggest that the first 10 years of the disorder are marked by exacerbations and remissions, but symptoms substantially remit in over half of the individuals with schizophrenia in later life. This improvement is likely a result of many factors. For example, biological changes such as age-related decreases in the neurotransmitter dopamine may result in symptom reductions. This model posits that many of the symptoms of schizophrenia result from an imbalance in opposing neurotransmitter systems, such as a relative excess of dopamine (as well as norepinephrine and serotonin) compared to acetylcholine (and the inhibitory neurotransmitter GABA). Hence, psychotic symptoms may remit with age due to a restoration of the balance between dopaminergic and cholinergic neurotransmitter systems caused by generalized reduction of dopamine (and relative maintenance of acetylcholine) that normally occurs with aging (Finch & Morgan, 1987).

Other factors that may contribute to improvement of symptoms with aging for some individuals with EOS include learned coping and symptom management skills. For example, individuals may acquire disorder management skills including strategies to reduce stress and to improve symptom recognition and medication compliance (McEvoy et al., 1989). In addition, individuals may learn over time to avoid the use of alcohol and street drugs that are associated with symptom exacerbation and poorer functioning (Zisook et al., 1992). Overall, there is greater optimism for favorable long-term outcomes for many individuals afflicted with schizophrenia, though a subgroup remains that continues to require intensive treatment and supervision in late life.

Assessment and treatment

Early intervention is now considered a priority in the treatment of EOS with the goal of improving long-term outcomes. There is a critical period of three to five years after the onset of psychosis in which interventions are most likely to be effective and have the maximum impact on recovery. Contemporary treatment for EOS individuals includes both pharmacological therapy and psychosocial rehabilitation with the goal of improving functional outcome and quality of life for young individuals. Specific areas of emphasis include community and social functioning, employment and education, and financial and housing independence (Malla & Payne, 2005). The following section provides an overview of pharmacological and psychosocial treatment options for individuals with EOS.

Pharmacological   The treatment of EOS is typically divided into two types of treatment including pharmacological and psychosocial rehabilitation. Pharmacological treatment for EOS is comprised of two tiers of medication including first-generation antipsychotics (FGAs) and second-generation antipsychotics (SGAs). First-generation antipsychotics (e.g., haloperidol, perphenazine, and thioridazine) are associated with neurological side effects including tardive dyskinesia (a disorder that involves involuntary movements, especially of the lower face and tongue), neuroleptic malignant syndrome (a rare but life-threatening idiosyncratic reaction characterized by fever, muscular rigidity, altered mental status, and autonomic dysfunction), and arrhythmia (a problem with the rate or rhythm of the heartbeat) (Palmer et al., 1999). Second-generation antipsychotics (e.g., clozapine, risperidone, olanzapine, aripiprazole) are associated with fewer neurological side effects, yet are much more likely to result in metabolic side effects including weight gain, high cholesterol, high blood sugar, and resistance to insulin (resulting in type 2 diabetes) and related cardiovascular disease (Vitiello et al., 2009). Despite early claims of substantially greater efficacy of SGAs compared to FGAs, a large-scale comparative effectiveness trial (i.e., CATIE: Clinical Antipsychotic Trials of Intervention Effectiveness) found no major differences in alleviating the primary symptoms of schizophrenia between the older and newer agents (Carpenter & Buchanan, 2008; Swartz et al., 2008).

Psychosocial rehabilitation Psychosocial rehabilitation refers to the range of social, educational, occupational, behavioral, and cognitive interventions designed to improve functioning and enhance recovery for persons with a serious mental disorder (Bartels & Mueser, 2008; Bartels & Pratt, 2009; Bellack & Mueser 1993; Pratt, Bartels, Mueser, & Forester, 2008; Pratt, Van Citters, Mueser, & Bartels, 2008). Effective psychosocial rehabilitation models developed for young adults with a serious mental disorder include assertive community treatment, social skills training, cognitive-behavioral therapy and cognitive remediation therapy, integrated dual diagnosis treatment of mental disorder and substance abuse disorder, family psychoeducation, disorder self-management, and supported employment. Psychosocial rehabilitation for older adults with severe mental disorders is focused on enhancing independent living skills, self-management of both psychiatric and medical problems, engaging in meaningful and fulfilling activities, improving quality of life, and living independently in the community.

Several promising skills training interventions for older adults with severe psychiatric disorders have been systematically evaluated and reviewed (Pratt, Van Citters et al., 2008). These include FAST, a social skills training program for middle-aged and older adults with chronic psychotic disorders (Patterson et al., 2003); CBSST, a combined skills training and cognitive-behavioral treatment program for older adults with schizophrenia (Granholm et al., 2005); and ST + HM, a combined skills training and health management intervention for community-dwelling older adults with a severe mental disorder (Bartels et al., 2004). Functional Adaptation Skills Training (FAST) consists of a 24-week skills training program to improve community functioning in middle-aged and older adults with persistent psychotic disorders. Cognitive-Behavioral Social Skills Training (CBSST) consists of an integrated treatment program for older adults with schizophrenia that combines cognitive-behavioral therapy (CBT) and social skills training (SST). Skills Training and Health Management (ST + HM) includes skills training (ST) to enhance functioning and health management (HM) to improve physical health outcomes. ST consists of weekly skills training classes in community living skills, social skills, and medication self-management occurring over 12 months. HM consists of a nurse case management intervention aimed at preventive health care and identification and monitoring of acute and chronic medical problems. Based on highly promising findings from the ST + HM pilot study, ST + HM has been further developed into the HOPES Program (Helping Older People Experience Success). HOPES consists of nurse health care management combined with skills training modules addressing healthy living, making and keeping friends, making the most of doctor visits, communicating effectively, making the most of leisure time, using medications effectively, and living independently in the community (Pratt, Bartels et al., 2008). Two-year psychosocial outcomes of a large randomized trial of the HOPES intervention found that this intervention is effective in improving self-efficacy, social skills, and community functioning (Mueser, Bartels et al., 2010).

The Aging Person with Schizophrenia: Late-Onset Schizophrenia (LOS)

Historical overview

A second group is composed of older adults who have the onset of their disorder in middle or old age, or "late-onset schizophrenia" (LOS). The following section contains an in-depth overview of LOS. The diagnosis of LOS evolved from early descriptions of a disorder called "paraphrenia." Kraepelin (1919/1971) used the term paraphrenia to describe a group of individuals, frequently older in age, with symptoms similar to "dementia praecox," but with fewer negative and cognitive symptoms. Kay and Roth (1961) later described "late paraphrenia" as a paranoid syndrome occurring in late life that was not accompanied by co-occurring dementia. Late paraphrenia was characterized by onset after age 45 of a well-organized paranoid delusional system, with or without auditory hallucinations, and often occurred with preserved personality. Late paraphrenia was more common among women than men. More recently, psychiatric diagnostic criteria have been revised to reclassify most individuals formally diagnosed with late paraphrenia as late-onset schizophrenia. For example, the *Diagnostic and Statistical Manual of Mental Disorders* (DSM-IV-TR; American Psychiatric Association, 2000) allows for a diagnosis of schizophrenia with the first onset of symptoms after age 45.

Course and outcomes of late-onset schizophrenia

The following clinical anecdote illustrates many of the characteristics of late-onset schizophrenia in an older individual.

> Mrs. W is a 63-year-old widowed woman who lives alone in her house. She has two daughters who live in the next town. During much of her life, she worked as a librarian until she retired at the age of 60. She was seen by many as somewhat odd and eccentric, yet never had any psychiatric hospitalizations or mental health treatment history during her younger years. Her husband died five years earlier from a myocardial infarction. Her own health is quite good, though her hearing

has substantially deteriorated. Over the last two years, Mrs. W has become increasingly concerned for her safety. She initially believed that there were prowlers or burglars trying to get into her house at night due to strange noises that she heard in the yard. She also reported that the potential prowlers recently began yelling derogatory sexual comments directed at her. She made repeated calls to the local police department, who inspected the grounds and found no signs of intruders and no evidence of anyone yelling at Mrs. W. Her concerns escalated when she began to believe that a group of men were constantly monitoring her every move with the plan to torture and murder her. She believed that these men regularly entered her bedroom at night and attempted to physically accost her as she slept. She resolved this problem by sitting up most of the night in her living room, and falling asleep in her chair – avoiding her bedroom at night.

Attempts to involve mental health professionals in her treatment were unsuccessful. Mrs. W insisted that her problems were due to a group of "criminals and rapists" who had targeted her house and complained that she only needed better police protection. She refused a psychiatric evaluation or psychiatric medications. By day Mrs. W functioned relatively well. She went out for lunch with her daughters on a regular basis and played cards one night a week with a small group of women friends. Her speech and thinking appeared entirely normal, except when discussion turned to issues having to do with crime or her personal safety. Family and friends dealt with the problem by avoiding conversation about these issues altogether.

At the age of 70, Mrs. W began to have unexplained episodes of losing consciousness, followed by transient weakness on her right side. Though she was convinced this was due to the group of men who were trying to kill her, an astute mental health case manager insisted on taking Mrs. W to her medical physician, who quickly diagnosed transient ischemic attacks (TIAs) and placed her on anticoagulant medication, preventing subsequent attacks. During the hospitalization, her physician was able to convince her to attempt a trial of low-dose risperidone. In addition, she was evaluated by audiology and was fitted for a hearing aid that substantially improved her hearing. Following discharge, her case manager and a visiting nurse regularly visited her in her home and ensured that Mrs. W continued to take her medications as prescribed. Within one month, she reported no further auditory hallucinations (no more strange noises in her yard and no more perceptions of derogatory statements directed at her) and was significantly less paranoid. Within several months, she reported that she no longer believed that she was at risk, as the men had "left" the neighborhood.

This case example demonstrates several key points about the assessment and treatment of older adults with LOS. First, Mrs. W had the onset of her psychiatric symptoms in late life (age 63) and in the absence of any significant signs of cognitive impairment or a neurological problem. As noted earlier, almost one-quarter (23 percent) of individuals with schizophrenia have the onset of their disorder after age 40 (Harris & Jeste, 1988). Consistent with early descriptions of paraphrenia, her premorbid personality was generally preserved, so that she maintained many of the appearances of her daily social routine and function. Hence, she did not seek or receive treatment for her psychiatric disorder until she was medically hospitalized for an unrelated disorder.

Second, this case typifies LOS since women are overrepresented among those affected by the disorder (Harris & Jeste, 1988). In contrast, most studies of EOS report similar proportions of women to men. Several explanations for this difference have been proposed. One view suggests that EOS and LOS are different forms of schizophrenia with different characteristics, including different rates among men and women. An alternative view suggests that biological factors are responsible for a later onset of schizophrenia in women, resulting in an overrepresentation of women compared to men for LOS. This later hypothesis is supported by findings in studies of EOS showing that the onset in women is approximately five years later than in men (Lewine, 1988). Among LOS this difference may be even greater. In a community study that included EOS and LOS, Castle and Murray (1993) found that 16 percent of men had the onset of schizophrenia after age 45, compared to 38 percent of women. Speculation about the difference in age of onset between men and women includes a possible protective effect of estrogens or a precipitating effect of androgens (Castle & Murray, 1993).

Third, this case illustrates the symptoms of LOS, which typically include relatively well-circumscribed, non-bizarre delusions, in the absence of a formal disorder in thought processes. Non-bizarre delusions involve situations that may occur in real life such as being poisoned, afflicted with an incurable disease, stalked, attacked, or deceived by a spouse or lover. In contrast, bizarre delusions involve phenomena that are considered totally implausible within one's culture (American Psychiatric Association, 2000). Mrs. W's delusions and hallucinations are relatively clearly defined and involve the psychotic (though theoretically possible) belief that she is in danger of being attacked by a group of criminals who are stalking her. In addition, her thinking processes remain well organized. When she is not focusing on her delusions, her speech and function are almost indistinguishable from her friends who do not have a major mental disorder. This is in marked contrast to the examples of EOS where thought disorder and difficulties in basic living skills were prominent. Delusions and hallucinations are common symptoms in late-onset schizophrenia and occur at a rate comparable to those found in young adults with early-onset schizophrenia. Delusions tend to be paranoid and are often systematized (Almeida, Howard, Levy, & David, 1995; Howard, Castle, Wessely, & Murray, 1993; Kay & Roth, 1961). Auditory hallucinations are substantially more common than visual or somatic hallucinations, similar to young adults with EOS (Almeida et al., 1995). In contrast to EOS, LOS is significantly less likely to manifest formal thought disorder, negative symptoms, or inappropriate affect (Almeida et al., 1995; Howard et al., 1993; Kay & Roth, 1961; Pearlson & Rabins, 1988; Pearlson et al., 1989).

The fourth point demonstrated by the case of Mrs. W relates to her premorbid (pre-disorder) level of functioning and subsequent ability to continue to function at a relatively good level during the course of her disorder. Compared to EOS, individuals with LOS are more likely to show better premorbid occupational adjustment (Post, 1966) and higher marriage rates. However, compared to normal comparison groups, individuals with LOS are frequently socially isolated and often have schizoid, schizotypal, or paranoid premorbid personalities (Harris & Jeste, 1988; Kay & Roth,

1961). Mrs. W's reputation for being "odd and eccentric" is consistent with this view of her personality. Nonetheless, her abilities to function independently and engage in some social relationships continued even after the onset of her disorder.

Mrs. W's case also illustrates the presence of sensory impairment that appears to predate the onset of the disorder. Mrs. W has marked sensory (hearing) impairment, a risk factor for LOS. In a review of 27 articles that assess visual and hearing abilities in older adults with late-onset disorders, Prager and Jeste (1993) concluded that sensory deficits are overrepresented in older adults with late-onset psychotic disorders. An association between visual impairment and visual hallucinations is suggested by the literature, although a specific relationship between visual impairment and late-onset paranoid psychosis remains controversial. On the other hand, the majority of studies reviewed support a specific association between hearing deficits and late-onset paranoid psychosis. Moderate to severe hearing deficits have been reported in approximately 40 percent of those with late-onset paranoid psychoses (Kay & Roth, 1961). As in Mrs. W's case, significant reductions in psychotic symptoms have been reported for some individuals who have late-onset paranoid disorders after fitting with a hearing aid, suggesting that deafness may precipitate or worsen symptoms (Almeida, Förstl, Howard, & David, 1993).

Clinically, the strong association between sensory impairments, psychotic symptoms, and LOS suggests that these individuals may benefit from systematic instruction in coping strategies for the management of positive symptoms. In recent years, growing evidence has emerged that younger individuals with schizophrenia employ a wide range of different strategies for coping with positive symptoms (Carr, 1988; Falloon & Talbot, 1981; Mueser & Gingerich, 1994). Methods for managing positive symptoms typically involve either disattention or relaxation, with coping efficacy strongly related to the number of coping strategies employed by the individual. A study by Tarrier and his colleagues (1993) indicated that young individuals with schizophrenia who were taught coping strategies experienced significant reductions in positive symptoms compared to individuals who received training in social problem-solving. This encouraging study suggests that older persons with schizophrenia characterized by persistent psychotic symptoms might benefit from receiving similar training in coping skills. However, studies are yet to be conducted on the potential benefit of skills training and other psychosocial rehabilitative interventions for older persons with schizophrenia.

Finally, Mrs. W eventually showed significant improvement when treated with a combination of mental health outreach support services and antipsychotic medications. Older adults with LOS have been shown to be as responsive to antipsychotic medications as young individuals with schizophrenia when treated with appropriate agents and dosages. For example, response rates of late-onset schizophrenia to antipsychotic medications range from 62 percent (Post, 1966) to 86 percent (Rabins, Pauker, & Thomas, 1984).

In general, the assessment and treatment of late-onset schizophrenia parallels the principles and practices used in the treatment of early-onset schizophrenia, incorporating a biopsychosocial perspective. This perspective assumes that optimal assessment and treatment addresses the biological, psychological, and social aspects of the person. For the older person with a severe mental disorder, this broad spectrum approach is particularly critical. Aging is associated with substantial biological changes that directly affect medication metabolism and side effects. Furthermore, the presence of multiple medical problems and all medications must be considered in treatment. The psychological impact of mental disorder and the effects of aging must also be carefully weighed in designing a program of treatment. The individual's cognitive abilities must be comprehensively assessed in order to inform the choice of intervention. Finally, social supports and stressors are a major consideration in assessing needed services. One of the most important factors determining whether an older person remains in the community or permanently resides in a nursing home is the presence of social and instrumental supports. In summary, the biopsychosocial perspective should be the foundation to assure a comprehensive clinical assessment and effective plan of treatment.

Future Challenges

The aging of the population of adults with schizophrenia and other serious mental disorders will challenge the future system of care for mental health, physical health, and long-term care in the United States. Recent studies suggest that the fifth decade of life for people with a serious mental disorder is a period of special vulnerability and risk. Between the ages of 50 and 65, adults with a serious mental disorder are three and a half times more likely to be admitted to nursing homes compared to other disabled or financially challenged adults who are Medicaid beneficiaries. At the same time, individuals with a mental disorder receiving services in public mental health settings have a life span that is 25 to 30 years shorter than the general population. This reflects a dramatic health disparity largely due to greater rates of cardiovascular disease and diabetes, which translates to an average life expectancy of approximately 54 years of age for people with a serious mental disorder. At the same time, the aging of the current "Baby Boomer" generation will result in a substantial increase in the numbers of adults with major mental disorders reaching middle and old age over the coming decade.

These converging trends will require new models of care and services that are specifically tailored for the needs of the older adult with a serious mental disorder. Home and community-based alternatives to nursing homes will need to be developed that respond to the special psychiatric, rehabilitative, and medical needs of the aging person with a severe mental disorder. Integrated health promotion, prevention, and health care management will need to become core components of the future mental health service delivery system for middle-aged and older adults. Psychiatric and medical needs will need to be considered "coequal" priorities for future models of mental health care that explicitly recognize interdependence of physical and mental health. This will require the development of competency in primary health care and prevention as a central mission for publicly funded mental health services.

Finally, future models of psychosocial rehabilitation will need to incorporate strategies to enhance cognition or to compensate for cognitive and physical limitations associated with the aging process. In addition to cognitive remediation and pharmacological agents developed to enhance cognition, novel applications of technology may have the potential to assist individuals with physical and cognitive limitations to remain in the community. New models of vocational rehabilitation, supported employment, and skill development will need to be developed to respond to the desires of older adults to engage in meaningful activities in late life. Consistent with the goals of older adults, future services should emphasize not simply "adding more years to life, but instead adding more life to years."

Summary and Conclusions

Despite recent advances, remarkably little is known about factors affecting the course or outcome of schizophrenia in older age. Schizophrenia can occur in late life as part of a lifelong disorder (early-onset schizophrenia), or first appear in older age (late-onset schizophrenia). Important factors that may affect the clinical presentation and treatment needs of the older person with schizophrenia (regardless of age of onset) include past history of treatment and cohort effects, comorbid medical illness, cognitive impairment, and the availability of social supports. Late-onset schizophrenia (LOS) is less common than early-onset schizophrenia (EOS) and is characterized by several distinct differences. Individuals with LOS compared to EOS are more likely to be women and to have better premorbid functioning, including better occupational history and a greater likelihood of having been married. The clinical presentation of LOS is more likely to include a predominance of positive symptoms such as paranoid delusions and auditory hallucinations and less likely to have negative symptoms. Formal thought disorder is rare in LOS, but common in EOS. Among those with LOS who have the onset of their disorder after age 60, there is a greater incidence of hearing loss compared to the general population. Finally, the limited data on treatment suggest that response to antipsychotic medication among individuals with LOS is comparable to EOS.

In general, there remains a paucity of research on treatments and services for older persons with severe and persistent mental disorders, particularly in the area of psychosocial treatment. In particular, little attention has focused on the individual with lifelong early-onset schizophrenia who is now in late middle age or old age. Further research is needed to determine the most effective and appropriate pharmacological and psychosocial interventions for the older person with schizophrenia.

10

Anxiety, Sexual, and Sleep Disorders

George still remembers the horror of World War II on a daily basis, although he never talks about it. One by one his buddies "went down" when their ship was sunk. How he survived he'll never quite know, but he prays daily for help living with the memories and the guilt.

Every day Genevieve struggles to make herself do the daily routine. She is so shaky all of the time; if she could just feel safe. The neighborhood is deteriorating, and her fear of what the kids will do to her is growing. She imagines all kinds of torture they could inflict if they decided to, and no one would know. The worst part is the terror she feels when her heart speeds up. She is just sure that this is the final curtain call. If her heart acts up when she is out and about, she gets particularly scared. So recently, she has prevailed upon her son and daughter-in-law to bring her groceries and supplies into the house, which she rarely leaves anymore.

John's diabetes has created erectile dysfunction that has undermined the sexual satisfaction that has always been an important part of his relationship with Morris. He avoids physical touch now, fearing that Morris will want it to "lead somewhere" that he can no longer go. Losing sex has brought a devastating loss of intimacy to a relationship that was remarkable for its decades of closeness.

Marion is awakened at least four or five times each night when Stephen gets up to wander around trying to figure out whether it is night or day. She has tried to sleep through his wanderings, but is just too afraid he will walk out the door or do something else unsafe. She's starting to have trouble falling asleep now, and has become so exhausted from lack of sleep that she looks like a wreck.

Anxiety, sleep, and sex are normal aspects of life in which dysfunctions can occur that can be devastating. The choice to combine the three in one chapter is primarily an organizational convenience, but there are also logical reasons for linking them. Anxiety is a major cause of disruption of normal sleep and sexual functioning, although many other factors produce a wide range of problems that are best viewed within the biopsychosocial model that informs this book. The vignettes noted above depict abnormal problems that are producing functional shifts in life patterns and decline in overall well-being.

For each of the three areas, the classifications and epidemiology of the disorders or difficulties will be presented, followed by a description of problems experienced by older adults, theories that explain the disorders or problems, and approaches to assessment and treatment in older adults.

Anxiety

Normal anxiety is experienced by all of us and is useful. Anxiety motivates us to be safe and perform adaptive behaviors that reduce anxiety (e.g., studying to reduce worry about an upcoming exam). However, when anxiety gets out of control or is excessive, then an anxiety disorder may be diagnosed. The disorders that make up the anxiety category bring significant distress to adults of any age. The hallmarks of anxiety are the combination of cognitive symptoms such as ruminative thinking, somatic symptoms such as racing heart or other signs of arousal, and affective symptoms such as low mood, fear, or worry. The cost of anxiety to the individual is high. Anxiety is associated with perceived difficulties with daily life, elevated levels of postoperative pain, and with a lower quality of life than is experienced by older adults with chronic illnesses such as diabetes or heart attack (Feeney, 2004; Wetherell et al., 2004). Not surprisingly, anxious individuals seek more medical services, thus generating large health care costs (Deacon, Lickel, & Abramowitz, 2008). Given the higher rates of anxiety than depression in older adults, the relatively recent upsurge of research on the nature of these disorders as well as strategies to assess and treat them effectively are desperately needed.

Types of Anxiety Disorders

The classification of anxiety disorders within the DSM-IV-TR includes several diverse disorders that are listed in Table 10.1, along with their essential features (American Psychiatric Association, 2000). *Phobias* are characterized by persistent fears and avoidance of a particular object or situation. *Generalized anxiety disorder* is the descriptor for the broadest set of anxiety symptoms that includes pervasive, excessive, or unrealistic worry on most days for six months or longer. *Panic disorder* is characterized by recurrent episodes of severe anxiety evidenced by several somatic and cognitive symptoms (e.g., shortness of breath, increased heart rate, sweating, tingling in hands and feet, fear of dying, fear of losing control, or fear of going crazy). The episodes often lack any warning signals, although they may occur in predictable situations (e.g., in an elevator, at a son's house, in a grocery store line). A common characteristic

Table 10.1 Diagnostic features for the most common anxiety disorders

Generalized Anxiety Disorder

Excessive anxiety or worry, occurring more days than not for at least 6 months, about multiple things.

Person finds it difficult to control the worry.

The anxiety is associated with 3 or more of the following 6 symptoms:

- Restlessness or feeling keyed up or on edge
- Fatigued easily
- Difficulty concentrating
- Irritability
- Muscle tension
- Sleep disturbance

Anxiety or worry causes significant distress or impairment in social, occupational, or aspects of functioning.

Specific Phobia

Marked and persistent fear that is excessive or unreasonable, cued by the presence or anticipated presence of a specific object or situation (e.g., flying, heights, animals, blood).

Exposure to the feared stimulus almost invariably provokes an immediate anxiety response.

Person recognizes that the fear is excessive or unreasonable.

The situation is avoided or else endured with intense anxiety or distress, and the avoidance or anxiety response interferes significantly with daily functioning.

Social Phobia

A marked and persistent fear of social or performance situations in which the person is exposed to unfamiliar people or to possible scrutiny by others. The person fears that he/she will act in a way that will be humiliating or embarrassing.

Exposure to the feared situation provokes anxiety.

The person recognizes that the fear is excessive or unreasonable.

The feared situations are avoided or else endured with intense anxiety and distress, and the avoidance or distress interferes with daily functioning.

Post-Traumatic Stress Disorder

Person was exposed to a traumatic event in which both were present:

* Person experienced, witnessed, or was confronted with life-threatening event or physical injury, or a threat to physical integrity of self or others
* Person's response involved intense fear, helplessness, or horror

The traumatic event is persistently re-experienced in 1 or more ways:

* Recurrent and intrusive distressing recollections
* Recurrent distressing dreams of the event
* Acting or feeling as if the event were recurring
* Intense psychological distress at the internal or external cues that symbolize or resemble the event
* Physiological reactivity on exposure to those cues

Persistent avoidance of stimuli associated with the trauma and numbing of general responsiveness in 3 (or more) of the following ways:

* Efforts to avoid thoughts, feelings, or conversations associated with the trauma
* Efforts to avoid activities, places, or people associated with the trauma
* Inability to recall important aspect(s) of the trauma
* Markedly diminished interest in significant activities
* Feeling detached or estranged from others
* Restricted range of affect
* Sense of short future

Persistent symptoms of increased arousal (new after the trauma) in 2 or more ways:

* Difficulty falling or staying asleep
* Irritability or outbursts of anger
* Difficulty concentrating
* Hypervigilance
* Exaggerated startle response

Source: Criteria summaries are adapted from the DSM-IV-TR (APA, 2000).

of the setting in which panic attacks tend to occur is that escape is difficult. As a strategy for coping with the fear of panic, some individuals restrict their activities to safe areas, thus developing agoraphobia over time. *Post-traumatic stress disorder* can occur following a traumatic event, and is diagnosed when the individual re-experiences the traumatic event in intrusive ways, avoids certain stimuli related to the event, experiences a numbing of feeling in response to specific stimuli, and experiences increased arousal generally. *Obsessive-compulsive disorder* is characterized by recurring obsessive thoughts and/or compulsive behaviors performed in response to the obsessive thoughts. Common obsessive thought patterns focus on fears of hurting someone or being contaminated by germs or dirt. Common compulsions include hand washing, counting, and repetitive checking.

Prevalence

Prevalence rates for anxiety disorders are higher than for depressive disorders, with 2–19 percent of older community residents reporting symptoms sufficient for diagnosis (Flint, 1994). The fact that anxiety is more prevalent than depression was found in the earliest community epidemiological study in the United States that included older adults, and frankly surprised the clinical community. A more recent national study in Canada that includes mental health epidemiological data on 12,792 adults shows similar rates of anxiety among the population (Streiner, Cairney, & Veldhuizen, 2006), as does the National Comorbidity Survey Replication study in the United States (Kessler, Berglund, Demler, Jin, & Walters, 2005). Although the prevalence of onset among the population age 60 and older is lower than at earlier points in adulthood, anxiety can occur for the first time even in advanced old age (Streiner et al., 2006). Lifetime prevalence rates of over 28.8 percent suggest that anxiety has affected the life experience of a substantial portion of the population, typically beginning in youth or early adulthood (Kessler et al., 2005). Even if the prevalence rate of diagnosable anxiety disorders is in the mid-range of estimates (e.g., approximately 10 percent), the prevalence of clinically significant anxiety hovers at approximately 20 percent among older adults. Figure 10.1 depicts prevalence variation across the most common anxiety disorders, and shows the powerful effects of age and gender on prevalence of all of these disorders.

Among the diagnostic categories for anxiety, phobias are the most common, with almost 5 percent of a national sample reporting them at time of interview (Regier, Rae, Narrow, Kaelber, & Schatzerg, 1988), and 9 percent of a multiracial Brooklyn neighborhood sample reporting a phobia at the time of interview (Cohen, Magai, Yaffee, Huangthaison, & Walcott-Brown, 2006a). Almost 5 percent of adults will have one particular phobia called social phobia in their lifetime, although only 1.3 percent report experiencing it in the past 12 months (Cairney et al., 2007). Agoraphobia (fear of leaving home) was found in 0.61 percent of the Canadian population study (McCabe, Cairney, Veldhuizen, Herrmann, & Streiner, 2006).

Generalized anxiety disorder (GAD) is the next most common, showing prevalence rates as high as 7.1 percent (Flint, 1994). Adults can develop GAD at any age, including later life. As is true with most psychological disorders, earlier onset of GAD is associated with greater severity of worry, higher rate of psychiatric comor-

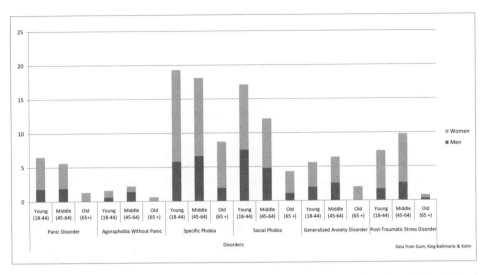

Figure 10.1   Gender and age differences in prevalence of anxiety disorders in the United States.
Source: Data from Gum, King-Kallimanis, and Kohn (2009).

bidities, and greater psychotropic medication use (Wetherell, LeRoux, & Gatz, 2003).

Similar to depression, older adults who do not reach criteria for diagnosis with a clinical disorder continue to report disturbingly high rates of symptoms that are now identified as subsyndromal anxiety. Subsyndromal anxiety was evident in 13 percent of one urban sample of older adults (Cohen, Magai, Yaffee, Huangthaison, & Walcott-Brown, 2006b).

Age differences in prevalence rates for anxiety disorders show somewhat lower rates in older than in younger adults (Streiner et al., 2006). Although age may actually mitigate anxiety, other explanations for the lower rates found in older adults are also plausible. For example, older adults may be underreporting their symptoms in community-based surveys. Alternatively, the cross-sectional nature of the studies may be capturing real differences among birth cohorts in their experience of anxiety, as could be the case if the "greatest generation" compensated for their early experiences of the Great Depression and World War II by becoming less anxious about subsequent routine problems in daily living. Yet another option is that older adults with anxiety and the comorbid physical and psychological problems that can accompany anxiety may be more likely to migrate toward congregate living facilities (e.g., assisted living) and thus be less available to epidemiological research. Multiple studies conducted over time with varied cohorts will be required to verify this finding.

Anxiety disorders appear to be relatively stable over time. A six-year longitudinal study in Amsterdam that followed 112 persons diagnosed with anxiety disorders found that 23 percent maintained their diagnosis six years later, and another 47 percent showed subclinical levels of anxiety disorders (Schuurmans et al., 2005).

Presentation in older adults

The presence of comorbid medical illnesses that produce symptoms similar to anxiety disorders creates a challenging differential diagnosis for many health providers. Effective means of assessing anxiety exist, as described below, but primary care providers who are the first source of help-seeking for most older adults often rely on patient self-report to identify anxiety. The symptoms reported by older adults may be somatic, overlapping symptoms of existing medical illnesses, or may be affective, overlapping with depression. Cognitive symptoms such as worry may lead the older adult as well as the health providers to focus on the content of the worry (e.g., racing heart, shortness of breath) rather than the pattern of worry that exemplifies anxiety. To complicate matters further, anxiety can also be a contributing factor to a variety of medical illnesses (e.g., gastrointestinal disorders), and anxiety symptoms are commonly present in older adults who are not diagnosable with an anxiety disorder. Sleep difficulties provide a good example, because aging adults often experience insomnia but not with the frequency, intensity, or impact as is the case for persons with GAD, for example (Wetherell et al., 2003).

Other mental disorders present with symptoms that overlap anxiety symptoms and anxiety disorders. For example, depression has a high rate of comorbidity with anxiety (Beekman et al., 2000; Mehta et al., 2003), and is hypothesized to share certain psychological and perhaps neurological underpinnings with anxiety (Teachman, Siedlecki, & Magee, 2007). Other psychological disorders are also comorbid with anxiety. Personality disorders are more prevalent in persons with anxiety disorders (Coolidge, Segal, Hook, & Stewart, 2000). Dementia (and in some cases, milder forms of cognitive impairment) produces high rates of anxiety symptoms, particularly restlessness, agitation, and fears. The relationship between anxiety and agitation in persons with dementia is still being clarified (Twelftree & Qazi, 2006). What is clear is that anxiety symptoms in demented persons warrant particular concern given that the poor problem-solving skills available to the patients can result in resistant and even assaultive behavior (Fisher & Noll, 1996).

The relationship between cognition and anxiety is emerging as an interesting area for research. Certainly, the content of thought is influenced by anxiety. The worries of the oldest old focus on health and memory, but considerable variation exists in the worry pattern over time (Jeon, Dunkle, & Roberts, 2006). Anxiety creates hypervigilance to threat in older adults as in young (Fox & Knight, 2005), suggesting that age does not fully influence the content of worry. The anxiety disorders shape the cognitive processes involved in worry, as evidenced by data showing that the worry of older adults with GAD is distinct from that of other older adults in frequency, uncontrollability, distress, and content (Wetherell et al., 2003). Anxiety is also associated with loss of inhibitory control, suggesting that age-related brain changes may be another source of important investigation in anxiety research (Price & Mohlman, 2007).

What is the effect of anxiety on health and disability? Certainly, anxiety is associated with high rates of medical service utilization, especially among persons suffering from panic attacks (Deacon et al., 2008). Medical help-seeking occurs for both the anxiety symptoms and comorbid medical symptoms that generate more worry among persons with anxiety. Anxiety actually increases mortality and risk of disease, including coronary artery disease in men (Van Hout et al., 2004). Anxiety also has been investigated as having a role in the development of functional disability. Some studies using objective measures of physical mobility and movement (e.g., Mehta et al., 2003) have found that older adults reporting anxiety do not decline functionally any faster than other older adults. However, that same study found that anxious older adults perceive their functional abilities to be declining faster than other older adults. In contrast, a study of rates of decline in ability to manage activities of daily living showed that anxiety was associated with declines in functioning (Brenes et al., 2005).

Theories of etiology

Several models for conceptualizing anxiety in older adults inform research and clinical work. Cognitive-behavioral models view anxiety behaviors as reflecting an absence of effective skills, distortions in thinking, and/or behavior patterns that avoid or circumvent more useful ways of addressing fearful thoughts about threat. Cognitive-behavioral models focus on thought processes as the mechanisms by which difficult situations are turned into anxiety symptoms (Beck, Emery, & Greenberg, 1985). Specifically, anxiety symptoms are viewed as a natural consequence of irrational thoughts (e.g., "My children must approve of me at all times"; "I must take care of everybody in the family").

More recently, an overarching model has been proposed that focuses on broad emotion regulation deficits as the core problem (Borkovec, Alcaine, & Behar, 2004; Roemer & Orsillo, 2002). Worry may be a strategy used to try to reduce arousal that is poorly tolerated by a subset of persons. The poor tolerance of arousal or negative emotional states may be the core problem rather than worry itself. This model would address other anxious behaviors as similar manifestations of coping strategies intended to reduce the undesirable negative affect or arousal. Poor interpersonal functioning, such as social isolation or conflict, are common negative outcomes of the coping strategies used by highly anxious persons that can perpetuate negative thought patterns and arousal that are characteristic of anxiety.

The high rate of comorbidity of anxiety with depression has led to efforts to conceptualize the common and distinct characteristics of these two disorders. A tripartite model suggests that anxiety shares with depression a higher-order factor of negative affect, along with lower-order factors of low positive affect (primary relevant to depression) and arousal (primarily relevant to anxiety) (Teachman et al., 2007).

Assessment

Assessment of anxiety can be accomplished through clinical interviews as well as self-report measures. Clinical interviews such as the Structured Clinical Interview for DSM-IV Axis I Disorders (First, Spitzer, Gibbon, & Williams, 2002) or the Anxiety Disorders Interview Schedule for DSM-IV (DiNardo, Brown, & Barlow, 1994) generate specific diagnoses by asking about presence, intensity, longevity, and impact on daily life of particular anxiety symptoms. Self-rating scales are used for screening for anxiety, yielding scores that are not informative for diagnosis, but provide an indicator of the presence and intensity of anxiety as a problem. Self-report measures for anxiety in older adults are currently in development because measures appropriate for the general population, such as the Beck Anxiety Inventory (Beck, Epstein, Brown, & Steer, 1988), have serious limitations in uses with older adults for whom physical illness symptoms can inflate anxiety scores if the measure has several somatic items (Wetherell & Gatz, 2005). Other commonly used measures include the State-Trait Anxiety Inventory (Spielberger, Gorsuch, Lushene, Vagg, & Jacobs, 1983) and the Hamilton Anxiety Rating Scale (Hamilton, 1969) because they are frequently used with other populations or in pharmacological studies and thus allow comparisons across studies. Cognitive symptoms of anxiety need to be heavily weighted in order for a self-report scale to offer discriminant validity from physical illness or depression. The existing cognitively focused measure, the Penn State Worry Questionnaire (Meyer et al., 1990), focuses on trait pathological worry and is thus not sensitive to changes over time that are important when using self-report scales as indicators of treatment progress. New self-report measures include the Geriatric Anxiety Inventory (Pachana et al., 2007) and the Geriatric Anxiety Scale (GAS; Segal, June, Payne, Coolidge, & Yochim, 2010). Both measures were developed specifically for use with older adults and have been successfully normed and validated. The GAS (Segal et al., 2010) includes 30 items of which 25 items represent three common domains of anxiety symptoms among older adults (cognitive, somatic, and affective) and 5 items represent common content areas of worry. Notably, the 25 symptom items were designed from the anxiety disorder diagnostic criteria from the DSM-IV-TR, providing broad-range coverage of diverse anxiety symptoms which can be teased apart by the three subscales.

Interventions for anxiety disorders

A recent upsurge in psychotherapy outcome research testing interventions for various anxiety disorders has produced an array of options for effective treatment (Mohlman, 2004; Nordhus & Pallesen, 2003; Wetherell, Lenze, & Stanley, 2005; Wetherell, Sorrell, Thorp, & Patterson, 2005). Although many studies have shown effectiveness, a variety of research methodologies have been used, some of which are informative but do not meet the criteria set for evidence-based treatment (EBT). Recently, four psychotherapy approaches were found to meet standards for EBT for anxiety disorders in older adults in a limited number of studies: relaxation training, cognitive-behavioral therapy (CBT), supportive therapy, and cognitive therapy (Ayers, Sorrell, Thorp, & Wetherell, 2007). These four treatments were applied to a mix of disorders, although their patient samples were primarily suffering from GAD, or having subjective distress over anxiety symptoms across diagnostic categories. Outcome research on phobias, panic disorder, obsessive-compulsive disorder, and post-traumatic stress disorder is lacking in strength to achieve EBT criteria.

CBT effectiveness studies are the most numerous, and the stronger support was found for CBT use with older adults experiencing GAD. The typical intervention protocol was short term (8–15 sessions) of individual or group intervention. Some studies experimented effectively with between-session prompts to complete homework (e.g., Mohlman et al., 2003). Researchers are currently working with tailored therapy approaches in which the treatment protocol consists of modules that are selected for use with particular patients based on the patient's particular needs (Wetherell, Sorrell et al., 2005).

Cognitive therapy and relaxation therapy studies were less numerous but showed similar benefits. Relaxation therapy is particularly promising because it can be conducted in a few sessions of training in a variety of settings, and shows benefits for up to a year (Rickard, Scogin, & Keith, 1994). Supportive therapy showed benefits but was not more effective than other EBTs.

Improvement across the studies was found in anxiety symptom reduction, overall quality of life improvement, and on measures of depression. To date, only a moderate effectiveness can be claimed for the various interventions because effect sizes vary across studies from small to large, with lower response rates than desired (Mohlman, 2004). No research to date has examined the mechanisms by which interventions achieve desired outcomes, nor have studies followed the samples over a period of years to study long-term effectiveness.

Pharmacological interventions continue to be the most commonly used approach for anxiety, at least in part because primary care is the most common site for help-seeking. In particular, the benzodiazepines (e.g., valium, xanax) are the most commonly prescribed for anxiety symptoms and disorders. Their calming effect occurs because of decrease in central nervous system activity, placing users at risk for loss of alertness and balance, and thus are considered risk factors for falls. They are also typically addicting. Antidepressants, particularly the selective serotonin reuptake inhibitors (SSRIs), are also prescribed to manage anxiety symptoms, with lower safety risks.

Although pharmacological interventions continue to be the most commonly used, significant concerns exist for their efficacy as well as safety. Many of the EBTs tested above were compared against pharmacological agents, either alone or in a combined treatment (EBT plus pharmacological agent). In general, the pattern of findings was that the EBTs demonstrated stronger effectiveness than the medications.

Sexual Disorders and Difficulties

Definitions of sexuality are heavily influenced by cultural images that promote definitions of what is normative and desirable. Historically, older adults were portrayed as asexual beings with neither interest nor ability to give or receive pleasure through sexual interactions. More recently, intensive marketing of pharmaceuticals designed to assist men in achieving and maintaining erections is affecting our images of aging to include not only the opportunity, but also the social imperative to maintain a particular type of sexual functioning (Potts, Grace, Vares, & Gavey, 2006).

Reduced rates of sexual activity with advancing age are normative, apparently for a very diverse set of reasons outlined below that do not necessarily relate to sexual disorders. Starting in late midlife, sexual activity rates drop dramatically from 73 percent to a low adulthood rate of 26 percent in persons aged 75–85 (Lindau et al., 2007). The decline in rate of sexual behavior is not necessarily an indicator of sexual disorder or difficulty, because loss of partners and onset of medical conditions and disabilities impact access and opportunity as well. Indeed, cross-national data show that almost two-thirds of older adults in Western countries are satisfied with their sexual relationships (Laumann et al., 2005).

Definitions

Sexual disorders are diagnosed using the same categories in the DSM-IV-TR (APA, 2000) for persons of all ages. Among the many possible sexual disorders, those more commonly associated with aging include male erectile disorder, and in women a disorder related to pain during sex that is known as dyspareunia. Men and women are also vulnerable to *sexual dysfunction due to a general medical condition* that interferes with sexual responses.

A unique set of problems arises when the onset of cognitive impairment introduces difficulties with intimacy into the lives of its victims and their caregivers. Over time, affection and sexual functioning both decline more rapidly for couples including a person with dementia than same-age couples without dementia (Wright, 1998). Caregiving partners may be confused about the ethics of continuing to be sexually active with a partner who is so dependent on the caregiver that the person may be unwilling to risk displeasing the caregiver by declining sexual activity. On the other hand, sexual intimacy between a person with any disability and his or her caregiving partner is a powerful validation of relationship endurance in the face of permanent disability (Davies, Zeiss, Shea, & Tinklenberg, 1998). Although persons with dementia can become less inhibited sexually, the probability of inappropriate sexual behaviors is quite low. Professional caregivers often have significant control over the care recipient's access to sexual partners as well as his or her opportunity to engage in sexual behavior, especially within institutional settings where the attitudes of the caregiver have full control over social relationships.

Prevalence

Prevalence of sexual activity and sexual satisfaction decline with advancing age in both men and women (Araujo, Mohr, & McKinlay, 2004; Laumann et al., 2005). Almost one-half of a national probability sample of adults age 57–85 report having a bothersome problem with their sexuality (Lindau et al., 2007).

Variability in the prevalence of dissatisfaction varies by gender and culture. A large, international study of sexual attitudes and behaviors in 29 diverse countries indicated that women report less physical pleasure, emotional pleasure, satisfaction with sexual functioning, and importance of sex compared with men (Laumann et al., 2005). Substantial cross-national variation was also evident in this study, with Western countries reporting more satisfaction overall, and Asian countries reporting the lowest levels of satisfaction by both men and women.

The sexual experience of older lesbian, gay, bisexual, and transgendered persons (LGBT) is poorly researched (Kimmel, Rose, & David, 2006). Not surprisingly, there is a serious paucity of data on sexual disorders in this group (Garnets & Peplau, 2006; Wierzalis, Barret, Pope, & Rankins, 2006). The current cohort of LGBT older adults experienced their sexuality in a context of powerful stigma that often made it impossible to be open about their sexuality if they wanted to be socially engaged. Cohort experience thus is one of the more powerful factors in understanding what may be viewed as normal or disordered about sexual functioning among LGBT older adults. Persons who early in life found that they experienced other than exclusively opposite-sex attraction were highly unlikely to have received appropriate education within which to interpret their own sexual experiences. This absence of developmental support is particularly powerful for all non-heterosexuals because it so profoundly influences identity development, which is shaped by a person's understanding of his or her sexual orientation, gender, and gender identity. Thus, the current cohort of older adults who identify as LGBT is likely to have had particularly challenging identity and intimacy paths through life, often maintaining separate public and private identities, or experiencing significant social marginalization when claiming their own sexual identity.

The aging experience of sexuality is shaped by changes in one's body and psychological representations of one's body identity or image, regardless of sexual orientation. Because sexual identity is usually expressed interpersonally, persons who identify as LGBT often face unique challenges because of internalized stigma as well as social stigmas that can interfere with normal sexual exploration. For some older adults, receipt of professional or personal care reveals aspects of their sexual identity that they had not previously revealed or prefer not to reveal (e.g., a transgendered person being bathed in a nursing home no longer has an option of choosing who knows what). Mental health among older persons who identify as LGBT is shaped by the same myriad factors as heterosexual adults, with a strong overlay of cohort-bound experiences that shaped identity and interpersonal relationship formation.

Risk factors

Risk factors for sexual disorders and difficulties again follow the biopsychosocial model, falling into physiological factors, psychological factors, and social factors, with high likelihood of interactions among the categories of risk.

Normal aging is associated with physiological changes in the sexual response cycle (outlined in Table 10.2) that create risk for sexual disorders and difficulties. Menopause in women is associated with reduced estrogen production, which can reduce desire and arousal, along with reduced production of lubrication that creates discomfort. Thinning of the vaginal wall also creates risk of discomfort during intercourse. However, marital problems are more strongly associated with sexual difficulties in women than are physiological changes (Dunn, Croft & Hackett, 1999). Significant

Table 10.2 Sexual response cycle

The sexual response cycle is typically divided into the following phases:

1 Desire – fantasies about, and desire for, sexual activity
2 Excitement – subjective sense of sexual pleasure; physiological changes characteristic of sexual arousal
3 Orgasm – peaking of sexual pleasure; release of sexual tension; rhythmic contractions
4 Resolution – muscular relaxation and a sense of general well-being

deterioration in sexual functioning was documented over a nine-year period in men aged 40–70 (Araujo et al., 2004). In late midlife men report reduced frequency of sexual thoughts and decreased sexual enjoyment, along with decreased erectile and orgasmic functioning. The functional decline is evident in slower response time in the earlier stages of the cycle, and reduced penile circumference during arousal. Although erectile problems result from these physiological changes, premature ejaculation is associated with anxiety. Despite these declines in the intensity and frequency of sexual responses, most people describe their sexuality as satisfying. Thus, as in other aspects of life, most people adapt to the changes of aging without identifying themselves as experiencing disorder or difficulty.

Sexual disorders and difficulties can occur as secondary effects of chronic illnesses and the medications used to treat them. Erectile dysfunction is commonly comorbid with diabetes mellitus, hypertension, coronary artery disease, radical prostatectomy, or pelvic trauma. Medications that increase risk for erectile dysfunction include anti-hypertensives, antiepileptic, antianxiety, or antidepressant agents. As explained below, the impact of these diseases and medications on sexual functioning is due to the fact that sexual responses are essentially vascular responses, thus decline in cardiovascular functioning almost always has a negative effect on sexual responsiveness. Alcohol use is an additional risk factor (Rowland, van Diest, Incrocci, & Slob, 2005).

Theories of etiology

Physical aging and age-related illness, medications, and over-the-counter agents are all primary causes of sexual dysfunction onset in later life. Each specific category of sexual dysfunction represents a descriptive category of some component of the sexual response cycle that is not working well. The mechanics of the sexual response cycle are complex, involving every major organ system of the body so almost any physiological difficulties can contribute to sexual dysfunctions.

Ageism and stereotypes of aging also contribute to sexual dysfunction in later life by shaping expectations for what is normal or even possible. Indeed, attitudes are stronger predictors of sexual desire than biomedical factors (DeLamater & Sill, 2005). Negative biases about the appropriateness of desiring sexual intimacy inhibit relationship exploration. Whereas a younger person might seek alternative strategies for remaining sexually active even after disability, an older person with beliefs that sexual desire is abnormal or unnecessary in later life may not even investigate the information or strategies available to adapt to the disability. Ageism in care providers can exert powerful influence on older adults as well.

Social causes are also significant factors as age increases the probability that women, in particular, will lose their husbands as sexual partners due to serious illness or death. The gender imbalance in later life poses a serious barrier for heterosexual women who might wish to partner again and influences sexual desire (DeLamater & Sill, 2005). LGBT partners may lose the privacy that afforded them social safety if either member of the couple requires assistance of formal service providers or residential placement.

Finally, anxiety about performance has deleterious effects on sexual functioning in both men and women. Often, anxiety about changes in sexual functioning can exacerbate the negative impact of what otherwise would have been a mild change. The compounding effect of anxiety can lead to avoidance of intimacy that can lead to sexual experiences as well as to poorly organized or structured sexual behaviors that are not satisfying.

Assessment

Sexual functioning should be assessed regularly in primary care as well as in mental health and relationship counseling. Physicians are less likely to ask older persons about their sexual well-being although the question would be welcomed by their patients (Nusbaum, Singh, & Pyles, 2004). Screening assessment can be as simple as a single question; questions simply need to be asked. Once a problem has been disclosed, assessment typically engages multiple disciplines, ideally in the context of an inter-professional team (Zeiss, Zeiss, & Davies, 1999).

Clinical interview is the first step in assessment of sexual disorders and difficulties. Initially, a broad lens is cast on the life circumstance of the client to look for causal factors in all spheres of biopsychosocial functioning. Physical health is an obvious area to research, with detailed assessment of illness history, current health status, use of medications, substance abuse, and medicinal uses of non-traditional health substances (e.g., herbs) or over-the-counter medications (e.g., laxatives). Psychological well-being is also evaluated with particular attention to the presence of anxiety, depression, and cognitive impairment. Characteristics of intimate social relationships are assessed along with the aspects of the broader social environment that might influence accessibility or comfort with sexual activity.

The interview also includes detailed assessment of the sexual functioning of the client using questions that elicit very specific descriptions of sexual behavior sequences. Disorders or difficulties may result from misunderstanding of normal age-related changes in physiological functioning (e.g., decreased lubrication) or from inadequate adaptation to physical disabilities that interfere with familiar ways of interacting sexually. General attitudes about sexuality, values, and language used to discuss sexual activity need to be documented because they shape the choice of interventions. The client's view of the problem is also detailed, along with previous efforts to address the problem and their results. Finally, the goal of the intervention needs to be developed explicitly. A thorough semi-structured interview format is outlined by Zeiss et al. (1999).

When partners are interviewed together, the interview detailed above would elicit information from both persons with follow-up assessment of discrepancies in viewpoint, experience, attitude, and previous solution attempts. Partners may discover during a joint interview that their efforts have been conflicted enough to actually undermine the potential efficacy of either person's approach. Joint interviews provide rich relationship information available only when observing two people who are seeking help for a particularly intimate aspect of their relationship. The assessment interview affords the opportunity to intervene in small ways by offering permission to state one's own view or experience without judgment, or to ask questions of a partner in non-judgmental ways that reduce shame or defensiveness. Of course, the clinical interview may or may not include partner(s), depending on their availability and the intervention goals.

Older adults experiencing sexual dysfunction should be examined carefully by a physician to determine whether the difficulty is primary or secondary to a chronic illness or medication. Because the sexual response cycle is particularly sensitive to functional losses in the cardiovascular or neurological systems due to illness or medication, the physical exam is of particular importance to older clients.

Interventions for sexual disorders

The focus of sex therapy is directed to problems identified in a thorough multidisciplinary assessment. Therapy may be undertaken with an individual or couple, and may focus heavily on sexual functioning or more broadly address intimacy and other social aspects of primary relationships. In general, talk therapy interventions for sexual dysfunctions have not been well researched; the clinical literature relies on case studies primarily.

Cognitive-behavior therapy offers an organized basis for treatment of sexual disorders in older adults (Crowther & Zeiss, 1999). The Permission, Limited Information, Specific Suggestion, Intensive Therapy (PLISSIT) model creates a framework for starting with the least necessary intervention and progressing toward more intensive treatment only as needed (Annon, 1974). Starting with Permission, the interventions proceed through sharing Limited Information, Specific Suggestions, and, when necessary, Intensive Therapy. Permission addresses sexual problems created by attitudinal factors as well as by poor adjustment to disability or illness that interrupted familiar ways of being sexually active. More recently, the opposite focus of permission also became relevant – permission *not* to demand hyperperformance from oneself just because pharmaceutical companies use media advertising to raise expectations (Potts et al., 2006). Informational interventions often address the particular educational need of the individual, although they can also be offered in a group context. Specific suggestions may be particularly useful to older adults seeking to adapt to age-related physiological changes in sexual responsiveness. Intensive Therapy would engage an individual or couple in extensive changes in the relationship, sexual behaviors, or in adjusting to the impact of loss of particular types of sexual functioning.

Pharmacological and prosthetic interventions are also available to restore sexual functioning. In women, the focus of these interventions is on hormonal enhancement of desire or genital arousal via enhancement of vascular functioning in the clitoral area. Topical application of vaginal estrogen in cream or ring decreases dryness and discomfort, and mechanical devices such as vibrators and vacuum systems stimulate clitoral engorgement. Recent public marketing of erectile dysfunction medications for men (e.g., Viagra) has generated remarkable sales. The effects on satisfaction with sexual functioning and relationship well-being have not yet been evaluated. Penile prostheses are available that create rigidity in the penis sufficient to engage in intercourse, with positive benefits for sexual and psychological well-being (Bettocchi et al., 2010). The rate of success of erectile dysfunction treatments among cancer patients demonstrates that although men prefer non-surgical treatment such as medication, success rates may be higher with the invasive treatments (Schover et al., 2002).

Education and training of health providers are obviously needed to enhance their comfort and skill in assessing and treating sexual problems in older adults (Davies et al., 1998). Staff in long-term care facilities are somewhat knowledgeable about sexual functioning but tend to deny interest in sexual behavior among residents. Administrators in institutional settings particularly need to be proactive in formulating policies for protection of resident rights to be sexually active along with appropriate resources to assess capacity to consent to sexual behavior among persons with cognitive impairments (Lyden, 2007). An excellent set of resources to support education about aging and sexuality is available on the American Psychological Association's Office on Aging web site at http://www.apa.org/pi/aging/sexuality.html.

Sleep Disorders and Difficulties

Complaints of sleep difficulties are more common in older adults than any other age group, occurring in approximately half of all older adults at any moment in time (Ohayon, 2002). The consequences of sleep disorders are significant: greater risk of physical and mental health comorbidities, higher health service utilization, greater functional disability, reduced quality of life, and, indeed, mortality (Dew et al., 2003). Obviously, healthy sleep is a significant component of mental health as well as a predictor of well-being that warrants attention in later life.

Before examining disorders of sleep, the normal effects of aging on sleep patterns needs to be understood. Sleep is divided into rapid eye movement (REM) sleep and four stages of non-REM sleep. The non-REM stages are simply numbered 1–4, with each larger number indicating a deeper stage of sleep characterized by slower brain waves. The percentage of slow-wave sleep decreases linearly by approximately 2 percent per decade in adulthood up to age 60, after which the decline levels off (Ohayon et al., 2004). However, these changes are insufficient to account for the sleep complaints of older adults, which primarily focus on decreased ability to maintain sleep (Ancoli-Israel & Ayalon, 2006).

Definitions and prevalence

Sleep disorders include various types of disrupted sleep patterns and various causes of those disruptions. In other words, sleep disorders are categorized according to descriptions of a disordered pattern (e.g., sleep initiation problems), an etiology (e.g., sleep apnea), or a behavioral consequence (e.g., excessive daytime sleepiness). The major categories of sleep disorders included in the DSM-IV-TR are listed in Table 10.3.

Insomnias are defined as difficulties initiating or maintaining normal sleep, or non-restorative sleep that leaves the person functioning poorly the next day. Patterns may include trouble falling asleep, difficulty falling back to sleep after nighttime awakening, or very early morning wakening without ability to fall back to sleep. Among community-dwelling older adults, prevalence rates range from 15–45 percent for difficulties initiating sleep, 20–65 percent for disrupted sleep, and 15–54 percent for terminal insomnia, whereas non-restorative sleep is reported by 10 percent of older

Table 10.3 Major sleep disorders in the DSM-IV-TR

Primary Insomnia	Nightmare Disorder
Primary Hypersomnia	Sleep Terror Disorder
Narcolepsy	Sleepwalking Disorder
Breathing-Related Sleep Disorder	Sleep Disorder Due to General Medical Conditions
Circadian-Rhythm Sleep Disorder	Substance-Induced Sleep Disorder

persons (Ohayon, 2002). Advancing age does not predict significant increases in these rates, but women report more sleep disruption than men.

Disrupted nighttime sleep disorders include sleep-disordered breathing, periodic limb movements, restless leg syndrome, and REM behavior disorder. Sleep-disordered breathing (SDB) problems involve either partial or full disruption of respiration 10–15 or more times per hour during sleep, conditions commonly called hypopneas or apneas. SDB prevalence increases dramatically from middle age (4–9 percent) to older adults (age 60+), for whom 45–62 percent meet criteria for diagnosis (Ancoli-Israel et al., 1991; Young et al., 1993). Periodic limb movements in sleep (PLMS) is characterized by repetitive leg movements occurring at least five times per hour, and as often as every 20–40 seconds throughout the night. Community-dwelling older adults show rates of 25–58 percent compared with 5–6 percent in younger adults across several studies (e.g., Foley et al., 1995). Restless leg syndrome (RLS) describes the patient's leg movements that are the only relief available to deal with the unpleasant sensation of "pins and needles" or "creepy, crawly feelings." RLS increases with age, with almost twice the prevalence in women as in men (Ohayon & Roth, 2002). Another movement disorder, REM behavior disorder (RBD), is a sleep disorder that results in complex motor movements and actions that may even harm the patient or others, apparently caused by lack of muscle inhibition during dream states. The highest prevalence of RBD is in older men, although it occurs in persons of all ages (Montplaisir, 2004).

Excessive daytime sleepiness (EDS) is a consequence of other sleep disorders or may be caused by other physiological, psychological, or social factors that disrupt sleep. EDS is associated with a myriad of risks, including driving accidents, mortality from cardiovascular accidents, psychiatric disorders, falls, and cognitive deficits. Daily functioning is also impaired in areas such as social functioning, activity level, general productivity, and vigilance, especially in those with multiple medical conditions or multiple medications (Gooneratne et al., 2003).

Risk factors

Although age-related changes in the sleep cycle are often lamented as disruptive of good restfulness, aging *per se* is not the cause of sleep disturbances although it may be a risk factor (Foley et al., 1995). Multiple biopsychosocial factors that are age related are implicated, however, and need to be evaluated carefully when older adults complain of sleep problems (Ancoli-Israel & Ayalon, 2006). Risk for almost all of the sleep disorders increases with diagnosis of multiple chronic illnesses, use of multiple medications, presence of psychiatric disorders (especially depression and anxiety), as well as changes in the timing and chronicity of sleep. Ironically, any sleep disorder also increases risk for other sleep problems.

Theories of etiology

Sleep disorders are best explained within the biopsychosocial model because their etiology can be purely physiological, as occurs with medication-induced insomnia, or may occur because of purely psychological factors (e.g., depression) or social factors (e.g., disruption due to household activity).

Physiological sources of sleep disorders are particularly common in later life, when aging itself reduces the robustness and satisfaction of sleep at the same time that chronic illnesses that disrupt sleep become normative. As described above, aging-induced changes in the brain reduce the amount of time spent in deeper stages of sleep. With available deep sleep time, all other interruptions of sleep can have greater disruptive impact on sleep. Thus, for example, PLMS and RLS create behavioral disruptions that lead to wakening and have a disproportionately interruptive impact on sleep in older persons.

Chronic illnesses and medications have direct negative effects on sleep. A remarkably wide range of illness conditions add to risk of sleep problems (Ancoli-Israel & Ayalon, 2006). Two illnesses that have particularly high rates of sleep disorders associated with them are Parkinson's disease and Alzheimer's disease, both of which are increasingly prevalent in later life (Garcia-Borreguero, Larrosa, & Bravo, 2003; McCurry et al., 1999). The medications prescribed for these and other conditions can also contribute to sleep problems. Additionally, medications can have diuretic effects that increase urinary frequency during the night, resulting in multiple trips to the bathroom that also interrupt the sleep cycle.

Aging reduces synchronization of circadian rhythms with external cues of the time of day or behavior patterns that structure day/night behavior sequences. These biological dysregulations lead older adults to sleep off-time with the social norms for sleep cycles, often with the urge to sleep early in the evening followed by middle of the night wakening for the "day." The causes of circadian disruption range from genetics to decreased light exposure, core body temperature cycle changes, and a range of environmental factors.

Sleep apneas and other SDBs are caused by temporary collapse of the airway that is often accompanied by loud snoring and breathing cessation. The impact on sleep has multiple pathways, including reduced oxygen intake (intermittent nighttime hypoxemia), self-awakening from the sounds of snoring, and the sudden awakening that terminates the cessation of breathing.

Psychological causes of sleep disruption include worry, anxiety, loneliness, and especially depression (Quan et al., 2005). Additionally, wakefulness rather than sleep induction may be promoted psychologically if the sleep environment stimulates mental activation. Anxiety and depression are also possible contributors to poor sleep because both include sleep disturbance within the constellation of symptoms within several disorders.

Social causes are also potential factors in sleep disorders in older adults. Any activity in the environment that forces awakening will also disrupt the sleep cycle and put the person more at risk for sleep disorder. Research on spousal caregivers, for example, has shown that sleep disruption is one of their most common and problematic sources of distress (McCurry, Logsdon, Vitiello, & Teri, 1998). A cognitively impaired spouse who wanders in the night not only makes noise that awakens the caregiver, but also poses a safety risk that keeps the caregiver too vigilant to sleep well. Nursing home residents who spend large proportions of their day in bed also have unusual sleep–wake patterns that disrupt successful sleep.

Assessment

As a natural consequence of the etiological complexity of sleep disorders, assessment of sleep problems requires a multidisciplinary approach to evaluation. Morgan (2000) recommends distinguishing between normal age-related changes in sleep, the most likely treatable causes (among many, potentially), and long-term sleep difficulties that have been present prior to aging. An obvious beginning point for assessment is a thorough medical examination, including both history and physical. Although not recommended routinely in primary care, polysomnography provides the gold standard of sleep cycle patterns and is available in specialty sleep clinics. Physiological sleep assessments typically involve nighttime monitoring of breathing, physiological measurement of brain activity using electroencephalograph (EEG) readings, and urine analysis during the night.

Self-report questionnaires are very useful to identify potential clinical disorders as well as for reporting of subjective perceptions of sleep cycle disruption and distress (McCrae et al., 2003). For example, self-reported daytime sleepiness or chronic tiredness in patients willing to undergo a sleep evaluation produced high prevalence of diagnosable disorders (77 percent of women and 98 percent of men were diagnosed in one study; Bailes, Baltzan, Alapin, Fichten, & Libman, 2005). Questionnaires include the Sleep Impairment Index and the Pittsburgh Sleep Quality Index (see Morin & Espie, 2003). Depression and anxiety questionnaires also are used consistently by clinicians and researchers studying sleep.

Sleep diaries track sleep/wake patterns in detail repeatedly over a period of days or weeks to identify the variation in sleep patterns that help identify social as well as psychological sources of disruption. Multiple measures can be attained in diaries, including perceived sleep latency, number of nighttime awakenings, amount of time spent awake, sleep time, sleep efficiency (% of in-bed time spent asleep), nap patterns, and sleep quality ratings.

Psychosocial interviews are used to obtain diagnostic information as well as detailed descriptions of thoughts and behaviors prior to and during difficult sleep periods, food/drink ingestion patterns, and nighttime awakening patterns. Sleep management strategies also are assessed to determine what the older person already uses successfully or without benefit. Finally, assessment of consequences of sleep disturbances can examine effects as diverse as daytime sleepiness, cognitive functioning, and activity rate.

A successful assessment produces a detailed description of the sleep pattern, subjective perceptions of sleep problems, subjective distress about sleep problems, and data that assist with diagnosis of the etiology of the disorder(s) as well as treatment planning.

Interventions for sleep disorders

Consistent with the assessment model described above, interventions begin with treatment of any primary condition that produces sleep disorders as a secondary consequence. Careful review of medication alternatives can sometimes produce options for treating chronic conditions that do not produce adverse sleep effects.

Pharmacological interventions are commonly prescribed when sleep problems are reported in primary care settings. Benzodiazepines are the most commonly prescribed and recommended pharmacological sleep agents despite limited evidence of their effectiveness (Bain, 2006; Simon & Ludman, 2006). Medications that depress central nervous system functioning are not good choices because there is no evidence of efficacy and side effects can be quite dangerous. Newer non-benzodiazepine sleep medications are now available, but comparative research shows poorer outcomes from these than cognitive-behavioral therapies (Sivertsen et al., 2006).

Non-pharmacological approaches to intervention offer fewer potential medical complications and better evidence of long-term efficacy than pharmacological approaches (Bain, 2006; Nau, McCrae, Cook, & Lichstein, 2005). Controlled clinical trials document the impact of cognitive-behavioral therapies for older adults on several aspects of sleep quality and quantity, primarily on self-report measures but with growing evidence of physiological impact as well (Lichstein, Riedel, Wilson, Lester, & Aguillard, 2001; Pallesen et al., 2004; Sivertsen et al., 2006). Sivertsen and colleagues (2006) demonstrated the impact of CBT on sleep efficiency (% time asleep) as well as increased time in slow-wave sleep (stages 3 and 4). Impressively, maintenance of gains has generally extended months or years beyond the end of treatment (e.g., Pallesen et al., 2004).

Cognitive-behavioral therapy techniques included in outcome studies showing positive benefits include sleep hygiene, sleep restriction, stimulus control, cognitive therapy, sleep compression, and relaxation (Nau et al., 2005). Some evidence suggests that patient characteristics predict which type of intervention helps most. For example, Lichstein et al. (2001) found that patients with high daytime fatigue responded best to interventions that extended sleep, whereas others responded best to interventions focused on sleep compression.

Recent data suggest that these approaches are also successful in challenging populations such as caregivers of persons with dementia who still experience the demands of providing care (McCrae, Tierney, & McNamara, 2005). Dementia patients also benefit from behavioral interventions (McCurry et al., 1998) to improve sleep. Finally, other approaches to sleep quality improvement that show potential include increases in morning or evening activity (Benloucif et al., 2004), music (Lai & Good, 2005), and napping (Campbell, Murphy, & Stauble, 2005).

Summary and Conclusions

Three categories of disorders were addressed in this chapter. Anxiety disorders are the most common type of mental disorders found in older adults. Assessment tools can be used to more consistently identify anxiety in older adults, and to track treatment. Researchers have generated empirically supported treatments for only a limited set of these disorders for older adults, but research is progressing rapidly. Research on sexual disorders in older adults is growing, generating effective strategies for assessment and intervention of the most common disorders. Sleep disorders are extremely common in older adults and produce a wide range of deleterious effects. Strategies to improve sleep quantity and quality have been demonstrated to have benefits for older adults. All three areas of psychopathology warrant additional research to develop a sufficient evidence base to treat the full range of disorders that are known to affect adults in later life.

11

Substance Abuse, Personality Disorders, and Marital/Family Conflict

Substance abuse, personality disorders, and marital conflict are often *hidden* problems in later life because many older adults with difficulties in these areas are either not detected by mental health professionals or the symptoms are not recognized by the older adults themselves. The vignettes described below depict the challenging nature of these types of problems because none of the cases shows a clear route to appropriate mental health assessment and treatment. For the areas of substance abuse and personality disorders, a description of the disorders, epidemiology, presentation of the disorders in later life, theories of etiology, and approaches to assessment and treatment in older adults will be depicted. The chapter concludes with a discussion of marital conflict and family problems among older adults, with a focus on the challenges of caregiving.

Substance Abuse

Lincoln and Lois rarely fought until after his retirement, although their marriage has always been filled with tension. She rarely misses a chance now to let him know just how unhappy she is with his drinking. He tells her to shut up, that there is no problem, and that she should quit trying to take away one of the peaceful pleasures of his retirement. Lincoln doesn't miss the pressure of work but he does miss the peaceful hours of driving that were a daily occurrence in his job as a salesman. Lois used to think she couldn't wait until Lincoln retired, but now is frustrated every afternoon when she hears the whiskey decanter rattle about 3 o'clock. She knows that by dinner he will be pretty out of it, and he will fall asleep by 7 p.m. What kind of retirement is this?

Jim never was much of a drinker throughout his adult years, although he enjoyed a beer or two here or there. But after his wife Ella died from cancer a couple of

Aging and Mental Health, 2e. Daniel L. Segal, Sara Honn Qualls, and Michael A. Smyer
© 2011 Daniel L. Segal, Sara Honn Qualls, and Michael A. Smyer

years ago, he has become increasingly lonely and isolated. After all, it was Ella who was the "social planner" for the couple, and it seems as if Jim's friends have slowly disappeared from his life. Now, in the evenings, Jim finds himself drinking more and more, thinking to himself that he does not have anything else to do to "pass the time." He has also been "doubling up" on his prescription pain medication, because he likes the way it relaxes him. Recently, he has fallen down a couple of times during periods of intoxication, breaking his arm the last time, but his doctors do not know about his drinking and increased pill popping, and Jim does not want to bring it up.

Many categories of psychoactive substances can be used and abused, including alcohol and other central nervous system depressants (e.g., benzodiazepines, barbiturates), cannabinoids (e.g., marijuana, hashish), hallucinogens (e.g., LSD, mescaline), inhalants (e.g., nitrous oxide), opioid analgesics (e.g., heroin, morphine), dissociative anesthetics (e.g., ketamine, PCP), entactogens (e.g., MDMA or "Ecstasy"), and stimulants (e.g., cocaine, amphetamines). By far, however, alcohol is the most commonly abused substance in later life.

Substance-related disorders in the DSM-IV-TR (American Psychiatric Association, 2000) are classified into either *substance abuse* or *substance dependence*. Substance abuse is defined as a maladaptive pattern of substance use involving negative social or legal consequences that are also associated with clinically significant impairment or distress. The diagnosis requires the person to show at least one of the following four criteria in a 12-month period:

- recurrent substance use resulting in a failure to fulfill major role obligations at work, school, or home;
- recurrent use in situations in which it is physically hazardous;
- recurrent substance-related legal problems;
- continued use despite having persistent or recurrent social problems caused or exacerbated by the substance use.

Alternatively, a diagnosis of *substance dependence* requires the person to show at least three of the following seven criteria in a 12-month period:

- tolerance (needing more of the substance to achieve intoxication);
- withdrawal (painful physical and psychological symptoms experienced when the substance is discontinued);
- taking the substance in larger amounts or over a longer period than intended;
- a persistent desire or unsuccessful efforts to cut down or eliminate substance use;
- spending a great deal of time in activities associated with substance use;
- reduction in important activities due to substance use;
- continued use despite persistent psychological or physical problems caused by use.

Substance abuse in older adults tends to focus on a different set of psychoactive substances than those abused by younger adults, with the exception of alcohol, which is commonly abused across the adult life span. Compared with younger adults, older adults are far less likely to abuse illegal drugs (e.g., cocaine, LSD, marijuana), but they are far more likely to misuse or abuse prescription medications and over-the-counter medications (Johnson-Greene & Inscore, 2005). The consequences of this "legal" drug abuse can be as serious as illegal drug use, but has generated far less attention from substance abuse intervention programs.

Prevalence

In the United States, substance abuse is a pervasive and costly problem. According to the 2007 National Survey on Drug Use and Health (US Department of Health and Human Services, 2008), approximately 23 million people aged 12 and older met criteria for substance abuse or dependence in the past year. The substance abuse problem among older adults is serious as well, although definitive prevalence data for community-dwelling older adults are lacking. In general, older adults consume less alcohol and have fewer alcohol-related problems than younger adults. However, it appears that drinking patterns remain relatively stable with age, likely reflecting the social and cultural norms that prevailed when the person began drinking, and that the negative effects of alcohol misuse among older adults remain substantial. Rates for alcohol problems among older adults are high in specific settings, such as among older patients admitted to hospitals (6–11 percent), older patients in psychiatric wards (20 percent), and older patients in emergency rooms (14 percent) (Council on Scientific Affairs, American Medical Association, 1996). Despite these high rates, substance abuse is likely underdiagnosed and underreported in the older adult population, due to the tendency among older adults toward denial, inadequate case-finding strategies, and limited relevance of some diagnostic criteria for substance abuse (King, Van Hasselt, Segal, & Hersen, 1994). Unfortunately, lack of accurate detection and diagnosis is a major barrier to adequate intervention.

Young adulthood is the life period associated with heavy alcohol use. The 2007 National Survey on Drug Use and Health (US DHHS, 2008) revealed that 21-year-olds reported the highest levels of current alcohol use (72 percent of the sample). Rates of current alcohol use tended to decline with advancing age, but were still significant in older age groups (67 percent in 25-year-olds; 62 percent in adults aged 30–34; 48 percent in adults aged 60–64; and 38 percent in individuals 65 years old and older). Although rates of heavy alcohol use are known to decrease with age, heavy drinking at an early age may have long-lasting consequences, influencing the level of education attained, subsequent employment, and involvement with the legal system. Regarding the life span history of alcohol problems, about 20–30 percent of individuals with alcohol problems in young adulthood continue to have problems in later adulthood, but those diagnosed with alcohol problems in middle age are more likely to continue to have problems over time (Larimer & Kilmer, 2000). However, as we describe in more detail below, some individuals develop alcohol problems in later life, problems that were not evident earlier in life.

Abuse of substances intended as medications is another area of serious concern for older adults. Older adults are the recipients of 34 percent of all prescribed medications and the consumers of 30 percent of all over-the-counter (OTC) medications, a percentage far greater than their proportion of the population (13 percent) (National Center for Health Statistics, 2003). Because older adults commonly take numerous medications prescribed by multiple providers and metabolize medications more slowly than younger adults, they are at a much greater risk for adverse reactions to a medication or combination of medications than younger adults. Although not necessarily involved in abuse or misuse patterns, these high rates of usage combined with physiological changes render older adults vulnerable to a variety of substance-induced symptoms and disorders such as the falls experienced by Jim. In contrast, illicit drug use among older adults is less common, although future usage patterns in older adults may be more widespread as the current cohort of young adults with much greater drug experiences reaches later life.

Presentation in older adults

Two patterns of onset are evident in older adult alcohol abusers: early- and late-onset alcohol abuse (Fingerhood, 2000). About two-thirds of older adult alcohol abusers fall into the early-onset group, with alcohol problems evident earlier in life. This group is more likely to have been in alcohol treatment, more likely to have serious financial, legal, and occupational consequences of drinking, more likely to have chronic health problems and impaired cognition, and less likely to have a solid support system in place. Among many early-onset problem drinkers, aging appears not to lead to resolution of the problem. Whereas rates of alcohol abuse appear to be relatively stable over the life span, the current cohorts of older adults have been less intensive users of alcohol than current young adults. In other words, there is a cohort effect with later-born cohorts using significantly more alcohol than earlier-born cohorts, but all evidence points to stability over time for each cohort.

Late-onset alcohol abuse is defined as beginning after the age of 60. Late-onset abusers usually enter treatment in a state of crisis and they are more likely to report feelings of depression, more likely to deny they have a problem with alcohol, and are more likely to have a supportive network in place (Fingerhood, 2000). Regardless of the time of onset, substance abuse by older adults usually developed as a mechanism for coping. Alcohol use is associated with efforts to enhance socialization, cope with widowhood, manage the loss of esteem associated with retirement, control social anxiety, cope with financial or health problems, and to avoid problems (Dupree & Schonfeld, 1996).

The two cases presented above illustrate this pattern. Lincoln increased his rate of drinking following retirement because he lacked sufficiently compelling alternative activities to fill his time and to avoid conflict with his wife, whereas Jim increased his drinking and pain medication use in response to the loneliness that followed the death of his spouse. Prescribed and OTC medications are primarily used to cope with pain, although insomnia, family problems, and other mental disorders are also prominent reasons for substance usage.

A key factor in abuse patterns is the different physiological responses of aging bodies to chemical substances. Due to changes in the efficiency with which substances are processed in the body, older adults are more susceptible to adverse drug reactions, drug interactions, and drug toxicity as compared to younger adults. Mental health professionals must be aware of the vulnerability of aging bodies to even the most innocent-appearing substances (e.g., aspirin) in altering the psychological functioning of older persons (for a review of what professionals should know, see Smyer & Downs, 1995).

Theories of etiology

The behavioral theory of substance abuse suggests that people use substances to increase positive moods, decrease negative moods, or both. When the desired psychological effect of the ingested substance is achieved, the substance use is reinforced. The behavioral model also suggests that many people begin using a psychoactive substance by following the modeling of peers or family members who abuse substances. The cognitive model emphasizes the role of thought processes in initiating and maintaining substance use behavior. In particular, thoughts may include *expectancies* about intoxication. To the extent the person holds positive beliefs about the effects of the substance (e.g., "A few drinks will help me relax and cope with my problems"), then the person will be more likely to use the substance. Conversely, to the extent the person holds negative beliefs about his or her ability to abstain from substance use (e.g., "I can't control myself"), then the person will be more likely to use the substance.

There is also a strong biological basis to the development of substance abuse problems. Specifically, a great deal of research has sought to determine the genetic contributions of substance abuse, with the vast amount of this research focusing on alcohol problems. The risk of developing serious alcohol problems is about 15 percent for daughters of people with alcohol abuse and 30 percent for sons of people with alcohol abuse. The overall heritability of alcohol dependence is estimated to be at about 50 to 60 percent, meaning that at least half of the tendency to develop severe alcohol problems can be attributed to one's genetics (see review by Dick & Bierut, 2006). It is presently unclear, however, exactly how many specific genes are implicated, their locations, and the exact mechanisms by which genes exert their influence on the development of substance problems.

Assessment of substance abuse

Assessment of substance abuse is a challenge because of the abuser's tendency to fail to recognize the quantity of substance used or to fail to fully appreciate the negative impact of the substance use, despite ample evidence to the contrary. Health care providers may also tend to overlook alcohol problems and medication mismanagement or endorse negative stereotypes of older adults with addiction problems. Even families may not be willing to address substance abuse, trivializing it due to ageism (e.g., "Grandpa only has a few years left. So what if he takes an extra drink here or there?"). In addition, the symptoms or expressions of substance abuse problems among older adults may be mistaken for those of other problems associated with later life, such as depression or dementia. In addition, relatives of older adults with a substance abuse problem may be ashamed of the problem and choose to ignore it.

Another challenge to assessment is the poor match between older adult substance abuse patterns and the diagnostic criteria for abuse and dependence provided by the DSM-IV-TR (APA, 2000). The DSM criteria emphasize impact of the substance use on occupation and on social relationships and responsibilities, which may not be as readily recognized in older adults as in young adults who fulfill multiple roles publicly. Also, mental health professionals who rely on traditional criteria are unlikely to recognize the patterns of substance abuse most problematic among older adults, whose substances are far more likely to be OTC or prescribed medications.

Clinicians typically try to draw out information about substance use in the course of clinical interviews. As rapport is established, clients have a greater likelihood of sharing accurate information. Asking a broad, non-judgmental, open-ended question such as "Would you tell me a little bit about your use of alcohol or drugs?" in a matter-of-fact way may serve to create an open dialogue about the person's substance use patterns rather than using a more punitive style such as "How often do you get drunk?" or even more direct questions about how much is ingested. When an older adult presents with a history of frequent falls, depression, insomnia, cognitive changes, or poor nutrition, he or she should certainly be assessed to rule out the possibility of substance abuse either causing the problem or making an existing problem worse.

Two brief self-report measures of alcohol are available to aid in the screening and detection of alcohol problems. The CAGE (Mayfield, McLeod, & Hall, 1974) is a mnemonic for four non-incriminating questions with good validity as a gross screening instrument for alcohol abuse among older adults:

- Have you ever felt you needed to *Cut* down on drinking?
- Have people *Annoyed* you by criticizing your drinking?
- Have you ever felt *Guilty* about drinking?
- Have you ever had a drink first thing in the morning (*Eye-opener*) to steady your nerves or to get rid of a hangover?

A positive (yes) response to even one CAGE item warrants further evaluation in a clinical interview.

The Michigan Alcoholism Screening Test (MAST) has a geriatric version (MAST-G; Blow et al., 1992), which is the most widely and successfully used measure in clinical practice. The MAST-G is presented in Table 11.1. As can be seen in the table, the measure contains 24 simple yes/no items unique to older problem drinkers. In all cases, "yes" is the pathological response and a cutoff of five positive responses indicates an alcohol problem (Blow et al., 1992). The MAST-G has excellent psychometric properties. For example, the MAST-G was found to have a sensitivity of 94 percent and specificity of 78 percent when the DSM diagnosis of alcohol dependence was used as the validation criteria. Factor analysis of the MAST-G has indicated five dimensions: loss and loneliness, relaxation, dependence, loss of control with drinking, and rule-making.

A rich clinical picture can also be generated with Gerontology Alcohol Project Drinking Profile (GAP-DP; Dupree, Broskowski, & Schonfeld, 1984), which is an elder-specific structured behavioral assessment tool. Clearly, a thorough evaluation

Table 11.1 Michigan Alcoholism Screening Test – Geriatric Version (MAST-G)

	Yes (1)	No (0)
1. After drinking have you ever noticed an increase in your heart rate or beating in your chest?		
2. When talking with others, do you ever underestimate how much you actually drink?		
3. Does alcohol make you sleepy so that you often fall asleep in your chair?		
4. After a few drinks, have you sometimes not eaten or been able to skip a meal because you didn't feel hungry?		
5. Does having a few drinks help decrease your shakiness or tremors?		
6. Does alcohol sometimes make it hard for you to remember parts of the day or night?		
7. Do you have rules for yourself that you won't drink before a certain time of the day?		
8. Have you lost interest in hobbies or activities you used to enjoy?		
9. When you wake up in the morning, do you ever have trouble remembering part of the night before?		
10. Does having a drink help you sleep?		
11. Do you hide your alcohol bottles from family members?		
12. After a social gathering, have you ever felt embarrassed because you drank too much?		
13. Have you ever been concerned that drinking might be harmful to your health?		
14. Do you like to end an evening with a night cap?		
15. Did you find your drinking increased after someone close to you died?		
16. In general, would you prefer to have a few drinks at home rather than go out to social events?		
17. Are you drinking more now than in the past?		
18. Do you usually take a drink to relax or calm your nerves?		
19. Do you drink to take your mind off your problems?		
20. Have you ever increased your drinking after experiencing a loss in your life?		
21. Do you sometimes drive when you have had too much to drink?		
22. Has a doctor or nurse ever said they were worried or concerned about your drinking?		
23. Have you ever made rules to manage your drinking?		
24. When you feel lonely, does having a drink help?		

Scoring: 5 or more "yes" responses indicative of alcohol problem.
For further information, contact Frederic C. Blow, PhD, at University of Michigan Mental Health Services, 4250 Plymouth Road, SPC 5765, Ann Arbor, MI 48109, tel. (734) 232-0404.

Source: © The Regents of the University of Michigan, 1991.

of substance abuse should be a part of any standard clinical evaluation with an older adult because substance abuse can be severe and debilitating in its own right, but it also can make other comorbid conditions such as anxiety and depression worse. In addition, substance abuse is linked to increased rates of suicide.

Interventions for substance abuse

Substance abuse treatments focus on three goals: stabilization and reduction of substance consumption, treatment of coexisting problems, and arrangement of appropriate social interventions (Atkinson, Ganzini, & Bernstein, 1992). With older adults, education rather than confrontation is usually used to reduce denial of the abuse pattern. For example, education about the changes in drug metabolism, the interaction of medications, and the importance of compliance with physician instructions can lead to increased compliance. Research demonstrates the role of cognitive factors in determining medication compliance (Gould, 2004). Evidence from laboratory experimentation suggests that altering the presentation of drug usage information can increase understanding and compliance with medication instructions, thus reducing the opportunity for substance misuse.

Education of physicians is an important component of a treatment plan for prescription and OTC drug abuse. Physicians may not recognize the potential for medication interactions to produce psychological symptoms. Physicians also may be unaware of all of the prescribed medications a patient is using if the patient is obtaining prescriptions from more than one physician. Thus, engaging physician cooperation is critical when attempting to intervene with prescription or OTC misuse.

Treatment of coexisting problems (e.g., depression, pain, or social isolation) can reduce the motivation for using substances inappropriately. This strategy is similar to that used with younger adult substance abusers, although the specific problems that need to be addressed may vary with age. In the case of Lincoln, marital therapy and, possibly, treatment of depression would be critical elements of the treatment plan. As long as home life is stressful, and Lincoln lacks a sense of purpose or skill for creating separateness from Lois, then he is likely to try to avoid conflict and unpleasant feelings in a familiar way – alcohol. Jim needs help with social skills so that he can begin to reconnect with old friends and develop new relationships to reduce his isolation.

The CBT approach to treatment focuses on behavioral interventions to help the client learn new, healthier patterns of behavior to replace substance use, and cognitive restructuring to reduce positive expectancies and to increase negative expectancies regarding the effects of substance use. Finally, training in self-management skills will generate more effective coping skills, again reducing the urge to use psychoactive substances to manage problem situations. For example, Dupree and Schonfeld (1996) present a case of excessive pain medication usage by an older woman. The treatment followed the social learning model in which the antecedents (situations, thoughts, feelings, and cues) that provoked the substance use behavior, and the short-term and long-term consequences of substance abuse, were first identified. Specific behavior therapy techniques such as assertion training, self-monitoring, behavior contracting, and reinforcement were used to modify the patient's use of medication.

Treatment outcome studies suggest that older patients stay in treatment longer and respond as well to alcohol interventions as do younger patients (Atkinson, Tolson, & Turner, 1993; Satre, Mertens, Areán, & Weisner, 2003). As could be expected, the outcomes are more favorable among persons with shorter histories of problem drinking (i.e., late onset). Although the data are not definitive, it appears that outcomes may be improved by treating older patients in age-segregated settings (e.g., Blow, Walton, Chermack, Mudd, & Brower, 2000).

Despite good success rates for those older adults who enter treatment, the vast majority of older adults with a substance abuse problem either do not receive adequate treatment or do not perceive the need for treatment. Treatment needs are expected to increase greatly in the coming years due to the large population of Baby Boomers who have higher abuse rates than the current cohort of older adults. In particular, the rates of illicit drug use among older adults are expected to greatly increase as younger cohorts with greater drug problems enter older adulthood.

Personality Disorders

Alice has had relational problems most of her adult life. Nobody ever seemed to be good enough for her or to appreciate her talents. But her life and relationships were manageable when she was able to throw herself into her work, having had a successful career as an attorney in a prestigious firm. Things began to crumble when she retired one year ago and now she is having an especially hard time adjusting to life in the rehabilitation facility after having heart surgery. She refuses to participate in the physical rehab exercises, thinking that "the doctors are ignorant" and that they don't understand how hard it is for her to be ill. Alice also is having problems with her roommate – "she is so rude talking to her family and friends on the phone several times a day and not paying any attention to me." She also despises the staff and becomes enraged when they request that she attempt to do some care activities herself like feeding herself and bathing – "Don't these fools understand who I am? I expect good service and will not put up with their attempts to get out of taking care of me. Instead of being the patient here, I should be running this whole place. I'd fire them all and get a top notch staff to replace them." The staff dread having to take care of Alice.

The DSM-IV-TR (APA, 2000) defines a personality disorder as "an enduring pattern of inner experience and behavior that deviates markedly from the expectations of the individual's culture, is pervasive and inflexible, has an onset in adolescence or early adulthood, is stable over time, and leads to distress or impairment" (p. 685). Essentially, a personality disorder (PD) is diagnosed when one's own personality traits (defined as characteristic ways of thinking, feeling, perceiving, and behaving) become inflexible, maladaptive, and pervasive across a broad range of situations. Patterns of inner experiences and behaviors that represent expectable or typical reactions to particular life experiences or represent a normal part of a developmental stage are not considered part of a PD. The DSM defines 10 prototypical PDs, which are described in Table 11.2.

Table 11.2   Description of the 10 DSM-IV-TR personality disorders

Antisocial	A pervasive pattern of disregard for, and violation of, societal norms and the rights of others, as well as lack of empathy.
Avoidant	A pervasive pattern of social inhibition, low self-esteem, and hypersensitivity to negative evaluation.
Borderline	A pervasive pattern of instability in interpersonal relationships, self-image, and emotions, as well as marked impulsivity.
Dependent	A pervasive and excessive need to be taken care of and a perception of being unable to function without the help of others, leading to submissive and clinging behaviors.
Histrionic	A pervasive pattern of excessive emotionality and attention-seeking behavior, with superficiality.
Narcissistic	A pervasive pattern of grandiosity, need for admiration, and lack of empathy and compassion for others.
Obsessive-compulsive	A pervasive pattern of preoccupation with orderliness, perfection, and control at the expense of flexibility, openness, and efficiency.
Paranoid	A pattern of pervasive distrust and suspicion of others such that their motives are perceived as malevolent.
Schizoid	A pervasive pattern of detachment from social relationships and a restricted range of emotional expression.
Schizotypal	A pervasive pattern of social deficits marked by acute discomfort with close relationships, as well as eccentric behavior and cognitive and perceptual distortions.

Source: Adapted from the DSM-IV-TR (APA, 2000).

Although the knowledge base about PDs in older adults has grown significantly in recent years, including publication of two books solely devoted to this topic (Rosowsky, Abrams, & Zweig, 1999; Segal, Coolidge, & Rosowsky, 2006), PDs in older adults remain a relatively understudied area for several reasons. Changing definitions of PDs across the various editions of the DSM have hampered longitudinal studies. The field of personality psychology has also struggled with the extent to which personality should be conceptualized as a set of enduring traits versus situationally influenced behaviors, especially patterns of coping with stress. Apparently, personality traits (including adaptive and maladaptive ones) are both stable and adaptable across the life span (Clark, 2009; Vaillant, 2002). Obviously, models of personality serve as a backdrop for models of PDs. Thus, stability in personality traits could be construed as a backdrop for PDs, which are also considered generally stable but not immutable, with shifting amounts of distress and dysfunction depending on contextual variables, especially stressors. Although the formal definition of PD requires an onset of the PD no later than early adulthood, in some cases a PD is not diagnosed or treated until later life, often when the stressors associated with later life prompt an exacerbation of the person's maladaptive behaviors (Molinari & Segal, 2011).

Despite methodological and conceptual challenges, it is clinically important to understand PDs in older adults for a number of reasons (Molinari & Segal, 2011). First, because PDs affect the way a person copes with the vicissitudes of life, older individuals with a PD are likely to have less success in negotiating age-related losses. Consider, for example, a histrionic person who has characteristically relied on her physical attractiveness and sexual seductiveness to acquire attention for herself. With advancing age, such a person may feel increasingly neglected, dejected, and angry as she loses some of her seductiveness and its attendant attention from others. As another example, a narcissistic person may feel a particularly painful loss of esteem and prestige when faced with retirement from a high-powered position, becoming severely angry and depressed. This was the case for Alice, who was also having difficulty coping with physical illness.

Second, because PD affects one's social functioning, older individuals with a PD are likely to be less effective in managing the social and interpersonal compromises necessary for peaceful institutional living (Molinari & Segal, 2011). For example, an avoidant older adult may dread the increased social "opportunities" provided by living at an assisted living facility, instead perceiving such occurrences as "more opportunities for rejection." Third, PDs typically influence the presentation of clinical disorders (coded on Axis I of the DSM-IV-TR) such as anxiety, depression, and substance abuse, thus hampering effective diagnosis and treatment. Molinari and Segal (2011) provide the example of disruptive behavior in a nursing home resident, which camouflages the fact that the resident is suffering from severe depression that is exacerbating premorbid antisocial PD features. In general, the presence of PDs that are comorbid with Axis I clinical disorders makes treatment more difficult and results in a worse prognosis for the older individual (Molinari & Segal, 2011; Segal et al., 2006).

Prevalence

The prevalence of PDs in the general adult population is estimated to be about 10 percent (Lenzenweger, 2008), indicating that PDs are actually quite common. However, the prevalence among the older population is presently unclear and a source of considerable debate in the literature. In an attempt to lend clarity to this issue, Abrams and Horowitz (1996) conducted a meta-analysis of the most methodologically sophisticated epidemiological studies among older adults, reporting an overall PD prevalence rate of 10 percent (with a range of 6 percent to 33 percent), neither confirming nor disputing an age effect on prevalence. However, Abrams and Horowitz concluded that the bulk of the evidence supports a modest decline in the frequency and intensity with age, at least for certain PDs. The exact cause for this decline is presently unknown, and is a current source of controversy and debate (Molinari & Segal, 2011).

Changing definitions and conceptualizations of PDs, poorly normed assessment devices, and the limited number of large studies among older adults all make prevalence estimates confusing and of limited value. Most studies have been conducted on inpatient units, examining the comorbidity of PDs with other clinical disorders. PDs are believed to be much more common than is generally recognized by outpatient mental health professionals. For example, among older outpatients with a depression diagnosis, one-third were diagnosed with PD (Thompson, Gallagher, & Czirr, 1988), most commonly avoidant and dependent PDs. Much higher rates of PD prevalence (e.g., 56 percent) are found in studies of older psychiatric inpatients (e.g., Molinari, Ames, & Essa, 1994). Coolidge et al. (2000) found similarly high PD rates among young (66 percent) and old (58 percent) chronically mentally ill patients, but the younger group was more likely to be specifically diagnosed with antisocial, borderline, and schizotypal PD. A combined inpatient and outpatient sample of depressed older adults yielded a prevalence rate of 63 percent (Molinari & Marmion, 1995).

The question of how PDs are affected by aging has been debated, but has lacked a research base on which to anchor a definitive answer. Some evidence points to a decline in expression of the symptoms associated with the cluster of PDs labeled *dramatic and erratic* (including borderline, histrionic, and narcissistic PDs) in midlife with an increase in symptoms again in later life (Reich, Nduaguba, & Yates, 1988). Others suggest that the decline in dramatic PDs relates to increased mortality rates among severely impulsive and erratic individuals, a decrease in energy and stamina needed to maintain the high-energy symptoms (e.g., brawling with others), and the poor fit of the DSM diagnostic criteria to accurately detect geriatric variants of the PDs (Segal et al., 2006).

Presentation in older adults

The stresses of old age are believed to produce personality regressions that mimic PDs and to exacerbate the expression of symptoms in some older adults (Rosowsky & Gurian, 1992; Segal et al., 2006). Loss of control of the environment that is characteristic of the increasing dependency that comes with loss of mobility and declining resources can provoke anxiety that generates PD symptoms. However, the symptom criteria used by the DSM system include life circumstances that may be irrelevant to older adults. For example, difficulties in the work environment and with residential family life may be less relevant because of the lower rate of participation in the work force and the tendency not to co-reside with family members. Thus, the behavioral expressions of PDs in older adults may not match the template typically used to identify PDs in younger adults.

In some cases, there is an emergence of PD symptoms that were "hidden" earlier in life (Segal et al., 2006). Consider, for example, a highly dependent woman who married young and was essentially nurtured along and taken care of by her more dominant spouse throughout their marriage. In such a case, it would only be after her husband's death that her struggles to take care of herself and the extent of her "disorder" would be recognized and perhaps diagnosed. A theorized pattern for each of the PDs is depicted in Table 11.3.

Theories of etiology

Because PDs and PD features begin relatively early in life and generally persist across adulthood and later life, it can be assumed that the etiology of PDs includes significant psychosocial and biological factors.

Table 11.3 Theorized patterns for the personality disorders in later life

Antisocial	For this type, there is a diminished chance of surviving into later life due to a lifestyle of recklessness, impulsivity, and risky behaviors. The underlying trait of psychopathy does not seem to change with age but there is a reduction of impulsive and physically aggressive behaviors due to physiological declines associated with aging. Physical disability, sensory decline, and cognitive impairment can be particularly problematic for older antisocial individuals who are incarcerated because their limitations make them especially vulnerable to exploitation from other prisoners.
Avoidant	This type commonly arrives at later life lonely, inhibited, and disconnected from others, having missed out on the normal developmental pathway to social confidence experienced by others. They are particularly vulnerable to the social losses that are commonly a part of later life (e.g., death of family members; migration of children) because their networks are generally constricted to begin with and they typically have great trouble replacing relationships that have been lost. Avoidant individuals can easily become more alone and frightened as their limited networks inevitably shrink.
Borderline	Physical fights, substance abuse, sexual acting out, self-mutilation, and other impulsive and physically taxing behaviors will typically become muted in later life. Geriatric variants of self-harming behaviors may include intentional anorexia, self-prescribed polypharmacy, refusal of needed medical attention, or sabotage of medical care. Aging typically has little impact on the chronic feelings of emptiness and unstable and intense interpersonal relationships. This type is especially likely to cause havoc upon their move to assisted living facilities, rehabilitation hospitals, or nursing facilities. They may intensely attach themselves to unsuspecting residents and staff only to turn against them in a brief period.
Dependent	This type experiences extreme difficulty with widowhood, leaving the person in the threatening and unfamiliar position of having to depend on himself or herself. After such a loss, dependent older adults commonly appear helpless, unable to perform the most mundane of functions after decades of relying excessively on their partners. Feeling lost and vulnerable, these older adults often turn to their adult children to fill the void left by the deceased spouse. In many cases, their excessive neediness quickly becomes burdensome, frequently leading to their children feeling overwhelmed.
Histrionic	This type is particularly intolerant of the physical declines that come with age (e.g., wrinkles, hair loss) because their self-worth is based largely on superficial characteristics such as physical appearance. Due to their lifelong reliance on their physical attributes to attract attention, many older people with this disorder respond to normal physical changes by becoming excessive users of plastic surgery and other anti-aging techniques. They also become depressed or angry when their flirtatious and seductive style becomes less rewarded.

Continued

Table 11.3 *Continued*

Narcissistic	One pattern is for the narcissistic type to come to old age alone, isolated, and bitter about their lack of success. Another pattern is for them to come to old age with great histories of accomplishment, although they often can no longer maintain that success. "Narcissistic injuries" due to the loss of power and prestige and general ageism in society often lead to depression, anxiety, and anger. The aging narcissist typically has trouble coping with age-related physical declines (e.g., hair loss, wrinkles, shrinking muscle mass) because they perceive these signs as detracting from their superiority over others. When older people with this disorder need care and support from others due to illness, rageful reactions are common, resulting in increased negative feedback and further blows to the narcissist's sense of self.
Obsessive-compulsive	Increased dependency on others is likely to be a difficult stressor for this type because their lifelong pattern of "doing things their own way" makes them resistant to change and unable to tolerate needing help from others. Believing there is only one way to accomplish tasks, they typically have great difficulty being flexible with lost or reduced physical and cognitive functions. Older adults with this disorder may feel resentful or be offended when offered help, which is interpreted by them as a statement that they are not in complete control. When having to receive help becomes inevitable, obsessive-compulsive older adults may react with catastrophic depression.
Paranoid	Sensory impairments (e.g., declines in hearing and vision) are likely to make the underlying paranoia more pronounced. The emergence of cognitive dysfunction due to a cognitive disorder may also worsen premorbid paranoid traits. Dealing with increased dependency on others will also likely be problematic because people with this disorder are not used to and are uncomfortable with accepting help from others. The paranoid type will have a particularly difficult time with aging due to the loss of the few relationships they may have developed earlier in life and the subsequent increasing isolation.
Schizoid	Increased dependency on others will be especially difficult for the schizoid older adult to manage. Because the person's disconnected style is ego-syntonic, it will likely cause marked distress when the person must by necessity depend on relationships with others for their care (e.g., as a resident in an assisted living facility or nursing home). A typical pattern is that of the lifelong recluse becoming more reclusive with advancing age, usually lasting for as long as the person can manage being alone until changes with aging require increased contact with others.
Schizotypal	This type responds particularly poorly to increased dependency on others due to the older schizotypal person's acute social anxiety. People with this disorder are likely to become agitated if physical infirmities force them to endure relationships with health care professionals, staff, and residents in congregate living settings. Their unusual and bizarre behaviors also make them an easy target for rejection in communal social settings. Some schizotypal adults become increasingly reclusive and isolated with advancing age, frequently becoming even more bizarre due to the complete or near complete lack of social contact.

Source: Adapted from Segal et al. (2006).

Psychosocial factors   From his psychoanalytic perspective, Sigmund Freud embedded the idea of personality within his psychosexual stages (i.e., oral, anal, oedipal, latency, and genital stages). Freud suggested that inborn temperamental traits combine with parental influences during these psychosexual periods to shape one's personality. How early figures react to the growing child's needs forges a rigid template that is operative throughout the person's life. These templates reflect whether a person will satisfy his or her psychological and social needs in an adaptive manner or in an exaggerated, repetitious, maladaptive manner that is a hallmark of PDs. Acute symptomatology erupts when current stressors intersect with the psychosocial dynamics and interpersonal sensitivities laid out early in life that create a hard bedrock of personality traits (Molinari & Segal, 2011).

The cognitive model of psychopathology suggests that PDs are characterized by *cognitive distortions* that are derived from biases in information processing and dysfunctional *schemas* or core beliefs that influence people's perceptions and thoughts at the conscious level (Beck, Freeman, Davis, & Associates, 2003). As described in Chapter 4, some cognitive distortions include all-or-none thinking, catastrophizing, magnification and minimization, and personalization. Some examples of cognitive distortions and schemas relevant to specific PDs include the following:

- An individual with antisocial PD perceives the rules of society as not pertaining to him, and as such, he is free to violate the rights of others and engage in criminal-type behavior with little or no remorse or guilt.
- An individual with borderline PD is prone to sort people into categories of either "all good" or "all bad" and is further preoccupied with feelings of abandonment and emptiness.
- An individual with dependent PD sees herself as weak, incompetent, and inadequate, requiring constant reassurance, nurturance, and direction.
- An individual with obsessive-compulsive PD tends to be a slave to the belief that he must be perfect and always in control.
- An individual with paranoid PD is prone to habitually and chronically perceive others as deceitful, abusive, and threatening.

Biological factors   The biological factor most extensively studied for the PDs is that of genetics. Jang, Livesley, Vernon, and Jackson (1996) studied 483 adult twin pairs, reporting a median heritability coefficient estimate of .44 for 66 of 69 PD facet traits. A related twin study by Jang, Livesley, and Vernon (1996) found that genetic contributions to PD traits actually increase with age. Torgersen et al. (2000) used a structured interview to diagnose the full range of PDs among 221 adult twin pairs, finding an overall heritability estimate of .60. In an interesting study of 112 child twin pairs, Coolidge, Thede, and Jang (2001) reported a median heritability coefficient of .75 for 12 specific PDs. Most recently, Kendler et al. (2008) studied 2,794 adult twins in Norway. The results indicated that one genetic factor reflected a broad vulnerability to PD pathology and negative emotionality whereas two other genetic factors more specifically reflected high impulsivity/low agreeableness and introversion. To summarize this genetic data, heritable traits certainly play a significant role in the formation of PDs, but heritability alone does not directly cause an individual to develop a specific PD. In a sense, genetics "loads the gun" but environment "pulls the trigger."

Assessment of personality disorders

The assessment of PDs is known to be particularly challenging across the life span. Specifically, it is generally difficult to distinguish one PD from another (Coolidge & Segal, 1998), since most people have a mix of diverse PD features and rarely present with all the prototypical features of one specific PD with no features of other PDs. The context of aging and later life further complicates the assessment of PDs because all of the standardized instruments used to screen for and measure specific PDs were developed for younger populations and thus do not adequately consider the context of later life (Balsis, Segal, & Donahue, 2009; Segal et al., 2006).

According to Molinari and Segal (2011), PDs are commonly seen in diverse mental health settings yet are seldom formally diagnosed. It is possible that some mental health professionals are reluctant to diagnose PDs in older adults due to pessimistic beliefs about the prospects of therapeutic change for older individuals with a PD and concerns over pejorative biases associated with a PD diagnosis. It is also possible that some professionals tend to focus their assessments on other disorders that are more easily identified, such as anxiety, depression, and cognitive disorders (Molinari & Segal, 2011).

Zweig (2008) recently described three special challenges in the assessment of older adults with PD. First, differentiating PD from co-occurring Axis I disorders (e.g., the state vs. trait problem) can be an arduous task, particularly when heightened irritability and interpersonal dysfunction are related at least in part to a mood change due to a recent loss. Second, differentiating PD from context-dependent roles and behaviors can pose a major diagnostic undertaking. For example, poor adaptation to a changing role such as becoming overwhelmed after the death of a spouse may reflect the anxiety of an acute adjustment disorder rather than the emergence of a dependent PD. Third, differentiating PD from personality change due to a neurological or medical condition can require an exhaustive medical work-up. Indeed, in a geriatric setting, somatic presentations of PD are common, which can complicate "teasing out" true comorbid medical/cognitive problems from personality dysfunction.

A final assessment challenge is that the diagnostic criteria sets do not fit older adults as well as they do younger adults (Balsis et al., 2009; Segal et al., 2006). In an empirical investigation of potential age-bias using item analysis, Balsis, Gleason, Woods, and Oltmanns (2007) found evidence of age-bias in 29 percent of the criteria for seven PDs. In this study, some diagnostic criteria were differentially endorsed by younger and older adults with equivalent PD pathology, suggesting a bias. To aid in the screening of general PD pathology (not specific PDs) in later life, a brief specialized self-report measure called the Gerontological Personality Disorders Scale (Van Alphen, Engelen, Kuin, Hoijtink, & Derksen, 2006) has recently been developed and preliminarily examined, but further validation studies are needed. At present there is no "gold standard" of diagnosis for PDs in older adults.

Interventions for personality disorders

Persons with PD primarily seek treatment when their familiar methods of coping and meeting their own needs can no longer be enacted or are distressing someone else, who then demands that treatment occur. For example, upon widowhood, they might be on their own for the first time in their lives. They might find themselves entering a new community, needing to make new friends and establish a social network for the first time in many years. As they come to experience that their lifelong ways of coping are no longer working for them, they become even more distressed, function even less well, and their behavior worsens. This vicious cycle is one component of treatment that typically makes intervention quite challenging (Segal et al., 2006).

Older adults with PD who seek professional help generally present for symptom relief or to address a specific problem, typically related to interpersonal conflicts. They frequently come to treatment secondary to the loss of autonomy and control, or upon the strong suggestion of another person on whom they need to depend, for example an adult child, a housing manager, or a primary care physician. They do not generally self-refer for psychotherapy, as their psychopathology is experienced as ego-syntonic (Segal et al., 2006).

According to Livesley (2004), a guiding principle to treatment is the recognition of a PD as being chronic and as defining the essence of the individual. Thus, the aim of treatment is not to cure but rather to reduce distress and improve function. Livesley has proposed four "principles" as inherent to PDs, each of which needs be considered in the treatment plan.

- A PD is central and involves all aspects of the personality structure. Therefore, an effective treatment plan must incorporate a range of interventions, and not just be a response to a specific problem. An implication of this is that the treatment indicated is typically more long term rather than brief.
- There exist core features common to all PDs as well as other features common to specific PDs. Therefore, treatment needs to incorporate strategies to manage the PD as a general psychopathology, as well as to offer customized strategies to address the more specific and idiosyncratic manifestations of specific PDs.
- Because PDs reflect a biopsychosocial etiology, interventions must reflect multiple contributing factors with the overarching goals of reducing distress and facilitating adaptation and functionality.
- Because those with PDs are especially vulnerable to poor reactions to stressors common to later life, interventions also must address the consequences of the particular stressors impacting the person.

As is evident, PD complicates treatment across the life span. As such, the goal of treatment is directed more at management of the PD than at full remission. In other words, the goal is to help the older individual move from personality *disorder* to personality *style* (Segal et al., 2006). Finally, although no medications are specifically approved for treating PDs, medications can be used to target symptoms that resemble clinical problems such as agitation, anxiety, depression, and loose thinking.

Marital Conflicts

Jack and Louisa never had a great relationship, but it did not seem to matter so much when they were both busy raising their children and working, with Jack having a high-powered career as a lawyer and Louisa working at the cafeteria at the local elementary school. But things have gotten much worse between them after Jack had a stroke, was forced to retire from work, and is now at home all day, feeling grouchy and expecting Louisa to take care of him. Louisa feels alternatively sympathetic to Jack's condition but also despondent because of the overwhelming burdens placed on her. She thought with the kids out of the house she could finally have some time to develop her own interests, but now that Jack is home all day, she does nothing but take care of him, as she sinks deeper and deeper into depression. She does not know where to turn for help.

Conflict and difficulties within the intimate domain of marital and family relationships can be very distressing to older adults. The distress may provoke the emergence of psychiatric symptoms (e.g., anxiety, depression, sleep problems, sexual problems) or declines in daily functioning. Just as marriage and family relationships can provide support for optimal mental well-being, so too can they undermine mental health. In this section, we describe the events and tasks that challenge marital and family functioning in the latest stages of life and discuss strategies for assessing difficulties and designing effective interventions.

Despite the higher probability of widowhood with advancing age, older men are much more likely to be married than older women. For example, in the 65–74-year-old group, 78 percent of men are married compared to 57 percent of women, in the 75–84-year-old group, 74 percent of men are married compared to 38 percent of women, and in the 85+ group, 60 percent of men are married compared to only 15 percent of women (Federal Interagency Forum on Aging-Related Statistics, 2008). Thus it is apparent that the gender gap in marriage becomes more severe in the oldest-old group. Although not as prevalent among older adults as among young adults, marriage is one of the intimate relationships that is of vital importance to older adults (Carstensen, 1992).

Changes in physical health, retirement, and disruptions in the lives of adult children can all challenge the familiar patterns of marital functioning (Qualls, 1995b). These life events spawn changes in the contexts, meaning, and practices of marriage that are experienced by the couple as developmental challenges or tasks (Cole, 1986). For example, Lincoln's retirement eliminated his structure for creating separateness: business trips. Unless he renegotiates another method of securing separateness, he and Lois will both continue to feel intruded upon and annoyed. In their case, alcohol use is a method they employ to maintain separateness without fighting, but it is a self-destructive method. Jack and Louisa are struggling with a different context, namely, one of impaired health and disability in one partner that is causing the strain. Table 11.4 shows the effects of three categories of events on key areas of marital functioning: time structure, roles, communication, power balance, nurturance, and relationships with children. Obviously, the last phase of life brings challenges to even long-term relationships.

Table 11.4 Impact of events of later life on marital processes

Events	Marital processes					
	Time structure	Roles	Communication	Power balance	Nurturance	Relationships with children
Retirement	• End of work-structured separateness • Increase in togetherness at home	• Dedifferentiation (decreased uniqueness, increased overlap) • Potential to decrease gender typing	• Need strategies to negotiate separateness and role transition • More shared experience decreases need for oral reporting	• Role transition provokes shift in power balance • Power from previous domain may be altered • Potential of egalitarianism increased in traditional couples	• Increased opportunity for small daily expressions	• Opportunity for increased contact and more directly involved roles • Visits with children often occur on distant turf
Onset of Impairment from Chronic Illness	• Usually increased portion of time devoted to basic care • Health constrains activity options	• Ill spouse experiences role loss • Well spouse experiences role gain	• Anger expressions are more threatening or complicated • Impairment may constrain ill spouse's capacity to communicate (e.g., stroke, cognitive impairment, decreased initiation)	• Source of power for ill spouse decreases • Well spouse's increase in responsibility brings increased power	• Ill spouse's opportunity to nurture may be constrained • Well spouse's caregiving role creates imbalance in time spent nurturing	• Children may be more "inside" the marriage than previously (boundary issues salient) • Children's role in supporting primary caregiver or ill parent may threaten spouse
Disruptions in Children's Lives	• Increased time spent experiencing and expressing concern as co-parents • Potential for increase in responsibility and decrease in leisure time	• Ambiguity in parenting roles increases • May provoke increase in financial, child care, or other support responsibilities	• Need for problem-solving communications may increase • Negotiating support within appropriate boundaries challenges communication patterns	• Boundary around marital dyad may be stretched • Can triangulate the marriage	• Nurturance often needs to be redirected outside marriage again (increased strain on marital satisfaction)	• Complex roles • Opportunity for reciprocity salient as aging parents again are giving

Source: Qualls (1995). Reprinted with permission from International Universities Press.

An important distinction should be made between distressed marriages that have a long history of conflict and those for whom distress is a recent phenomenon. Long-term conflicted marriages are those that settled into entrenched but stable patterns of conflict. The patterns that maintained the long-term conflict are difficult to treat successfully. However, later-life events can unsettle the stability enough to create crises that can be addressed. Long-term satisfied marriages are likely to have been increasingly satisfied with the marriage as the years progressed (Anderson, Russell, & Schumm, 1983). Conflicts seen in the later years are a direct indicator of difficulty adapting to the developmental tasks of later life. Research studies focusing on changes in marital satisfaction across the life span suggest that with increasing age, married couples generally report higher levels of marital satisfaction (Levenson, Carstensen, & Gottman, 1993). Recent conflict within a long-term satisfied marriage may occur if the couple lack understanding of how to adapt to changes in their life circumstances or change in their individual functioning (e.g., due to disability).

Regardless of marital satisfaction history, a key question for someone seeking to help a conflicted couple is: Why is the couple seeking therapy now? Indeed, some event or change in the structure or functioning of their marriage must have occurred in order to trigger the current help-seeking efforts. The goal of intervention may be merely to restore equilibrium and a tolerable level of distance and/or conflict. In higher-functioning couples, interventions may reap benefits beyond just immediate coping, by promoting deeper intimacy within the marriage (Wolinsky, 1990). A special problem for aging couples can occur within the sexual aspects of their relationship. The sexual disorders and their treatments are described in Chapter 10.

Family Problems

Viola has had serious health problems since midlife. Currently, heart and lung disease severely limit her physical capabilities. She becomes short of breath after only a few steps, despite the help of oxygen to which she is tethered 24 hours a day. As long as Dad was alive, the children were buffered fairly well from the constancy of her needs. Since his death the extent of her dependency has become clearer. Viola can do very little basic household maintenance for herself. Fixing lunch exhausts her, and vacuuming is beyond her capability. On her limited income, she cannot hire household assistance. She is terrified of falling and losing her capacity to breathe. She has demanded that the children install emergency bells in every room, just in case she gets sick or someone tries to break in. The children are spread across the country, but each weekend one of them visits. Before their father's death, the children promised him that they would not place Viola in a nursing home. But the demands of caring are wearing them all out.

Problems in later-life families often focus on dependency needs of aging parents or their adult children. Families are trying to figure out how to assist adult members who would prefer to be autonomous and whose disabilities usually limit some but not all autonomous functioning. Often, the amount of assistance required is somewhat ambiguous, generating multiple interpretations of what should be done. For many families, the current generation of older adults is living longer, with more chronic illnesses than any previous generation. Thus, there typically is no model available in their own family for how to adapt to the current aging-related transitions within the family.

Researchers in the past two decades have documented the intensive involvement of older adults with their family members (Blieszner, 2009; Fingerman, Miller, & Seidel, 2009). The myth that families in Western civilizations now abandon their families has been effectively debunked by the repeated documentation of high rates of contact between adult children and aging parents and the high rates of assistance. Furthermore, patterns of assistance in families are multidirectional: Aging parents and their adult children are engaged in reciprocal giving and receiving of both instrumental (practical assistance with tasks or finances) and emotional support. Thus, the image of aging parents abandoned by their adult children at the time when they are dependent on them is a false one on several counts.

Despite the fact that most older adults are independent, giving as much as they receive, the family transition that is probably most disruptive to families in this phase of life relates to increasing dependency. As one person's needs for assistance become greater, other family members take on more of the caregiving function. Rarely does one become a caregiver or care receiver overnight. As depicted in Figure 11.1, the transition is a process that can be conceptualized as a career that "requires an orderly restructuring of responsibilities and activities that take place across time" (Aneshensel, Pearlin, Mullan, Zarit, & Whitlach, 1995). The case of Viola, described at the beginning of this section, is typical of the dilemmas and commitments faced by families of ill older adults.

The restructuring inherent to caregiving alters the family system, often in dramatic ways (Qualls & Noecker, 2009). When one or more members take on an increased role of monitoring the well-being of another, the caregivers are then limited in time and resources available for other relationships (e.g., siblings or children). Viola's children must balance the needs of their mother with other commitments in their lives (e.g., jobs, children, friends, and community responsibilities). The meaning of

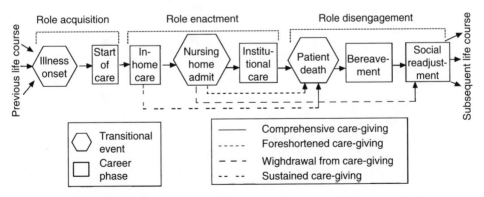

Figure 11.1   Progression of caregiving career.
Source: From Aneshensel et al. (1995). Adapted by permission.

the relationship between caregiver and care receiver also changes, as the balance of mutuality is altered. Whereas Viola may have been limited in the domains of relationship she could experience with her children in the past, she is even further limited now. The role of *care receiver* is most salient for her now, likely overshadowing other dimensions of their relationship. The more anxious and concerned the children become about their decisions regarding her care, the more caregiving will dominate the relationship.

Caregivers of frail older persons report high rates of stress from their role strain and role loss that result in negative consequences for their mental and physical health (Liu & Gallagher-Thompson, 2009; Schulz & Beach, 1999). Notably, caregivers who experience strain in the caregiving role have higher rates of mortality than age-matched controls who are not caregivers (Schulz & Beach, 1999) and African American caregivers seem to have worse health than White caregivers (Crowther & Austin 2009; Knight, Flynn Longmire, Dave, Kim, & David, 2007), which may be due to a combination of greater strain and fewer resources. The deleterious effects of caregiving vary over time as the demands of the caregiving career impact daily functioning. Despite the many potential challenges of caregiving, social support and coping are known to buffer caregivers against the stressor (Liu & Gallagher-Thompson, 2009; Zarit & Zarit, 2007). As shown in Figure 11.2, the impact of the caregiving responsibilities is mediated by cognitive appraisals of the situation and resource availability as well as by objective demands of the care recipient's needs (Gatz, Bengtson, & Blum, 1990).

Assessment of the caregiver and care recipient is the starting point for intervention (J. Zarit, 2009). Often caregivers bring the care recipient to the assessment session and it is vitally important that the care recipient's cognitive, emotional, medical, and psychological functioning is fully assessed and understood, which serves as a backdrop for the kinds of interventions that should be applied. The assessment of caregiver

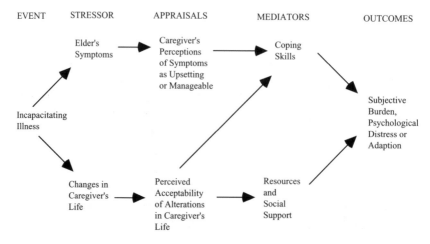

Figure 11.2 Conceptual framework for caregiver stress and coping.
Source: Adapted from Gatz et al. (1990).

emotional distress often includes measures of psychiatric symptoms, physical health difficulties, and patient-related burden (Zarit & Zarit, 2007). In addition, assessment should examine characteristics of the relationship between caregiver and care receiver and some exploration of the presence of support or conflict within the larger extended family network. Assessment of family functioning that extends beyond the caregiving role may focus on the structure and functioning of the family and on family history as it relates to current patterns of stressful interaction (Qualls & Noecker, 2009; see Chapter 6). The assessment should also determine what formal services the caregiver or care recipient has tried and the extent to which the services were helpful or not. In many cases, caregivers are unaware of some community services and they may derive significant benefits once such services are accessed. Clinicians therefore should be knowledgeable about local and national resources that may be available to the caregiver or care recipient.

Once the assessment is completed, interventions for caregiving families typically consist of education (especially about the care recipient's illness and the availability of care resources), problem-solving (including specific suggestions for managing the caregiving role in general, specific behavior problems exhibited by the care recipient, and other stressors in the caregiver's life), and support (S. Zarit, 2009). The primary treatment modalities include individual counseling or psychotherapy for the caregiver, family meetings, and support groups (Zarit & Zarit, 2007). On rare occasions, intensive family therapy is also indicated. Support groups for caregivers have become increasingly popular, especially groups for caregivers of patients with a cognitive disorder such as Alzheimer's disease. Although caregiver support groups are not as effective as individual counseling or a combination of counseling and family meetings in reducing caregiver burden, groups can provide ongoing support for caregivers during or after a more intensive period of treatment. Zarit and Zarit have identified several specific benefits of support groups:

- groups are an effective source for disseminating information;
- groups provide a venue for the sharing of experiences and feelings with others who are in similar situations;
- groups provide opportunities for the giving and receiving of support;
- groups often provide novel strategies and ideas for solving specific problems; and
- groups encourage caregivers to take better care of themselves.

One intervention that included support group participation as well as individual and family counseling reduced the deterioration in caregivers' mental and physical functioning that is typically seen over time, and also decreased the number of nursing home admissions (Mittelman, Haley, Clay, & Roth, 2006). Building on their model of the caregiving career, Aneshensel et al. (1995) recommend matching intervention strategies with the needs of the particular stage in the caregiving career. For example, during the *role acquisition* stage, caregivers need information and assistance identifying the varied parts of their role and building skill in the role. Later, during the *role enactment* stage, problem-solving and garnering assistance and support for the long haul of caregiving are likely to be more appropriate (see Figure 11.3).

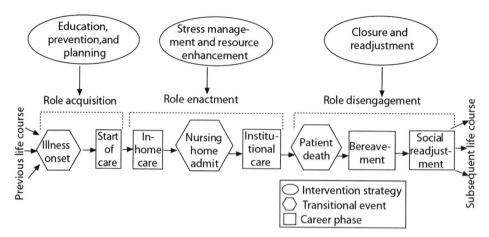

Figure 11.3 Intervention strategies across the caregiving career.
Source: From Aneshensel et al. (1995). Adapted by permission.

Summary and Conclusions

Although less thoroughly studied, the disorders and difficulties described in this chapter obviously also challenge some later-life individuals and families. It may well turn out to be the case that substance abuse, PDs, and marital and family problems are each as impactful and deleterious as other difficulties more commonly associated with aging (e.g., depression). Much more research is needed to determine the true prevalence and nature of these difficulties with older adults. Assessments and treatments, similarly, are areas in which considerable research is needed.

12

Settings and Contexts of Mental Health Services

You have just received a referral from the physician at a nursing home where you consult: "Please have Psychologist see Mr. Johnson for sexual acting out." Your initial discussion with the day shift nursing supervisor provides the following details.

Ralph Johnson is a 77-year-old retired mailman who has resided in the intermediate care section of the nursing home for 15 months. He was admitted from home because his wife was unable to care for him after he suffered a series of two cardiovascular accidents over an 11-month period. Mrs. Johnson visits one to two times per week, always with her daughter, Elaine, because Mrs. Johnson does not drive.

Mr. Johnson's strokes have left him with residual right-sided weakness and somewhat slurred speech. The supervisor states that he is confused at times. Other medical problems include high blood pressure, for which he takes Capaten 50 mg. b.i.d., and diabetes, which had been well controlled by diet until recently, when he began eating less and losing weight. He has now been put on insulin. He also suffers from some arthritis and carries a diagnosis of "chronic anxiety" for which he takes Xanax 1.0 mg. b.i.d. (scheduled) and hs. (p.r.n.).

Mr. Johnson is able to ambulate with a walker, but he has been walking less and less over the past several months. The supervisor remembers that he was initially fairly active in the home's recreational activities program, and assumes that he still attends programs regularly. He sleeps well, and enjoys watching television in his room and chatting with his one cognitively intact roommate.

When asked about the physician's referral, the supervisor provided very little direct information: "I really have no idea about that. We've never had any trouble with him. The nurses on second shift got the doctor to write that order." (Spayd, 1993)

This referral reflects the complexity of mental health consultation and service provision in the typical settings where older adults are served. Clinical services for Mr.

Aging and Mental Health, 2e. Daniel L. Segal, Sara Honn Qualls, and Michael A. Smyer
© 2011 Daniel L. Segal, Sara Honn Qualls, and Michael A. Smyer

Johnson will require highly skilled approaches to his illness comorbidity, interdisciplinary collaboration, and unique characteristics of particular settings that influence practice. Mental health practitioners not only must be competent in effective assessment and treatment, they also must know how to apply those skills within the settings where older adults live and are served. Indeed, the psychology discipline has defined setting-specific competencies as core to becoming a professional geropsychologist (Knight, Karel, Hinrichsen, Qualls, & Duffy, 2009), competencies that are relevant to all mental health professionals.

This chapter provides an overview of four settings where mental health services may be delivered: housing, social services, legal contexts, and health care. Each has distinct characteristics that include organizational structures, particular players, distinct mental health needs, and professional knowledge and skills specific to those settings. Each also represents a very large category with tremendous diversity in populations served, funding streams, and policies regulating the quality of care. We offer this bird's eye view of services settings for older adults where mental health issues are salient. Indeed, this overview illustrates how mental health services for older adults cannot solely occur in an outpatient office. The complexity of these settings suggests that aging populations provide some of the most intellectually intriguing, clinically demanding, and professionally diverse career opportunities available in the field of mental health.

Traditional outpatient mental health services require the older adult to seek the services following a rather complex set of tasks involved in help-seeking that include recognizing the symptom(s), naming the problem as mental health concern, identifying services resources, and accessing the service appropriately. Many older adults will not be able to accomplish at least one of those tasks. As one strategy to remove barriers, the integration of mental health providers into the settings where older adults already live and receive services offers a unique opportunity to influence well-being, bypassing the need for self-referral. Geriatric mental health services have long been encouraged to integrate mental health care with other service providers, and model programs are under development in each of the service industries described in this chapter.

In each setting described below, we identify the organizational characteristics of the service sector along with the key personnel or players, and then briefly discuss the distinctive mental health issues relevant to that service environment. Mental health providers will need to be knowledgeable about the settings in order to integrate care effectively.

Housing

The last quarter of the twentieth century witnessed a rapid expansion of housing available to older adults. Historically, older adults had the option of living in their own home, with family, or in an "old folks home." A shared myth in our culture portrays happy families living in multigenerational households in previous centuries, despite data that suggest that most families lived together due to economic necessity rather than preference. Since the advent of guaranteed pensions in the United States

Housing

Own Home

Own Home with Services

Senior Congregate Housing

Assisted Living

Nursing Home

Acute Care

Figure 12.1   Housing continuum for older adults.

and Europe, older adults have continually indicated that they prefer to live independently of their family.

Organizational structures

Diverse options now exist for supporting the desire for independent domicile. Housing is often portrayed as a continuum that ranges from fully independent (i.e., a house in a community neighborhood) to providing 100 percent support for all aspects of personal care for persons who are too ill to care for the most basic aspects of self-care (i.e., a skilled nursing facility). Figure 12.1 depicts a range of housing options. Each option actually represents a category containing multiple options that vary based on cost, architectural features, and lifestyle variations. For example, assisted living is a large category that includes massive apartment complexes with supportive services as well as neighborhood homes with a single provider supporting the lives of four to six residents who have single-occupancy or shared bedrooms. The cultural variety within that category is extraordinary.

Each level of housing operates within particular legal structures that influence the services that can be made available there. Housing options such as rehabilitation centers, acute hospitals, and skilled nursing facilities are highly regulated environments. In between are options whose organizational structures may be determined by architectural features, staffing, and programming more than by regulation. For example, a senior apartment building may have management staff, maintenance staff, resident council, and various service providers who come and go, all of whom shape the organizational context in which residents live.

Mental health providers must appreciate and understand the particular organizational structures of *each* housing setting in which they wish to provide services. Who has charge of which aspects of the residents' lives? Who provides hidden support for people who would require a different setting if that support person were not propping up the functioning of the most ill residents? What spaces are used for what purposes within this setting? How do spaces, staff, and transportation constrain resident behaviors or, alternatively, offer opportunities that foster well-being?

The players

Housing contexts that offer supportive services have a variety of staff roles that must be understood by mental health providers. Although residents of assisted living facilities may have difficulty discriminating among staff roles, in fact the housekeepers, medication managers, nurses, activities personnel, and personal care providers have *very* distinct roles. For example, the housekeeper typically is not allowed to prepare food, assist a resident with transferring from chair to wheelchair, or hand a resident the medications that are sitting on the counter out of the resident's reach. Despite restrictions on delivery of services to the resident, the housekeeper has intimate knowledge of the daily activities and needs of the residents because he/she is actually in each resident's apartment regularly and thus can observe readily each resident's self-care skills and errors.

Mental health providers need to understand the distinct as well as overlapping characteristics of staff job descriptions. At a practical level, staff will have opportunity to observe behaviors and situations that are highly relevant to mental health practice. Providers often use staff, families, and sometimes other residents to assist in implementing a care plan. The time taken to know staff, understand their roles and relationships with residents, and hear their concerns can pay off substantially.

Mental health providers often find it helpful to train staff, especially regarding the origins of "problem behaviors" and strategies to provide care when those are present. The traditional weekly psychotherapy hour is a limited intervention tool in many long-term care settings where 24/7 care patterns will have a far stronger influence on behavior than intermittent talk therapy. The high rate of cognitive impairment found in residents of long-term care facilities also points to the need for careful evaluation of whether psychotherapy is appropriate and useful for the resident. However, efforts to alter staff behavior require mental health providers to first and foremost understand the culture of the direct care staff, their motivations for doing the work and thus for responding to suggestions or recommended changes in work patterns, and the reward system in which they operate. Staff training requires multi-pronged approaches that are closely aligned with management practices as well.

Distinct mental health needs

Epidemiology of mental disorders varies considerably across housing types. As was reported in earlier chapters on the various disorders, the highest rates of mental disorder exist among the most frail and most ill residents of nursing homes. High rates of cognitive impairment and other mental disorders are also present in assisted living, as compared with community-dwelling populations. Among persons living in their own homes, mental disorder prevalence rises during times of physical illness or rehabilitation post-hospitalization, and drops as illness comorbidities are better controlled. However, living in one's own home can also set up an older person for social isolation and the psychological difficulties that accompany it, such as loneliness. Acute care settings such as hospitals are prime contexts for delirium that is a consequence of many illnesses and medications.

Mental health providers need to become familiar with the characteristics of the populations they will serve in each housing setting, the players, and the organizational structures of that setting. The case of Mr. Johnson described above illustrates the complexity of providing mental health services in a nursing facility where information about him is dispersed among staff on three shifts, family, his physician, and a myriad of other players who are not even mentioned in the vignette (e.g., dietician, activities director). This scenario depicts the common problem of identifying whether there really is a mental health problem or not, whether there are behavior problems that challenge a particular set of players, and who is able to help elucidate the picture. If Mr. Johnson turns out to be depressed, the treatment will similarly involve multiple players more than likely. How does one work with the multitude of participants in a way that is appropriate in protecting his dignity and confidentiality?

Social Services

Social services agencies offer older adults assistance designed to keep them living in the community independently. Ranging from meals-on-wheels programs to support completing insurance forms, social service providers offer non-medical assistance that supports Independent Activities of Daily Living (IADLs) needed to live independently in the community.

Organizational structures

Social services agencies are organized in very diverse ways that reflect idiosyncratic histories in a particular local community. In contrast to housing or health care where the organizational structures would be relatively consistent across regions (e.g., all cities have hospitals, outpatient surgery centers, assisted living facilities, senior housing campuses), social services are organized in quite varied ways. For example, transportation or respite care services may be provided by a home health agency, a housing facility, or a government agency. Large senior services organizations may coordinate several services or the services may be accessed from multiple providers. Not surprisingly, older persons and their families are often uncertain where to find and access services and agency providers often find it challenging to coordinate care.

The funding source for services influences eligibility for access. Publicly funded services tend to have age, income, or functional disability status as eligibility criteria. In the United States, public funding for aging services derives primarily from the Older Americans Act, which defines policies for social service access. As depicted in Figure 12.2, funding authority rests in the US Department of Health and Human Services, which distributes to the Administration on Aging, which funnels funds to state units on aging that disburse them throughout the state. In many cases, funds are distributed through a national network of Area Agencies on Aging (AAAs), which cover all geographic regions of the United States. The AAAs contract with service providers to actually deliver the vast majority of the services.

Privately funded social services are organized in even more diverse ways. Services are offered by faith-based organizations, fee-for-service private providers, and by

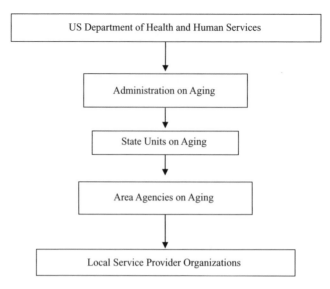

Figure 12.2   Aging services network: flow of funding and policies.

providers of health care and housing. Utilities companies may offer a discount subsidy for older adults on fixed incomes that is funded by company profits or customer donations. Churches may provide services directly (e.g., Stephen Ministries) or they may collaborate with other organizations to co-fund an agency. United Way collects funds for many member agencies and disburses based on local need. Member organizations such as AARP and Alzheimer's Association may be major providers in some locations but offer considerably less in others. Private service agencies may also set eligibility criteria or may offer services for set fees.

Many services are included in the social services category. Unfortunately, many consumers can feel blitzed by the sheer range of services that are offered in disjointed organizational structures. Family members often inquire about where to begin to learn about the array of options, along with eligibility criteria and cost. AAAs are a great starting point, because they offer Information and Assistance (I&A) services that at a minimum catalog the available resources in the region. Families can locate the options for adult day care, meals delivery, transportation, home repair, financial assistance, telephone reassurance, and employment service, among others.

The players

Social services agencies begin their work with an older adult by evaluating the need for services, sometimes during an in-home visit. The home visit offers unique opportunity for the evaluator to witness the home living conditions. Is there food in the refrigerator? Is the home clean? Are medications organized and appropriately accessible? Are pets cared for well? Do others live in the home? Are appropriate assistive devices available in the home to support mobility and sensory impairments? In the absence of a home visit, the intake evaluation relies on client report of functioning and challenges. A collateral interview often adds additional perspective on day to day life, particularly for people with any degree of cognitive impairment that limits their ability to provide a thorough, consistent history of functioning.

Based on the evaluation, a services plan would be developed and shared with the client who can select desired services. A case manager may have responsibility for developing and overseeing implementation of the plan. Agency workers are engaged to provide specific services in what is often a complex pattern of deliveries, installations, and ongoing services. The case manager tracks implementation, communicating regularly with clients to monitor satisfaction, benefits, and any change in condition that would affect eligibility or appropriateness of services.

Distinct mental health needs

Social service workers have the opportunity to witness mental health needs *in situ*. Observation of older adults sharing a meal at a congregate meal site may be the only opportunity anyone has to recognize signs of elder abuse, depression, anxiety, or substance abuse in persons who are otherwise socially isolated. In this way, social service providers are important gatekeepers for mental health services.

> The transportation volunteer was shocked when Millie opened her door without any clothing on the lower half of her body. Millie did not recall that the visitor was coming or that she even had an important medical appointment.

> Sandy and her children enjoy delivering meals to older adults on Saturday morning, but were distressed to find one older woman trying to share her meal with two teenage grandsons. Sandy wondered if the agency knew that the boys were living with this woman.

> The respite care worker worries that her 3 hours a week are a drop in the bucket compared with what Jack needs to support his full-time care of his developmentally disabled son. Since his last heart attack, Jack simply has less energy and strength to lift his son from bed to wheelchair. Every week Jack looks more depressed and worried, and is losing weight.

The value and impact of social services are influenced by the mental health of their older clients. The older person's cognitive ability, personality, and mood influence the perception of need for help and the subsequent utilization of services. Mental health problems pose striking challenges to providers whose efforts can be thwarted, denied, or confused by clients with mental disorders. Yet efforts to get clients to accept a referral are often met with resistance. If mental health problems continue unabated, social service agencies can become less effective while expending more resources.

Mental health providers have an important opportunity to partner with social service providers to create integrated care models. Social service providers value the insights of mental health professionals about the causes of behavior, and benefit significantly from consultations about how to adapt the service to better meet the needs of clients with mental disorders. Models of integrated care are needed to create innovative ways of partnering.

Health Care

About 16 percent of the economy goes for health care in the United States, of which a disproportionately high amount is spent on health care for older adults. The range of health care settings in which mental health services may be delivered is as broad as the range of housing. Mental health providers represent a small portion of health care services and of cost, but are increasingly valued as the role of self-directed behavior in health outcomes has been highlighted across the range of settings. Setting shapes the roles available to mental health professionals as well as the services that are needed or even possible. Rarely are mental health professionals able to provide services in isolation because physical health comorbidities almost inevitably lead older adults to receive services from more than one discipline. Integrated care is emerging as a standard of care that older adults deserve, but one that requires significant change in practices across settings (APA Task Force on Integrated Health Care, 2007).

Organizational structures

Health care settings include remarkably diverse contexts for mental health service delivery. Ranging from home health care delivered directly into the homes of older adults to intensive care in acute care hospitals, diverse settings establish distinct environments for mental health services. Nursing homes, for example, are both housing and health care, offering practice opportunities that are totally different from those offered in intensive care units of an acute care hospital. Mental health providers need to understand the organizational characteristics and contexts of the particular setting in which they seek to deliver services.

Among the myriad of organizational characteristics that differentiate health care settings are a few mentioned here. Public and private ownership create distinct funding streams that constrain or enable services options. For example, nursing homes that rely primarily on Medicaid funding (public funding for indigent persons) receive far lower reimbursements per resident than do nursing homes that only accept private pay, which can set any rate the market will bear. Not surprisingly, public and private nursing homes show different patterns of staffing, use of certain therapies, and outcomes (Amirkhanyan, 2008).

Each setting is constrained and supported by regulatory policies and the organizations that oversee compliance with them. For example, rehabilitation hospitals are regulated differently from acute care hospitals or home health providers. Regulations are structured at federal, state, and local levels, sometimes in competing networks of regulations and certification processes.

Other characteristics that vary across health settings are length of service (or length of stay), range of services provided, and level of acuity that can be addressed. Funding sources and staff expertise also vary by setting. Health care is an exceptionally complex industry with a particularly diverse set of roles, professions, and regulatory structures.

The players

In addition to funding source, the array of players who participate in health care in each setting is distinct. Nursing homes rely heavily on entry-level direct service personnel who provide intimate personal care to very ill persons who have high rates of mental disorder. In contrast, intensive care units are populated with highly technically skilled professionals whose expertise involves split-second life-and-death decisions with medically fragile individuals. Rarely could a neuropsychological evaluation or a psychotherapy session be performed in an intensive care unit, for example.

The roles of each discipline also vary across setting. Whereas physicians are highly involved and central to care in an intensive care unit, nursing staff or nursing assistants are more likely to have an authoritative voice in care decisions for home health patients or even nursing home residents. In most health settings, more than one discipline is involved in care, requiring some type of team structure, whether formally organized as an interprofessional team with shared governance and care responsibilities, or functioning as a virtual team of providers who never lay eyes on one another. The mental health provider's role varies significantly across those settings, as does the nature of the services delivered.

Health care inevitably involves multiple participants who can be conceptualized as a team (Takamura, 1985). Teams have many types of structures, including a non-communicating "virtual" team whose virtual members may not be aware of who else is on the team or how care is being delivered by other members of the team. Regardless of whether the team is virtual, multidisciplinary, or intensively interdisciplinary in structure, functioning of the team has a critical impact on care. Models for team development offer guidance about how to structure team membership and operation to maximize quality of care for patients (Heinemann & Zeiss, 2002). An example of a services system that places a strong emphasis on teams is hospice and palliative care (Kasl-Godley, 2011). In contrast, most settings have minimal support for coordination of care among the team of providers. Families may be the most commonly omitted members of the health care team despite their role in providing the vast majority of care, including health care. Considerable work is needed to build successful team models in real practice settings.

Distinct mental health needs

Older persons served in all health care settings have higher rates of mental disorders than are found in populations who are not accessing health care. As noted consistently throughout this book, physical health problems increase risk of mental disorders. Rates of disorder vary across settings, with highest rates in nursing homes and other long-term care settings. Rates are elevated in acute care and home health care as well. Yet more institutional settings, such as nursing homes, show the highest rates, likely due to a combination of institutional characteristics of the setting that reduce control and self-respect and the fact that the medical conditions that forced the residents into the setting also create comorbidities with mental disorders.

Many health care settings have renamed themselves *behavioral health services* to represent the many ways in which behavioral issues are key to health care. Assessment and treatment of mental disorders continue to be critical roles for mental health providers. However, behavioral health services also include the application of behavior change principles to behavioral aspects of chronic illness conditions such as diabetes or cardiovascular disease. Increasingly, the National Institutes of Health have invested substantial funding in understanding how to change self-care health behaviors that are key to managing chronic illness. Mental health professionals with expertise in behavior change have much to offer to the efforts to reduce health risk factors that are so predictive of health and functional outcomes for persons with chronic illness. For example, behavioral strategies to improve diet, exercise, stress management, and to reduce obesity are critical to controlling negative outcomes as well as health costs.

Mental health providers working with older adults inevitably encounter end-of-life care issues (Qualls & Kasl-Godley, 2011). Advanced care planning and other legal issues that arise at the end of life are discussed below. Mental health is a key factor in defining the quality of life during the last months of life when meaning, purpose, endings, and grief are salient issues. Mental health providers are often the team members who keep the patient, family, and care team aware of those issues and help them process psychosocial aspects of dying. Specialized practice competencies are now defined for persons whose work focuses on end-of-life care, and training materials are available to build those competencies even in persons who may encounter the issues only intermittently in practice.

Legal Contexts

Legal issues arise in later life primarily due to the increased risk of significant cognitive impairments that restrict self-care capacity. Although severe physical impairments may limit functional abilities, as long as cognition is intact, the severely impaired person retains all legal rights for self-determination. Mental health professionals play key roles in evaluating decision-making capacity (Qualls & Smyer, 2007), although the decision is ultimately a legal one that is made by a judge using criteria defined for the jurisdiction in which the decision is rendered. The legal procedures must be understood well by any mental health provider seeking to participate in the system.

A task force sponsored by the American Bar Association and the American Psychological Association has produced a rich model for conceptualizing the components of legal capacity, illustrated in Figure 12.3 (ABA and APA, 2008). Weighing in the balance are several domains that must be evaluated and considered by clinicians. The presence of an illness is not the defining factor; rather, capacity is ultimately a functional determination. Although state standards vary, common components of the definition of incapacity include cognitive limitations that render the individual functionally incapable of self-care without risk to health and safety, thus requiring assistance from another. Some states add the criterion that assistive technologies have been applied and found insufficient to build capacity. In this rapidly evolving field,

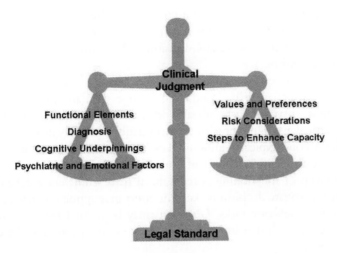

Figure 12.3 Components of evaluation of decision-making capacity.

mental health professionals must work to stay up to date on the legal standards, the professional standards for evaluation, and the alternative strategies that can be used to protect well-being in persons with compromised cognitive abilities without having to acquire a judicial guardianship decision.

> Dr. Johnson's evaluation of Lela Granger suggests that although she can state a preference about her health care, she lacks capacity to appreciate the scope or impact of those choices. Mrs. Granger's advanced directive empowers her oldest son, Tom, to take the role of surrogate decision-maker.

> A social services case manager found 7 inches of sewage back-up in Mr. Andrews' home. Mr. Andrews acted as surprised by her concern about the health risks as he was about the sewage problem. Further investigation showed little food in the house and a stack of unpaid bills. With no family to assist him, Mr. Andrews' safety and well-being was evaluated by Adult Protective Services, who subsequently petitioned the court to appoint a guardian for him.

The players

Ultimately, a clinical judgment is taken under consideration by a judge or jury who must weigh that clinical judgment against the rules of law to render a legal decision. Many people participate in the process prior to the final legal decision, however.

A petitioner raises the question of capacity initially. The petitioner may be a nurse in a nursing home who is concerned that a resident who is demanding to go home may not have the capacity to decide. Or a family member may petition the court for guardianship of finances if the family member believes that a loved one is at risk for financial fraud and abuse. The petition may be made directly to the Probate Court, with a request that the judge conduct a guardianship hearing. Alternatively, a physician may be asked to assess capacity and in the case of decision-making incapacity the physician may invoke a surrogate decision-maker without having to engage in a full guardianship hearing.

The petition requires an evaluation of the person's capacity for independent decision-making which may be conducted by one or many professionals. Nurses, physical therapists, psychologists, social workers, and other professionals may all be involved in particular components of that evaluation. Reports of the evaluations are submitted to the court typically, although lawyers for the petitioner or the older adult (defendant) may also hire independent evaluations.

Once a domain of functioning is recognized to be sufficiently deficient that the person needs a surrogate decision-maker, the court may appoint a guardian for a wide or narrow array of self-care tasks. Guardians may be mental health or other health providers, attorneys, or other interested parties who can ensure that the elders' well-being is protected.

Distinct mental health needs

Persons with cognitive impairment due to diseases such as Alzheimer's disease or other assault on the brain (e.g., traumatic brain injury or stroke) require increasing amounts of assistance to remain safe. The vast majority of supportive care provided to such persons occurs informally as families and other loved ones simply offer services that compensate for lost abilities. Mental health providers can coach individuals into providing more intensive interventions as cognitive ability declines, thus avoiding legal decisions as long as possible (Qualls, 2007).

Mental health providers are often involved in evaluation of a person's legal capacity to function independently. The evaluation must relate specifically to the needs of the legal decision-makers in order to be of value. In other words, the evaluator must understand the standards and know how to link his/her own evaluation data to the legal standard as well as to the practical concerns faced by the evaluators. Neuropsychologists conduct testing that identifies the level of ability and impairment in particular cognitive domains (e.g., different types of memory, attention, language, problem-solving, and executive function). Mental health providers may assess everyday abilities (see Table 12.1) to determine the domains for the guardianship as well as the values of the person in question. If family members are conflicted about who should be appointed as surrogate decision-makers, evaluation of family members or of relationships may be requested by the court. Finally, mental health providers may be called upon to provide treatment to determine whether limitations in functioning can be ameliorated.

The Roles of Mental Health Providers across Settings

Several common themes about mental health are evident in the four settings described in this chapter. Mental health issues appear in all settings, often complicating the delivery of services by other professionals and paraprofessionals. Staff in these settings

Table 12.1 Components of everyday functioning relevant for capacity evaluation

Domain	Description
1. Care of Self	Maintain adequate hygiene, bathing, dressing, toileting, dental hygiene
	Prepare meals and eat for adequate nutrition
	Identify abuse or neglect and protect self from harm
2. Financial	Protect and spend small amounts of cash
	Manage and use checks
	Give gifts and donations
	Make or modify will
	Buy or sell real property
	Deposit, withdraw, dispose, invest monetary assets
	Establish and use credit
	Pay, settle, prosecute, or contest any claim
	Enter into a contract, commitment, or lease arrangement
	Continue or participate in the operation of a business
	Employ persons to advise or assist him/her
	Resist exploitation, coercion, undue influence
3. Medical	Give/withhold medical consent
	Admit self to health facility
	Choose and direct caregivers
	Make or change an advance directive
	Manage medications
	Contact help if ill or in medical emergency
4. Home and Community Life	Choose/establish abode
	Maintain reasonably safe and clean shelter
	Be left alone without danger
	Drive or use public transportation
	Make and communicate choices about roommates
	Initiate and follow a schedule of daily and leisure activities
	Travel
	Establish and maintain personal relationships with friends, relatives, co-workers
	Determine degree of participation in religious activities
	Use telephone
	Use mail
	Avoid environmental dangers and obtain emergency help
5. Civil or Legal	Retain legal counsel
	Vote
	Make decisions about legal documents

Source: Adapted from Moye (2007).

play a key role in identifying potential mental health problems, screening for them, making referrals, and adjusting their own treatment plans to maximize effectiveness in the presence of mental disorder. Mental health providers also play key roles in conducting screening evaluations, responding to referrals with full evaluations and contributions to treatment plans, and initiating mental health services when needed. Additionally, mental health professionals offer consultation to organizations about mental health and well-being of clients and staff.

Consider again the case of Mr. Johnson which started this chapter. As the nursing home's mental health specialist, one of your first tasks may be to assess both the individual nursing home resident and the organizational context in which the resident is functioning. In Mr. Johnson's case, the referral is for "sexual acting out." A series of questions follow from this simple description: What is meant by this term in this context? What is the pattern of sexual acting out (e.g., are there differences across times of day, places within the home, etc.)? Whose problem is this? The referral indicates that the "nurses on second shift got the doctor to write" the referral, so speaking with that particular crew may be an important place to start. What will success look like in this case? Will a reduction in the acting out be success? Will a shift in Mr. Johnson's pattern of activity (e.g., from the day room to his own semi-private room) be successful? The complexities of these questions represent well a typical mental health referral in an agency setting.

In earlier chapters, we identified major treatment approaches for major categories of psychopathology (e.g., anxiety, depression, cognitive impairment). These approaches also form the context for treatment of nursing home residents. Spayd and Smyer (1996) outline five procedural steps for selecting an appropriate and effective intervention for a mentally ill nursing home resident:

1   Identify the problem in behavioral terms.
2   Determine realistic and mutually agreeable goals for intervention.
3   Identify all available mental health resources.
4   Assess the available interventions, in light of the individual resident's problem and characteristics.
5   Consider the potential problems with available treatments and the possibility of not intervening.

Spayd and Smyer (1996) begin with the specific elements of the problem. By focusing on specific behaviors, they urge us to avoid global complaints from staff such as the referral problem for Mr. Johnson: "sexual acting out." In following up on this referral, a first step would be to become clearer about what specific activities were involved and under what conditions (e.g., time of day, particular persons present, etc.).

The second step – determining *mutually* agreeable goals – requires assessing whose problem needs to be addressed. In Mr. Johnson's case, the nursing director suggests that the problem only occurs on second shift. Thus, one of the key elements in setting the goals will be to identify those who must be involved in developing the agreement: the resident, the relevant staff, other residents and family members (as appropriate), and the psychologist.

The third step – identifying all available mental health resources – reminds us that the treatment plan may include other members of the nursing home community (e.g., residents, staff, family members, visitors) as well as outside expertise. Finally, an assessment of the resident's own capacities as resources is also essential (e.g., does the resident have sufficient cognitive capacity to be actively engaged in the therapeutic process?).

Given an appreciation of both the appropriate goals and resources available for this resident's problem situation, an essential next step is to assess the available interventions. In this step, the clinician serves as the scientist practitioner: assessing what is known from the literature, gauging what is feasible within the constraints of the individual resident and his or her context, and the professional and paraprofessional resources of the setting.

The final step is a variation on the first rule of medical intervention: First do no harm. With a clear understanding of the problem, the resources, and potential interventions available, we will be able to consider the limitations of treatment, as well as the benefits. Brink (1979) highlighted the *principle of minimal interference*, with a goal of disturbing established patterns of living as little as possible. Thus, we should consider the full range of options – including the option of not intervening – before we undertake treatment.

Mental health clinicians need to leverage their expertise by engaging resources consistently available in the setting. Professional mental health providers are limited in most of these settings, so an appropriate use of talent is to serve as a consultant to the setting, seeking to engage key members of the nursing home community as elements of the mental health treatment team (Cohn & Smyer, 1988). Furthermore, the daily staff–resident interaction is a more powerful influence on behavior than an infrequent (e.g., weekly) professional interaction.

There are several steps in the consultation process: (1) preparation; (2) relationship development; (3) problem assessment; (4) formulation and delivery of interventions; and (5) follow-up (Caplan, 1970). For clinicians, starting a consultation practice in any of these settings requires background knowledge and experience – learning the territory of the industry, mental health reimbursement, and developing relationships with administrators and staff, and other key referral sources. Thus, in addition to mental health intervention skills, consultants also need skill in organizational behavior. The latter perspective provides frameworks and tools for influencing the culture of the setting, including staff hiring, development, and training as well as management organization and communication.

Mental health consultants in community settings must clarify several elements in the consultation:

- Who is the consumer or client (e.g., older adult, staff members, family members)?
- When does the consultation occur in the cycle of the problem process (e.g., prior to a problem occurring or in the midst of a crisis)?
- At what level does the consultation occur (e.g., at the case level or at the administrative level)?
- What is the route of expected intervention (e.g., directly with the older adult or indirectly through working with other staff members)?

- Perhaps most importantly, what is the goal for the consultative intervention (e.g., treatment of a specific older adult; development of a policy)?

Resources to guide mental health clinicians working in long-term care offer an array of approaches to consultation as well as other aspects of clinical work (Hyer & Intrieri, 2006; Norris, Molinari, & Ogland-Hand, 2002; Rosowsky et al., 2008).

Summary and Conclusions

Mental health professionals are increasingly drawn to offer services within the community organizational settings where older adults live and access services. The concept of integrated care is gaining momentum as the need for coordination among professionals, agencies, and family members is obvious. Electronic communication tools demonstrate the value of shared information and decision-making across settings. Successful teamwork makes evident the risks of poorly coordinated service by professionals operating in silos. As practice patterns evolve, mental health providers will be key participants in creating new opportunities for collaboration, integration of care, and communication. Models emerging in recent years include the hospice and palliative care, the Program for All-Inclusive Care for the Elderly (PACE), and primary care integration demonstration projects. Each of these has unique policy constraints on funding and services dissemination that make it challenging to broaden their impact.

Key policy issues threaten the potentials of integrated care models and require intensive advocacy in the next few years. The absence of a funding system for mental and behavioral health training comparable to that in other health disciplines is a major concern. Without such funding, the work force in geriatric mental health cannot keep pace with the growing demand. Early career psychologists also are not drawn to the field because of inadequate funding of the services they provide. An absence of parity in mental health services reimbursement has been a major disincentive for use of those services by older adults who have been charged a 50 percent co-pay for mental health services in contrast to 20 percent for all other health services. Current policies have scheduled a gradual phase-in of parity that may rectify this disparity if funding continues. Furthermore, indigent older adults and those relying on Medicaid for long-term care funding will continue to be underserved given the shockingly low reimbursement rates for mental health services and ineligibility of many needed services (e.g., staff consultation). Other examples of policy challenges facing providers are the nearly complete disconnect between disabilities and aging services networks, the silos in funding and services between public mental health and other components of health care, the omission of families from the health care team, and the absence of a model or funding for home-based primary care. The policy advocacy priorities of the National Coalition on Mental Health and Aging are shown in Table 12.2, where the broad range of issues that are prioritized by a national organization is evident.

The field of geriatric mental health is also evolving rapidly in ways that will help establish its credibility and position in the marketplaces of science and practice. For

Table 12.2 Advocacy priorities of the National Coalition on Mental Health and Aging (March, 2010)

1 Assure access to an affordable and comprehensive range of quality mental health and substance abuse services, including:
   - outreach
   - home and community-based services
   - prevention, and
   - intervention, coordinated with acute and long-term services and supports.
2 Assure that these services are age, gender, and linguistically appropriate, culturally competent, and consumer driven.
3 Promote the development and implementation of home and community-based services as an alternative to institutionalization through a variety of public and private funding mechanisms.
4 Promote older adult mental health and substance abuse services research, and coordinate and finance the movement of evidence-based prevention, early intervention, and treatment from research into services, including healthy aging and chronic disease management programs.
5 Support the integration of older adult mental health and substance abuse services into primary health care, long-term services and supports, and community-based service systems.
6 Promote screening for co-occurring mental and substance use disorders by primary health, mental health, and substance abuse providers and encourage the development of integrated treatment strategies.
7 Increase collaboration among aging, health, mental health, and substance abuse consumer organizations, disability organizations, veterans', women's, LGBT, and advocacy groups, professional associations, academic institutions, research entities, and all relevant government agencies to promote more effective use of resources and to reduce fragmentation of services.
8 Conduct a public/private education campaign to educate consumers, family members, providers, and the public on healthy aging and mental wellness and the identification and promise of effective treatments for mental health disorders in older adults, incorporating consumer choice/empowerment and involving consumers to promote the benefits of mental health prevention and treatment in older adults.
9 Reduce the stigma associated with mental disorders in older adults, and reduce age-related prejudice and discrimination regarding mental disorders.
10 Develop and implement a national strategy for older adult suicide prevention.
11 Ensure services and supports for family caregivers that provide access to vital support services, including mental health and substance abuse services.
12 Promote the health and well-being of older adults through the prevention, detection, treatment, intervention, and prosecution of elder abuse, neglect, and exploitation.
13 Promote the capacity of state long-term care ombudsman programs to recognize and respond to complaints of elder abuse and neglect and mental health and substance abuse concerns.
14 Designate an older adult mental health leader or coordinator in AoA and other appropriate HHS, federal, state, and local agencies responsible for mental health services.
15 Address severe provider and faculty shortages in mental health, behavioral health, and substance abuse for older adults by expanding geriatric traineeships for a broad range of mental health and health professionals, and targeting national financial incentives such as loan forgiveness programs and continuing education funding.

Source: National Coalition on Mental Health and Aging (2010). Reprinted with permission.

example, professional psychologists have established the Pikes Peak Model for Training in Professional Geropsychology that focuses on competencies to practice (Knight et al., 2009) along with guidelines for practice (American Psychological Association, 2003) and an organizational network for programs training geropsychologists (Council of Professional Geropsychology Training Programs). Another example is the strong advocacy organization in geriatric psychiatry, the American Association for Geriatric Psychiatry. The science of aging and mental health has also built a substantial corpus of findings on which to base practice patterns. The content of this book illustrates the growing scientific base for identifying practices that warrant policy support, funding, and integration into training programs.

In short, the oft-touted "future" aging demographic revolution is here. The opportunities and challenges to have an impact on the lives of older adults and their families are now urgent. A diversity of professional providers, policymakers, and scientists have considerable work ahead to integrate findings and practice opportunities into services policies and structures.

Epilogue

In this book we have tried to provide a framework for assessing effective mental health treatments for older adults. In doing so, we have provided a snapshot of theoretical and practice concepts at the beginning of the twenty-first century. Effective geriatric intervention will continue to evolve as a function of three elements: the changing characteristics of cohorts of older adults in the future; developments in the basic understanding of the processes that affect geriatric mental health; and alterations in the public policy contexts that affect the provision of mental health services for older adults.

Today's older adults represent a unique intersection of individual and historical time. There are some indications that tomorrow's older adults may arrive in later life with different patterns of mental health and disorder. For example, some have suggested that today's younger and middle-aged adults have higher rates of depression than the current older adults did at a comparable point in their lives and are bringing higher rates of mental disorder with them into later life. In addition, the older adults of the future may arrive in later life with increased experience of and increased expectations regarding mental health treatment: They may rely more upon mental health services, thereby demanding greater access and efficacy from the mental health system. Finally, tomorrow's older adults will arrive in later life with a different set of experiences of historical and personal life stresses. Together, these patterns may alter the rates and presentation of mental disorders in the future.

Whereas the older adults of the future will change, so will our understanding of three areas that shape the development and implementation of mental health services for older adults: gerontology; mental disorder; and effective mental health treatment. Study of the basic processes of aging continues to uncover a more differentiated view of the processes and prospects of normal aging. At the same time, inquiry regarding the precursors of mental disorder in later life remains an important part of the scientific agenda. These investigations of the processes of aging and mental disorder will be accompanied by continued scrutiny of the most effective treatment approaches for older adults and their families. Increasingly, these will involve interdisciplinary collaboration. In short, the knowledge base for effective practice will continue to evolve.

Changes in the older adults themselves and in our understanding of the processes of aging will force changes in the public policies that affect geriatric mental health practice. For example, current debates regarding the fiscal health of Medicare, Medicaid, and social security will shape the scope and costs of mental health services for older adults in the future, as well as access to those services. For example, we may see an increase in funding for interdisciplinary collaboration to serve older adults more effectively.

Whatever the emerging policy consensus, the provision of geriatric mental health services will be a function of that policy context, along with the characteristics of the older adults of the future and the evolving understanding of aging and mental health. This book provides a foundation for treatment today and the unfolding of treatment options in the future.

References

Abrams, R. C., & Horowitz, S. V. (1996). Personality disorders after age 50: A meta-analysis. *Journal of Personality Disorders, 10,* 271–281.

Agency for Health Care Policy and Research. (1993). *Depression guideline panel. Depression in primary care: Vol. 2. Treatment of major depression. Clinical practice guideline, Number 5.* Rockville, MD: US Department of Health and Human Services, Public Health Service, Agency for Health Care Policy and Research. AHCPR Publication No. 93-0551.

Aldwin, C. M. (1990). The Elders Life Stress Inventory: Egocentric and nonegocentric stress. In M. A. Parris Stephens, J. H. Crowther, S. E. Hobfoll, & D. L. Tennenbaum (Eds.), *Stress and coping in later-life families* (pp. 49–69). New York: Hemisphere.

Aldwin, C. M. (2007). *Stress, coping, and development: An integrative perspective* (2nd ed.). New York: Guilford.

Aldwin, C. M., Park, C. L., & Spiro, A. (Eds.). (2007). *Handbook of health psychology and aging.* New York: Guilford.

Aldwin, C. M., Yancura, L. A., & Boeninger, D. A. (2007). Coping, health, and aging. In C. M. Aldwin, C. L. Park, & A. Spiro (Eds.), *Handbook of health psychology and aging* (pp. 210–226). New York: Guilford.

Aleman, A., Kahn, R. S., & Selten, J. P. (2003). Sex differences in the risk of schizophrenia: Evidence from meta-analysis. *Archives of General Psychiatry, 60,* 565–571.

Alexopoulos, G. S., Meyers, B. S., Young, R. C., Campbell, S., Silbersweig, D., & Charlson, M. (1997). The "vascular depression" hypothesis. *Archives of General Psychiatry, 54,* 915–922.

Alexopoulos, G. S., Raue, P. J., Kanellopoulos, D., Mackin, S., & Areán, P. A. (2008). Problem solving therapy for the depression-executive dysfunction syndrome of late life. *International Journal of Geriatric Psychiatry, 23,* 782–788.

Allen-Burge, R., Stevens, A. B., & Burgio, L. D. (1999). Effective behavioral interventions for decreasing dementia-related challenging behavior in nursing homes. *International Journal of Geriatric Psychiatry, 14,* 213–232.

Almeida, O. P., Förstl, H., Howard, R., & David, A. S. (1993). Unilateral auditory hallucinations. *British Journal of Psychiatry, 162,* 262–264.

Almeida, O. P., Howard, R. J., Levy, R., & David, A. (1995). Psychotic states arising in late life (late paraphrenia): The role of risk factors. *British Journal of Psychiatry, 166,* 215–228.

Alzheimer's Association. (2009a, May). Alzheimer's disease facts and figures. *Alzheimer's and Dementia: The Journal of the Alzheimer's Association, 5,* 234–270.

Alzheimer's Association. (2009b). *2009 Alzheimer's disease facts and figures*. Retrieved October 28, 2009, from http://www.alz.org/national/documents/report_alzfactsfigures2009.pdf.

American Association of Suicidology. (2008). *Elderly suicide fact sheet*. Washington, DC: American Association of Suicidology. Retrieved from http://www.suicidology.org/c/document_library/get_file?folderId=232&name=DLFE-158.pdf.

American Bar Association Commission on Law & Aging and American Psychological Association. (2008). *Assessment of older adults with diminished capacity: A handbook for psychologists*. Washington, DC: American Bar Association and American Psychological Association.

American Geriatrics Society & American Association for Geriatric Psychiatry. (2003). Consensus statement on improving the quality of mental health care in US nursing homes: Management of depression and behavioral symptoms associated with dementia. *Journal of the American Geriatrics Society, 51*, 1287–1298.

American Psychiatric Association. (2000). *Diagnostic and statistical manual of mental disorders* (4th ed., text revision). Washington, DC: Author.

American Psychological Association. (2003, July). *Mental health care and older adults: Facts and policy recommendations*. Washington, DC: Author. Retrieved from http://www.apa.org/ppo/issues/oldermhfact03.html.

American Psychological Association, Presidential Task Force on the Assessment of Age-Consistent Memory Decline and Dementia. (1998). *Guidelines for the evaluation of dementia and age-related cognitive decline*. Washington, DC: American Psychological Association.

Amirkhanyan, A. (2008). Privatizing public nursing homes: Examining the effects on quality and access. *Public Administration Review, 68*(4), 665–680.

Ancoli-Israel, S., & Ayalon, L. (2006). Diagnosis and treatment of sleep disorders in older adults. *American Journal of Geriatric Psychiatry, 14*, 95–103.

Ancoli-Israel, S., Kripke, D. F., Klauber, M. R. et al. (1991). Sleep-disordered breathing in community-dwelling elderly. *Sleep, 14*, 486–495.

Anderson, S. A., Russell, C. S., & Schumm, W. A. (1983). Perceived marital quality and family life-cycle categories: A further analysis. *Journal of Marriage and the Family, 45*, 127–139.

Anderson, V. C., Litvack, Z. N., & Kaye, J. A. (2005). Magnetic resonance approaches to brain aging and Alzheimer disease-associated neuropathology. *Topics in Magnetic Resonance Imaging, 16*, 439–452.

Andrews, A. O., Bartels, S. J., Xie, H., & Peacock, W. J. (2009). Increased risk of nursing home admission among middle-aged and older adults with schizophrenia. *American Journal of Geriatric Psychiatry, 17*, 697–705.

Aneshensel, C. S., Pearlin, L. I., Mullan, J. T., Zarit, S. H., & Whitlatch, C. J. (1995). *Profiles in caregiving: The unexpected career*. San Diego, CA: Academic Press.

Annon, J. F. (1974). *The behavioral treatment of sexual problems*. Honolulu, HI: Enabling Systems, Inc.

Antonucci, T. C., & Akiyama, H. (1995). Convoys of social relations: Family and friendships within the lifespan context. In R. Blieszner & V. H. Bedford (Eds.), *Handbook on aging and the family* (pp. 355–371). Westport, CT: Greenwood Press.

APA Task Force on Integrated Health Care. (2007). *Blueprint for change: Achieving integrated health care for an aging population*. Washington, DC: American Psychological Association.

APA Working Group on the Older Adult. (1998). What practitioners should know about working with older adults. *Professional Psychology: Research and Practice, 29*, 413–427.

Araujo, A. B., Mohr, B. A., & McKinlay, J. B. (2004). Changes in sexual function in middle-aged and older men: Longitudinal data from the Massachusetts Male Aging Study. *Journal of the American Geriatrics Society, 52*, 1502–1509.

Areán, P. A., Hegel, M., Vannoy, S., Fan, M. Y., & Unuzter, J. (2008). Effectiveness of problem-solving therapy for older, primary care patients with depression: Results from the IMPACT project. *The Gerontologist, 48*, 311–323.

Areán, P. A., Perri, M. G., Nezu, A. M., Schein, R. L., Christopher, F., & Joseph, T. X. (1993). Comparative effectiveness of social problem-solving therapy and reminiscence therapy as treatments for depression in older adults. *Journal of Consulting and Clinical Psychology, 61*, 1003–1010.

Atkinson, R. M., Ganzini, L., & Bernstein, M. J. (1992). Alcohol and substance-use disorders in the elderly. In J. E. Birren, R. B. Sloane, & G. D. Cohen (Eds.), *Handbook of mental health and aging* (2nd ed., pp. 515–555). San Diego, CA: Academic Press.

Atkinson, R. M., Tolson, R. L., & Turner, J. A. (1993). Factors affecting outpatient treatment compliance of older male problem drinkers. *Journal of Studies on Alcohol, 54*, 102–106.

Avorn, J., Soumerai, S. B., Everitt, D. E., & Ross, D. D. (1992). A randomized trial of a program to reduce the use of psychoactive drugs in nursing homes. *New England Journal of Medicine, 327*, 168–173.

Ayers, C. R., Sorrell, J. T., Thorp, S. R., & Wetherell, J. L. (2007). Evidence-based psychological treatments for late-life anxiety. *Psychology and Aging, 22*(1), 8–17.

Bailes, S., Baltzan, M., Alapin, I., Fichten, C. S., & Libman, E. (2005). Diagnostic indicators of sleep apnea in older women and men: A prospective study. *Journal of Psychosomatic Research, 59*, 365–373.

Baillargeon, J. G., Paar, D. P., Wu, H., Giordano, T. P., Murray, O., Raimer, B. G., Avery, E. N., Diamond, P. M., & Pulvino, J. S. (2008). Psychiatric disorders, HIV infection and HIV/hepatitis co-infection in the correctional setting. *AIDS Care, 20*(1), 124–129.

Bain, K. T. (2006). Management of chronic insomnia in elderly persons. *American Journal of Geriatric Pharmacotherapy, 4*, 168–192.

Balsis, S., Gleason, M. E. J., Woods, C. M., & Oltmanns, T. F. (2007). An item response theory analysis of DSM-IV personality disorder criteria across younger and older age groups. *Psychology and Aging, 22*, 171–185.

Balsis, S., Segal, D. L., & Donahue, C. (2009). Revising the personality disorder diagnostic criteria for the *Diagnostic and Statistical Manual of Mental Disorders-Fifth Edition (DSM-V)*: Consider the later life context. *American Journal of Orthopsychiatry, 79*, 452–460.

Baltes, M. (1988). The etiology and maintenance of dependency in the elderly: Three phases of operant research. *Behavior Therapy, 19*, 301–320.

Baltes, M. M., & Wahl, H. W. (1996). Patterns of communication in old age: The dependence-support and independence-ignore script. *Health Communication, 8*, 217–231.

Baltes, P. B. (1987). Theoretical propositions of life-span developmental psychology: On the dynamics between growth and decline. *Developmental Psychology, 23*, 611–626.

Baltes, P. B., & Baltes, M. M. (1990a). Selective optimization with compensation. In P. B. Baltes & M. M. Baltes (Eds.), *Successful aging: Perspectives from the behavioral sciences* (pp. 1–34). New York: Cambridge University Press.

Baltes, P. B., & Baltes, M. M. (Eds.). (1990b). *Successful aging: Perspectives from the behavioral sciences.* Cambridge: Cambridge University Press.

Bandura, A. (1977). Self-efficacy: Toward a unifying theory of behavioral change. *Psychological Review, 84*, 191–215.

Barlow, D. H., Nock, M. K., & Hersen, M. (2008). *Single-case experimental designs: Strategies for studying behavior change* (3rd ed.). Boston: Allyn & Bacon.

Bartels, S. J. (1989). Organic mental disorder: When to suspect medical illness as a cause of psychiatric symptoms. In J. M. Ellison (Ed.), *Psychopharmacology: A primer for the psychotherapist.* Chicago: Year Book Medical Publishers.

Bartels, S. J. (2004). Caring for the whole person: Integrated health care for older adults with severe mental illness and medical comorbidity. *Journal of the American Geriatrics Society, 52,* S249–S257.

Bartels, S. J., & Drake, R. E. (1988). Depressive symptoms in schizophrenia: Comprehensive differential diagnosis. *Comprehensive Psychiatry, 29,* 467–483.

Bartels, S. J., & Drake, R. E. (1989). Depression in schizophrenia: Current guidelines to treatment. *Psychiatric Quarterly, 60,* 333–345.

Bartels, S. J., & Mueser, K. T. (2008). Psychosocial rehabilitation for older adults with serious mental illness: Introduction to special series. *American Journal of Psychiatric Rehabilitation, 11*(1), 1–6.

Bartels, S. J., & Pratt, S. I. (2009). Psychosocial rehabilitation and quality of life for older adults with serious mental illness: Recent findings and future research directions. *Current Opinion in Psychiatry, 22,* 381–385.

Bartels, S. J., & Van Citters, A. D. (2005). Community-based alternatives for older adults with serious mental illness: The Olmstead decision and deinstitutionalization of nursing homes. *Ethics, Law, and Aging Review, 11,* 3–22.

Bartels, S. J., Clark, R. E., Peacock, W. J., Dums, A. R., & Pratt S. I. (2003). Medicare and Medicaid costs for schizophrenia patients by age cohort compared with depression, dementia, and medically ill patients. *American Journal of Geriatric Psychiatry, 11,* 648–657.

Bartels, S. J., Forester, B., Mueser, K. T., Miles, K. M., Dums, A. R., Pratt, S. I., Littlefield, C., O'Hurley, S., White, P., & Perkins, L. (2004). Enhanced skills training and health care management for older persons with severe mental illness. *Community Mental Health Journal, 40*(1), 75–90.

Bartels, S. J., Miles, K. M., Dums, A. R., & Levine, K. J. (2003). Are nursing homes appropriate for older adults with severe mental illness? Conflicting consumer and clinician views and implications for the Olmstead decision. *Journal of the American Geriatrics Society, 51,* 1571–1579.

Bartels, S. J., Mueser, K. T., & Miles, K. M. (1997a). Functional impairments in elderly with schizophrenia and major affective disorder living in the community: Social skills, living skills, and behavior problems. *Behavior Therapy, 28,* 43–63.

Bartels, S. J., Mueser, K. T., & Miles, K. M. (1997b). A comparative study of elderly patients with schizophrenia and bipolar disorder in nursing homes and the community. *Schizophrenia Research, 27*(2–3), 181–190.

Bartels, S. J., Teague, G. B., Drake, R. E., Clark, R. E., Bush, P., & Noordsy, D. L. (1993). Service utilization and costs associated with substance abuse among rural schizophrenic patients. *Journal of Nervous and Mental Disease, 181,* 227–232.

Beaudreau, S. A., & O'Hara, R. (2008). Late-life anxiety and cognitive impairment: A review. *American Journal of Geriatric Psychiatry, 16,* 790–803.

Beck, A. T., Emery, G., & Greenberg, R. L. (1985). *Anxiety disorders and phobias: A cognitive perspective.* New York: Basic Books.

Beck, A. T., Epstein, N., Brown, G., & Steer, R. (1988). An inventory for measuring clinical anxiety: Psychometric properties. *Journal of Consulting and Clinical Psychology, 56,* 893–897.

Beck, A. T., Freeman, A., Davis, D. D., & Associates. (2003). *Cognitive therapy of personality disorders* (2nd ed.). New York: Guilford.

Beck, A. T., Kovacs, M., & Weissman, A. (1979). Assessment of suicidal ideation: The Scale for Suicidal Ideation. *Journal of Consulting and Clinical Psychology, 47,* 343–352.

Beck, A. T., Rush, A. J., Shaw, B. F., & Emery, G. (1979). *Cognitive therapy of depression.* New York: Guilford.

Beck, A. T., Steer, R. A., & Brown, G. K. (1996). *Manual for the Beck Depression Inventory-II.* San Antonio, TX: Psychological Corporation.

Bedford, V. H. (1995). Siblings in middle and later adulthood. In R. Blieszner & V. H. Bedford (Eds.), *Handbook on aging and the family* (pp. 201–222). Westport, CT: Greenwood Press.

Beekman, A. T. F., de Beurs, E., van Balkom, A. J. L. M., Deeg, D. J. H., Van Dyck, R., & Van Tilburg, W. (2000). Anxiety and depression in later life: Co-occurrence and communality of risk factors. *American Journal of Psychiatry, 157,* 89–95.

Bellack, A. S., & Mueser, K. T. (1993). Psychosocial treatment of schizophrenia. *Schizophrenia Bulletin, 19,* 317–336.

Bellack, A. S., Morrison, R. L., Wixted, J. T., & Mueser, K. T. (1990). An analysis of social competence in schizophrenia. *British Journal of Psychiatry, 156,* 809–818.

Belle, S. H., Burgio, L., Burns, R., Coon, D., Czaja, S. J., Gallagher-Thompson, D. et al. (2006). Enhancing the quality of life of dementia caregivers from different ethnic or racial groups: A randomized, controlled trial. *Annals of Internal Medicine, 145,* 727–738.

Bengtson, V. L., & Kuypers, J. A. (1984). The family support cycle: Psychosocial issues in the aging family. In J. M. A. Munnichs, P. Mussen, E. Olbrich, & P. G. Coleman (Eds.), *Life-span and change in a gerontological perspective* (pp. 257–273). Orlando, FL: Academic Press.

Bengtson, V. L., Rosenthal, C., & Burton, L. (1995). Paradoxes of families and aging. In R. H. Binstock & L. K. George (Eds.), *Handbook of aging and the social sciences* (4th ed., pp. 253–282). San Diego, CA: Academic Press.

Benloucif, S., Orbeta, L., Ortiz, R., Janssen, I., Finkel, S. I., Bleiberg, J., & Zee, P. C. (2004). Morning or evening activity improves neuropsychological performance and subjective sleep quality in older adults. *Sleep, 27,* 1542–1551.

Berezin, M. A. (1972). Psychodynamic considerations of aging and the aged: An overview. *American Journal of Psychiatry, 128,* 1483–1491.

Bertram, L., McQueen, M. B., Mullin, K., Blacker, D., & Tanzi, R. E. (2007). Systematic meta-analyses of Alzheimer disease genetic association studies: The AlzGene database. *Nature Genetics, 39,* 17–23.

Bettocchi, C., Palumbo, F., Spilotros, M., Lucarelli, G., Palazzo, S., Battaglia, M., Selvaggi, F. P., & Ditonno, P. (2010). Patient and partner satisfaction after AMS inflatable penile prosthesis implant. *Journal of Sexual Medicine, 7,* 304–309.

Bierman, E. J. M., Comijs, H. C., Jonker, C., & Beekman, A. T. F. (2005). Effects of anxiety versus depression on cognition in later life. *American Journal of Geriatric Psychiatry, 13,* 686–693.

Binder, E. F., & Robbins, L. N. (1990). Cognitive impairment and length of hospital stay in older persons. *Journal of American Geriatrics Society, 38,* 759–776.

Birren, J. E., & Renner, V. J. (1980). Concepts and issues of mental health and aging. In J. E. Birren & R. B. Sloane (Eds.), *Handbook of mental health and of aging* (pp. 3–33). Englewood Cliffs, NJ: Prentice-Hall.

Blazer, D. G. (2003). Depression in later life: Review and commentary. *Journals of Gerontology: Series A: Biological Sciences and Medical Sciences, 58,* 249–265.

Blazer, D. G., Woodbury, M., Hughes, D. C., George, L. K., Manton, K. G. et al. (1989). A statistical analysis of the classification of depression in a mixed community and clinical sample. *Journal of Affective Disorders, 16,* 11–20.

Blechman, E. A. (2009). Personal health records for older adults with chronic conditions and their informal caregivers. In S. H. Qualls & S. H. Zarit (Eds.), *Aging families and caregiving* (pp. 287–310). Hoboken, NJ: John Wiley & Sons, Inc.

Blieszner, R. (2009). Who are the aging families. In S. H. Qualls & S. H. Zarit (Eds.), *Aging families and caregiving* (pp. 1–18). Hoboken, NJ: John Wiley & Sons.

Blieszner, R., Roberto, K., Wilcox, K., Barham, E., & Winston, B. (2007). Dimensions of ambiguous loss in couples coping with mild cognitive impairment. *Family Relations, 56,* 196–209.

Blow, F. C., Brower, K. J., Schulenberg, J. E., Demo-Dananberg, L. M., Young, J. P., & Beresford, T. P. (1992). The Michigan Alcoholism Screening Test – Geriatric Version (MAST-G): A new elderly-specific screening instrument. *Alcoholism, 16,* 372.

Blow, F. C., Walton, M. A., Chermack, S. T., Mudd, S. A., & Brower, K. J. (2000). Older adult treatment outcome following elder-specific inpatient alcoholism treatment. *Journal of Substance Abuse Treatment, 19,* 67–75.

Bohlmeijer, E., Roemer, M., Cuijpers, P., & Smit, F. (2007). The effects of reminiscence on psychological well-being in older adults: A meta-analysis. *Aging and Mental Health, 11,* 291–300.

Bonanno, G. A. (2004). Loss, trauma, and human resilience: Have we underestimated the human capacity to thrive after extremely adverse events? *American Psychologist, 59,* 20–28.

Bonanno, G. A. (2009). *The other side of sadness: What the new science of bereavement tells us about life after loss.* New York: Basic Books.

Borkovec, T. D., Alcaine, O., & Behar, E. (2004). Avoidance theory of worry and generalized anxiety disorder. In R. G. Turk, C. L. Turk, & D. S. Mennin (Eds.), *Generalized anxiety disorder* (pp. 77–108). New York: Guilford.

Boszormenyi-Nagy, I., & Spark, G. M. (1984). *Invisible loyalties.* New York: Brunner/Mazel.

Bowen, M. (1978). *Family therapy in clinical practice.* New York: J. Aronson.

Bowlby, J. (1969). *Attachment and loss. Vol. 1: Attachment.* New York: Basic Books.

Brault, M. W. (2008). *Americans with disabilities: 2005, Current Population Reports, P70–117.* Washington, DC: US Census Bureau.

Brenes, G. A., Guralnik, J. A., Williamson, J. D., Friend, L. P., Simpson, C., Simonsick, E. M., & Penninx, B. W. J. H. (2005). The influence of anxiety on progression of disability. *Journal of the American Geriatrics Society, 53,* 34–39.

Brink, T. L. (1979). *Geriatric psychotherapy.* New York: Human Sciences Press.

Brouwers, N., Sleegers, K., & Van Broeckhoven, C. (2008). Molecular genetics of Alzheimer's disease: An update. *Annals of Medicine, 40*(8), 1–22.

Brown, S., Inskip, H., & Barraclough, B. (2000). Causes of the excess mortality of schizophrenia. *British Journal of Psychiatry, 177,* 212–217.

Buracchio, T., & Kaye, J. (2009). Early diagnosis of Alzheimer's disease and mild cognitive impairment: Imaging, biomarkers, and technology. *Generations, 33*(1), 18–23.

Burgio, L. D., Burgio, K. L., Engel, B. T., & Tice, L. M. (1986). Increasing distance and independence of ambulation in elderly nursing home residents. *Journal of Applied Behavior Analysis, 19,* 357–366.

Burgio, L. D., Stevens, A., Burgio, K., Roth, D., Paul, P., & Gerstle, J. (2002). Teaching and maintaining behavior management in the nursing home. *The Gerontologist, 42,* 487–496.

Burns, D. D. (1999). *Feeling good: The new mood therapy.* New York: HarperCollins.

Burns, D. D., Shaw, B. F., & Crocker, W. (1987). Thinking styles and coping strategies of depressed women: An empirical investigation. *Behavioral Research and Therapy, 25,* 223–225.

Butler, R. (1974). Successful aging and the role of life review. *Journal of the American Geriatric Society, 22,* 529–535.

Butler, R. N., Lewis, M., & Sunderland, T. (1991). *Aging and mental health: Positive psychosocial and biomedical approaches.* New York: Merrill.

Butler, R. N., Lewis, M., & Sunderland, T. (1998). *Aging and mental health: Positive psychosocial and biomedical approaches* (5th ed.). Boston: Allyn & Bacon.

Caine, E., Lyness, J., & Conwell, Y. (1996). Diagnosis of late-life depression: Preliminary studies in primary care settings. *American Journal of Geriatric Psychiatry, 4*, 45–50.

Cairney, J., McCabe, L., Veldhuizen, S., Corna, L. M., Streiner, D., & Herrmann, N. (2007). Epidemiology of social phobia in later life. *American Journal of Geriatric Psychiatry, 15*, 224–233.

Camp, C. (2006). Spaced retrieval: A model for dissemination of a cognitive intervention for persons with dementia. In D. K. Attix & K. A. Welsh-Bohmer (Eds.), *Geriatric neuropsychology: Assessment and intervention* (pp. 275–292). New York: Guilford.

Campbell, S. S., Murphy, P., & Stauble, T. N. (2005). Effects of a nap on nighttime sleep and waking function in older subjects. *Journal of the American Geriatrics Society, 53*, 48–53.

Caplan, G. (1970). *The theory and practice of mental health consultation*. New York: Basic Books.

Carpenter, W. T., & Buchanan, R. W. (2008). Lessons to take home from CATIE. *Psychiatric Services, 59*, 523–525.

Carr, V. (1988). Patients' techniques for coping with schizophrenia: An exploratory study. *British Journal of Medical Psychology, 61*, 339–352.

Carstensen, L. L. (1992). Social and emotional patterns in adulthood: Support for socioemotional selectivity theory. *Psychology and Aging, 7*, 331–338.

Carstensen, L. L., & Fisher, J. E. (1991). Problems of the elderly in nursing homes. In P. Wisocki (Ed.), *Handbook of clinical behavior therapy with the elderly client* (pp. 337–362). New York: Plenum.

Carstensen, L. L., Fung, H., & Charles, S. (2003) Socioemotional selectivity theory and the regulation of emotion in the second half of life. *Motivation and Emotion, 27*, 103–123.

Carstensen, L. L., Isaacowitz, D. M., & Charles, S. T. (1999). Taking time seriously: A theory of socioemotional selectivity. *American Psychologist, 54*, 165–181.

Carter, E., & McGoldrick, M. (1988). *The changing family life cycle: A framework for family therapy* (2nd ed.). New York: Gardner Press.

Carver, C. S. (1997). You want to measure coping but your protocol's too long: Consider the Brief COPE. *International Journal of Behavioral Medicine, 4*, 92–100.

Carver, C. S., Scheier, M. F., & Weintraub, J. K. (1989). Assessing coping strategies: A theoretically based approach. *Journal of Personality and Social Psychology, 56*, 267–283.

Castle, D. J., & Murray, R. M. (1993). The epidemiology of late-onset schizophrenia. *Schizophrenia Bulletin, 19*, 691–700.

Centers for Disease Control and Prevention (CDC). (2007). *Behavioral risk factor surveillance system survey data*. Atlanta, GA: US Department of Health and Human Services, Centers for Disease Control and Prevention.

Centers for Disease Control and Prevention (CDC). Web-Based Injury Statistics Query and Reporting System (WISQARS) [Online]. (2005). National Center for Injury Prevention and Control, CDC. Retrieved April 27, 2009, from http://www.cdc.gov/injury/wisqars/.

Centers for Disease Control and Prevention & Alzheimer's Association. (2007). *The healthy brain initiative: A national public health road map to maintaining cognitive health.* Chicago: Alzheimer's Association.

Centers for Disease Control and Prevention & The Merck Company Foundation. (2007). *The state of aging and health in America 2007.* Whitehouse Station, NJ: The Merck Company Foundation. Retrieved from http://www.cdc.gov/aging/pdf/saha_2007.pdf.

Centers for Disease Control and Prevention & the National Association of Chronic Disease Directors. (2008). *The state of mental health and aging in America issue brief 1: What do the data tell us?* Atlanta, GA: National Association of Chronic Disease Directors. Retrieved from http://www.cdc.gov/aging/pdf/mental_health.pdf.

Centers for Medicare and Medicaid Services (CMS). (2010). *Medicare and you, 2010.* Baltimore: US Department of Health and Human Services.

Charney, D. S., Reynolds, C. F. III, Lewis, L., Lebowitz, B. D., Sunderland, T., Alexopoulos, G. S., Blazer, D. G., Katz, I. R., Meyers, B. S., Areán, P. A., Borson, S., Brown, C., Bruce, M. L., Callahan, C. M., Charlson, M. E., Conwell, Y., Cuthbert, B. N., Devanand, D. P., Gibson, M. J., Gottlieb, G. L., Krishnan, K. R., Laden, S. K., Lyketsos, C. G., Mulsant, B. H., Niederehe, G., Olin, J. T., Oslin, D. W., Pearson, J., Persky, T., Pollock, B. G., Raetzman, S., Reynolds, M., Salzman, C., Schulz, R., Schwenk, T. L., Scolnick, E., Unützer, J., Weissman, M. M., & Young, R. C. (2003). Depression and Bipolar Support Alliance consensus statement on the unmet needs in diagnosis and treatment of mood disorders in late life. *Archives of General Psychiatry, 60,* 664–672.

Ciompi, L. (1980). The natural history of schizophrenia in the long term. *British Journal of Psychiatry, 136,* 413–420.

Clark, L. A. (2009). Stability and change in personality disorder. *Current Directions in Psychological Science, 18,* 27–31.

Clotfelter, C. T. (2004). *After Brown: The rise and retreat of school desegregation.* Princeton, NJ: Princeton University Press.

Cohen, C. I. (2000). Practical geriatrics: Directions for research and policy on schizophrenia and older adults: Summary of the GAP committee report. *Psychiatric Services, 51,* 299–302.

Cohen, C. I., Magai, C., Yaffee, R., Huangthaison, P., & Walcott-Brown, L. (2006a). The prevalence of phobia and its associated factors in a multiracial aging urban population. *American Journal of Geriatric Psychiatry, 14,* 507–514.

Cohen, C. I., Magai, C., Yaffee, R., Huangthaison, P., & Walcott-Brown, L. (2006b). The prevalence of anxiety and associated factors in a multiracial sample of older adults. *Psychiatric Services, 57,* 1719–1725.

Cohen, G. D. (1992). The future of mental health and aging. In J. E. Birren, R. B. Sloane, & G. D. Cohen (Eds.), *Handbook of mental health and aging* (2nd ed., pp. 893–914). San Diego, CA: Academic Press.

Cohen, S., Kamarck, T., & Mermelstein, R. (1983). A global measure of perceived stress. *Journal of Health and Social Behavior, 24,* 385–396.

Cohen-Mansfield, J., & Jensen, B. (2008). Nursing home physicians' knowledge of and attitudes toward nonpharmacological interventions for treatment of behavioral disturbances associated with dementia. *Journal of American Medical Directors Association, 9,* 491–498.

Cohen-Mansfield, J., & Libin, A. (2004). Assessment of agitation in elderly patients with dementia: Correlations between informant rating and direct observation. *International Journal of Geriatric Psychiatry, 19,* 881–891.

Cohler, B. J. (1993). Aging, morale, and meaning: The nexus of narrative. In T. R. Cole, W. A. Achenbaum, P. L. Jakobi, & R. Kastenbaum (Eds.), *Voices and visions of aging: Toward a critical gerontology* (pp. 107–133). New York: Springer.

Cohler, B. J., & Hostetler, A. J. (2003). Linking life course and life story: Social change and the narrative study of lives. In J. Mortimer & R. Shanahan (Eds.), *Handbook of the life course* (pp. 555–578). New York: Kluwer Academic/Plenum.

Cohn, M. D., & Smyer, M. A. (1988). Mental health consultation: Process, professions, and models. In M. A. Smyer, M. D. Cohn, & D. Brannon (Eds.), *Mental health consultation in nursing homes* (pp. 46–63). New York: New York University Press.

Cohn, M. D., Smyer, M. A., & Horgas, A. L. (1994). *The ABCs of behavior change: Skills for working with behavior problems in nursing homes.* State College, PA: Venture Publishing.

Colarusso, C. A., & Nemiroff, R. A. (1979). Some observations and hypotheses about the psychoanalytic theory of adult development. *International Journal of Psycho-Analysis, 60*, 59–71.

Cole, C. L. (1986). Developmental tasks affecting the marital relationship in later life. *American Behavioral Scientist, 29*, 389–403.

Colton, C. W., & Manderscheid, R. W. (2006). Congruencies in increased mortality rates, years of potential life lost, and causes of death among public mental health clients in eight states. *Preventing Chronic Disease, 3*, 1–14.

Conwell, Y. (1994). Suicide in elderly patients. In L. S. Schneider, C. F. Reynolds, B. D. Lebowitz, & A. J. Friedhoff (Eds.), *Diagnosis and treatment of depression in late life: Results of the NIH consensus development conference* (pp. 397–418). Washington, DC: American Psychiatric Press.

Coolidge, F. L., & Segal, D. L. (1998). Evolution of the personality disorder diagnosis in the *Diagnostic and Statistical Manual of Mental Disorders. Clinical Psychology Review, 18*, 585–599.

Coolidge, F. L., Segal, D. L., Hook, J. N., & Stewart, S. (2000). Personality disorders and coping among anxious older adults. *Journal of Anxiety Disorders, 14*, 157–172.

Coolidge, F. L., Segal, D. L., Pointer, J. C., Knaus, E. A., Yamazaki, T. G., & Silberman, C. S. (2000). Personality disorders in older adult inpatients with chronic mental illness. *Journal of Clinical Geropsychology, 6*, 63–72.

Coolidge, F. L., Thede, L. L., & Jang, K. L. (2001). Heritability of personality disorders in childhood: A preliminary investigation. *Journal of Personality Disorders, 15*, 33–40.

Coon, D. W., Gallagher-Thompson, D., & Thompson, L. W. (2003). *Innovative approaches to reduce dementia caregiver distress: A clinical guide.* New York: Springer.

Costa, P. T., & McCrae, R. R. (1994). Depression as an enduring disposition. In L. S. Schneider, C. F. Reynolds, B. D. Lebowitz, & A. J. Friedhoff (Eds.), *Diagnosis and treatment of depression in late life: Results of the NIH consensus development conference* (pp. 155–167). Washington, DC: American Psychiatric Press.

Council on Scientific Affairs, American Medical Association. (1996). Alcoholism in the elderly. *Journal of the American Medical Association, 275*, 797–801.

Crowther, M., & Austin, A. (2009). The cultural context of clinical work with aging caregivers. In S. H. Qualls & S. H. Zarit (Eds.), *Aging families and caregiving* (pp. 45–60). Hoboken, NJ: John Wiley & Sons, Inc.

Crowther, M. R., & Zeiss, A. M. (1999). Cognitive-behavior therapy in older adults: A case involving sexual functioning. *In Session: Psychotherapy in Practice, 55*, 961–975.

Cuijpers, P., van Straten, A., Andersson, G., & van Oppen, P. (2008). Psychotherapy for depression in adults: A meta-analysis of comparative outcomes studies. *Journal of Consulting and Clinical Psychology, 76*, 909–922.

Cutler, L. (2007). Physical environments of assisted living: Research needs and challenges. *The Gerontologist, 47*, 68–82.

Dale, W., Hougham, G. W., Hill, E. K., & Sachs, G. A. (2006). High interest in screening and treatment for mild cognitive impairment in older adults: A pilot study. *Journal of American Geriatrics Society, 54*, 1388–1394.

Daruna, J. H. (2004). *Introduction to psychoneuroimmunology.* San Diego, CA: Elsevier Academic Press.

David-Ferdon, C., & Kaslow, N. (2008). Evidence-based psychosocial treatments for child and adolescent depression. *Journal of Clinical Child and Adolescent Psychology, 37*, 162–104.

Davidson, M., Harvey, P. D., Powchick, P., Parrella, M., White, L., Knobler, H. Y., Losonczy, M. F., Keefe, R. S., Katz, S., & Frecska, E. (1995). Severity of symptoms in chronically institutionalized geriatric schizophrenic patients. *American Journal of Psychiatry, 152,* 197–207.

Davies, H. D., Zeiss, A. M., Shea, E. A., & Tinklenberg, J. R. (1998). Sexuality and intimacy in Alzheimer's patients and their partners. *Sexuality and Disability, 16,* 193–203.

Davis, M. C., Zautra, A. J., Johnson, L. M., Murray, K. E., & Okvat, H. A. (2007). Psychosocial stress, emotion regulation, and resilience among older adults. In C. M. Aldwin, C. L. Park, & A. Spiro (Eds.), *Handbook of health psychology and aging* (pp. 250–266). New York: Guilford.

Day, K. L., McGuire, L. C., & Anderson, L. A. (2009). The CDC Healthy Brain Initiative: Public health and cognitive impairment. *Generations, 33*(1), 11–17.

Deacon, B., Lickel, J., & Abramowitz, J. S. (2008). Medical utilization across the anxiety disorders. *Journal of Anxiety Disorders, 22,* 344–350.

DeLamater, J. D., & Sill, M. (2005). Sexual desire in later life. *Journal of Sex Research, 42,* 138–149.

Dew, M. A., Hoch, C. C., Buysse, D. J., Monk, T. H., Begley, A. E., Housck, P. R., Hall, M., Kupfer, D. J., & Reynolds, C. F. (2003). Healthy older adults' sleep predicts all-cause mortality at 4 to 19 years of follow-up. *Psychosomatic Medicine, 65,* 63–72.

Dick, D. M., & Bierut, L. J. (2006). The genetics of alcohol dependence. *Current Psychiatry Reports, 8,* 151–157.

Diehl, M., Coyle, N., & Labouvie-Vief, G. (1996). Age and sex differences in strategies of coping and defense across the life span. *Psychology and Aging, 11,* 127–139.

DiNardo, P. A., Brown, T. A., & Barlow, D. H. (1994). *Anxiety Disorders Interview Schedule for DSM-IV: Lifetime Version (ADIS-IV-L).* San Antonio, TX: Psychological Corporation/ Graywind Publications Incorporated.

Dobson, K. S., & Dozois, D. J. A. (2001). Historical and philosophical bases of the cognitive-behavioral therapies. In K. S. Dobson (Ed.), *Handbook of cognitive-behavioral therapies* (2nd ed., pp. 3–39). New York: Guilford.

Dozois, D. J. A., Frewen, P. A., & Covin, R. (2006). Cognitive theories. In J. C. Thomas & D. L. Segal (Eds.), Personality and everyday functioning. Vol. *1* in M. Hersen & J. C. Thomas (Eds.-in-Chief), *Comprehensive handbook of personality and psychopathology* (pp. 173–191). Hoboken, NJ: John Wiley & Sons, Inc.

Drake, R. E., Osher, F. C., & Wallach, M. A. (1989). Alcohol use and abuse in schizophrenia: A prospective community study. *Journal of Nervous and Mental Disease, 177,* 408–414.

Drake, R. E., Wallach, M. A., & Hoffman, J. S. (1989). Housing instability and homelessness among aftercare patients of an urban state hospital. *Hospital and Community Psychiatry, 40*(1), 46–51.

Druss, B. G., Marcus, S. C., Campbell, J., Cuffel, B., Harnett, J., Ingoglia, C., & Mauer, B. (2008). Medical services for clients in community mental health centers: Results from a national survey. *Psychiatric Services, 59,* 917–920.

Duberstein, P. R., Conwell, Y., Conner, K. R., Eberly, S., & Caine, E. D. (2004). Suicide at 50 years and older: Perceived physical illness, family discord and financial strain. *Psychological Medicine, 34,* 137–146.

Dunn, K. M., Croft, P. R., & Hackett, G. I. (1999). Association of sexual problems with social, psychological, and physical problems in men and women: A cross-sectional population survey. *Journal of Epidemiology and Community Health, 53,* 144–148.

Dupree, L. W., & Schonfeld, L. (1996). Substance abuse. In M. Hersen & V. B. Van Hasselt (Eds.), *Psychological treatment of older adults* (pp. 281–297). New York: Plenum.

Dupree, L. W., Broskowski, H., & Schonfeld, L. (1984). The Gerontology Alcohol Project: A behavioral treatment program for elderly alcohol abusers. *The Gerontologist, 24,* 510–516.

Dworkin, R. H. (1994). Pain insensitivity in schizophrenia: A neglected phenomenon and some implications. *Schizophrenia Bulletin, 20*, 235–248.

D'Zurilla, T. J., & Nezu, A. M. (2007). *Problem-solving therapy: A positive approach to clinical intervention* (3rd ed.). New York: Springer.

Edelstein, B. A., Woodhead, E. L., Segal, D. L., Heisel, M. J., Bower, E. H., Lowery, A. J., & Stoner, S. A. (2008). Older adult psychological assessment: Current instrument status and related considerations. *Clinical Gerontologist, 31*(3), 1–35.

Eisdorfer, C., Czaja, S. J., Loewenstein, D. A., Rubert, M. P., Arguelles, S., Mitrani, V. B., & Szapocznik, J. (2003). The effect of a family therapy and technology-based intervention on caregiver depression. *The Gerontologist, 43*, 521–531.

Eisenberg, L. (2005). Violence and the mentally ill: Victims, not perpetrators. *Archives of General Psychiatry, 62*, 825–826.

Elder, G. H., Jr. (1974). *Children of the Great Depression: Social change and life experiences.* Chicago: University of Chicago Press.

Ellis, A. (1991). *Reason and emotion in psychotherapy.* New York: Citadel.

Ellis, A., & Dryden, W. (2007). *The practice of rational emotive behavior therapy* (2nd ed.). New York: Springer.

Elson, P. (2005). Do older adults presenting with memory complaints wish to be told if later diagnosed with Alzheimer's disease? *International Journal of Geriatric Psychiatry, 21*, 419–425.

Elwood, W. N. (Ed.). (1999). *Power in the blood: A handbook on AIDS, politics, and communication.* Mahwah, NJ: Erlbaum.

Engels, G. I., & Vermey, M. (1997). Efficacy of non-medical treatment of depression in elders: A quantitative analysis. *Journal of Clinical Geropsychology, 3*, 17–34.

Epictetus. (1955). *The enchiridion.* (G. Long, Trans.). New York: Promethean Press. (Original c.101 AD.)

Erikson, E. H. (1963). *Childhood and society* (2nd ed.). New York: Norton.

Erikson, E. H., Erikson, J. M., & Kivnick, H. Q. (1986). *Vital involvement in old age.* New York: Norton.

Fairchild, K., & Scogin, F. (2008). Assessment and treatment of depression. In K. Laidlaw & B. G. Knight (Eds.), *Handbook of emotional disorders in later life: Assessment and treatment* (pp. 213–231). New York: Oxford University Press.

Falloon, I., & Talbot, R. E. (1981). Persistent auditory hallucinations: Coping mechanisms and implications for management. *Psychological Medicine, 11*, 329–339.

Farias, S. T., Mungas, D., & Jagust, W. (2005). Degree of discrepancy between self and other-reported everyday functioning by cognitive status: Dementia, mild cognitive impairment, and healthy elders. *International Journal of Geriatric Psychiatry, 20*, 827–834.

Fazel, S., & Danesh, J. (2002). Serious mental disorder in 23,000 prisoners: A systematic review of 62 surveys. *Lancet, 359*, 545–550.

Federal Interagency Forum on Aging-Related Statistics. (2008). *Older Americans 2008: Key indicators of well-being.* Federal Interagency Forum on Aging-Related Statistics. Washington, DC: United States Government Printing Office.

Feeney, S. L. (2004). The relationship between pain and negative affect in older adults: Anxiety as a predictor of pain. *Journal of Anxiety Disorders, 18*, 733–744.

Ferri, C. P., Prince, M., Brayne, C., Brodaty, H., Fratiglioni, L., Ganguli, M. et al. (2005). Global prevalence of dementia: A Delphi consensus study. *The Lancet, 366*, 2112–2117.

Fillenbaum, G. G., van Belle, G., Morris, J. C., Mohs, R. C., Mirra, S. S., Davis, P. C., et al. (2008). Consortium to Establish a Registry for Alzheimer's Disease (CERAD): The first twenty years. *Alzheimer's and Dementia, 4*, 96–109.

Finch, C. E., & Morgan, D. (1987). Aging and schizophrenia: A hypothesis relating to asynchrony in neural aging processes to the manifestations of schizophrenia and other neurologic diseases with age. In N. E. Miller & G. Cohen (Eds.), *Schizophrenia and aging* (pp. 97–108). New York: Guilford.

Fingerhood, M. (2000). Substance abuse in older people. *Journal of the American Geriatrics Society, 48,* 985–995.

Fingerman, K. L., Miller, L. M., & Seidel, A. J. (2009). Functions families serve in old age. In S. H. Qualls & S. H. Zarit (Eds.), *Aging families and caregiving* (pp. 19–44). Hoboken, NJ: John Wiley & Sons, Inc.

First, M. B., Spitzer, R. L., Gibbon, M., & Williams, J. B. W. (2002). *Structured Clinical Interview for DSM-IV-TR Axis I Disorders, Research Version, Patient Edition (SCID-I/P).* New York: Biometrics Research, New York State Psychiatric Institute.

Fisher, J. E., & Noll, J. P. (1996). Anxiety disorders. In L. L. Carstensen, B. A. Edelstein, & L. Dornbrand (Eds.), *The practical handbook of clinical gerontology* (pp. 304–323). Thousand Oaks, CA: Sage.

Fiske, A., Wetherell, J. L., & Gatz, M. (2009). Depression in older adults. *Annual Review of Clinical Psychology, 5,* 363–389.

Flint, A. (1994). Epidemiology and comorbidity of anxiety disorders in the elderly. *American Journal of Psychiatry, 151,* 640–649.

Floyd, M., Scogin, F., McKendree-Smith, N. L., Floyd, D. L., & Rokke, P. D. (2004). Cognitive therapy for depression: A comparison of individual psychotherapy and bibliotherapy for depressed older adults. *Behavior Modification, 28,* 297–318.

Foley, D. J., Monjan, A. A., Brown, S. I. et al. (1995). Sleep complaints among elderly persons: An epidemiological study of three communities. *Sleep, 18,* 425–432.

Folkman, S., & Lazarus, R. S. (1988). *Manual for the Ways of Coping Questionnaire.* Palo Alto, CA: Consulting Psychologists Press.

Folkman, S., Lazarus, R. S., Pimley, S., & Novacek, J. (1987). Age differences in stress and coping processes. *Psychology and Aging, 2,* 171–184.

Folsom, D. P., Depp, C., Palmer, B. W., Mausbach, B. T., Golshan, S., Fellows, I., Cardenas, V., Patterson, T. L., Kraemer, H. C., & Jeste, D. V. (2009). Physical and mental health-related quality of life among older people with schizophrenia. *Schizophrenia Research, 108,* 207–213.

Folsom, D. P., McCahill, M., Bartels, S. J., Lindamer, L. A., Ganiats, T. G., & Jeste, D. V. (2002). Medical comorbidity and receipt of medical care by older homeless people with schizophrenia or depression. *Psychiatric Services, 53,* 1456–1460.

Folstein, M., Bassett, S., Romanoski, A., & Nestadt, G. (1991). The epidemiology of delirium in the community: The Eastern Baltimore Mental Health Survey. *International Psychogeriatrics, 3*(2), 169–176.

Folstein, M. F., Folstein, S. E., & McHugh, P. R. (1975). "Mini-Mental State": A practical method for grading the cognitive state of patients for the clinician. *Journal of Psychiatric Research, 12,* 189–198.

Fortinsky, R. H., Tennen, H., Frank, N., & Affleck, G. (2007). Health and psychological consequences of caregiving. In C. M. Aldwin, C. L. Park, & A. Spiro (Eds.), *Handbook of health psychology and aging* (pp. 227–249). New York: Guilford.

Foster, S. M., Cornwell, R. E., Kisley, M. A., & Davis, H. P. (2006). Cognitive changes across the lifespan. In S. H. Qualls & M. A. Smyer (Eds.), *Changes in decision-making capacity in older adults: Assessment and intervention* (pp. 25–60). Hoboken, NJ: John Wiley & Sons, Inc.

Fox, L. S., & Knight, B. G. (2005). The effects of anxiety on attentional processes in older adults. *Aging and Mental Health, 9,* 585–593.

Fry, P. S. (1986). Assessment of pessimism and despair in the elderly: A Geriatric Scale of Hopelessness. *Clinical Gerontologist, 5*, 193–201.

Futterman, A., Thompson, L. W., Gallagher-Thompson, D., & Ferris, R. (1995). Depression in later life: Epidemiology, assessment, etiology and treatment. In E. Beckham & R. Leber (Eds.), *Handbook of depression* (2nd ed., pp. 494–525). New York: Guilford.

Gabryelewicz, T., Styczynska, M., Pfeffer, A., Wasiak, B., Barczak, A., Luczywek, E., Androsiuk, W., & Barcikowska, M. (2004). Prevalence of major and minor depression in elderly persons with mild cognitive impairment – MADRS factor analysis. *International Journal of Geriatric Psychiatry, 19*, 1168–1172.

Gallagher, D., & Frankel, A. S. (1980). Depression in older adult(s): A moderate structuralist viewpoint. *Psychotherapy: Theory, Research and Practice, 17*(1), 101–104.

Gallagher, D., & Thompson, L. W. (1981). *Depression in the elderly: A behavioral treatment manual.* Los Angeles: University of Southern California Press.

Gallagher-Thompson, D., & Coon, D. W. (2007) Evidence-based psychological treatments for distress in family caregivers of older adults. *Psychology and Aging, 22*, 37–51.

Gallagher-Thompson, D., & Steffan, A. M. (1994). Comparative effects of cognitive-behavioral and brief psychodynamic psychotherapies for depressed family caregivers. *Journal of Consulting and Clinical Psychology, 62*, 543–549.

Gallagher-Thompson, D., Steffan, A. M., & Thompson, L. W. (Eds.). (2008). *Handbook of behavioral and cognitive behavioral therapies with older adults.* New York: Springer.

Gallagher-Thompson, D., & Thompson, L. W. (2010). *Treating late-life depression: A cognitive-behavioral therapy approach: Therapist guide.* New York: Oxford University Press.

Garcia-Borreguero, D., Larrosa, O., & Bravo, M. (2003). Parkinson's disease and sleep. *Sleep Medicine Reviews, 7*, 115–129.

Garnets, L., & Peplau, L. A. (2006). Sexuality in the lives of aging lesbian and bisexual women. In D. Kimmel, T. Rose, & S. David (Eds.), *Lesbian, gay, bisexual and transgender aging: Research and clinical perspectives* (pp. 70–90). New York: Columbia University Press.

Gatz, M. (1992). Stress, control, and psychological interventions. In M. L. Wykle, E. Kahana, & J. Kowal (Eds.), *Stress and health among the elderly* (pp. 209–222). New York: Springer.

Gatz, M., Bengtson, V. L., & Blum, M. J. (1990). Caregiving families. In J. E. Birren & K. W. Schaie (Eds.), *Handbook of psychology and aging* (3rd ed., pp. 404–426). San Diego, CA: Academic Press.

Gatz, M., Fiske, A., Fox, L. S., Kaskie, B., Kasl-Godley, J., McCallum, T. J., & Wetherell, J. (1998). Empirically validated psychological treatments for older adults. *Journal of Mental Health and Aging, 4*, 9–46.

Gatz, M., Kasl-Godley, J. E., & Karel, M. J. (1996). Aging and mental disorders. In J. E. Birren & K. W. Schaie (Eds.), *Handbook of the psychology of aging* (4th ed., pp. 365–382). San Diego, CA: Academic Press.

Gatz, M., Kasl-Godley, J., & Karel, M. (1996). Aging and mental disorders. In J. E. Birren & K. W. Schaie (Eds.), *Handbook of the psychology of aging* (4th ed., pp. 365–382). San Diego, CA: Academic Press.

Gatz, M., & Smyer, M. A. (1992). The mental health system and older adults in the 1990s. *American Psychologist, 47*, 741–751.

Gatz, M., & Smyer, M. A. (2001). Mental health and aging at the outset of the twenty-first century. In J. E. Birren & K. W. Schaie (Eds.), *Handbook of the psychology of aging* (5th ed., pp. 523–544). San Diego, CA: Academic Press.

Gaugler, J., Roth, D., Haley, W., & Mittelman, M. (2008). Can counseling and support reduce burden and depressive symptoms in caregivers of people with Alzheimer's disease during the transition to institutionalization? Results from the New York University Caregiver Intervention Study. *Journal of the American Geriatrics Society, 56*, 421–428.

Gellis, Z. D., McGinty, J., Horowitz, A., Bruce, M. L., & Misener, E. (2007). Problem-solving therapy for late-life depression in home care: A randomized field trial. *American Journal of Geriatric Psychiatry, 15*, 968–978.

George, L. K. (1994). Social factors and depression in late life. In L. S. Schneider, C. F. Reynolds, B. D. Lebowitz, & A. J. Friedhoff (Eds.), *Diagnosis and treatment of depression in late life: Results of the NIH consensus development conference* (pp. 131–153). Washington, DC: American Psychiatric Press.

Gilford, R., & Bengtson, V. (1979). Measuring marital satisfaction in three generations: Positive and negative dimensions. *Journal of Marriage and the Family, 41*, 387–398.

Gitlin, L. N., Belle, S. H., Burgio, L. D., Czaja, S. J., Mahoney, D., Gallagher-Thompson, D., Burns, R., Hauck, W. W., Zhang, S., Schulz, R., & Ory, M. G. (2003). Effect of multicomponent interventions on caregiver burden and depression: The REACH multisite initiative at 6-month follow-up. *Psychology and Aging, 18*, 361–374.

Goldberg, J. H., Breckenridge, J. N., & Sheik, J. I. (2003). Age difference in symptoms of depression and anxiety: Examining behavioral medicine outpatients. *Journal of Behavioral Medicine, 26*(2), 119–132.

Goldberg, T. E., Hyde, T. M., Kleinman, J. E., & Weinberger, D. R. (1993). Course of schizophrenia: Neuropsychological evidence for a static encephalopathy. *Schizophrenia Bulletin, 19*, 797–804.

Goldstein, J. M. (1988). Gender differences in the course of schizophrenia. *American Journal of Psychiatry, 145*, 684–689.

Gonyea, J. G., O'Connor, M. K., & Boyle, P. A. (2006). Project CARE: A randomized controlled trial of a behavioral intervention group for Alzheimer's disease caregivers. *The Gerontologist, 46*, 827–832.

Gooneratne, N. S., Weaver, T. E., Cater, J. R., Pack, F. M., Arner, H. M., Greenberg, A. S., & Pack, A. I. (2003). Functional outcomes of excessive daytime sleepiness in older adults. *Journal of the American Geriatrics Society, 51*, 642–649.

Gould, O. N. (2004). Aging, cognition, and medication adherence. In C. Spielberger (Ed.-in-Chief), *Encyclopedia of applied psychology* (pp. 111–116). New York: Elsevier.

Gould, R. L. (1978). *Transformations: Growth and change in adult life*. New York: Simon & Schuster.

Grabowski, D. C., Aschbrenner, K. A., Feng, Z., & Mor, V. (2009). Mental illness in nursing homes: Variations across states. *Health Affairs, 28*, 689–700.

Granholm, E., McQuaid, J. R., McClure, F. S., Auslander, L. A., Perivoliotis, D., Pedrelli, P., Patterson, T., & Jeste, D. V. (2005). A randomized, controlled trial of cognitive behavioral social skills training for middle-aged and older outpatients with chronic schizophrenia. *American Journal of Psychiatry, 162*, 520–529.

Green, J. (2006). Feedback. In D. K. Attix & K. A. Welsh-Bohmer (Eds.), *Geriatric neuropsychology: Assessment and intervention* (pp. 223–236). New York: Guilford.

Green, R. C. (2005). *Diagnosis and management of Alzheimer's disease and other dementias* (2nd ed.). Caddo, OK: Professional Communications.

Grisso, T. (2003). *Evaluating competences* (2nd ed.). New York: Plenum.

Grossman, L. S., Harrow, M., Rosen, C., & Faull, R. (2006). Sex differences in outcome and recovery for schizophrenia and other psychotic and nonpsychotic disorders. *Psychiatric Services, 57*, 844–850.

Gruenewald, T. L., & Kemeny, M. E. (2007). Psychoneuroimmunological processes in aging and health. In C. M. Aldwin, C. L. Park, & A. Spiro (Eds.), *Handbook of health psychology and aging* (pp. 97–118). New York: Guilford.

Grundmann, M. (1996). Historical context of father absence: Some consequences for the family formation of German men. *International Journal of Behavioral Development, 19*, 415–431.

Gum, A. M., Areán, P. A., Hunkeler, E., Tang, L., Katon, W., Hitchcock, P. et al. (2006). Depression treatment preferences in older primary care patients. *The Gerontologist, 46,* 14–22.

Gum, A. M., King-Kallimanis, B., & Kohn, R. (2009). Prevalence of mood, anxiety, and substance-abuse disorders for older Americans in the National Comorbidity Survey-Replication. *American Journal of Geriatric Psychiatry, 17,* 769–781.

Gutmann, D. L. (1987). *Reclaimed powers: Toward a new psychology of men and women in later life.* New York: Basic Books.

Gutmann, D. L. (1992). Toward a dynamic geropsychology. In J. W. Barron, M. N. Eagle, & D. L. Wolitzky (Eds.), *Interface of psychoanalysis and psychology* (pp. 284–296). Washington, DC: American Psychological Association.

Hagestad, G. O. (1986). The aging society as a context for family life. *Daedalus, 115,* 119–139.

Hagestad, G. O. (1988). Demographic change and the life course: Some emerging trends in the family realm. *Family Relations, 37,* 405–410.

Halgin, R. P., & Whitbourne, S. K. (2010). *Abnormal psychology: Clinical perspectives on psychological disorders* (6th ed.) New York: McGraw-Hill.

Hamilton, M. (1969). Diagnosis and rating of anxiety. *British Journal of Psychiatry* (Special Publication 3), 76–79.

Harding, C. M., Brooks, G. W., Ashikaga, T., Strauss, J. S., & Breier, A. (1987a). The Vermont longitudinal study of persons with severe mental illness, I: Methodology, study sample, and overall status 32 years later. *American Journal of Psychiatry, 144,* 718–726.

Harding, C. M., Brooks, G. W., Ashikaga, T., Strauss, J. S., & Breier, A. (1987b). The Vermont longitudinal study of persons with severe mental illness, II: Long-term outcome of subjects who retrospectively met DSM-III criteria for schizophrenia. *American Journal of Psychiatry, 144,* 727–735.

Hargrave, T. D., & Anderson, W. T. (1992). *Finishing well: Aging and reparation in the intergenerational family.* New York: Brunner/Mazel.

Harris, M., & Jeste, D. (1988). Late-onset schizophrenia: An overview. *Schizophrenia Bulletin, 14,* 39–55.

Hartman, A. (1997). Aging Holocaust survivors and PTSD. *Dimensions, 4*(3), 3–5.

Hasin, D. S., Goodwin, R. D., Stinson, F. S., & Grant, B. F. (2005). Epidemiology of major depressive disorder: Results from the National Epidemiologic Survey on Alcoholism and Related Conditions. *Archives of General Psychiatry, 62,* 1097–1106.

Heaton, R., Paulsen, J. S., McAdams, L. A., Kuck, J., Zisook, S., Braff, D., Harris, M. J., & Jeste, D. V. (1994). Neuropsychological deficits in schizophrenics: Relationship to age, chronicity, and dementia. *Archives of General Psychiatry, 51,* 469–476.

Heinemann, G. D., & Zeiss, A. (2002). A model of team performance. In G. D. Heinemann & A. M. Zeiss (Eds.), *Team performance in health care: Assessment and development* (pp. 29–42). New York: Kluwer Academic/Plenum.

Heisel, M. J., & Flett, G. L. (2006). The development and initial validation of the Geriatric Suicide Ideation Scale. *American Journal of Geriatric Psychiatry, 14,* 742–751.

Herbert, T. B., & Cohen, S. (1993). Stress and immunity in humans: A meta-analytic review. *Psychosomatic Medicine, 55,* 364–379.

Herr, J. J., & Weakland, J. H. (1979). *Counseling elders and their families.* New York: Springer.

Hinrichsen, G. A. (2008). Interpersonal psychotherapy as a treatment for depression in later life. *Professional Psychology: Research and Practice, 39,* 306–312.

Hinrichsen, G. A., & Clougherty, K. F. (2006). *Interpersonal psychotherapy for depressed older adults.* Washington, DC: American Psychological Association.

Hinrichsen, G. A., & Emery, E. (2005). Interpersonal factors and late life depression. *Clinical Psychology: Science and Practice, 12,* 264–275.

Holmes, T., & Rahe, R. (1967). The social readjustment rating scale. *Journal of Psychosomatic Research, 11*, 213–218.

Hootman, J. M., Bolen, J., Helmick, C. G., & Langmaid, G. (2006). Prevalence of doctor-diagnosed arthritis and arthritis-attributable activity limitation: United States, 2003–2005. *Morbidity and Mortality Weekly Report, 55*, 1089–1092.

Hootman, J. M., & Helmick, C. G. (2006). Projections of US prevalence of arthritis and associated activity limitations. *Arthritis and Rheumatism, 54*, 226–229.

Howard, R., Castle, D., Wessely, S., & Murray, R. (1993). A comparative study of 470 cases of early- and late- onset schizophrenia. *British Journal of Psychiatry, 163*, 352–357.

Hughes, J. R., Hatsukami, D. K., Mitchell, J. E., & Dahlgren, L. A. (1986). Prevalence of smoking among psychiatric outpatients. *American Journal of Psychiatry, 143*, 993–997.

Hutchinson, L. C., & O'Brien, C. E. (2007). Changes in pharmacokinetics and pharmacodynamics in the elderly patient. *Journal of Pharmacy Practice, 20*, 4–12.

Hyer, L., & Intrieri, R. (2006). *Geropsychological interventions in long-term care.* New York: Springer.

Institute of Medicine. (2009). *Integrative medicine and the health of the public.* Washington, DC: National Academies Press.

Jackson, J. H. (1984). Remarks on the evolution and dissolution of the nervous system. *Journal of Mental Science, 33*, 25–48.

Jahoda, M. (1958). *Current concepts of positive mental health.* New York: Basic Books.

Jang, K. L., Livesley, W. J., & Vernon, P. A. (1996). The genetic basis of personality at different ages: A cross-sectional twin study. *Personality and Individual Differences, 21*, 299–301.

Jang, K. L., Livesley, W. J., Vernon, P. A., & Jackson, D. N. (1996). Heritability of personality disorder traits: A twin study. *Acta Psychiatrica Scandinavica, 94*, 438–444.

Jeon, H.-S., Dunkle, R., & Roberts, B. L. (2006). Worries of the oldest old. *Health and Social Work, 31*, 256–265.

Jeste, D. V., Alexopoulos, G. S., Bartels, S. J., Cummings, J. L., Gallo, J. J., Gottlieb, G. L., Halpain, M. C., Palmer, B. W., Patterson, T. L., Reynolds, C. F., & Lebowitz, B. D. (1999). Consensus statement on the upcoming crisis in geriatric mental health: Research agenda for the next 2 decades. *Archives of General Psychiatry, 56*, 848–853.

Jeste, D. V., Gladsjo, J. A., Lindamer, L. A., & Lacro, J. P. (1996). Medical comorbidity in schizophrenia. *Schizophrenia Bulletin, 22*, 413–430.

Jeste, D. V., Harris, M. J., Krull, A., Kuck, J., McAdams, L. A., & Heaton, R. (1995). Clinical and neuropsychological characteristics of patients with late-onset schizophrenia. *American Journal of Psychiatry, 152*, 722–730.

Jeste, D. V., Lacro, J. P., Gilbert, P. L., Kline, J., & Kline, N. (1993). Treatment of late-life schizophrenia with neuroleptics. *Schizophrenia Bulletin, 19*, 817–830.

Jeste, D. V., & Nasrallah, H. A. (2003). Schizophrenia and aging: No more dearth of data? *American Journal of Geriatric Psychiatry, 11*, 584–587.

Jeste, D. V., Twamley, E. W., Eyler Zorrilla, L. T., Golshan, S., Patterson, T. L., & Palmer, B. W. (2003). Aging and outcome in schizophrenia. *Acta Psychiatrica Scandinavica, 107*, 336–343.

Johnson, C. J., & Johnson, F. A. (1992). Psychological distress among inner-city American elderly: Structural, developmental, and situational contexts. *Journal of Cross-Cultural Gerontology, 7*, 221–236.

Johnson-Greene, D., & Inscore, A. B. (2005). Substance abuse in older adults. In S. S. Bush & T. A. Martin (Eds.), *Geriatric neuropsychology: Practice essentials* (pp. 429–451). New York: Taylor & Francis.

Jorm, A., Korten, A., & Henderson, A. (1987). The prevalence of dementia: A quantitative integration of the literature. *Acta Psychiatrica Scandinavica, 76,* 465–479.

Jung, C. G. (1933). *Modern man in search of a soul.* New York: Harcourt Brace.

Kahana, E., & Kahana, B. (1996). Conceptual and empirical advances in understanding well through proactive adaptation. In V. Bengtson (Ed.), *Adulthood and aging: Research on continuities and discontinuities* (pp. 18–41). New York: Springer.

Kahana, E., & Kahana, B. (2003). Contextualizing successful aging: New directions in age-old search. In R. Settersten, Jr. (Ed.), *Invitation to the life course: A new look at old age* (pp. 225–255). Amityville, NY: Baywood.

Kahn, R. L. (1975). The mental health system and the future aged. *The Gerontologist, 15*(2), 24–31.

Kaiser Family Foundation. (2009, June). *Explaining health care reform: What is Medicaid?* Washington, DC: The Henry J. Kaiser Family Foundation. Retrieved from http://www.kff.org/healthreform/upload/7920.pdf.

Karel, M. J., Ogland-Hand, S., Gatz, M., & Unützer, J. (2002). *Assessing and treating late-life depression: A casebook and resource guide.* New York: Basic Books.

Kasl-Godley, J. E. (2011). Health care teams. In S. H. Qualls & J. E. Kasl-Godley (Eds.), *End-of-life issues, grief, and bereavement: What clinicians need to know.* Hoboken, NJ: John Wiley & Sons, Inc.

Kaufer, D. I., & Cummings, J. L. (2003). Delirium and dementia: An overview. In T. E. Feinberg & M. J. Farah (Eds.), *Behavioral neurology and neuropsychology* (2nd ed., pp. 495–500). New York: McGraw-Hill.

Kaufman, D. W., Kelly, J. P., Rosenberg, L., Anderson, T. E., & Mitchell, A. A. (2002). Recent patterns of medication use in the ambulatory adult population of the United States: The Slone survey. *Journal of the American Medical Association, 287,* 337–344.

Kay, D., & Roth, M. (1961). Environmental and hereditary factors in the schizophrenias of old age ("late paraphrenia") and their bearing on the general problem of causation in schizophrenia. *Journal of Mental Science, 107,* 649–686.

Kazdin, A. E. (2001). *Behavior modification in applied settings* (6th ed.). Belmont, CA: Wadsworth/Thompson Learning.

Kelly, C., & McCreadie, R. G. (1999). Smoking habits, current symptoms, and premorbid characteristics of schizophrenic patients in Nithsdale, Scotland. *American Journal of Psychiatry, 156,* 1751–1757.

Kelly, K. G., & Zisselman, M. (2000). Update on electroconvulsive therapy (ECT) in older adults. *Journal of the American Geriatrics Society, 48,* 560–566.

Kemp, B. J., & Mitchell, J. M. (1992). Functional impairment in geriatric mental health. In J. E. Birren, R. B. Sloane, & G. D. Cohen (Eds.), *Handbook of mental health and aging* (2nd ed., pp. 671–697). San Diego, CA: Academic Press.

Kendler, K. S., Aggen, S. H., Czajkowski, N., Røysamb, E., Tambs, K., Torgersen, S., Neale, M. C., & Reichborn-Kjennerud, T. (2008). The structure of genetic and environmental risk factors for DSM-IV personality disorders: A multivariate twin study. *Archives of General Psychiatry, 65,* 1438–1446.

Kendler, K. S., Gatz, M., Gardner, C. O., & Pedersen, N. L. (2006). A Swedish national twin study of lifetime major depression. *American Journal of Psychiatry, 163,* 109–114.

Kessler, R. C., Berglund, P. A., Demler, O., Jin, R., & Walters, E. E. (2005). Lifetime prevalence and age-of-onset distributions of DSM-IV disorders in the National Comorbidity Survey Replication (NCS-R). *Archives of General Psychiatry, 62,* 593–602.

Kiecolt-Glaser, J. K. (2009). Psychoneuroimmunology: Psychology's gateway to the biomedical future. *Perspectives on Psychological Science, 4,* 367–369.

Kim, J. H., Knight, B. G., & Longmire, C. V. (2007). The role of familism in stress and coping processes among African American and White dementia caregivers: Effects on mental and physical health. *Health Psychology, 26,* 564–576.

Kimmel, D., Rose, T., & David, S. (Eds.). (2006). *Lesbian, gay, bisexual and transgender aging: Research and clinical perspectives.* New York: Columbia University Press.

King, C., Van Hasselt, V. B., Segal, D. L., & Hersen, M. (1994). Diagnosis and assessment of substance abuse in older adults: Current strategies and issues. *Addictive Behaviors, 19,* 41–55.

Kinsella, K. (1995). Aging and the family: Present and future demographic issues. In R. Blieszner & V. H. Bedford (Eds.), *Handbook on aging and the family* (pp. 32–56). Westport, CT: Greenwood Press.

Kivnick, H. Q. (1985). Grandparenthood and mental health. In V. L. Bengtson & J. F. Robertson (Eds.), *Grandparenthood* (pp. 211–224). Beverly Hills, CA: Sage.

Kivnick, H. Q. (1993). Everyday mental health: A guide to assessing life strengths. In M. A. Smyer (Ed.), *Mental health and aging* (pp. 19–36). New York: Springer.

Klerman, G. L., Weissman, M. M., Rounsaville, B. J., & Chevron, E. S. (1984). *Interpersonal psychotherapy of depression.* Northvale, NJ: Jason Aronson.

Knight, B. G. (2004). *Psychotherapy with older adults* (3rd ed.). Thousand Oaks, CA: Sage.

Knight, B. G., Flynn Longmire, C. V., Dave, J., Kim, J. H., & David, S. (2007). Mental health and physical health of family caregivers: A comparison of African American and White caregivers. *Aging and Mental Health, 11,* 538–546.

Knight, B. G., Karel, M., Hinrichsen, G., Qualls, S. H., & Duffy, M. (2009). Pikes Peak model for training in professional geropsychology. *American Psychologist, 64,* 205–214.

Knight, B. G., Lutzky, S. M., & Macofsky-Urban, F. (1993). A meta-analytic review of interventions for caregiver distress: Recommendations for future research. *The Gerontologist, 33,* 240–248.

Knight, B. G., & Qualls, S. H. (1995). The older client in developmental context: Life course and family systems perspectives. *Clinical Psychologist, 48*(2), 11–17.

Knight, B. G., & Satre, D. D. (1999). Cognitive behavioral psychotherapy with older adults. *Clinical Psychology: Science & Practice, 6,* 188–203.

Knopman, D., Donohue, J. A., & Gutterman, E. M. (2000). Patterns of care in the early stages of Alzheimer's disease: Impediments to timely diagnosis. *Journal of the American Geriatrics Society, 48,* 300–304.

Kohut, H. (1971). *The analysis of the self.* New York: International Universities Press.

Kong, E., Evans, L., & Guevara, J. (2009). Nonpharmacological intervention for agitation in dementia: A systematic review and meta-analysis. *Aging and Mental Health, 13,* 512–520.

Koran, L. M., Sox, H. C., Marton, K. I. et al. (1989). Medical evaluation of psychiatric patients. *Archives of General Psychiatry, 46,* 733–740.

Kraepelin, E. (1971). *Dementia praecox and paraphrenia* (R. M. Barclay, Trans.). Huntington, NY: Rovert E. Kreiger. (Original work published in 1919.)

Krause, N. (1995a). Stress and well-being in later life: Using research findings to inform intervention design. In L. A. Bond, S. J. Cutler, & A. Grams (Eds.), *Promoting successful and productive aging* (pp. 203–219). Thousand Oaks, CA: Sage.

Krause, N. (1995b). Stress, alcohol use, and depressive symptoms in later life. *The Gerontologist, 35,* 296–307.

Kumar, R., Dear, K. B. G., Christensen, H., Ilschner, S., Jorm, A. F., Meslin, C. et al. (2005). Prevalence of mild cognitive impairment in 60–64-year-old community-dwelling individuals: The Personality and Total Health through Life 60+ Study. *Dementia and Geriatric Cognitive Disorders, 19,* 67–74.

Lai, H.-L., & Good, M. (2005). Music improves sleep in older adults. *Journal of Advanced Nursing, 49,* 234–244.

Laidlaw, K., Thompson, L. W., Dick-Siskin, L., & Gallagher-Thompson, D. (2004). *Cognitive behaviour therapy with older people.* Hoboken, NJ: John Wiley & Sons, Inc.

Lair, T., & Lefkowitz, D. (1990). Mental health and functional status of residents of nursing and personal care homes. In *National Medical Expenditure Survey Research Findings 7* (DHHS Publication No. PHS90-3470). Rockville, MD: Public Health Service, Agency for Health Care Policy and Research.

Larimer, M. E., & Kilmer, J. R. (2000). Natural history. In G. Zernig, A. Saria, M. Kurz, & S. O'Malley (Eds.), *Handbook of alcoholism* (pp. 13–28). Boca Raton, FL: CRC Press.

Laumann, E. O., Nicolosi, A., Glasser, D. B., Paik, A., Gingell, C., Moreira, E., Wang, T., & GSSAB Investigator's Group. (2005). Sexual problems among women and men aged 40–80 years: Prevalence and correlates identified in the Global Study of Sexual Attitudes and Behaviors. *International Journal of Impotence Research, 17,* 39–57.

Lawton, M. P. (1979). Therapeutic environments for the aged. In D. Canter & S. Canter (Eds.), *Designing for therapeutic environments* (pp. 233–276). New York: John Wiley & Sons, Inc.

Lawton, M. P. (1980). *Environment and aging.* Pacific Grove, CA: Brooks/Cole.

Lawton, M. P. (1982). Competence, environmental press, and the adaptation of old people. In M. P. Lawton, P. G. Windley, & T. O. Byerts (Eds.), *Aging and the environment: Theoretical approaches* (pp. 33–59). New York: Springer.

Lawton, M. P., & Nahemow, L. (1973). Ecology and the aging process. In C. Eisdorfer & M. P. Lawton (Eds.), *The psychology of adult development and aging* (pp. 619–673). Washington, DC: American Psychological Association.

Lazarus, R. S., & Folkman, S. (1984). *Stress, appraisal, and coping.* New York: Springer.

Lazarus, R. S., & Folkman, S. (1987). Coping and adaptation. In W. D. Gentry (Ed.), *Handbook of behavioral medicine* (pp. 282–325). New York: Guilford.

LeBlanc, L. A., Raetz, P. B., & Feliciano, L. (in press). Behavioral gerontology. In W. W. Fisher, C. C. Piazza, & H. S. Roane (Eds.), *Handbook of applied behavior analysis.* New York: Guilford.

Lenzenweger, M. F. (2008). Epidemiology of personality disorders. *Psychiatric Clinics of North America, 31,* 395–403.

Lesser, I., Miller, B., Swartz, R., Boone, K., Mehringer, C., & Mena, I. (1993). Brain imaging in late-life schizophrenia and related psychoses. *Schizophrenia Bulletin, 19,* 773–782.

Levenson, R. Q., Carstensen, L. L., & Gottman, J. M. (1993). Long-term marriage: Age, gender, and satisfaction. *Psychology and Aging, 8,* 301–313.

Levinson, D. J., Darrow, C. N., & Klein, E. B. (1978). *The seasons of a man's life.* New York: Alfred A. Knopf.

Levy, B. R. (2003). Mind matters: Cognitive and physical effects of aging self-stereotypes. *Journal of Gerontology: Psychological Sciences, 58B,* P203–P211.

Lewin, K. (1935). *A dynamic theory of personality: Selected papers of Kurt Lewin.* New York: McGraw-Hill.

Lewine, R. J. (1988). Gender in schizophrenia. In H. A. Nasrallah (Ed.), *Handbook of schizophrenia: Vol. 3* (pp. 379–397). Amsterdam: Elsevier.

Lewine, R. J., Gulley, L. R., Risch, S. C., Jewart, R., & Houpt, J. L. (1990). Sexual dimorphism, brain morphology, and schizophrenia. *Schizophrenia Bulletin, 16,* 195–203.

Lewinsohn, P. M., & Graf, M. (1973). Pleasant activities and depression. *Journal of Consulting and Clinical Psychology, 41,* 261–268.

Lewinsohn, P. M., Munoz, R. F., Youngren, M. A., & Zeiss, A. M. (1992). *Control your depression* (rev. ed.). New York: Fireside.

Lichstein, K. L., Riedel, B. W., Wilson, N. M., Lester, K. W., & Aguillard, R. N. (2001). Relaxation and sleep compression for late-life insomnia: A placebo-controlled trial. *Journal of Consulting and Clinical Psychology, 69*, 227–239.

Lichtenberg, P. (1998). *Mental health practice in geriatric health care settings.* Binghamton, NY: Haworth.

Lichtenberg, P. (2009). Controversy and caring: An update on current issues in dementia. *Generations, 33*(1), 5–10.

Lindau, S. T., Schumm, L. P., Laumann, E. O., Levinson, W., O'Muircheartaigh, C. A., & Waite, L. J. (2007). A study of sexuality and health among older adults in the United States. *New England Journal of Medicine, 357*, 762–774.

Lingler, J. H., Nightingale, M. C., Erlen, J. A., Kane, A. L., Reynolds, C. F., Schulz, R., & DeKosky, S. T. (2006). Making sense of mild cognitive impairment: A qualitative exploration of the patient's experience. *The Gerontologist, 46*, 791–800.

Linka, E., Bartkó, G., Agárdi, T., & Kemény, K. (2000). Dementia and depression in elderly medical inpatients. *International Psychogeriatrics, 12*, 67–75.

Liu, W., & Gallagher-Thompson, D. (2009). Impact of dementia caregiving: Risks, strains, and growth. In S. H. Qualls & S. H. Zarit (Eds.), *Aging families and caregiving* (pp. 85–111). Hoboken, NJ: John Wiley & Sons.

Livesley, W. J. (2004). A framework for an integrated approach to treatment. In J. Livesley (Ed.), *Handbook of personality disorders: Theory, research, and treatment.* New York: Guilford.

Logsdon, R. G., McCurry, S. M., & Teri, L. (2007). Evidence-based psychological treatments for disruptive behaviors in individuals with dementia. *Psychology and Aging, 22*, 28–36.

Lonie, J. A., Tierney, K. M., & Ebmeier, K. P. (2009). Screening for mild cognitive impairment: A systematic review. *International Journal of Geriatric Psychiatry, 24*, 902–915.

Lopez, O. L., Becker, J. T., Somsak, D., Dew, M. A., & DeKosky, S. T. (1994). Awareness of cognitive deficits and anosognosia in probable Alzheimer's disease. *Journal of Geriatric Psychiatry and Neurology, 4*, 189–193.

Lyden, M. (2007). Assessment of sexual consent capacity. *Sexuality and Disability, 25*, 3–20.

Mace, N. L., & Rabins, P. V. (2001). *The 36 hour day: A family guide to caring for persons with Alzheimer Disease, related dementing illnesses, and memory loss in later life.* Baltimore: Johns Hopkins University Press.

Malla, A., & Payne, J. (2005). First-episode psychosis: Psychopathology, quality of life, and functional outcome. *Schizophrenia Bulletin, 31*, 650–657.

Manton, K. G., Gu, X., & Lamb, V. L. (2006). Change in chronic disability from 1982 to 2004/2005 as measured by long-term changes in function and health in the US elderly population. *Proceedings of the National Academy of Sciences, 103*, 18374–18379. Retrieved from http://www.pnas.org/cgi/doi/10.1073/pnas.0608483103.

Mark, T. L., Harwood, H. J., McKusick, D. C., King, E. C., Vandivort-Warren, R., & Buck, J. A. (2008). Mental health and substance abuse spending by age, 2003. *Journal of Behavioral Health Services and Research, 35*, 279–289.

Marsiske, M., Lang, F. R., Baltes, P. B., & Baltes, M. M. (1996). Selective optimization with compensation: Life-span perspectives on successful human development. In R. A. Dixon & L. Backman (Eds.), *Compensating for psychological deficits and declines: Managing losses and promoting gains* (pp. 35–79). Mahwah, NJ: Erlbaum.

Martin, P., & Smyer, M. A. (1990). The experience of micro- and macroevents: A life span analysis. *Research on Aging, 12*, 294–310.

Mattis, S., Jurica, P. J., & Leitten, C. L. (2001). *Dementia Rating Scale-2.* Odessa, FL: Psychological Assessment Resources, Inc.

Mayfield, D., McLeod, G., & Hall, P. (1974). The CAGE questionnaire: Validation of a new alcoholism screening instrument. *American Journal of Psychiatry, 131*, 1121–1123.

McCabe, L., Cairney, J., Veldhuizen, S., Herrmann, N., & Streiner, D. L. (2006). Prevalence and correlates of agoraphobia in older adults. *American Journal of Geriatric Psychiatry, 14*, 515–512.

McCrae, C. S., Tierney, C. G., & McNamara, J. P. H. (2005). Behavioral intervention for insomnia: Future directions for nontraditional caregivers at various stages of care. *Clinical Gerontologist, 29*, 95–114.

McCrae, C. S., Wilson, N. M., Lichstein, K. L., Durrence, H. H., Taylor, D. J., Bush, A. J., & Riedel, B. W. (2003). "Young old" and "old old" poor sleepers with and without insomnia complaints. *Journal of Psychosomatic Research, 54*, 11–19.

McCurry, S. M., Logsdon, R. G., Teri, L., Gibbons, L. E., Kukull, W. A., Bowen, J. D., McCormick, W. C., & Larson, E. B. (1999). Characteristics of sleep disturbance in community-dwelling Alzheimer's disease patients. *Journal of Geriatric Psychiatry and Neurology, 12*, 53–59.

McCurry, S. M., Logsdon, R. G., Vitiello, M. V., & Teri, L. (1998). Successful behavioral treatment for reported sleep problems in elderly caregivers of dementia patients: A controlled study. *Journal of Gerontology B: Psychological and Social Sciences, 53*, 122–129.

McEvoy, J. P., Freter, S., Everett, G., Geller, J. L., Appelbaum, P., Apperson, L. J., & Roth, L. (1989). Insight and the clinical outcome of schizophrenic patients. *Journal of Nervous and Mental Disease, 177*, 48–51.

McGoldrick, M., Gerson, R., & Petrie, S. (2008). *Genograms: Assessment and intervention* (3rd ed.). New York: Norton Professional Books.

Meeks, S., Looney, S. W., Van Haitsma, K., & Teri, L. (2008). BE-ACTIV: A staff-assisted behavioral intervention for depression in nursing homes. *The Gerontologist, 48*, 105–114.

Meeks, S., Shah, S. N., & Ramsey, S. K. (2009). The Pleasant Events Schedule – nursing home version: A useful tool for behavioral interventions in long-term care. *Aging & Mental Health, 13*, 445–455.

Meeks, T. W., & Jeste, D. V. (2008). Older individuals. In K. T. Mueser & D. V. Jeste (Eds.), *Clinical handbook of schizophrenia* (pp. 390–397). New York: Guilford.

Mehta, K. M., Simonsick, E. M., Penninx, B. W. J. H., Schulz, R., Rubin, S. M., Satterfield, S., & Yaffe, K. (2003). Prevalence and correlates of anxiety symptoms in well-functioning older adults: Findings from the Healthy Aging and Body Composition Study. *Journal of the American Geriatrics Society, 51*, 499–504.

Mello, M. F., Mari, J. J., Bacaltchuk, J., Verdeli, H., & Neugebauer, R. (2005). A systematic review of research findings on the efficacy of IPT for depressive disorders. *European Archives of Psychiatry and Clinical Neuroscience, 255*, 75–82.

Meyer, T., Miller, M., Metzger, R. et al. (1990). Development and validity of the Penn State Worry Scale. *Behavior Research and Therapy, 28*, 487–495.

Minuchin, S. (1974). *Families and family therapy.* Cambridge, MA: Harvard University Press.

Mitrani, V. B., Lewis, J. E., Feaster, D. J., Czaja, S. J., Eisdorfer, C., Schulz, R., & Szapocznik, J. (2006). The role of family functioning in the stress process of dementia caregivers: A structural family framework. *The Gerontologist, 46*, 97–105.

Mittelman, M. S., Ferris, S. H., Shulman, E., Steinberg, G., & Levin, B. (1996). A family intervention to delay nursing home placement of patients with Alzheimer's disease: A randomized controlled trial. *Journal of the American Medical Association, 276*, 1725–1731.

Mittelman, M. S., Haley, W. E., Clay, O. J., & Roth, D. L. (2006). Improving caregiver well-being delays nursing home placement of patients with Alzheimer disease. *Neurology, 67*, 1592–1599.

Mittelman, M. S., Roth, D. L., Coon, D. W., & Haley, W. E. (2004). Sustained benefit of supportive intervention for depressive symptoms in caregivers of patients with Alzheimer's disease. *American Journal of Psychiatry, 161*, 850–856.

Mohlman, J. (2004). Psychosocial treatment of late-life generalized anxiety disorder: Current status and future directions. *Clinical Psychology Review, 24*, 149–169.

Mohlman, J., Gorenstein, E. E., Kleber, M., DeJesus, M., Gorman, J. M., & Papp, L. A. (2003). Standard and enhanced cognitive-behavioral therapy for late-life generalized anxiety disorder. *American Journal of Geriatric Psychiatry, 11*, 24–32.

Molinari, V. (Ed.). (2000). *Professional psychology in long term care: A comprehensive guide.* New York: Hatherleigh Press.

Molinari, V., Ames, A., & Essa, M. (1994). Prevalence of personality disorders in two geropsychiatric inpatient units. *Journal of Geriatric Psychiatry and Neurology, 7*, 209–215.

Molinari, V., & Marmion, J. (1995). Relationship between affective disorders and Axis II diagnoses in geropsychiatric patients. *Journal of Geriatric Psychiatry and Neurology, 8*, 61–64.

Molinari, V., & Segal, D. L. (2011). Personality disorders: Description, etiology, and epidemiology. In M. Abou-Saleh, C. Katona, & A. Kumar (Eds.), *Principles and practice of geriatric psychiatry* (3rd ed., pp. 649–654). Hoboken, NJ: John Wiley & Sons.

Molton, I. R., & Raichle, K. A. (2010). Psychophysiological disorders. In D. L. Segal & M. Hersen (Eds.), *Diagnostic interviewing* (4th ed., pp. 343–369). New York: Springer.

Montgomery, R. J. V., & Kosloski, K. (2009). Caregiving as a process of changing identity: Implications for caregiver support. *Generations, 33*(1), 47–52.

Montplaisir, J. (2004). Abnormal motor behavior during sleep. *Sleep Medicine, 5*, S31–S24.

Morden, N. E., Mistler, L. A., Weeks, W. B., & Bartels, S. J. (2009). Health care for patients with serious mental illness: Family medicine's role. *Journal of the American Board of Family Medicine, 22*, 187–195.

Morgan, K. (2000). Sleep and aging. In K. L. Lichstein & C. M. Morin (Eds.), *Treatment of late-life insomnia* (pp. 3–36). Thousand Oaks, CA: Sage.

Moriarty, P. J., Lieber, D., Bennett, A., White, L., Parrella, M., Harvey, P. D., & Davis, K. L. (2001). Gender differences in poor outcome patients with lifelong schizophrenia. *Schizophrenia Bulletin, 27*, 103–113.

Morin, C. M. (1993). *Insomnia: Psychological assessment and management.* New York: Guilford.

Morin, C. M., & Espie, C. A. (2003). *Insomnia: A clinical guide to assessment and treatment.* New York: Kluwer Academic/Plenum.

Morris, J. C., Heyman, A., Mohs, R. C., Hughes, J. P., van Belle, G., Fillenbaum, G. et al. (1989). The Consortium to Establish a Registry for Alzheimer's Disease (CERAD): Part 1 – Clinical and neuropsychological assessment of Alzheimer's disease. *Neurology, 39*, 1159–1165.

Mortensen, P. B., & Juel, K. (1990). Mortality and causes of death in schizophrenic patients in Denmark. *Acta Psychiatrica Scandinavica, 81*, 372–377.

Moye, J. (2007). Clinical frameworks for capacity assessment. In S. H. Qualls & M. A. Smyer, *Changes in decision-making capacity in older adults: Assessment and intervention* (pp. 177–190). Hoboken, NJ: John Wiley & Sons, Inc.

Moye, J., & Marson, D. C. (2007). Assessment of decision-making capacity in older adults: An emerging area of practice. *Journals of Gerontology: Psychological Sciences, 62B*, P3–P11.

Mrazek, P. J., & Haggerty, R. J. (Eds.). (1994). *Reducing risks for mental disorders: Frontiers for preventive intervention research.* Washington, DC: National Academy Press.

Mueser, K. T., Bartels, S. J., Pratt, S. I., Swain, K., Forester, B., Cather, C., & Feldman, J. (2010). Randomized trial of social rehabilitation and integrated health care for older people with severe mental illness. *Journal of Consulting and Clinical Psychology, 78*, 561–573.

Mueser, K. T., & Gingerich, S. (1994). *Coping with schizophrenia: A guide for families.* Oakland, CA: New Harbinger.

Mueser, K. T., Sayers, S. L., Schooler, N. R., Mance, R. M., & Haas, G. L. (1994). A multi-site investigation of the reliability of the Scale for the Assessment of Negative Symptoms. *American Journal of Psychiatry, 151,* 1453–1462.

Mueser, K. T., Yarnold, P. R., Levinson, D. F., Singh, H., Bellack, A. S., Kee, K., Morrison, R. L., & Yadalam, K. G. (1990). Prevalence of substance abuse in schizophrenia: Demographic and clinical correlates. *Schizophrenia Bulletin, 16,* 31–56.

Mui, A. C., Burnette, D., & Chen, L. M. (2001). Cross-cultural assessment of geriatric depression: A review of the CES-D and the GDS. *Journal of Mental Health and Aging, 7,* 137–164.

Murrell, S., Norris, F. H., & Hutchins, G. S. (1984). Distribution and desirability of life events in older adults: Population and policy implications. *Journal of Community Psychology, 12,* 301–311.

Mynors-Wallis, L. M., Gath, D. H., Day, A., & Baker, F. (2000). Randomised control trial of problem solving treatment, antidepressant medication, and combined treatment for major depression in primary care. *British Medical Journal, 320,* 26–30.

NASMHPD Medical Directors Council Publications and Reports. (2005). *Integrating behavioral health and primary care services: Opportunities and challenges for state mental health authorities.* Retrieved from http://www.nasmhpd.org/publicationsmeddir.cfm.

NASMHPD Medical Directors Council Publications and Reports. (2006). *Morbidity and mortality in people with serious mental illness.* Retrieved from http://www.nasmhpd.org/publicationsmeddir.cfm.

National Academy on an Aging Society. (2000, September). *Alzheimer's disease and dementia: A growing challenge.* Washington, DC: Author.

National Center for Health Statistics. (2003). *Health, United States, 2003.* Hyattsville, MD: US Department of Health and Human Services, Centers for Disease Control and Prevention.

National Coalition on Mental Health and Aging. (2010). 2010 Priorities of the National Coalition on Mental Health and Aging (NCMHA), Washington, DC. Retrieved from http://www.ncmha.org.

Nau, S. D., McCrae, C. S., Cook, K. G., & Lichstein, K. L. (2005). Treatment of insomnia in older adults. *Clinical Psychology Review, 25,* 546–672.

Nemiroff, R., & Colarusso, C. (1990). Frontiers of adult development in theory and practice. *New dimensions in adult development* (pp. 97–124). New York: Basic Books.

Neugarten, B. L. (1979). Time, age and the life cycle. *American Journal of Psychiatry, 136,* 887–895.

Newton, N., Brauer, D., Gutmann, D. L., & Grunes, J. (1986). Psychodynamic therapy with the aged: A review. *Clinical Gerontologist, 5,* 205–229.

Nezu, C. M., Nezu, A. M., & Areán, P. (1991). Assertiveness and problem-solving training for mildly mentally retarded adults. *Research on Developmental Disabilities, 12,* 371–386.

Nezu, C. M., Nezu, A. M., & Dudek, J. A. (1998). A cognitive behavioral model of assessment and treatment for intellectually disabled sexual offenders. *Cognitive Behavioral Practice, 5,* 25–64.

Nezu, A. M., & Perri, M. G. (1989). Social problem-solving therapy for unipolar depression: An initial dismantling investigation. *Journal of Consulting and Clinical Psychology, 57,* 408–413.

Nichols, L. O., & Martindale-Adams, J. (2006). The decisive moment: Caregivers' recognition of dementia. *Clinical Gerontologist, 30,* 39–52.

NIH Consensus Panel on Assessment. (1988). NIH Consensus Statement: Geriatric assessment methods for clinical decision-making. *Journal of the American Geriatrics Society, 36,* 342–347.

NIH Consensus Panel on Assessment & NIH Consensus Panel on Depression in Late Life. (1992). Diagnosis and treatment of depression in late life. *Journal of the American Medical Association, 268,* 1018–1024.

Noimark, D. (2009). Predicting the onset of delirium in the post-operative patient. *Age and Ageing, 38,* 368–373.

Norcross, J. C., Hedges, M., & Castle, P. H. (2002). Psychologists conducting psychotherapy in 2001: A study of the Division 29 membership. *Psychotherapy: Theory, Research, Practice, Training, 39,* 97–102.

Nordhus, I. H., & Pallesen, S. (2003). Psychological treatment of late-life anxiety: An empirical review. *Journal of Consulting and Clinical Psychology, 71,* 643–651.

Norris, M. P. (2009). Integrating families into long-term care psychology services: Orchestrating cacophonies and symphonies. In S. H. Qualls & S. H. Zarit (Eds.), *Aging families and caregiving* (pp. 189–208). Hoboken, NJ: John Wiley & Sons, Inc.

Norris, M. P., Molinari, V., & Ogland-Hand, S. (2002). *Emerging trends in psychological practice in long-term care.* Binghamptom, NH: Haworth Press.

Nusbaum, M. R. H., Singh, A. R., & Pyles, A. A. (2004). Sexual healthcare needs of women aged 65 and older. *Journal of the American Geriatrics Society, 52,* 117–122.

Ohayon, M. M. (2002). Epidemiology of insomnia: What we know and what we still need to learn. *Sleep Medicine Reviews, 6,* 97–111.

Ohayon, M. M., Carskadon, M. A., Guilleminault, C. et al. (2004). Meta-analysis of quantitative sleep parameters from childhood to old age in healthy individuals: Developing normative sleep values across the human lifespan. *Sleep, 27,* 1255–1273.

Ohayon, M. M., & Roth, T. (2002). Prevalence of restless legs syndrome and periodic limb movement disorder in the general population. *Journal of Psychosomatic Research, 53,* 547–554.

Olfson, M., Mechanic, D., Hansell, S., Boyer, C. A., & Walkup, J. (1999). Prediction of homelessness within three months of discharge among inpatients with schizophrenia. *Psychiatric Services, 50,* 667–673.

Olfson, M., Sing, M., & Schlesinger, H. J. (1999). Mental health/medical care cost offsets: Opportunities for managed care. *Health Affairs, 18,* 79–90.

Olson, D. (1996). Clinical assessment and treatment using the family circumplex model. In F. W. Kaslow (Ed.), *Handbook in relational diagnosis* (pp. 59–80). New York: John Wiley & Sons, Inc.

Oxman, T. E., Barret, J. E., Barret, J., & Gerber, T. (1990). Symptomatology of late-life minor depression among primary care patients. *Psychosomatics, 31,* 174–180.

Pachana, N., Byrne, G., Siddle, H., Koloski, N., Harley, E., & Arnold, E. (2007). Development and validation of the Geriatric Anxiety Inventory. *International Psychogeriatrics, 19,* 103–114.

Pallesen, S., Nordhus, I. H., Kvale, G., Nielsen, G. H., Havik, O. E., Johnsen, B. H., & Skjøtskift, S. (2004). Behavioral treatment of insomnia in older adults: An open clinical trial comparing two interventions. *Behavior Research and Therapy, 41,* 31–48.

Palmer, B. W., Heaton, S. C., & Jeste, D. V. (1999). Older patients with schizophrenia: Challenges in the coming decades. *Psychiatric Services, 50,* 1178–1183.

Parsons, T. (1949). The social structure of the family. In R. Anshen (Ed.), *The family: Its function and destiny* (pp. 173–201). New York: Harper & Row.

Patterson, T. L., McKibbin, C., Taylor, M., Goldman, S., Davila-Fraga, W., Bucardo, J. et al. (2003). Functional adaptation skills training (FAST): A pilot psychosocial intervention study in middle-aged and older patients with chronic psychotic disorders. *American Journal of Geriatric Psychiatry, 11*, 17–23.

Pearlson, G. D., Kreger, L., Rabins, P. V., Chase, G. A., Cohen, B., Wirth, J. B., Schlaepfer, T. B., & Tune, L. E. (1989). A chart review study of late-onset and early-onset schizophrenia. *American Journal of Psychiatry, 146*, 1568–1574.

Pearlson, G. D., & Rabins, P. V. (1988). The late onset psychoses: Possible risk factors. *Psychiatric Clinics of North America, 11*, 15–33.

Penedo, F. J., & Dahn, J. R. (2005). Psychoneuroimmunology and aging. In K. Vedhara & M. Irwin (Eds.), *Human psychoneuroimmunology* (pp. 81–106). New York: Oxford University Press.

Pepin, R., Segal, D. L., & Coolidge, F. L. (2009). Intrinsic and extrinsic barriers to mental health care among community-dwelling younger and older adults. *Aging and Mental Health, 13*, 769–777.

Petersen, R. C. (2004). Mild cognitive impairment as a diagnostic entity. *Journal of Internal Medicine, 256*, 183–194.

Philibert, M. (1979). Philosophical approach to gerontology. In J. Hendricks & C. Davis Hendricks (Eds.), *Dimensions of aging* (pp. 379–394). Cambridge, MA: Winthrop.

Pinquart, M., Duberstein, P. R., & Lyness, J. M. (2006). Treatments for later-life depressive conditions: A meta-analytic comparison of pharmacotherapy and psychotherapy. *American Journal of Psychiatry, 163*, 1493–1501.

Pinquart, M., & Sörensen, S. (2001). How effective are psychotherapeutic and other psychosocial interventions with older adults? A meta-analysis. *Journal of Mental Health and Aging, 7*, 207–240.

Pinquart, M., & Sörensen, S. (2006). Helping caregivers of persons with dementia: Which interventions work and how large are their effects? *International Psychogeriatrics, 18*, 577–595.

Pinquart, M., & Sörensen, S. (2007). Correlates of physical health of informal caregivers: A meta-analysis. *The Journals of Gerontology: Series B: Psychological Sciences and Social Sciences, 62*(2), P126–P137.

Plassman, B. L., Langa, K. M., Fisher, G. G., Heeringa, S. G., Weir, D. R., Ofstedal, M. B. et al. (2007). Prevalence of dementia in the United States: The Aging, Demographics, and Memory Study. *Neuroepidemiology, 29*, 125–132.

Plassman, B. L., Langa, K. M., Fisher, G. G., Heeringa, S. G., Weir, D. R., Ofstedal, M. B. et al. (2008). Prevalence of cognitive impairment without dementia in the United States. *Annals of Internal Medicine, 148*, 427–434.

Post, F. (1966). *Persistent persecutory states of the elderly.* London: Pergamon Press.

Potts, A., Grace, V. M., Vares, T., & Gavey, N. (2006). "Sex for life"? Men's counter-stories on "erectile dysfunction," male sexuality and ageing. *Sociology of Health and Illness, 28*, 306–329.

Powers, D. V. (2008). Psychotherapy in long-term care: II. Evidence-based psychological treatments and other outcome research. *Professional Psychology: Research and Practice, 39*, 257–263.

Prager, S., & Jeste, D. V. (1993). Sensory impairment in late-life schizophrenia. *Schizophrenia Bulletin, 19*, 755–772.

Pratt, S. I., Bartels, S. J., Mueser, K. T., & Forester, B. (2008). Helping older people experience success: An integrated model of psychosocial rehabilitation and health care management for older adults with serious mental illness. *American Journal of Psychiatric Rehabilitation, 11*, 41–60.

Pratt, S. I., Van Citters, A. D., Mueser, K. T., & Bartels, S. J. (2008). Psychosocial rehabilitation in older adults with serious mental illness: A review of the research literature and recommendations for development of rehabilitative approaches. *American Journal of Psychiatric Rehabilitation, 11*, 7–40.

Price, R. B., & Mohlman, J. (2007). Inhibitory control and symptom severity in late life generalized anxiety disorder. *Behaviour Research and Therapy, 45*, 2628–2639.

Prigerson, H. G., Vanderwerker, L. C., & Maciejewski, P. K. (2007). Complicated grief as a mental disorder: Inclusion in DSM. In M. Stroebe, R. Hansson, H. Schut, & W. Stroebe (Eds.), *Handbook of bereavement research and practice*. Washington, DC: American Psychological Association.

Pruchno, R. A., Blow, F. C., & Smyer, M. A. (1984). Life events and interdependent lives: Implications for research and intervention. *Human Development, 27*, 31–41.

Qualls, S. H. (1995a). Clinical interventions with later life families. In R. Blieszner & V. H. Bedford (Eds.), *Handbook on aging and the family* (pp. 474–487). Westport, CT: Greenwood Press.

Qualls, S. H. (1995b). Marital therapy with later life couples. *Journal of Geriatric Psychiatry, 28*, 139–163.

Qualls, S. H. (2002). Defining mental health in later life. *Generations, 25*, 9–13.

Qualls, S. H. (2005). Mental health in later life, ecology of. In C. B. Fisher & R. M. Lerner (Eds.), *Applied developmental science: An encyclopedia of research, policies, and programs*. Thousand Oaks, CA: Sage.

Qualls, S. H. (2007). Clinical interventions for decision making with impaired persons. In S. H. Qualls & M. A. Smyer, *Changes in decision-making capacity in older adults: Assessment and intervention* (pp. 271–298). Hoboken, NJ: John Wiley & Sons, Inc.

Qualls, S. H., & Benight, C. C. (2007). The role of clinical health geropsychology in the health care of older adults. In C. M. Aldwin, C. L. Park, & A. Spiro (Eds.), *Handbook of health psychology and aging* (pp. 367–389). New York: Guilford.

Qualls, S. H., & Kasl-Godley, J. E. (2011). *End-of-life issues, grief, and bereavement: What clinicians need to know*. Hoboken, NJ: John Wiley & Sons, Inc.

Qualls, S. H., & Layton, H. (2010). Mental health and adjustment. In J. C. Cavanaugh & C. K. Cavanaugh (Eds.), *Aging in America. Vol. 2: Physical and mental health* (pp. 171–187). Santa Barbara, CA: Praeger.

Qualls, S. H., & Noecker, T. L. (2009). Caregiver family therapy for conflicted families. In S. H. Qualls & S. H. Zarit (Eds.), *Aging families and caregiving: A clinician's guide to research, practice, and technology* (pp. 155–188). Hoboken, NJ: John Wiley & Sons, Inc.

Qualls, S. H., Segal, D. L., Norman, S., Niederehe, G., & Gallagher-Thompson, D. (2002). Psychologists in practice with older adults: Current patterns, sources of training, and need for continuing education. *Professional Psychology: Research and Practice, 33*, 435–442.

Qualls, S. H., & Smyer, M. A. (1995). Mental health. In G. L. Maddox (Ed.), *The encyclopedia of aging* (2nd ed., pp. 629–631). New York: Springer.

Qualls, S. H., & Smyer, M. A. (2007). *Changes in decision-making capacity in older adults: Assessment and intervention*. Hoboken, NJ: John Wiley & Sons, Inc.

Qualls, S. H., & Zarit, S. H. (Eds.). (2009). *Aging families and caregiving: A clinician's guide to research, practice, and technology*. Hoboken, NJ: John Wiley & Sons, Inc.

Quan, S. F., Katz, R., Olson, J., Bonekat, W., Enright, P. L., Young, T., & Newman, A. (2005). Factors associated with incidence and persistence of symptoms of disturbed sleep in an elderly cohort: The Cardiovascular Health Study. *American Journal of Medical Science, 329*, 163–172.

Rabins, P. V. (1991). Psychosocial and management aspects of delirium. *International Psychogeriatrics, 3*, 319–324.

Rabins, P. V., Pauker, S., & Thomas, J. (1984). Can schizophrenia begin after age 44? *Comprehensive Psychiatry, 25*, 290–293.

Radloff, L. S. (1977). The CES-D scale: A self-report depression scale for research in the general population. *Applied Psychological Measurement, 1*, 385–401.

Rapp, S. R., Parisi, S. A., & Walsh, D. A. (1988). Psychological dysfunction and physical health among elderly medical inpatients. *Journal of Consulting and Clinical Psychology, 56*, 851–855.

Reeves, R. R., & Brister, J. C. (2008). Psychosis in late life: Emerging issues. *Journal of Psychosocial Nursing and Mental Health Services, 46*, 45–52.

Regier, D. A., Rae, D. S., Narrow, W. E., Kaelber, C. T., & Schatzerg, A. F. (1988). Prevalence of anxiety disorders and their comorbidity with mood and addictive disorders. *British Journal of Psychiatry, 173*, 24–28.

Reich, J., Nduaguba, M., & Yates, W. (1988). Age and sex distribution of DSM-III personality cluster traits in a community population. *Comprehensive Psychiatry, 29*, 298–303.

Reich, J. W., & Zautra, A. J. (1989). A perceived control intervention for at-risk older adults. *Psychology and Aging, 4*, 415–424.

Reich, J. W., & Zautra, A. J. (1990). Dispositional control beliefs and the consequences of a control-enhancing intervention. *Journal of Gerontology: Psychological Sciences, 45*, P46–P51.

Reinecke, M. A., & Clark, D. A. (Eds.). (2004). *Cognitive therapy across the lifespan: Theory, research and practice.* Cambridge: Cambridge University Press.

Reisberg, B., Ferris, S. H., De Leon, M. J., & Crook, T. (1982). The Global Deterioration Scale for assessment of primary degenerative dementia. *American Journal of Psychiatry, 139*, 1136–1139.

Reynolds, C. F., III, Frank, E., Perel, J. M., Imber, S. D., Cornes, C., Miller, M. D. et al. (1999). Nortriptyline and interpersonal psychotherapy as maintenance therapies for recurrent major depression: A randomized controlled trial in patients older than 59 years. *Journal of the American Medical Association, 281*, 39–45.

Rickard, H. C., Scogin, F., & Keith, S. (1994). A one-year follow-up of relaxation training for elders with subjective anxiety. *The Gerontologist, 34*, 121–122.

Robertson, J. F. (1995). Grandparenting in an era of rapid change. In R. Blieszner & V. H. Bedford (Eds.), *Handbook on aging and the family* (pp. 243–260). Westport, CT: Greenwood Press.

Robins, L. N., Cottler, L., Bucholz, K., & Compton, W. (1995). *The Diagnostic Interview Schedule, Version 4.* St. Louis, MO: Washington University.

Rodgers, R. H., & White, J. W. (1993). Family development theory. In P. G. Boss, W. J. Doherty, R. LaRossa, W. R. Schumm, & S. K. Steinmetz (Eds.), *Sourcebook of family theories and methods* (pp. 225–254). New York: Plenum.

Roemer, L., & Orsillo, S. M. (2002). Expanding our conceptualization of and treatment for generalized anxiety disorder: Integrating mindfulness/acceptance-based approaches with existing cognitive behavioral models. *Clinical Psychology: Science and Practice, 9*, 54–68.

Rosenstein, M. J., Milazzo-Sayre, L. J., & Manderscheid, R. W. (1990). Characteristics of persons using specialty inpatient, outpatient, and partial care programs in 1986. In R. W. Manderscheid & M. A. Sonnenschein (Eds.), *Mental health, United States, 1990* (pp. 139–172). Washington, DC: United States Government Printing Office.

Rosenzweig, A., Prigerson, H., Miller, M. D., & Reynolds, C. F. (1997). Bereavement and late-life depression: Grief and its complications in the elderly. *Annual Review of Medicine, 48*, 421–428.

Rosowsky, E., Abrams, R. C., & Zweig, R. A. (Eds.). (1999). *Personality disorders in older adults: Emerging issues in diagnosis and treatment.* Mahwah, NJ: Erlbaum.

Rosowsky, E., Casciani, J., & Arnold, M. (Eds.). (2008). *Geropsychology and long-term care: A practitioner's guide.* New York: Springer.

Rosowsky, E., & Gurian, B. (1992). Impact of borderline personality disorder in late life on systems of care. *Hospital and Community Psychiatry, 43,* 386–389.

Rowe, J. W., & Kahn, R. (1998). *Successful aging.* New York: Pantheon Books.

Rowland, D., van Diest, S., Incrocci, L., & Slob, A. K. (2005). Psychosexual factors that differentiate men with inhibited ejaculation from men with no dysfunction or another sexual dysfunction. *Journal of Sexual Medicine, 2*(3), 383–389.

Roy, A. (1986). Suicide in schizophrenia. In A. Roy (Ed.), *Suicide* (pp. 97–112). Baltimore: Williams & Wilkins.

Ryff, C. (1982). Successful aging: A developmental approach. *The Gerontologist, 22,* 209–214.

Ryff, C., & Keyes, C. L. (1996). The structure of psychological well-being revisited. *Journal of Personality and Social Psychology, 69,* 719–727.

Rystedt, I. B., & Bartels, S. J. (2008). Medical comorbidity. In K. T. Mueser & D. V. Jeste (Eds.), *Clinical handbook of schizophrenia* (pp. 424–436). New York: Guilford.

Saha, S., Chant, D., & McGrath, J. (2007). A systematic review of mortality in schizophrenia: Is the differential mortality gap worsening over time? *Archives of General Psychiatry, 64,* 1123–1131.

Salzman, C., Jeste, D. V., Meyer, R. E., Cohen-Mansfield, J., Cummings, J., Grossberg, G. T., Jarvik, L., Kraemer, H. C., Lebowitz, B. D., Maslow, K., Pollock, B. G., Raskind, M., Schultz, S. K., Wang, P., Zito, J. M., & Zubenko, G. S. (2008). Elderly patients with dementia-related symptoms of severe agitation and aggression: Consensus statement on treatment options, clinical trials methodology, and policy. *Journal of Clinical Psychiatry, 69,* 889–898.

Satre, D., Knight, B. G., & David, S. (2006). Cognitive behavioral interventions with older adults: Integrating clinical and gerontological research. *Professional Psychology: Research and Practice, 37,* 489–498.

Satre, D., Mertens, J., Areán, P. A., & Weisner, C. (2003). Contrasting outcomes of older versus middle-aged and younger adult substance abuse patients in a managed care treatment program. *Journal of Studies on Alcohol, 64,* 520–530.

Saxena, S., & Lawley, D. (2009). Delirium in the elderly: A clinical review. *Postgraduate Medicine Journal, 85,* 405–413.

Schaie, K. W. (1994). The course of adult intellectual development. *American Psychologist, 49,* 304–313.

Schaie, K. W. (1995). Training materials in geropsychology: Developmental issues. In B. G. Knight, L. Teri, P. Wohlford, & J. Santos (Eds.), *Mental health services for older adults: Implications for training and practice in geropsychology* (pp. 33–39). Washington, DC: American Psychological Association.

Schaie, K. W. (2005). *Developmental influences on adult intelligence: The Seattle longitudinal study.* New York: Oxford University Press.

Schaie, K. W., & Willis, S. L. (2002). *Adult development and aging* (5th ed.). New York: Prentice Hall.

Schaie, K. W., & Willis, S. L. (2005). *Intellectual functioning in adulthood: Growth, maintenance, decline and modifiability.* Philadelphia, PA: American Society on Aging and MedLife Foundation.

Schaie, K. W., & Zanjani, F. A. K. (2006). Intellectual development across adulthood. In C. Hoare (Ed.), *Handbook of adult development and learning* (pp. 99–114). Oxford: Oxford University Press.

Scharlach, A. E. (1987). Relieving feelings of strain among women with elderly mothers. *Psychology and Aging, 2,* 9–13.

Schiff, B., & Cohler, B. J. (2001). Telling survival backwards: Holocaust survivors narrate the past. In G. M. Kenyon, P. G. Clark, & B. de Vries (Eds.), *Narrative gerontology: Theory, research, and practice* (pp. 113–136). New York: Springer.

Schneider, J. A., Arvanitakis, Z., Bang, W., & Bennett, D. A. (2007). Mixed brain pathologies account for most dementia cases in community-dwelling older persons. *Neurology, 69,* 2197–2204.

Schover, L. R., Fouladi, R. T., Warneke, C. L., Neese, L., Klein, E. A., Zippe, C., & Kupelian, P. A. (2002). The use of treatments for erectile dysfunction among survivors of prostate carcinoma. *Cancer, 95,* 2397–2407.

Schulberg, H. C., Katon, W., Simon, G. E., & Rush, A. J. (1998). Treating major depression in primary care practice: An update of the Agency for Health Care Policy and Research practice guidelines. *Archives of General Psychiatry, 55,* 1121–1127.

Schuurmans, J., Comijs, H. C., Beekman, A. T. F., Deeg, D. J. H., Emmelkamp, P. M. G., & van Dyck, R. (2005). The outcome of anxiety disorders in older people at 6-year follow-up: Results from the Longitudinal Aging Study Amsterdam. *Acta Psychiatrica Scandinavica, 111,* 420–428.

Scogin, F. R., Jamison, C., & Davis, N. (1990). Two-year follow-up of bibliotherapy for depression in older adults. *Journal of Consulting and Clinical Psychology, 58,* 665–667.

Scogin, F., & McElreath, L. (1994). Efficacy of psychosocial treatments for geriatric depression: A quantitative review. *Journal of Consulting and Clinical Psychology, 62,* 69–74.

Scogin, F. R., Welsh, D., Hanson, A., Stump, J., & Coates, A. (2005). Evidence-based psychotherapies for depression in older adults. *Clinical Psychology: Science and Practice, 12,* 222–237.

Seeman, M. V. (1986). Current outcome in schizophrenia: Women vs. men. *Acta Psychiatrica Scandinavica, 73,* 609–617.

Seeman, M. V., & Lang, M. (1990). The role of estrogens in schizophrenia gender differences. *Schizophrenia Bulletin, 16,* 185–194.

Segal, D. L. (2010). Diagnostic and statistical manual of mental disorders (DSM-IV-TR). In I. Weiner & W. E. Craighead (Eds.), *The Corsini encyclopedia of psychology and behavioral science* (4th ed., pp. 495–497). Hoboken, NJ: John Wiley & Sons, Inc.

Segal, D. L., & Coolidge, F. L. (2007). Structured and semi-structured interviews for differential diagnosis: Issues and applications. In M. Hersen, S. M. Turner, & D. C. Beidel (Eds.), *Adult psychopathology and diagnosis* (5th ed., pp. 78–100). Hoboken, NJ: John Wiley & Sons.

Segal, D. L., Coolidge, F. L., Cahill, B. S., & O'Riley, A. A. (2008). Psychometric properties of the Beck Depression Inventory-II (BDI-II) among community-dwelling older adults. *Behavior Modification, 32,* 3–20.

Segal, D. L., Coolidge, F. L., & Hersen, M. (1998). Psychological testing of older people. In I. H. Nordhus, G. R. VandenBos, S. Berg, & P. Fromholt (Eds.), *Clinical geropsychology* (pp. 231–257). Washington, DC: American Psychological Association.

Segal, D. L., Coolidge, F. L., & Rosowsky, E. (2006). *Personality disorders and older adults: Diagnosis, assessment, and treatment.* Hoboken, NJ: John Wiley & Sons.

Segal, D. L., Hook, J. N., & Coolidge, F. L. (2001). Personality dysfunction, coping styles, and clinical symptoms in younger and older adults. *Journal of Clinical Geropsychology, 7,* 201–212.

Segal, D. L., June, A., Payne, M., Coolidge, F. L., & Yochim, B. (2010). Development and initial validation of a self-report assessment tool for anxiety among older adults: The Geriatric Anxiety Scale. *Journal of Anxiety Disorders, 24,* 709–714.

Serrano, J. P., Latorre, J. M., Gatz, M., & Montanes, J. (2004). Life review therapy using autobiographical retrieval practice for older adults with depressive symptomatology. *Psychology and Aging, 19,* 272–277.

Seshadri, S., Beiser, A., Kelly-Hayes, M., Kase, C. S., Au, R., Kannel, W. B., & Wolf, P. A. (2008). The lifetime risk of stroke: Estimates from the Framingham Study. *Stroke, 37,* 345–350.

Shanas, E. (1979). Social myth as hypothesis: The case of the family relations of old people. *The Gerontologist, 19*, 3–9.

Shanas, E. (1980). Older people and their families: The new pioneers. *Journal of Marriage and the Family, 42*, 9–15.

Shanmugham, B., Karp, J., Drayer, R., Reynolds, C. F., III, & Alexopoulos, G. (2005). Evidence-based pharmacologic interventions for geriatric depression. *Psychiatric Clinics of North America, 28*, 821–835.

Shaw, B. A., & Krause, N. (2002). Exposure to physical violence during childhood, aging, and health. *Journal of Aging and Health, 14*, 467–494.

Sheikh, J. I., & Yesavage, J. A. (1986). Geriatric Depression Scale (GDS): Recent evidence and development of a shorter version. *Clinical Gerontologist, 5*, 165–173.

Shemmings, D. (2006). Using adult attachment theory to differentiate adult children's internal working models of later life filial relationships. *Journal of Aging Studies, 20*, 177–191.

Shields, C. G. (1992). Family interaction and caregivers of Alzheimer's disease patients: Correlates of depression. *Family Process, 31*, 19–33.

Shields, C. G., King, D. A., & Wynne, L. C. (1995). Interventions with later life families. In R. H. Mikesell, D. Lusterman, & S. H. McDaniel (Eds.), *Integrating family therapy: Handbook of family psychology and systems theory* (pp. 141–158). Washington, DC: American Psychological Association.

Shulz, R., & Beach, S. R. (1999). Caregiving as a risk for mortality: The caregiver health effects study. *Journal of the American Medical Association, 282*, 2215–2219.

Simon, G. E., & Ludman, E. J. (2006). Outcome of new benzodiazepine prescriptions to older adults in primary care. *General Hospital Psychiatry, 28*, 374–378.

Sivertsen, B., Omvik, S., Pallesen, S., Bjorvatn, B., Havik, O. E., Kvale, G., Nielsen, G. H., & Nordhus, I. H. (2006). Cognitive behavioral therapy vs. zopiclone for treatment of chronic primary insomnia in older adults: A randomized controlled trial. *Journal of the American Medical Association, 295*, 2851–2858.

Skaff, M. M. (2007). Sense of control and health: A dynamic duo in the aging process. In C. M. Aldwin, C. L. Park, & A. Spiro (Eds.), *Handbook of health psychology and aging* (pp. 186–209). New York: Guilford.

Skinner, B. F. (1953). *Science and human behavior*. New York: Free Press.

Smith, G., & Rush, B. K. (2006). Normal aging and mild cognitive impairment. In D. K. Attix & K. A. Welch-Bohmer (Eds.), *Geriatric neuropsychology: Assessment and intervention* (pp. 27–55). New York: Guilford.

Smyer, M. A. (1995). Formal support in later life: Lessons for prevention. In L. A. Bond, S. J. Cutler, & A. Grams (Eds.), *Promoting successful and productive aging* (pp. 186–202). Thousand Oaks, CA: Sage.

Smyer, M. A., & Downs, M. G. (1995). Psychopharmacology: An essential element in educating clinical psychologists for working with older adults. In B. G. Knight, L. Teri, P. Wohlford, & J. Santos (Eds.), *Mental health services for older adults: Implications for training and practice in geropsychology* (pp. 73–83). Washington, DC: American Psychological Association Press.

Smyer, M. A., & Shea, D. G. (1996). Mental health among the elderly. In L. A. Vitt & J. Siegenthaler (Eds.), *Encyclopedia of financial gerontology* (pp. 365–371). Westport, CT: Greenwood Press.

Snowden, M., Sato, K., & Roy-Byrne, P. (2003). Assessment and treatment of nursing home residents with depression or behavioral symptoms associated with dementia: A review of the literature. *Journal of the American Geriatrics Society, 51*, 1305–1317.

Spayd, C. S. (1993, June). *Psychological consultation in the nursing home: Group brainstorming case example*. Unpublished workshop material.

Spayd, C. S., & Smyer, M. A. (1996). Psychological interventions in nursing homes. In S. H. Zarit & B. G. Knight (Eds.), *A guide to psychotherapy and aging: Effective clinical interventions in a life-stage context* (pp. 241–268). Washington, DC: American Psychological Association.

Spielberger, C., Gorsuch, R., Lushene, R., Vagg, P. R., & Jacobs, G. A. (1983). *Manual of the State-Trait Anxiety Inventory*. Palo Alto, CA: Consulting Psychologists Press.

Stanford Center for Longevity & the Max Planck Institute for Human Development. (2009). *Expert consensus on brain health*. Retrieved November 30, 2009, from http://longevity.stanford.edu/mymind/cognitiveagingstatement.

Stanley, M. A., Hopko, D. R., Diefenbach, G. J., Bourland, S. L., Rodriegues, H., & Wagner, P. (2003). Cognitive-behavior therapy for late-life generalized anxiety disorder in primary care: Preliminary findings. *American Journal of Geriatric Psychiatry, 11*, 92–96.

Starr, B. D., Weiner, M. B., & Rabetz, M. (1979). *The Projective Assessment of Aging Method (PAAM)*. New York: Springer.

Streiner, D. L., Cairney, J., & Veldhuizen, S. (2006). The epidemiology of psychological problems in the elderly. *Canadian Journal of Psychiatry, 51*, 185–191.

Susser, M. B., & Susser, E. (1996). Choosing a future for epidemiology, II: From black box to Chinese boxes and eco-epidemiology. *American Journal of Public Health, 86*, 674–677.

Swartz, M. S., Stroup, T. S., McEvoy, J. P., Davis, S. M., Rosenheck, R. A., Keefe, R. S., Hsiao, J. K., & Lieberman, J. A. (2008). What CATIE found: Results from the schizophrenia trial. *Psychiatric Services, 59*, 500–506.

Takamura, J. (1985). Introduction: Health teams. In L. J. Campbell & S. Vivell (Eds.), *Interdisciplinary team training for primary care in geriatrics: An educational model for program development and evaluation* (pp. 64–67). Washington, DC: Government Printing Office.

Tarrier, N., Beckett, R., Harwood, S., Baker, A., Yusupoff, L., & Ugarteburu, I. (1993). A trial of two cognitive behavioral methods of treating drug-resistant residual psychotic symptoms in schizophrenic patients: I. Outcome. *British Journal of Psychiatry, 162*, 524–532.

Teachman, B. A., Siedlecki, K. L., & Magee, J. C. (2007). Aging and symptoms of anxiety and depression: Structural invariance of the tripartite model. *Psychology and Aging, 22*, 160–170.

Teri, L. (1996). Depression in Alzheimer's disease. In M. Hersen & V. B. Van Hasselt (Eds.), *Psychological treatment of older adults: An introductory text* (pp. 209–222). New York: Plenum.

Teri, L., & Lewinsohn, P. M. (1982). Modification of the pleasant and unpleasant event schedules for use with the elderly. *Journal of Consulting and Clinical Psychology, 50*, 444–445.

Teri, L., Logsdon, R. G., & McCurry, S. M. (2008). Exercise interventions for dementia and cognitive impairment: The Seattle protocols. *Journal of Nutrition, Health, and Aging, 12*(6), 391–394.

Teri, L., Logsdon, R. G., Uomoto, J., & McCurry, S. M. (1997). Behavioral treatment of depression in dementia patients: A controlled clinical trial. *Journal of Gerontology, 52B*, 349–367.

Teri, L., Logsdon, R., Wagner, A., & Uomoto, J. (1994). The caregiver role in behavioral treatment of depression in dementia patients. In E. Light, G. Niederehe, & B. D. Lebowitz (Ed.), *Stress effects on family caregivers of Alzheimer's patients* (pp. 185–204). New York: Springer.

Teri, L., Truax, P., Logsdon, R., Uomoto, J., Zarit, S., & Vitaliano, P. P. (1992). Assessment of behavioral problems in dementia: The Revised Memory and Behavior Problem Checklist. *Psychology and Aging, 7*, 622–631.

Teri, L., & Wagner, A. (1992). Alzheimer's disease and depression. *Journal of Consulting and Clinical Psychology, 60,* 379–391.

Thompson, L. W., Dick-Siskin, L., Coon, D. W., Powers, D. V., & Gallagher-Thompson, D. (2010). *Treating late-life depression: A cognitive-behavioral therapy approach: Workbook.* New York: Oxford University Press.

Thompson, L. W., Gallagher, D., & Czirr, R. (1988). Personality disorder and outcome in the treatment of late-life depression. *Journal of Geriatric Psychiatry, 21,* 133–146.

Thompson, L. W., Gallagher, D., Nies, G., & Epstein, D. (1983). Evaluation of the effectiveness of professionals and nonprofessionals as instructors of "Coping with Depression" classes for elders. *The Gerontologist, 23,* 390–396.

Thompson, L. W., Gallagher-Thompson, D. E., & Dick, L. P. (1995). *Cognitive-behavioral therapy for late-life depression: A therapist manual.* Palo Alto, CA: Older Adult and Family Center, Veterans Affairs Palo Alto Health Care System.

Topo, P. (2009). Technology studies to meet the needs of people with dementia and their caregivers: A literature review. *Journal of Applied Gerontology, 28*(1), 5–37.

Torgersen, S., Lygren, S., Øien, P. A., Skre, I., Onstad, S., Edvardsen, J., Tambs, K., & Kringlen, E. (2000). A twin study of personality disorders. *Comprehensive Psychiatry, 41,* 416–425.

Trenkle, D., Shankle, W., & Azen, S. (2007). Detecting cognitive impairment in primary care: Performance assessment of three screening instruments. *Journal of Alzheimer's Disease, 11,* 323–335.

Troll, L. E., & Bengtson, V. L. (1993). The oldest-old in families: An intergenerational perspective. In L. Burton (Ed.), *Families and aging* (pp. 79–89). Amityville, NY: Baywood Press.

Twelftree, H., & Qazi, A. (2006). Relationship between anxiety and agitation in dementia. *Aging and Mental Health, 10,* 362–367.

Uchino, B. N. (2009). Understanding the links between social support and physical health. *Perspectives on Psychological Science, 4,* 236–255.

United Nations, Department of Economic and Social Affairs, Population Division. (2006). *Population ageing wallchart 2006.* Retrieved March 15, 2009 from http://www.un.org/esa/population/publications/ageing/ageing2006chart.pdf.

Unverzagt, F., Kasten, L., Johnson, K., Rebok, G., Marsiske, M., Koepke, K. et al. (2007). Effect of memory impairment on training outcomes in ACTIVE. *Journal of the International Neuropsychological Society, 13,* 953–960.

US Bureau of the Census. (2003). *Statistical abstract of the United States.* Washington, DC: Author.

US Bureau of the Census. (2007, June). *Older adults in 2005.* Washington, DC: Author. Retrieved October 15, 2009, from http://www.census.gov/population/www/pop-profile/files/dynamic/OLDER.pdf.

US Census Bureau. (2009). *Statistical abstract of the United States.* Retrieved from http://www.census.gov/compendia/statab/.

US Department of Health and Human Services. (1999). *Mental health: A report of the Surgeon General.* Rockville, MD: US Department of Health and Human Services, Substance Abuse and Mental Health Services Administration, Center for Mental Health Services, National Institutes of Health, National Institute of Mental Health. Retrieved from http://www.surgeongeneral.gov/library/mentalhealth/home.html.

US Department of Health and Human Services. (2000). *Healthy people 2010.* Washington, DC: US Department of Health and Human Services. Retrieved from http://www.health.gov/healthypeople.

US Department of Health and Human Services. (2001). *Mental health: Culture, race, and ethnicity – A supplement to mental health: A report of the Surgeon General.* Rockville, MD:

US Department of Health and Human Services, Substance Abuse and Mental Health Services Administration, Center for Mental Health Services.

US Department of Health and Human Services. (2006). *2005 White House conference on aging.* Washington, DC: US Department of Health and Human Services. Retrieved from http://www.whcoa.gov/index.asp.

US Department of Health and Human Services, Substance Abuse and Mental Health Services Administration. (2008). *Summary of Findings from the 2007 National Survey on Drug Use and Health.* Retrieved January 10, 2008, from http://www.oas.samhsa.gov/WebOnly.htm#NSDUHtabs.

Vaillant, G. E. (1977). *Adaptation to life.* Boston: Little, Brown.

Vaillant, G. E. (2002). *Aging well: Surprising guideposts to a happier life from the landmark Harvard study of adult development.* Boston: Little, Brown.

Vaillant, G. E., & Vaillant, C. O. (1990). Natural history of male psychological health, XII: A 45-year study of predictors of successful aging at age 65. *American Journal of Psychiatry, 147,* 31–37.

Van Alphen, S. P. J., Engelen, G. J. J. A., Kuin, Y., Hoijtink, H. J. A., & Derksen, J. J. L. (2006). A preliminary study of the diagnostic accuracy of the Gerontological Personality disorders Scale (GPS). *International Journal of Geriatric Psychiatry, 21,* 862–868.

Van Hout, H. P., Beekman, A. F., de Beurs, E., Comijs, H., Van Marwijk, H., De Haan, M. et al. (2004). Anxiety and the risk of death in older men and women. *British Journal of Psychiatry, 185,* 399–404.

Vedhara, K., & Irwin, M. (Eds.). (2005). *Human psychoneuroimmunology.* New York: Oxford University Press.

Vitaliano, P. P., Zhang, J., & Scanlan, J. M. (2003). Is caregiving hazardous to one's physical health? A meta-analysis. *Psychological Bulletin, 129,* 946–972.

Vitiello, B., Correll, C., van Zwieten-Boot, B., Zuddas, A., Parellada, M., & Arango, C. (2009). Antipsychotics in children and adolescents: Increasing use, evidence for efficacy and safety concerns. *European Neuropsychopharmacology, 19,* 629–635.

Watzlawick, P., Beavin, J. H., & Jackson, D. D. (1967). *Pragmatics of human communication: A study of interactional patterns, pathologies, and paradoxes.* New York: Norton.

Watzlawick, P., Weakland, J. H., & Fisch, R. (1974). *Change.* New York: Norton.

Weissman, M. M., Markowitz, J. C., & Klerman, G. L. (2000). *Comprehensive guide to interpersonal psychotherapy.* New York: Basic Books.

Wetherell, J. L., & Gatz, M. (2005). The Beck Anxiety Inventory in older adults with Generalized Anxiety Disorder. *Journal of Psychopathology and Behavioral Assessment, 27,* 17–24.

Wetherell, J. L., Lenze, E. J., & Stanley, M. A. (2005). Evidence-based treatment of geriatric anxiety disorders. *Psychiatric Clinics of North America, 28,* 871–896.

Wetherell, J. L., LeRoux, H., & Gatz, M. (2003). DSM-IV criteria for Generalized Anxiety Disorder in older adults: Distinguishing the worried from the well. *Psychology and Aging, 18,* 622–627.

Wetherell, J. L., Sorrell, J. T., Thorp, S. R., & Patterson, T. L. (2005). Psychological interventions for late-life anxiety: A review and early lessons from the CALM Study. *Journal of Geriatric Psychiatry and Neurology, 18,* 72–82.

Wetherell, J. L., Thorp, S. R., Patterson, T. L., Golshan, S., Jeste, D. V., & Gatz, M. (2004). Quality of life in geriatric generalized anxiety disorder: A preliminary investigation. *Journal of Psychiatric Research, 38,* 305–312.

Whitchurch, G. G., & Constantine, L. L. (1993). Systems theory. In P. G. Boss, W. J. Doherty, R. LaRossa, W. R. Schumm, & S. K. Steinmetz (Eds.), *Sourcebook of family theories and methods* (pp. 325–355). New York: Plenum.

White, M., & Epston, D. (1990). *Narrative means to therapeutic ends.* New York: Norton.

Whitehouse, P., & Moody, H. (2006). Mild cognitive impairment: A "hardening of the categories"? *Dementia: The International Journal of Social Research and Practice, 5,* 11–25.

Wierzalis, E. A., Barret, B., Pope, M., & Rankins, M. (2006). Gay and bisexual men and aging: Sex and intimacy. In D. Kimmel, T. Rose, & S. David (Eds.), *Lesbian, gay, bisexual and transgender aging: Research and clinical perspectives* (pp. 91–109). New York: Columbia University Press.

Wilkinson, D. G. (2002). *Electroconvulsive therapy (ECT): Principles and practice of geriatric psychiatry* (2nd ed., pp. 433–437). Hoboken, NJ: John Wiley & Sons.

Williams, M., & Lewis, C. (2009). A platform for intervention and research on family communication in elder care. In S. H. Qualls & S. H. Zarit (Eds.), *Aging families and caregiving* (pp. 269–286). Hoboken, NJ: John Wiley & Sons, Inc.

Willis, S. L., Tennstedt, S. L., Marsiske, M., Ball, K., Elias, J., Koepke, K. M. et al. (2006). Long-term effects of cognitive training on everyday functional outcomes in older adults. *Journal of the American Medical Association, 296,* 2805–2814.

Wisniewski, S. R., Belle, S. H., Coon, D. W., Marcus, S. M., Ory, M. G., Burgio, L. D. et al. (2003). The Resources for Enhancing Alzheimer's Caregiver Health (REACH): Project design and baseline characteristics. *Psychology and Aging, 18,* 375–384.

Wisocki, P. (1991). Behavioral gerontology. In P. Wisocki (Ed.), *Handbook of clinical behavior therapy with the elderly client* (pp. 3–51). New York: Plenum.

Wolinsky, M A. (1990). *A heart of wisdom: Marital counseling with older and elderly couples.* New York: Brunner/Mazel.

Wood, J. M., Nezworski, M. T., Lilienfeld, S. O., & Garb, H. N. (2003). *What's wrong with the Rorschach? Science confronts the controversial inkblot test.* San Francisco: Jossey-Bass.

World Health Organization. (1948). *Constitution of the World Health Organization.* Geneva: Author. Retrieved from http://www.who.int/governance/eb/who_constitution_en.pdf.

World Health Organization. (2005). *Suicide prevention (SUPRE).* Geneva: Author. Retrieved from http://www.who.int/mental_health/prevention/suicide.

Wright, L. K. (1998). Affection and sexuality in the presence of Alzheimer's disease: A longitudinal study. *Sexuality and Disability, 16,* 167–179.

Yesavage, J. A., Brink, T. L., Rose, T. L., Lum, O., Huang, V., Adey, M. B., & Leirer, V. O. (1983). Development and validation of a geriatric depression screening scale: A preliminary report. *Journal of Psychiatric Research, 17,* 37–49.

Young, T., Palta, M., Dempsey, J. et al. (1993). The occurrence of sleep-disordered breathing among middle-aged adults. *New England Journal of Medicine, 328,* 1230–1235.

Zarit, J. (2009). Assessment and intervention with family caregivers. In S. H. Qualls & S. H. Zarit (Eds.), *Aging families and caregiving* (pp. 113–130). Hoboken, NJ: John Wiley & Sons.

Zarit, S. H. (2009). Empirically supported treatment for family caregivers. In S. H. Qualls & S. H. Zarit (Eds.), *Aging families and caregiving* (pp. 131–154). Hoboken, NJ: John Wiley & Sons, Inc.

Zarit, S. H., & Zarit, J. M. (2007). *Mental disorders in older adults* (2nd ed.). New York: Guilford.

Zautra, A. J., Reich, J. W., & Newsom, J. T. (1995). Autonomy and sense of control among older adults: An examination of their effects on mental health. In L. A. Bond, S. J. Cutler, & A. Grams (Eds.), *Promoting successful and productive aging* (pp. 153–170). Thousand Oaks, CA: Sage.

Zeiss, A. M., Zeiss, R. A., & Davies, H. M. (1999). Assessment of sexual function and dysfunction in older adults. In P. Lichtenberg (Ed.), *Handbook of assessment in clinical gerontology* (pp. 270–296). New York: John Wiley & Sons, Inc.

Zhu, C. W., Scarmeas, N., Torgan, R., Albert, M., Brandt, J., Blacker, D., Sano, M., & Stern, Y. (2006). Clinical features associated with costs in early AD: Baseline data from the Predictors Study. *Neurology, 66,* 1021–1028.

Zisook, S., Heaton, R., Moranville, J., Kuck, J., Jernigan, T., & Braff, D. (1992). Past substance abuse and clinical course of schizophrenia. *American Journal of Psychiatry, 149,* 552–553.

Zubin, J., & Spring, B. (1977). Vulnerability: A new view of schizophrenia. *Journal of Abnormal Psychology, 86*(2), 103–126.

Zweig, R. A. (2008). Personality disorder in older adults: Assessment challenges and strategies. *Professional Psychology: Research and Practice, 3,* 298–305.

Name Index

Subject Index